MURALS OF NEW YORK CITY

THE BEST OF NEW YORK'S PUBLIC PAINTINGS FROM BEMELMANS TO PARRISH

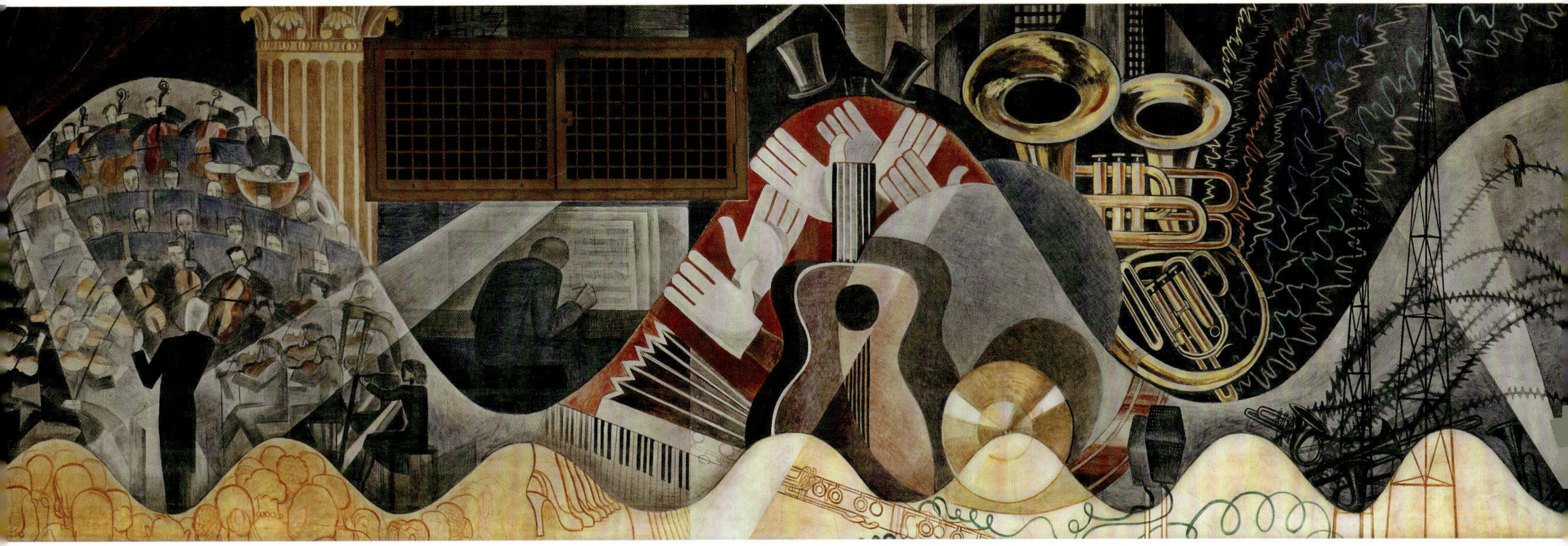

Written by **GLENN PALMER-SMITH** • Photographs by **JOSHUA McHUGH** • Introduction by **GRAYDON CARTER**

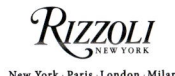

RIZZOLI
NEW YORK

New York · Paris · London · Milan

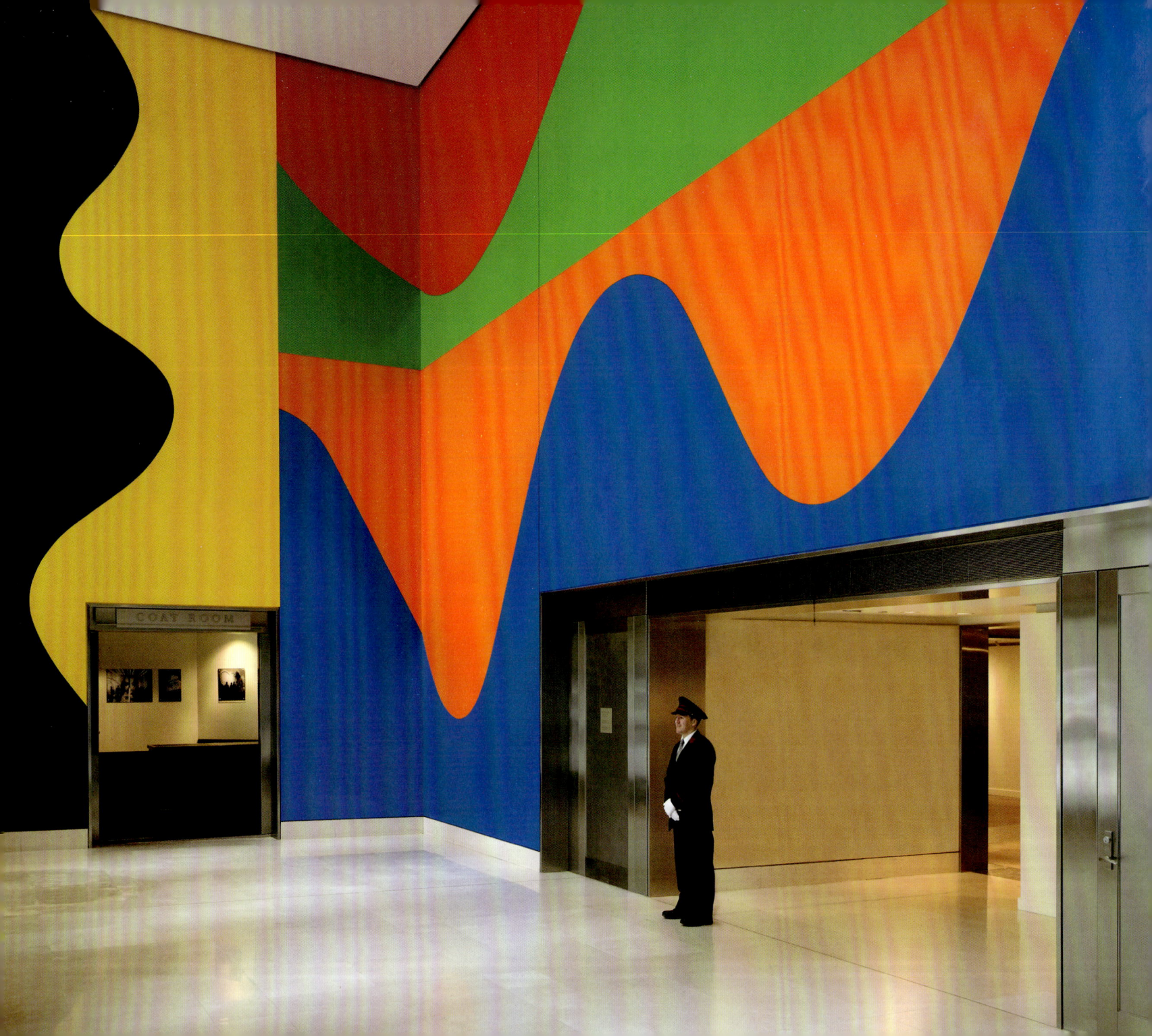

CONTENTS

INTRODUCTION

GRAYDON CARTER

In their purest form, murals have the ability to tell stories. And it is in this respect that they keep alive the epic tale of mankind in all its splendor and vanity. In their broadest form, they can be anything from the most primitive scratchings on the walls of caves in Northern Spain to Etruscan temples, Buddhist monasteries, and the palaces at Knossos and Samarra, and all the way up into the pantheon of muraldom inhabited by Giotto's Arena Chapel, in Padua, and Michelangelo's Sistine Chapel in Rome. Murals can be platforms for or against, everything from industrial boosterism and nation building to political oppression and war. The expanse of the canvas must be part of the appeal for their creators inasmuch as some of the finest painters of the past century have turned their hand to the art, including Picasso, Léger, Rivera, Sargent, and even Keith Haring. Picasso's reaction to the bombing of the Basque city of Guernica made its first appearance as a mural for the Spanish pavilion at the 1937 Paris Exposition. If there's a golden age for murals in this country, it would have to be the period between the Wars, when so many of the walls of our civic buildings, libraries, schools, and skyscraper lobbies were transformed into glorious showcases thanks largely to funding from the Federal Arts Program and the Works Progress Administration, two of the work-creating operations of F.D.R.'s New Deal.

That so many of the splendid examples of the muralist's art are in New York is a blessing to anyone who lives in the city. And in the pages of this splendid book, by Glenn Palmer-Smith and Joshua McHugh, they come alive, beckoning in miniature for the reader to make the journey to the sources. As much as each painting tells a story, there is a story behind each painting. I didn't know this, but the blue night sky on the ceiling of the main concourse of Grand Central was painted backward. It seems that the artist, Paul Hellue, a Frenchman and a member of the circle around Proust, turned over the execution of the project to an Australian painter, who composed the night sky the way it's seen on the other side of the earth. As Glenn has noted, this went largely unnoticed until an astronomy buff from New Rochelle pointed it out.

Maxfield Parrish's stunning 30-foot mural that runs the length of the King Cole Bar, in the St. Regis Hotel, was originally commissioned by John Jacob Astor for the bar of the Knickerbocker hotel in Times Square. When the Knickerbocker was converted to offices, the mural went on something of a journey, first to the Chicago Art Institute, then to the New York Racquet Club on Park Avenue, and finally to the place where it now watches over the St. Regis's bar patrons. Parrish, being a Quaker, was originally skittish about creating a mural for a drinking establishment, but Astor eased his concerns by paying him an unheard-of sum for the times: $5,000. He did have one stipulation, however. Astor wanted his face to be the basis for King Cole's.

There are so many delightful murals and stories behind them here, but this is Glenn's territory and it is terrain he knows well. Inasmuch as I had a minor hand in two of the murals he has chosen—the one at the Waverly Inn in Greenwich Village, and the one at the Monkey Bar in the East 50s between Madison and Park—perhaps a few words about these two would be appropriate. When my partners, Sean Macpherson, Eric Goode, and I took over the Waverly Inn in 2007, I called Ed Sorel, the dean of American illustrators, to see if he might be interested in doing a mural for our front dining room. Sorel and I had been working together for a number of years, and I thought the warm, lush coloring and devilish caricatures in his work would be perfect for the restaurant. I wanted to express, in mural form, the stretch of bohemian history that formed the mythology of the Village. And the Waverly was very much a part of that history. It opened during Prohibition and was once owned by the secretary to then *Vanity Fair* assistant editor Clare

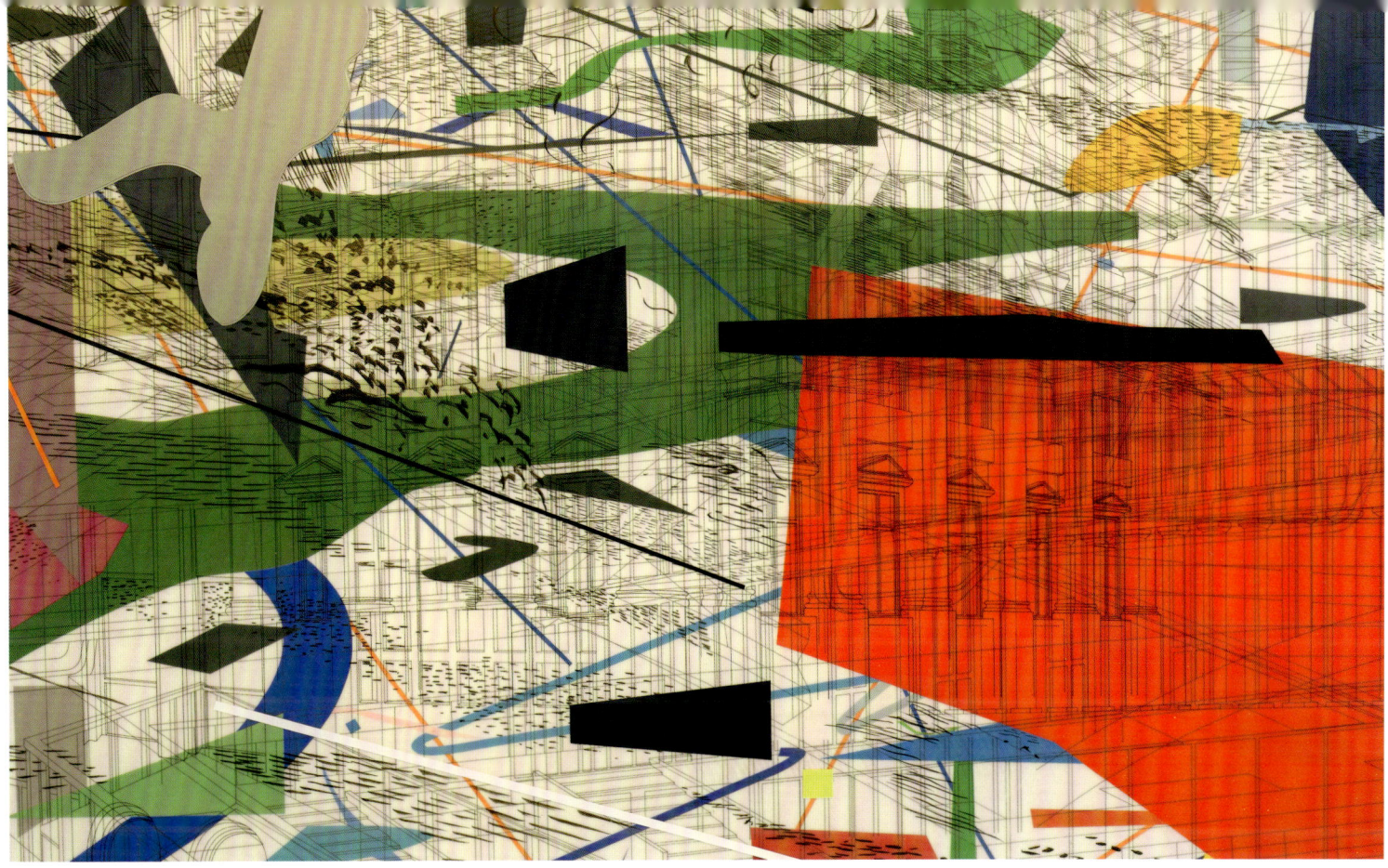

Boothe (later to add Luce to her name). And so, with a lot of back-and-forth, Ed and I worked up with a list of more than three dozen figures that hark back to the Village's early days, as a haven for free spirits, and carry forward to the postwar years. There is everyone from Edgar Allan Poe, John Reed, and Willa Cather, to Jack Kerouac, Norman Mailer, and Joan Baez.

A few years later, Jeff Klein and Jeremy King and I took over the venerable Monkey Bar, a restaurant with a raffish past, and what we thought was a promising future. Back in the day, Tallulah Bankhead and Tennessee Williams were two of the restaurant's many notable regulars. Both lived upstairs at the Hotel Elysée, itself a place with a slightly louche past, in that local wits referred to it as the Easy-Lay. Indeed, Williams died there, having choked to death trying to open a Visine top with his teeth. The walls of the front bar area of the restaurant had a playful mural with scenes of anthropomorphic monkeys that had been done by a series of artists. For the main dining room, I went back to Ed, and after many conversations, we agreed on a list, and from that he created a sweeping portrait of Jazz Age New York: Harold Ross, Moss Hart, Babe Ruth, Billy Rose, Scott Fitzgerald, Robert Benchley, and the like. I eat there a lot. And the first thing I do when I'm seated is to just look around the room and steep myself in the history of this great city. As it is with the other murals in this book, the panels at the Monkey Bar and the Waverly Inn form a tableaux of many stories. And they say to those who inspect them that they too are part of this magnificent continuum of human endeavor and achievement that is New York.

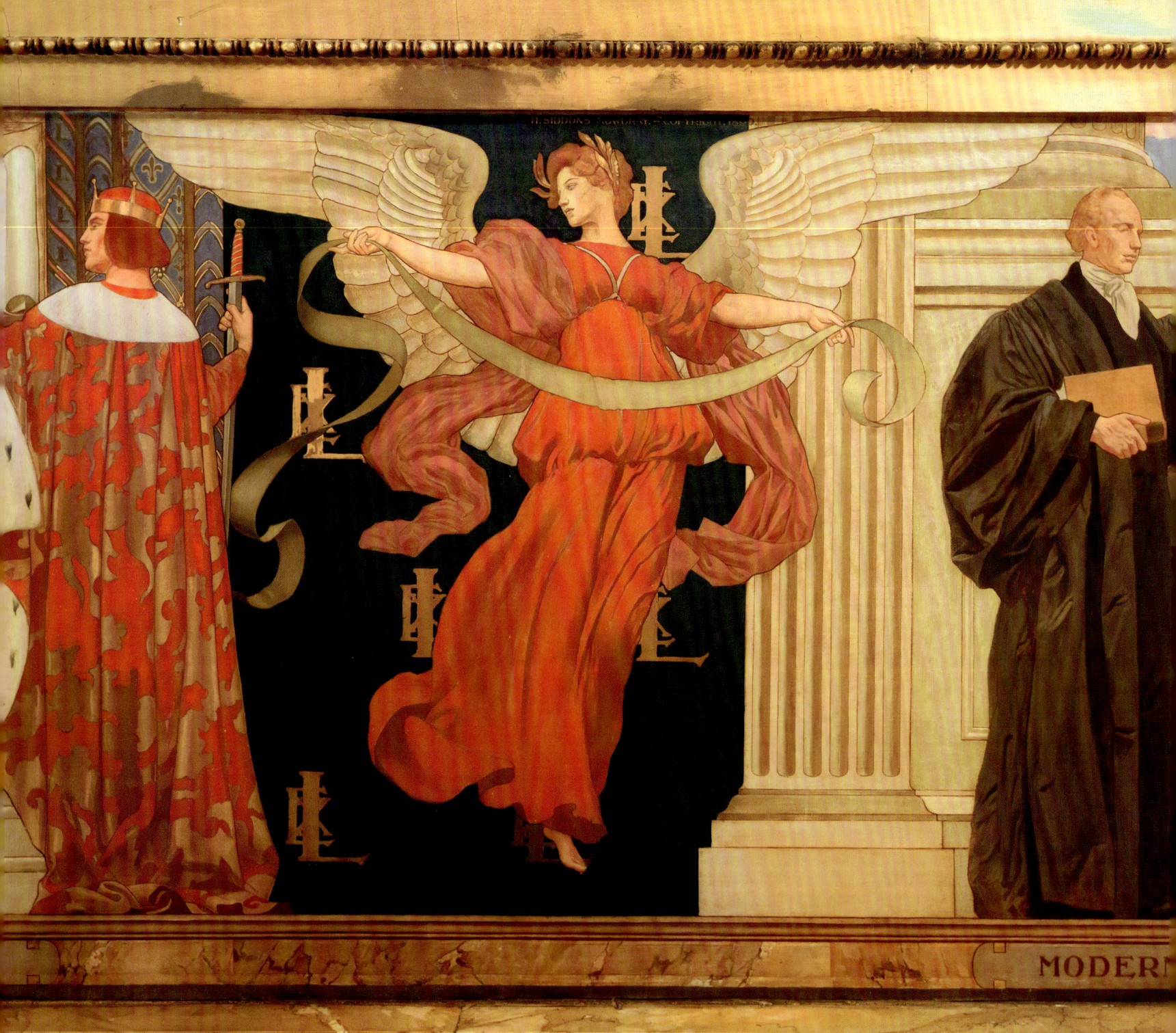

NYS SUPREME COURT, APPELLATE DIVISION

EDWIN BLASHFIELD · KENYON COX · JOSEPH LAUBER · H. SIDDONS MOWBRAY · WILLARD LEROY METCALF
ROBERT LEWIS REID · EDWARD EMERSON SIMMONS · CHARLES YARDLEY TURNER · HENRY O. WALKER

When he designed his monument to justice, architect James Brown Lord virtually copied the style of the great Italian Renaissance master builder Andrea Palladio. The majestic courthouse was wrought from the finest white and Sienna marble, onyx, gilded paneling, stained glass, and carved wood, all handcrafted by the last great generation of European artisans. Lord had complete artistic control over the project, including which painters' and sculptors' work would adorn the building. All of Lord's artists were forged from the same mold. Many were born before the Civil War in New England and made their way to New York and Paris. They studied classical painting during the Belle Époque at the l'École des Beaux-Arts, the Académie Julian, and the ateliers of the greatest artists of that time. They belonged to the same art societies, taught at the same schools, and shared a passion for traditional painting. They were the heart of the renaissance of American art that emerged as a force in the World's Columbian Exposition of 1893 in Chicago, which launched the golden age of American mural painting.

And because of this shared history, when it opened on the second day of the twentieth century, the Appellate Division courthouse was not only the grandest courthouse in America, it also represented the zenith of American mural painting. It is remarkable, and almost inconceivable in today's world of celebrity artists, that the ten leading painters of the day, all chosen by Lord to paint the courthouse murals, agreed to form a committee, headed by John La Farge, to ensure that their diverse styles could be modulated into a harmonious whole and to resolve any conflicts.

Henry Siddons Mowbray, a Paris-trained, classical artist with a flat, decorative style, painted a 62-foot-long frieze entitled *Transmission of the Law* in the center of the grand lobby. The 44-inch-high painting, which borders the top of the wall, follows the evolution of law through the centuries, beginning with Moses's descent from Mount Sinai. Ten winged angels with flowing draperies and scrolls form beautiful curvilinear patterns that provide the transitions between the eras and cultures.

Mowbray's Renaissance formality is in strong contrast to the two murals entitled *Justice* and *The Banishment of Discord*, painted on the lobby's west wall. Metcalf brought the Impressionist sensibilities and vigorous brushwork he had developed at Giverny with Claude Monet to the allegories he illustrated in these paintings, his first murals. Twelve dramatic figures of children and winged women, each rich with symbolism, portray the concepts of Law, Justice, and Equality and their impact on Oppression and Transgression. *The Banishment of Discord* presents the drama of Transgression and Discord being driven away by the forces of Justice and Goodness.

Robert Lewis Reid was another American Impressionist. In a dramatic departure from his usual subject—decorative images of young women with flowers—he illustrated his version of *Justice* on the opposite wall from Metcalf's *Justice*. Winged angelic women representing peace, prosperity, drama, music, education, and religion are flanked by men guarding the law, carrying banners and bundles of sticks. His second panel, *Fame*, exalts the arts.

Above the entrance are two spandrels by Charles Yardley Turner, the least-known painter of the group. As such, his contribution is small and, because of the placement, often overlooked if not unnoticeable. On the left, a woman representing Equity holds an orb and sword while a child at her feet balances the scales of justice. On the right is a woman holding a scroll bearing her name, Lex (Latin for "Law"). The child at her feet holds a mirror representing Truth.

An ornate triptych, placed on the eastern wall faces the judges' bench to remind them of their duty to justice. The three paintings, equal in size and separated by slender marble pilasters, show influences of Italian masters such as Raphael and Michelangelo and conform to a low-key palette of colors that harmonize with the room.

Edward Emerson Simmons created the painting on the left of the triptych, *The Justice of the Law*. Ralph Waldo Emerson's nephew and, at the time, the preeminent American muralist, Simmons achieved a beautiful effect by keeping the central figure in sharp focus while gradually softening the focus as he moved toward the outer edges and the other figures.

The central panel of the triptych is entitled *The Wisdom of the Law*, by Henry O. Walker. Walker uses soft, diffuse light and gentle colors to show Wisdom descending a staircase. The total effect is one of tranquility and peace.

The panel on the right, *The Power of the Law*, by Edwin Blashfield, is a highly decorative composition of Law, a woman dressed in white. Against the background of a faux mosaic is a visual cacophony of legal history and noble sentiments.

On the opposite wall, behind the judge's elaborately carved dark oak dais, is a four-panel frieze by Kenyon Cox, a devotee of classical painting. In *The Reign of Law*, women are the embodiment of justice, law, and peace, the very foundation of civilization—ironic, given that the mural was painted at a time when women did not have the right to vote.

On the north and south walls are sixteen Italianate panels painted by Joseph Lauber. The paintings, all of which could easily be imagined as hanging in the Sistine Chapel, explore the concepts of justice, courage, and patriotism.

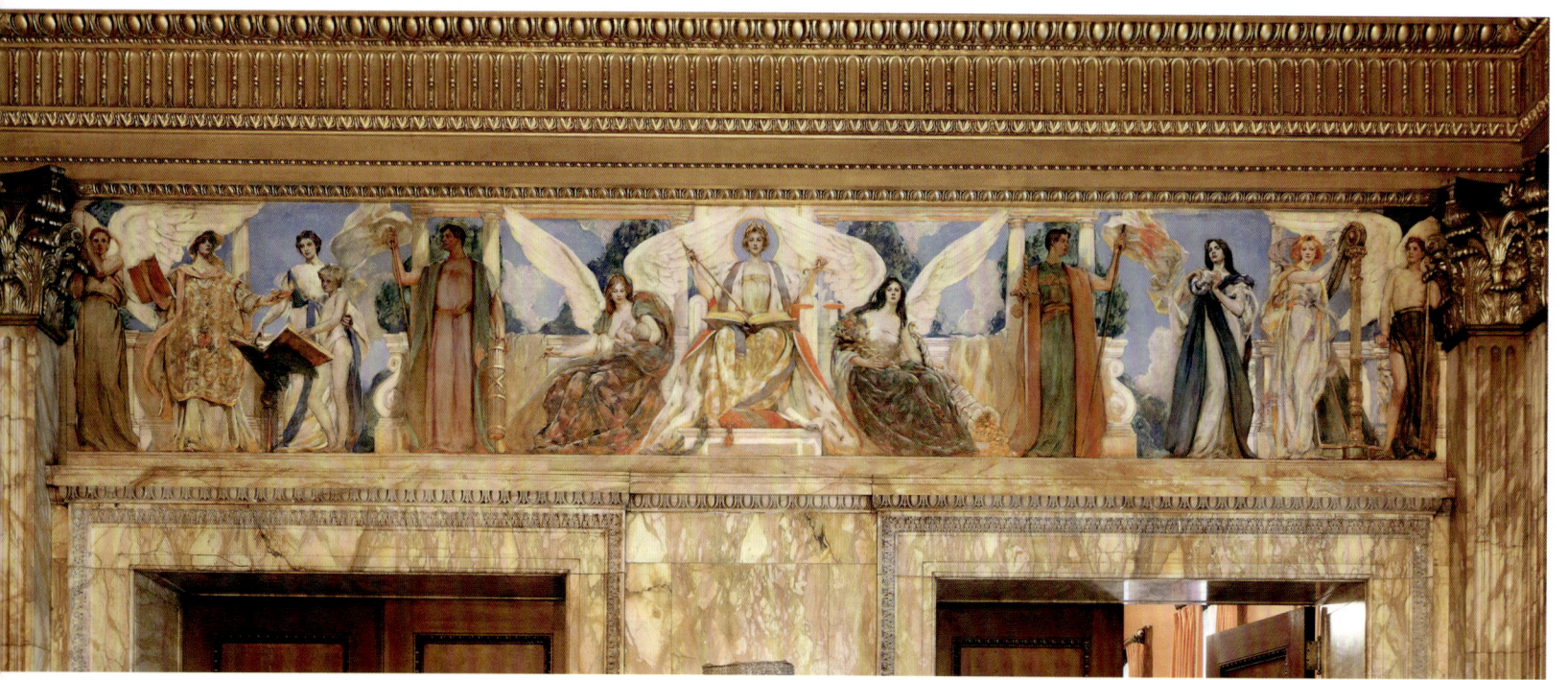

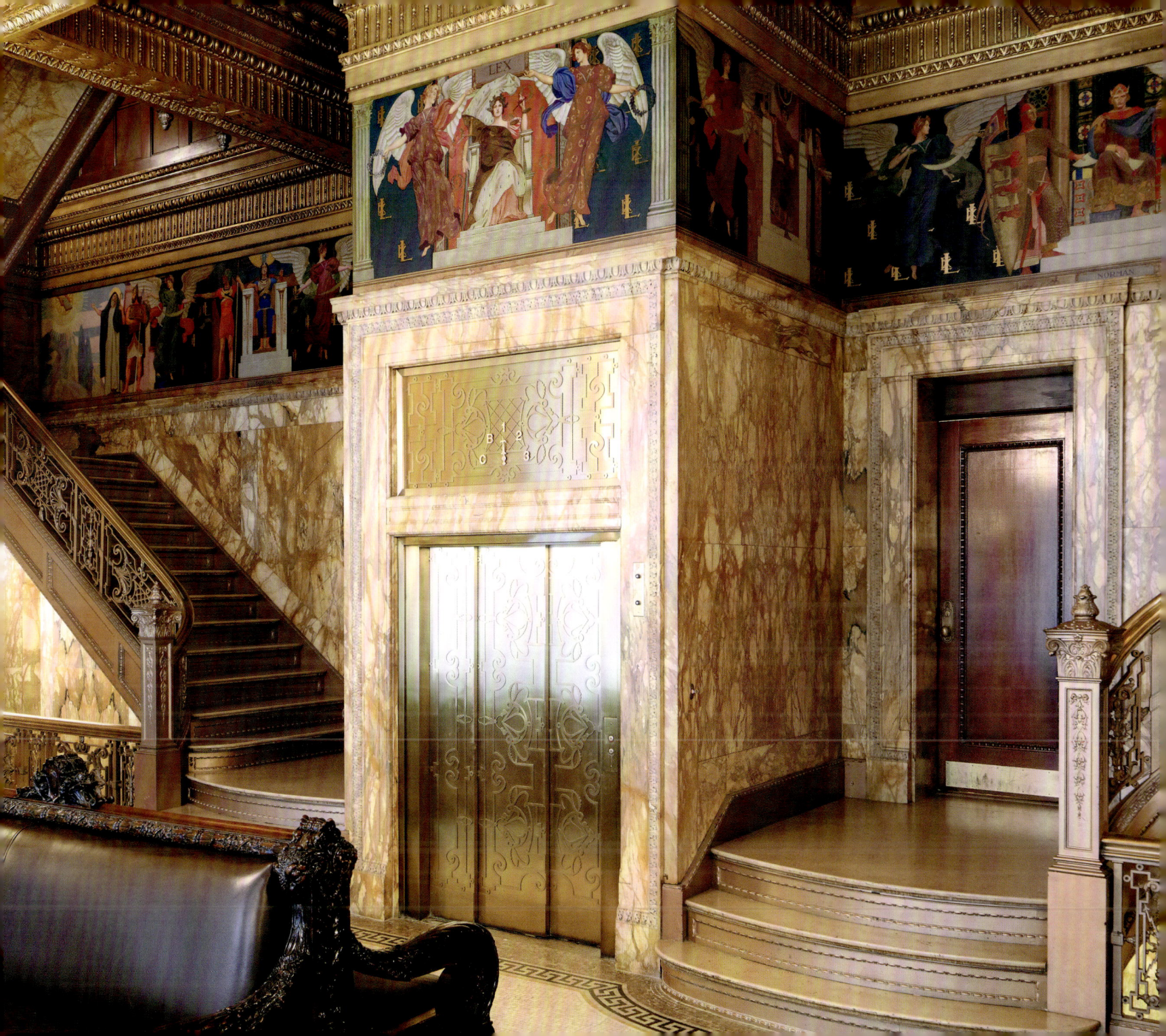

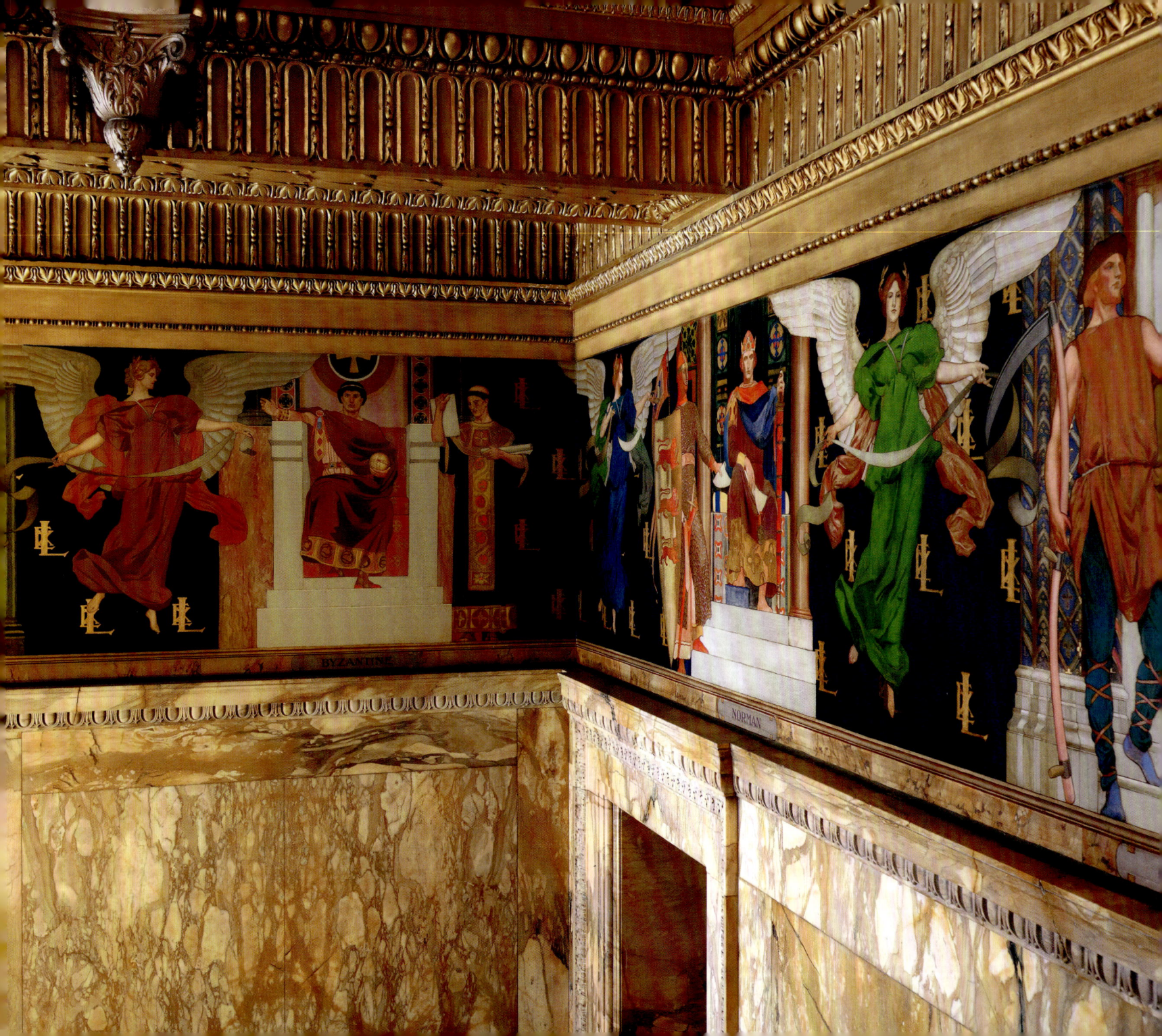

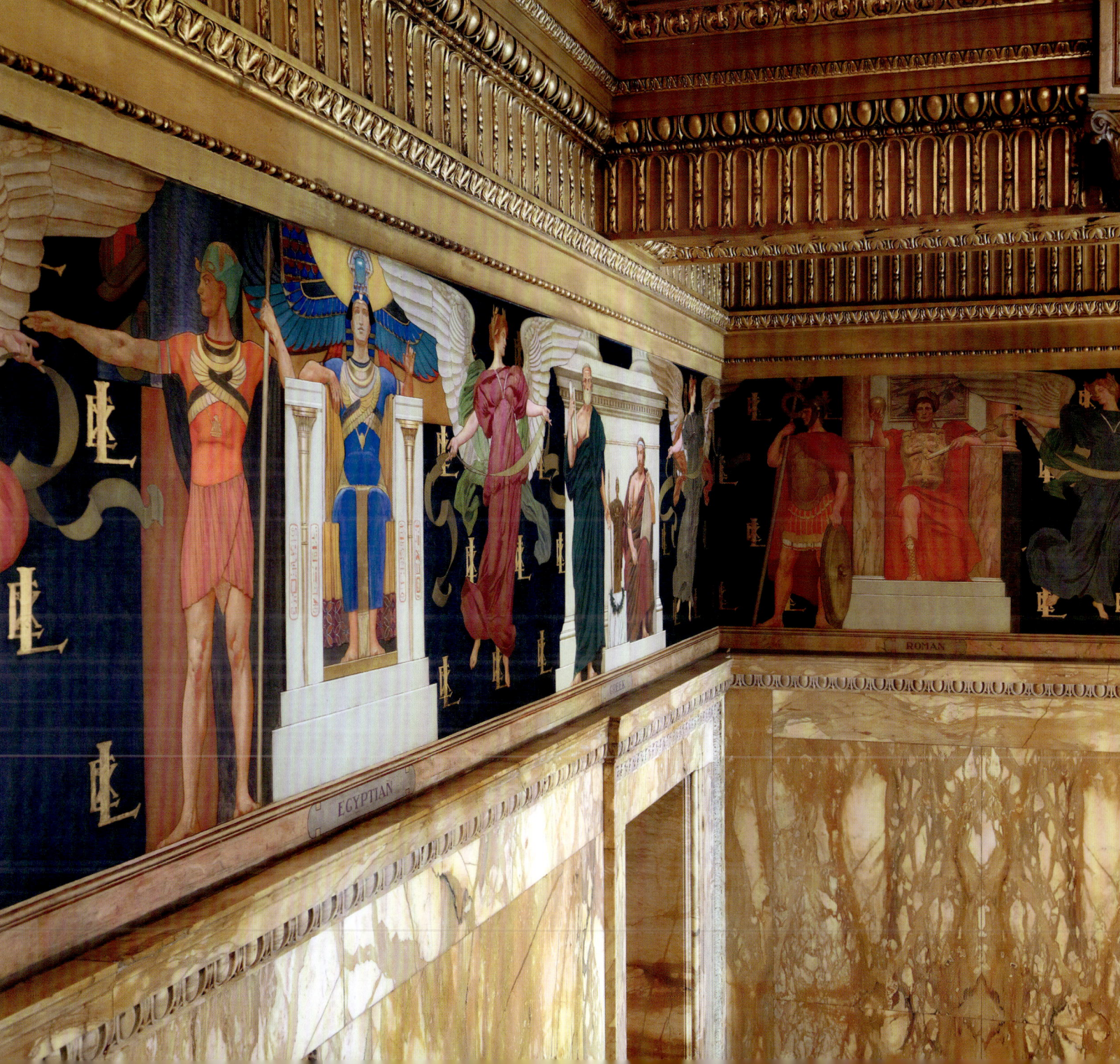

EGYPTIAN

ROMAN

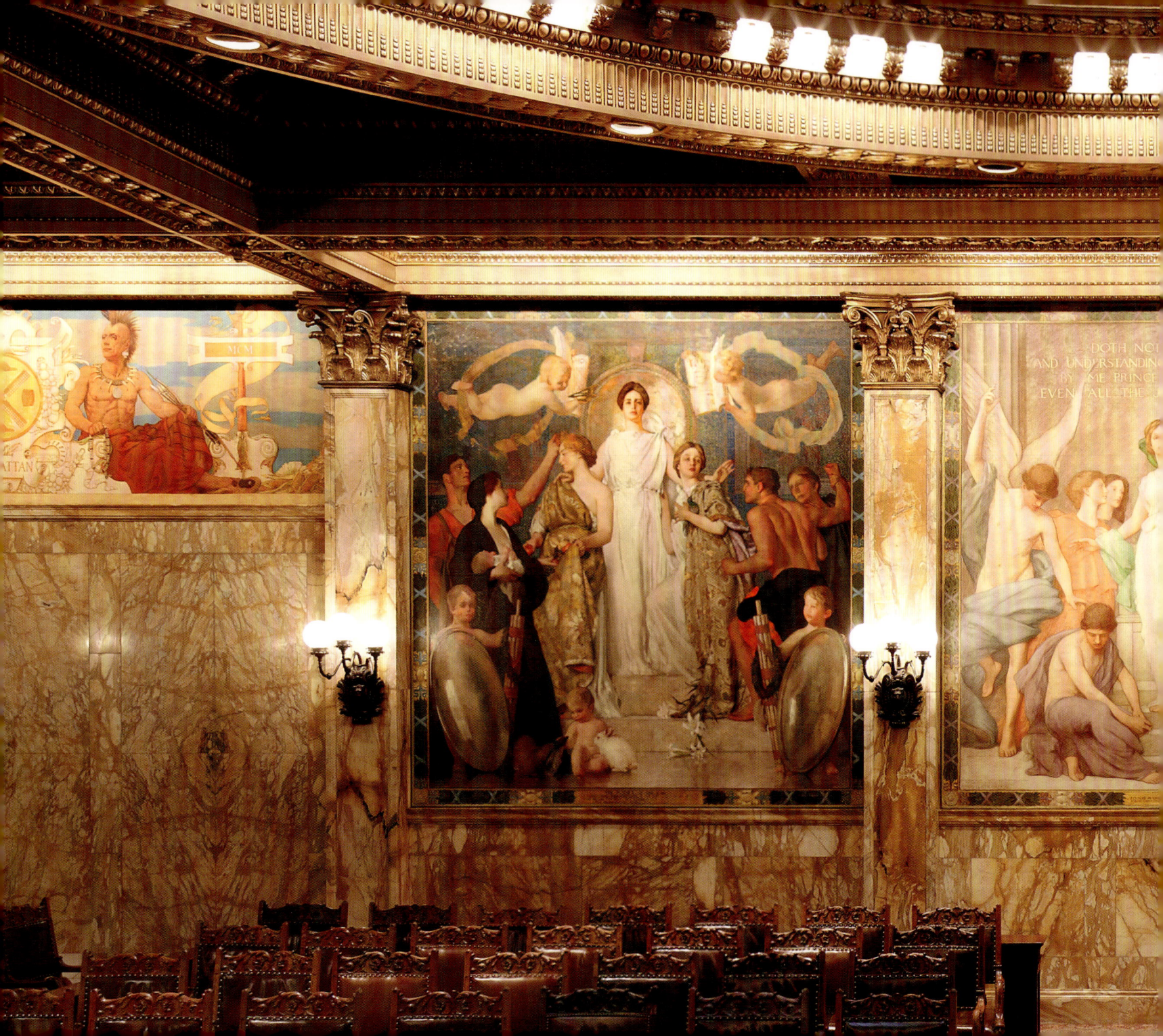

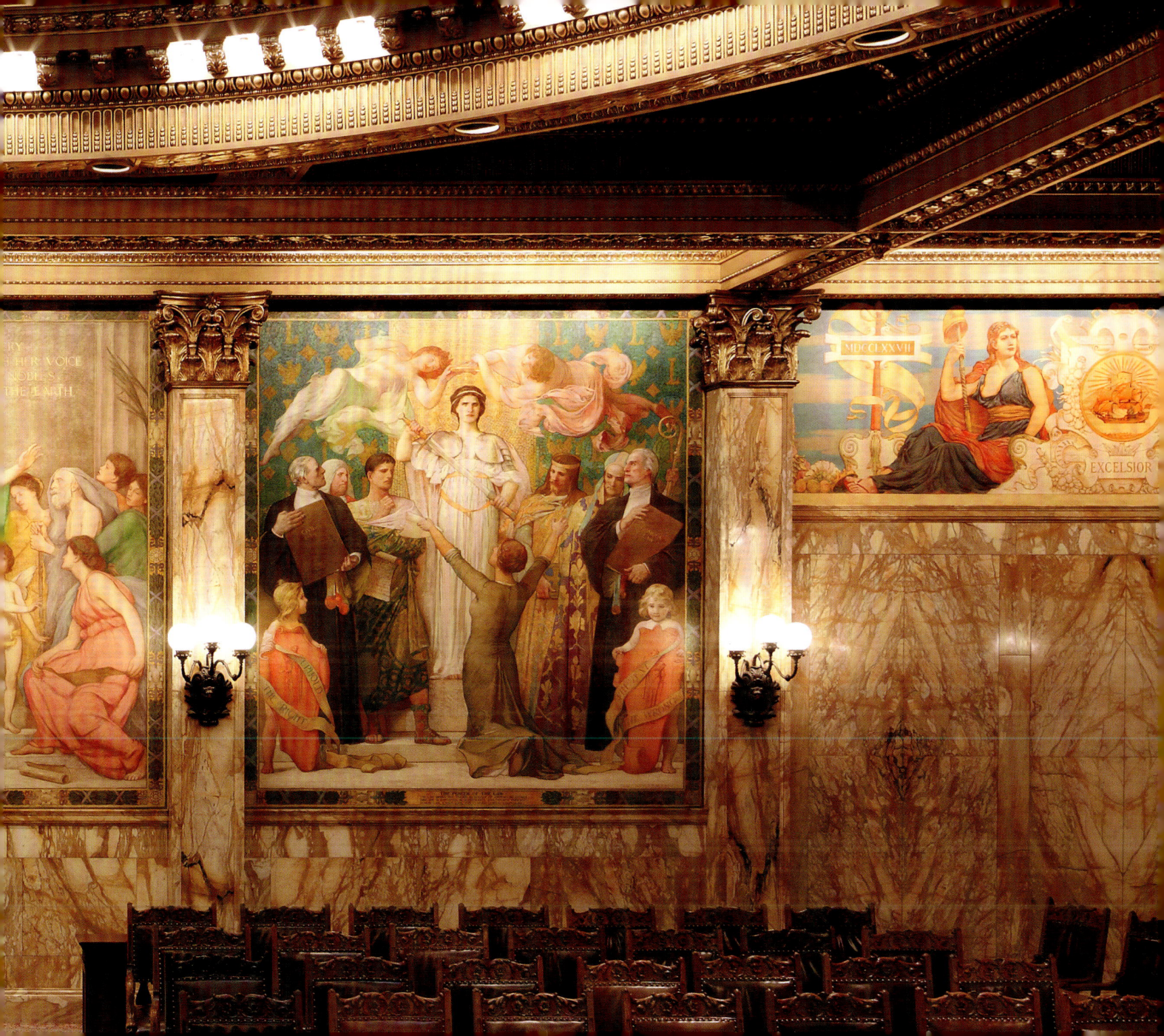

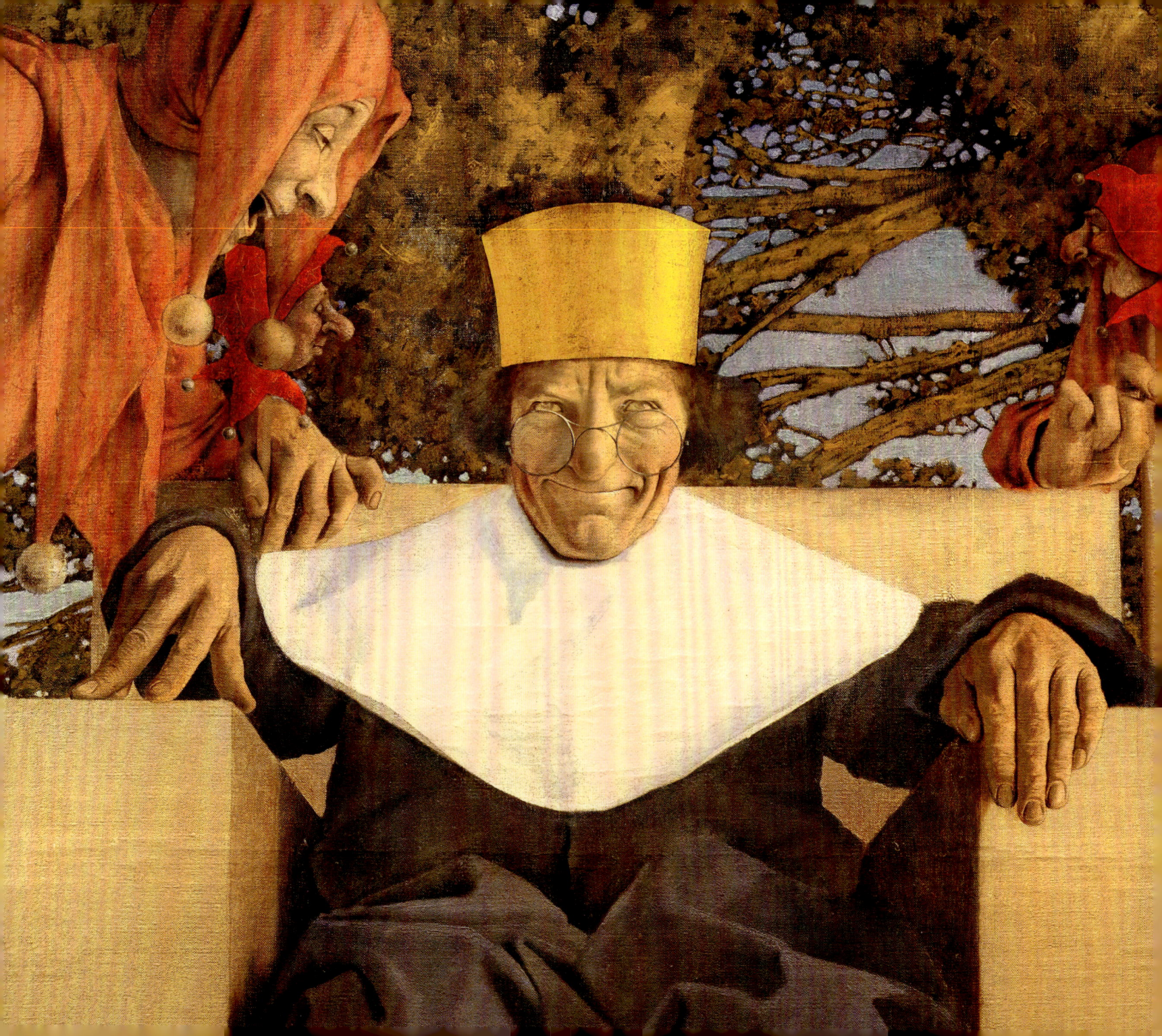

KING COLE BAR

One glides on marble polished to a liquid gloss toward Maxfield Parrish's luminous masterpiece glowing softly in the bar. The elegance and glitter of the St. Regis fades into the background. The hotel, patrons, bartenders—all of us—are in service to the king.

Maxfield Parrish was one of the most beloved artists during the golden age of American illustration. His dreamlike, surrealistic work has been called heroic realism. A little over a century ago, John Jacob Astor IV invited Maxfield Parrish to paint a mural for the bar in his new Knickerbocker Hotel, the American birthplace of the Bloody Mary. Parrish was a teetotaling Quaker and the idea of painting for a barroom offended his patrician sensibilities. But commerce trumped virtue, and Parrish agreed to accept the $5,000 commission. Soon after, Astor presented another challenge to Parrish. Astor reasoned that if he were going to shell out that kind of money, it would only be logical that he be portrayed as the king in the painting, which was to be of Old King Cole. Parrish agreed again and, in doing so, exacted his revenge and won a competition. His clique, composed of the major painters of the day, had wagered that it could come up with a subject that he couldn't possibly paint: a fart. Parrish accepted the challenge. In the mural that he painted for Astor and that was paid for by Astor, the king, as Astor, is sitting on his "throne" breaking wind. Parrish won the bet.

The twin jesters flanking the king are both self-portraits of Parrish ridiculing his patron's flatulence. In fact, all of the figures in the 8-by-30-foot painting resemble Parrish—the mural is a study in passive aggression. One of the secrets to the rich beauty of the painting is Parrish's use of the old masters' technique of glazing. Glazing is a process in which multiple, thin, transparent layers of pure color, separated with a layer of varnish, are applied over a white ground. As light passes through the colors, it is reflected back from the white base, mixing all the colors together. The brilliance of color derived from glazing is impossible to achieve by traditional methods of mixing pigments and applying them directly to a canvas. Light seems to emanate from the painting. And that unique cobalt blue of the work is a color that he created and often used in his paintings and which came to be known as "Parrish blue."

When the Knickerbocker Hotel became an office building, the painting was moved to the Chicago Art Institute. It returned to New York for a brief appearance at the New York Racquet and Tennis Club until finally, during the Depression, it found its way to its present home at the St. Regis Hotel. When the painting was taken down and cleaned for its hundredth birthday, it was appraised at $12 million.

We can safely assume that every celebrity of the past century has sat in front of "King Cole." Norman Rockwell loved the painting and referred to Parrish as his "idol." Ernest Hemingway, Salvador Dalí, Marlene Dietrich, John Lennon, Yoko Ono, Joe DiMaggio, and Marilyn Monroe all lived at the hotel and were regulars at the King Cole Bar. Just for fun, imagine meeting one of them for a drink in front of that wonderful piece of New York elegance. You can't miss.

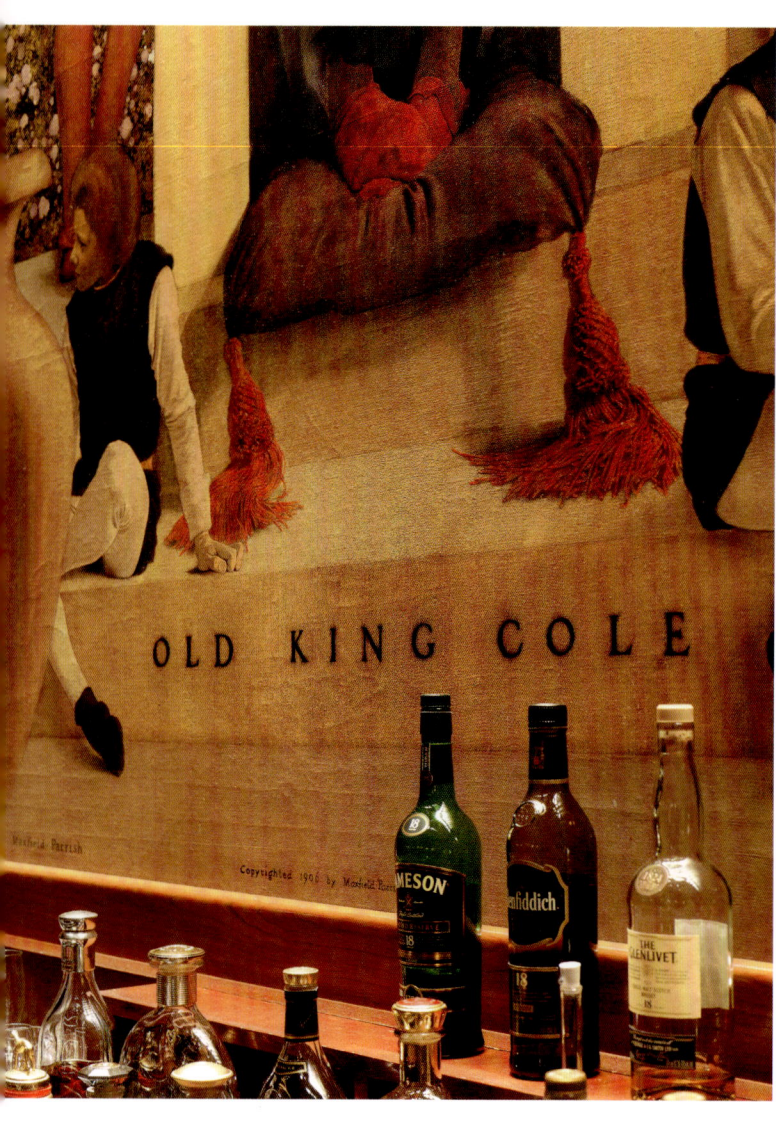

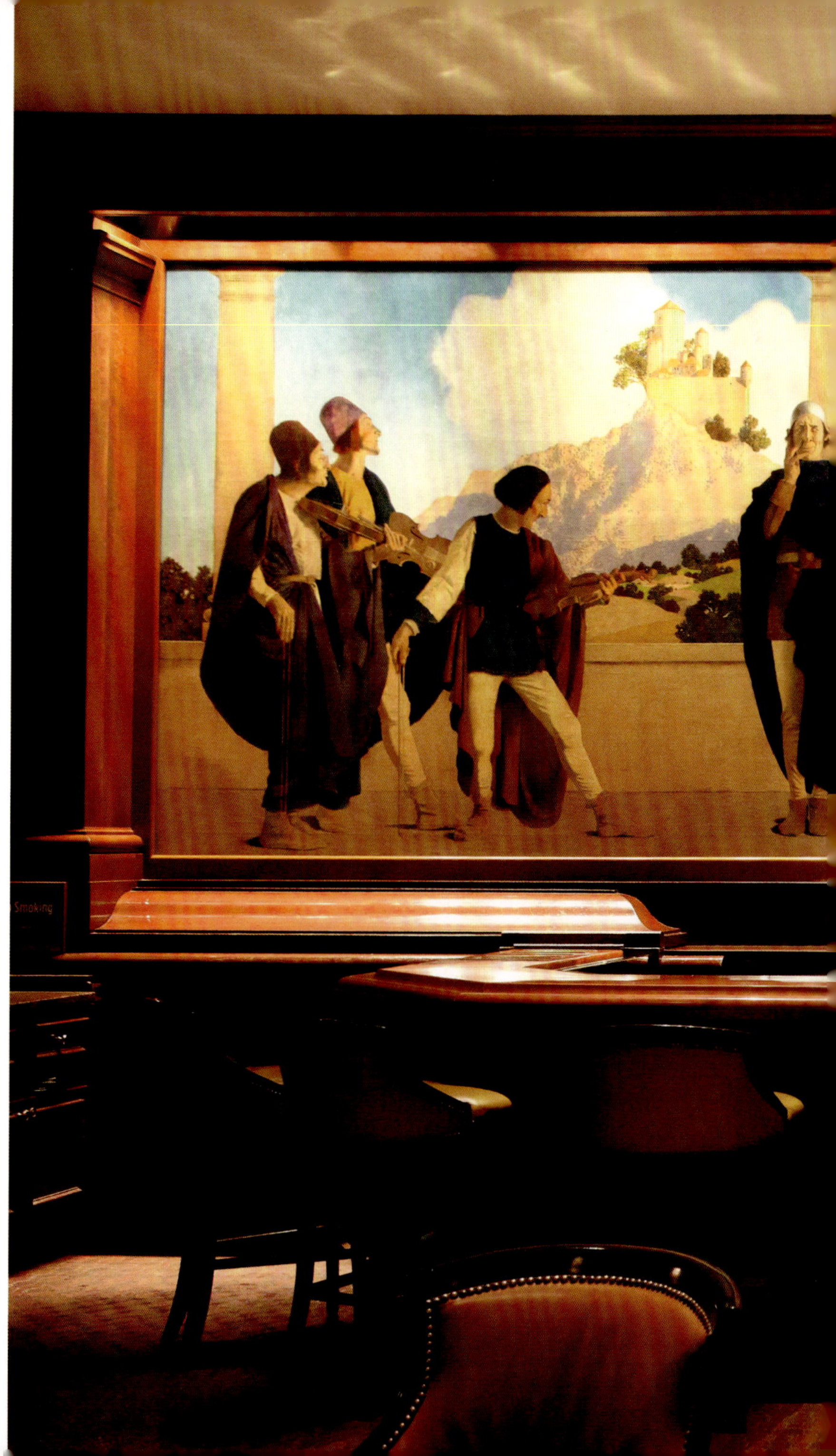

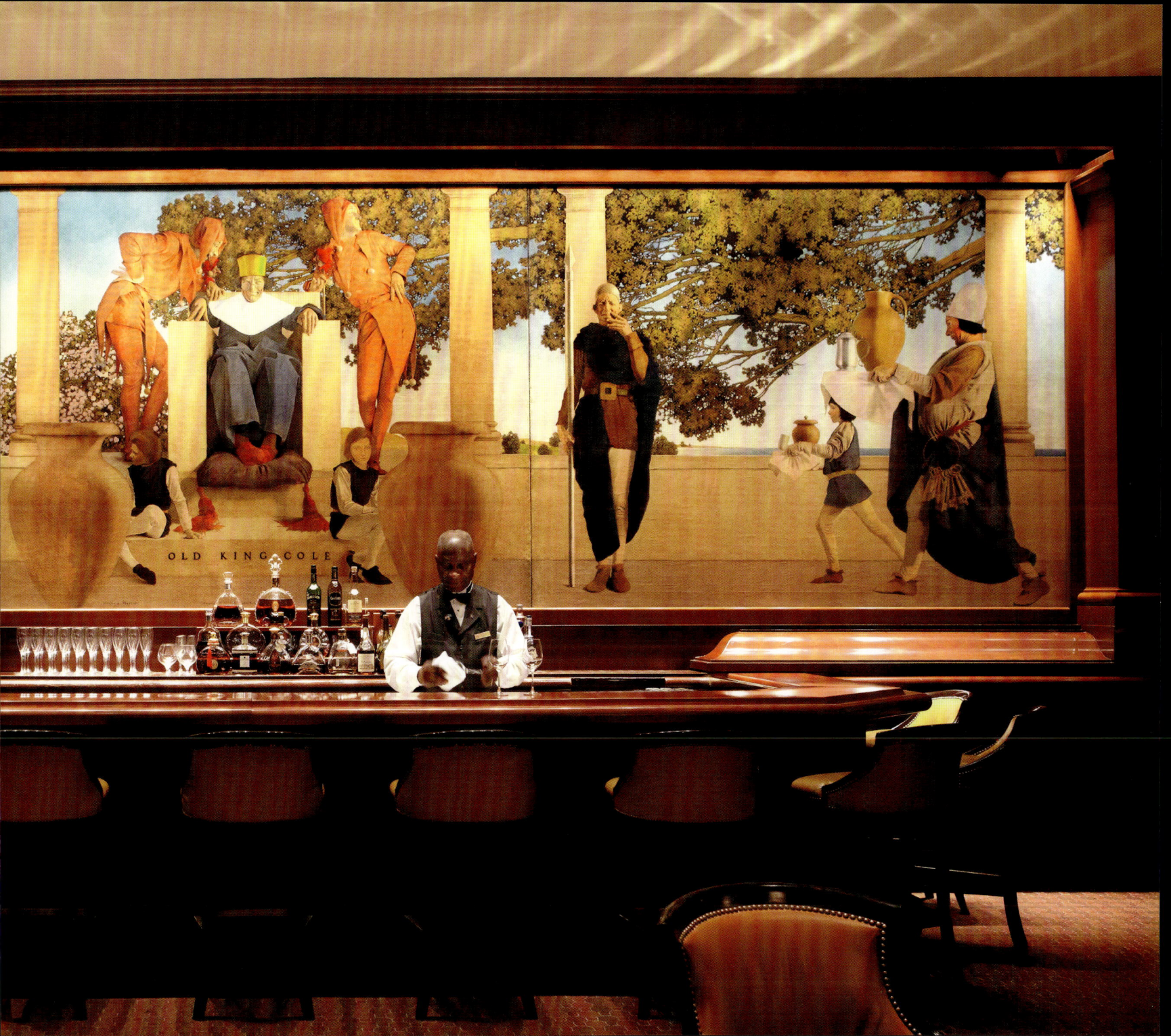

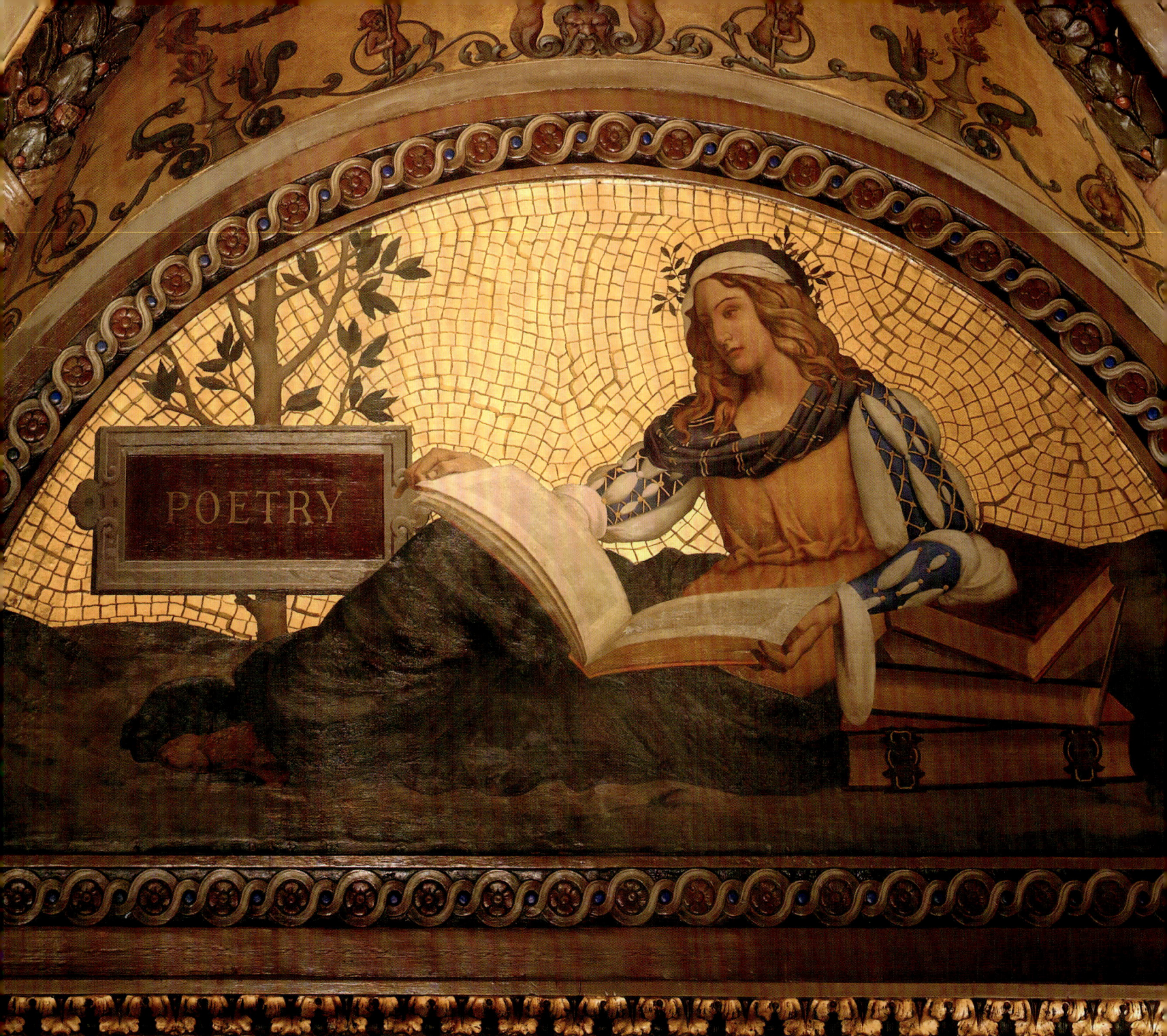

POETRY

THE MORGAN LIBRARY & MUSEUM

29 East 36th Street, Manhattan   •   H. SIDDONS MOWBRAY

Henry Siddons Mowbray was born in Alexandria, Egypt, to English parents in 1858. Adopted by his uncle George Mowbray, he was raised in Massachusetts. By the time he was twenty, he was studying classical painting in the Parisian studio of the influential painter and teacher Léon Bonnat. Mowbray returned to America at the height of the post Civil War building boom known as the American Renaissance. It was the perfect time for Mowbray, whose training and passion for the Italian Renaissance blended with the era's style of luxury homes and civic spaces.

Starting in the 1880s, Mowbray painted his first murals in the mansion of railroad magnate Collis Potter Huntington, located across the street from the Vanderbilt mansion. The Vanderbilts had to keep up with the Huntingtons, so they hired Mowbray to paint their Charles McKim–designed mansion in Hyde Park. McKim then used Mowbray to paint murals for the University Club. Soon thereafter, J. Pierpont Morgan, arguably the greatest art collector of the twentieth century, commissioned McKim to design the Morgan Library to house his magnificent collection. The library is now home to three Gutenberg bibles, extraordinary illuminated manuscripts, Charles Dickens's original manuscript of *A Christmas Carol*, the penned poems of Robert Burns and Percy Bysshe Shelley, scores of Beethoven, Mozart, and Verdi, drawings by Michelangelo and da Vinci, and recent acquisitions including scraps of paper upon which Bob Dylan wrote "Blowin' in the Wind."

McKim based his design on the beautiful Villa Madama in Rome. Mowbray had already spent two years in Rome studying decorative painting in preparation for the University Club murals. His depth of knowledge of fifteenth-century Italian art, coupled with his highly developed technical skills, taste, and discipline

made him the only artist to be entrusted with a commission of this magnitude. McKim, naturally, commissioned Mowbray to paint portions of the Library's Rotunda and East Room.

The commission carried with it the imperative that the work be completed no later than October 1, 1905, or within half a year of the plasterwork's completion, a deadline that was extended to accommodate construction delays and the reality of how long it took to paint at Mowbray's level of quality.

For his University Club murals, Mowbray had been criticized for copying Pinturicchio's paintings from the Liberal Arts Room of the Vatican's Borgia apartments. To avoid repeating himself and further inviting criticism, he composed unique compositions inspired by Italian Renaissance masters. The Rotunda lunettes and ceiling are a richly intricate paean to ancient, medieval, and Renaissance poetry. Characters from *The Iliad*, *The Odyssey*, *The Divine Comedy*, and the court of King Arthur appear in a richly complicated tableau.

The three-dimensional gilding of King Arthur's crown, sword, and chain are a particularly remarkable aspect in this tour de force. Each detail was sculpted out of a paste composite on the canvas and then gilded. Mowbray also employed trompe l'oeil to create an arch, complete with faux marble, to simulate the other arches.

Mowbray worked for three years on the canvases in his studio in Greenwich Village. They were finished and installed in 1906 as the major construction work was nearing completion. By the autumn of 1907, he returned to approve and adjust the lighting. When Morgan entered the finished library for the first time, he said, "This I used to consider as my library. Now it is Mowbray's."

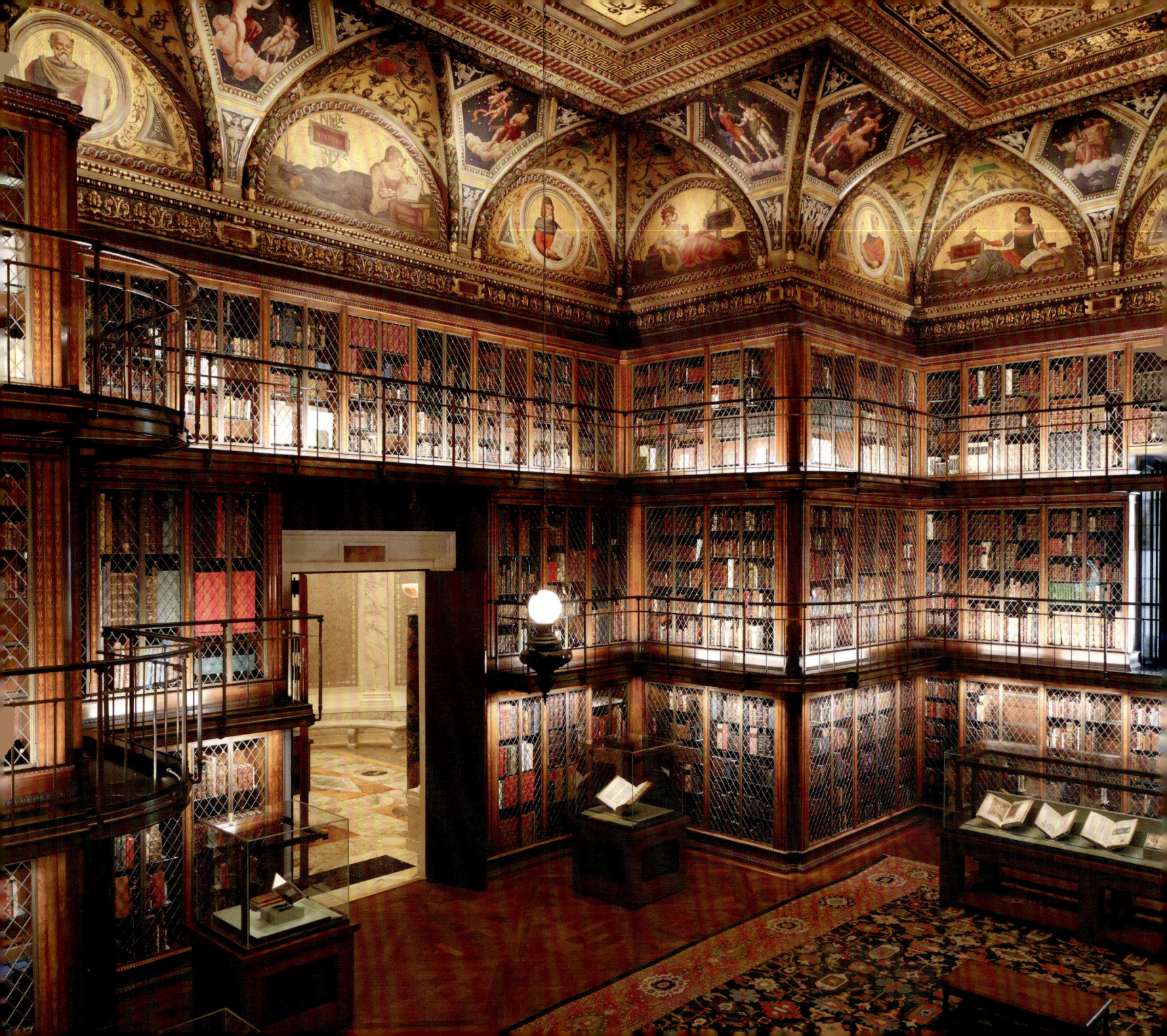

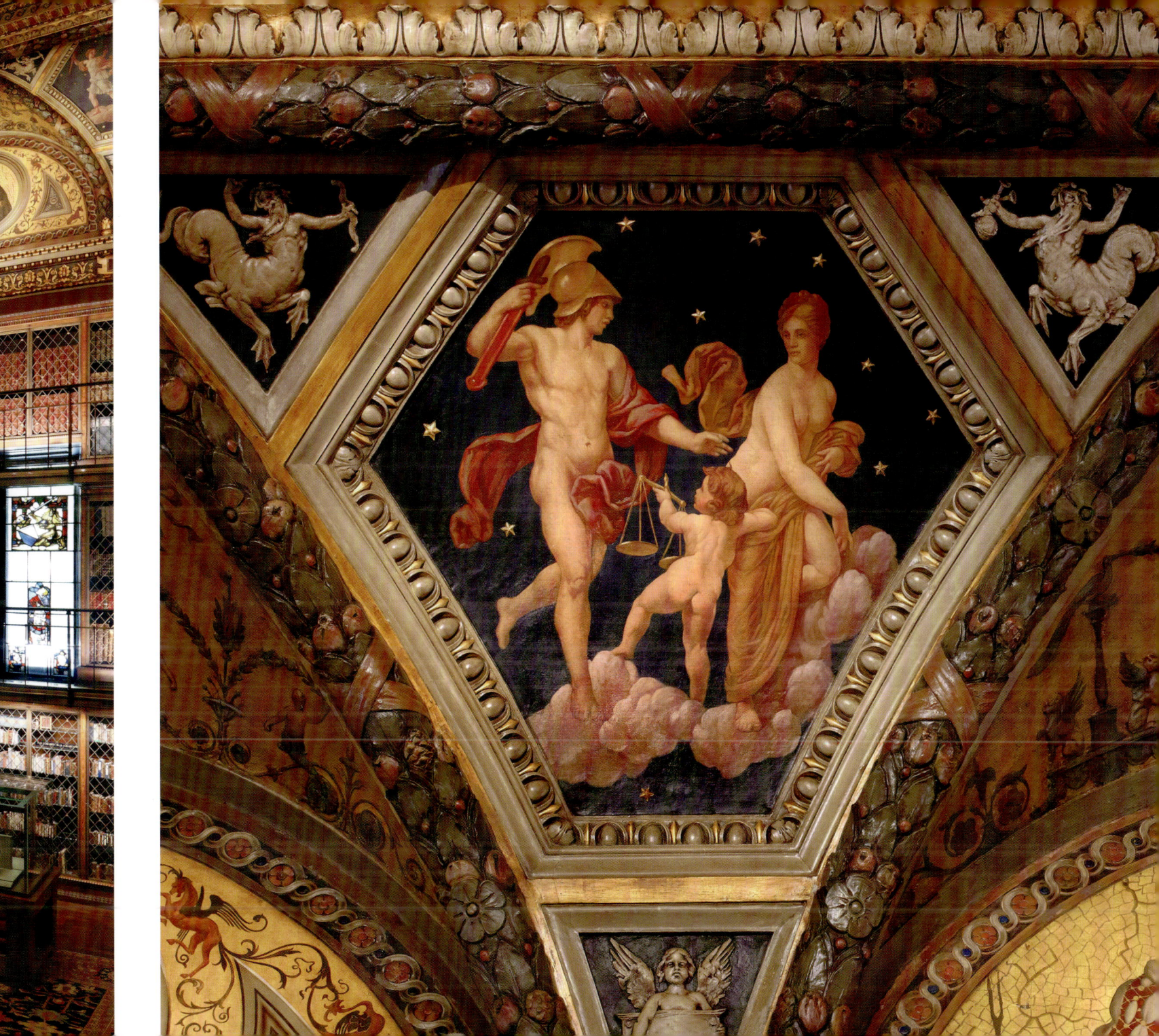

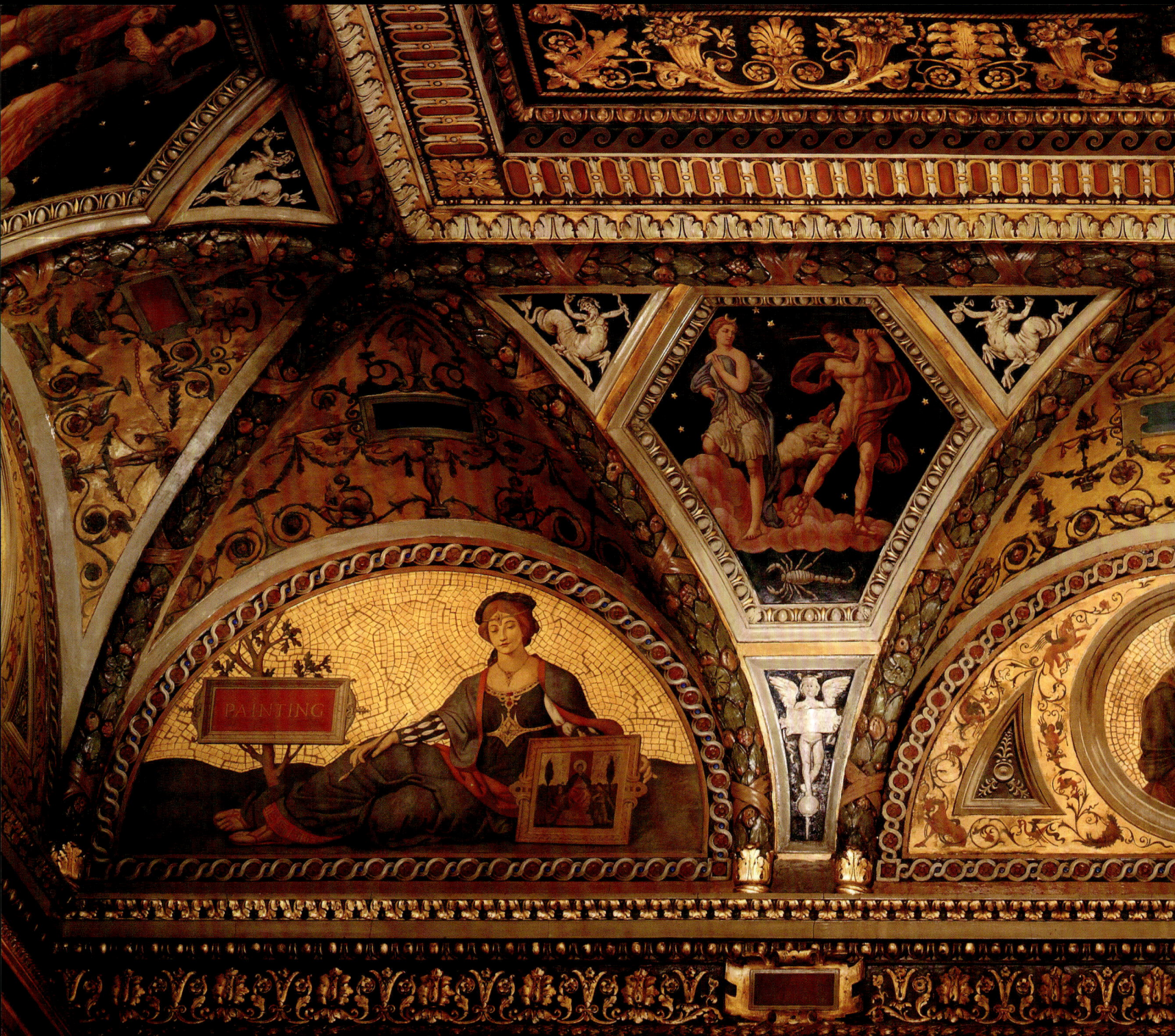

PAINTING

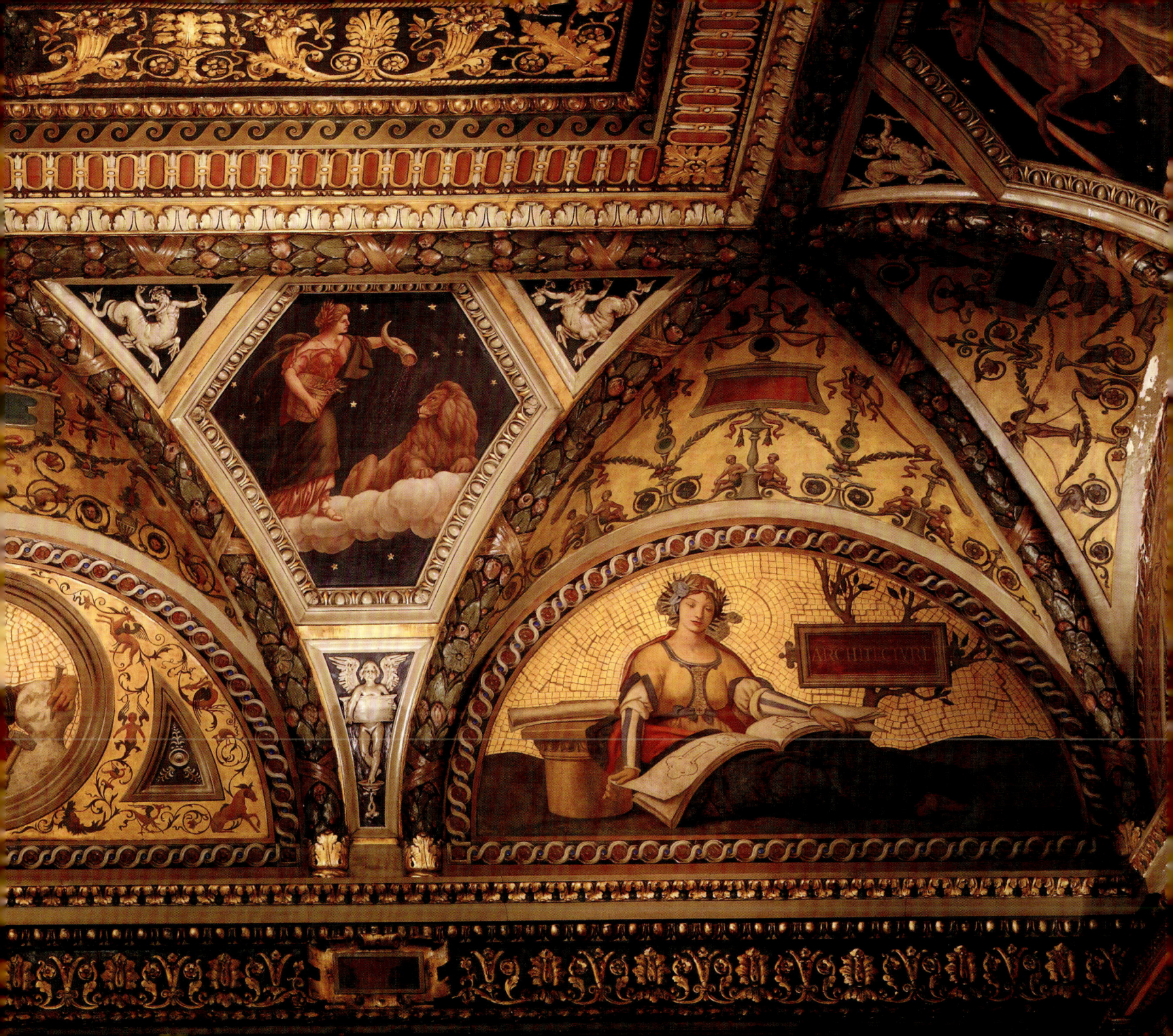

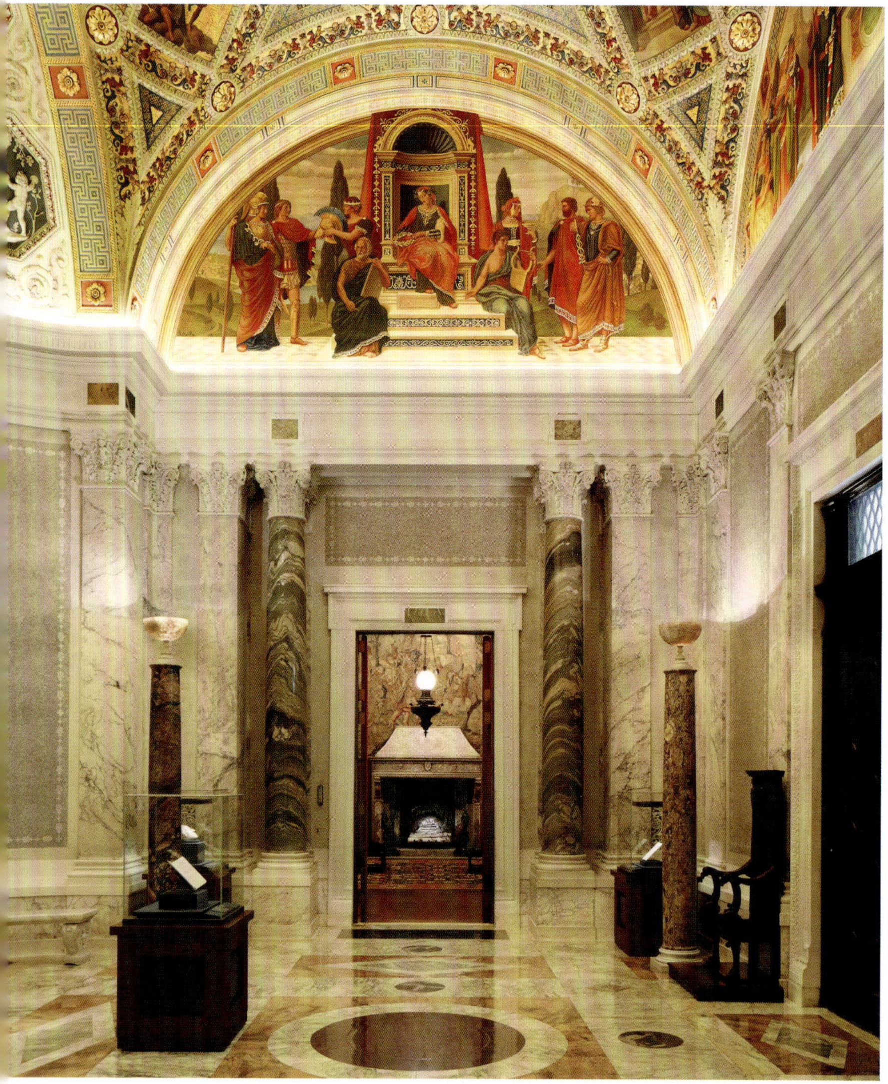

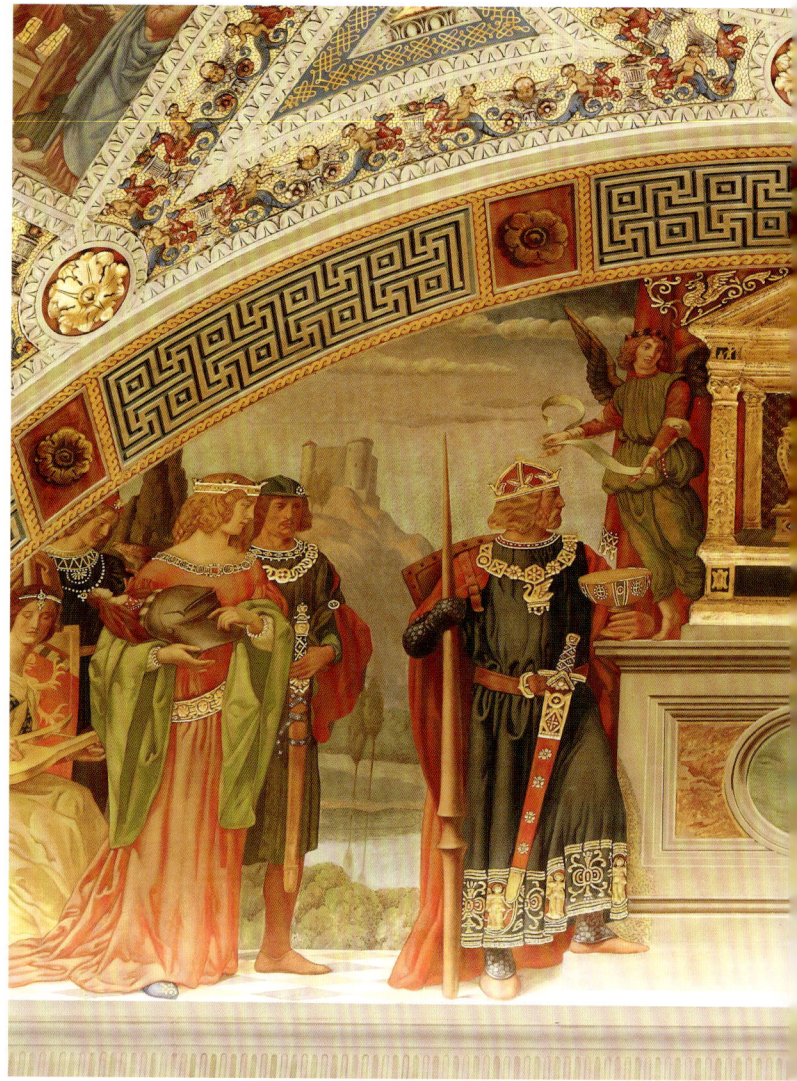

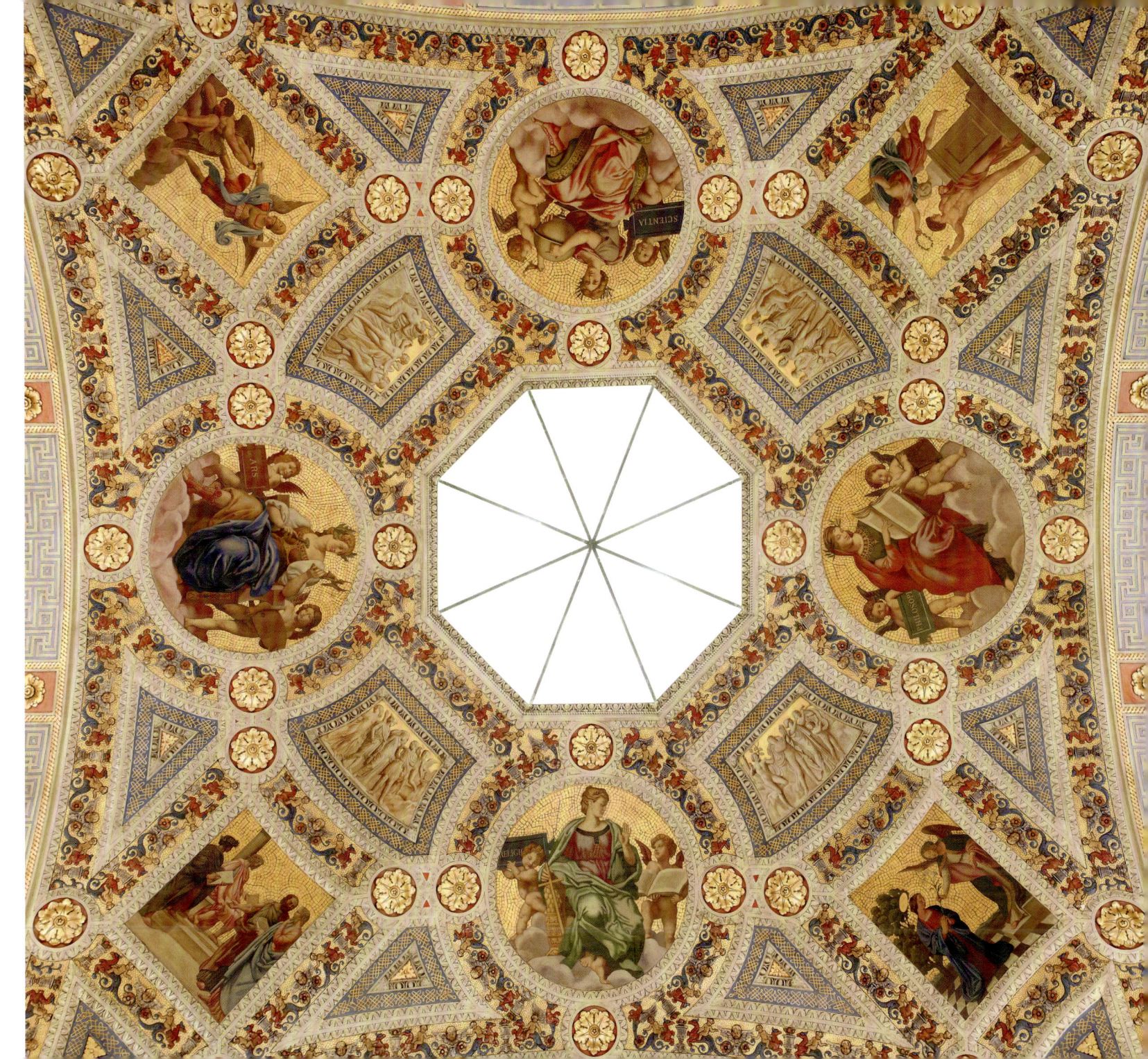

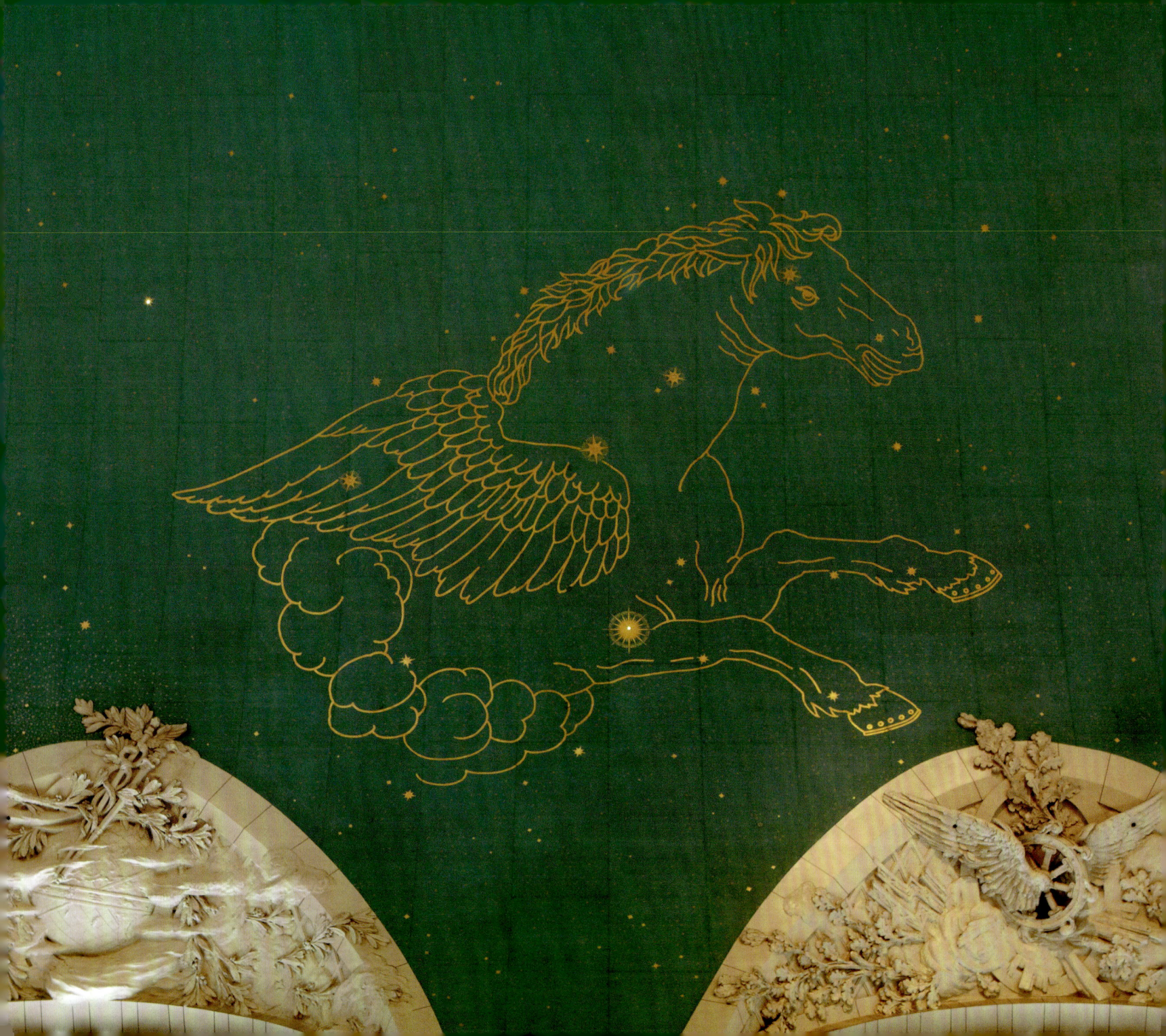

GRAND CENTRAL TERMINAL

The main room of Cornelius Vanderbilt's Grand Central Terminal was supposed to feature a skylight. But the architect, Whitney Warren, facing budgetary problems, opted to commission French artist Paul César Helleu to paint an 80,000-square-foot ceiling mural instead. No other artist epitomizes the elegance of the Belle Époque as Paul Helleu. A close friend of Marcel Proust, his social circle included James McNeill Whistler, John Singer Sargent, James Tissot, August Rodin, Edgar Degas, Pierre-Auguste Renoir, Oscar Wilde, Coco Chanel, and Charlie Chaplin.

Warren asked Helleu to create a stylized, Mediterranean-inspired starscape of the October-to-March zodiac and the equatorial line. Helleu was best known for his portraiture, so he hired a technical adviser, Professor of Astronomy Dr. Harold Jacoby, to assist. Jacoby presented Helleu with a diagram based on a map in the *Uranometria*, a seventeenth century astrological atlas by Johann Bayer. Bayer had reversed the anthropomorphic constellations, so in the atlas, Orion and the other humans and demigods are shown from the back, rather than the front, as they are seen in the night sky.

Helleu's vision of the nighttime heavens is painted a cerulean blue of daytime, embellished with gold leaf representing twenty-five thousand stars. The sixty stars indicating the astrological signs were originally illuminated by electric lights in the ceiling and later replaced by fiber-optic lights and then LEDs. Helleu surrendered the execution of his vision to Australian Charles Basing, who changed the heavens even more than Bayer had. Basing's final mural reverses the sky, so all the constellations are also reversed, save Orion the Hunter, which was shown incorrectly in the *Uranometria*, and which is now the only astronomically correct element in the mural. No one seemed to notice until, about a month after the terminal opened, an amateur astronomer commuting through Grand Central Terminal reported it to the *New York Times*. The embarrassed Vanderbilts insisted that the mistake was intentional, and this vision of the universe was from God's point of view.

Basing's apprentice, Charles Gulbrandsen, restored the mural in 1945. By the mid-1990s, the mural was so blackened that it was restored a second time. The restorer, John Canning, used sixty-five hundred cotton rags, fifteen hundred gallons of water, and the same cleaning agent used to clean the Sistine Chapel. In the northwest corner, a small rectangle remains to show what the ceiling looked like before the cleaning—and to remind us why we shouldn't smoke.

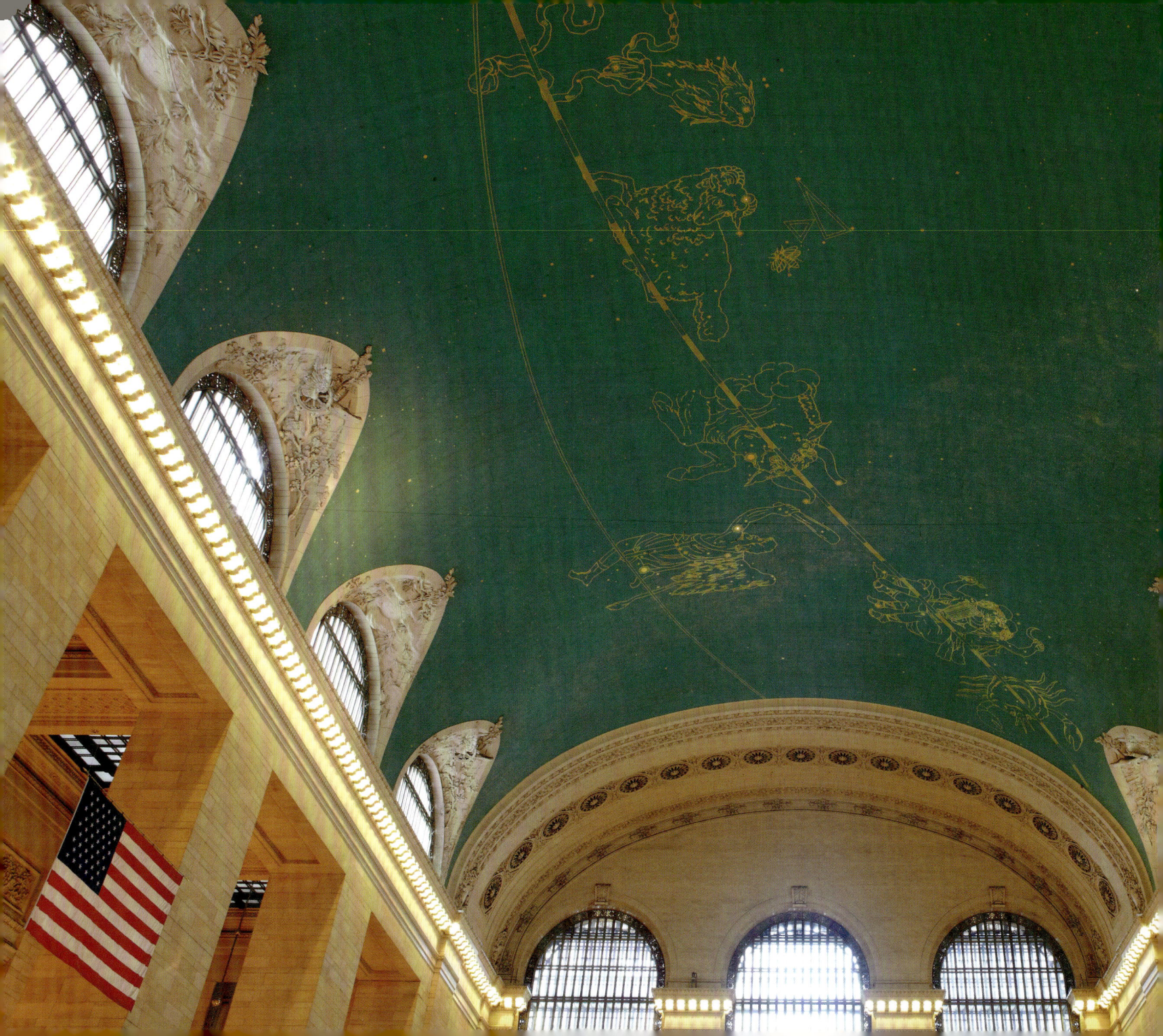

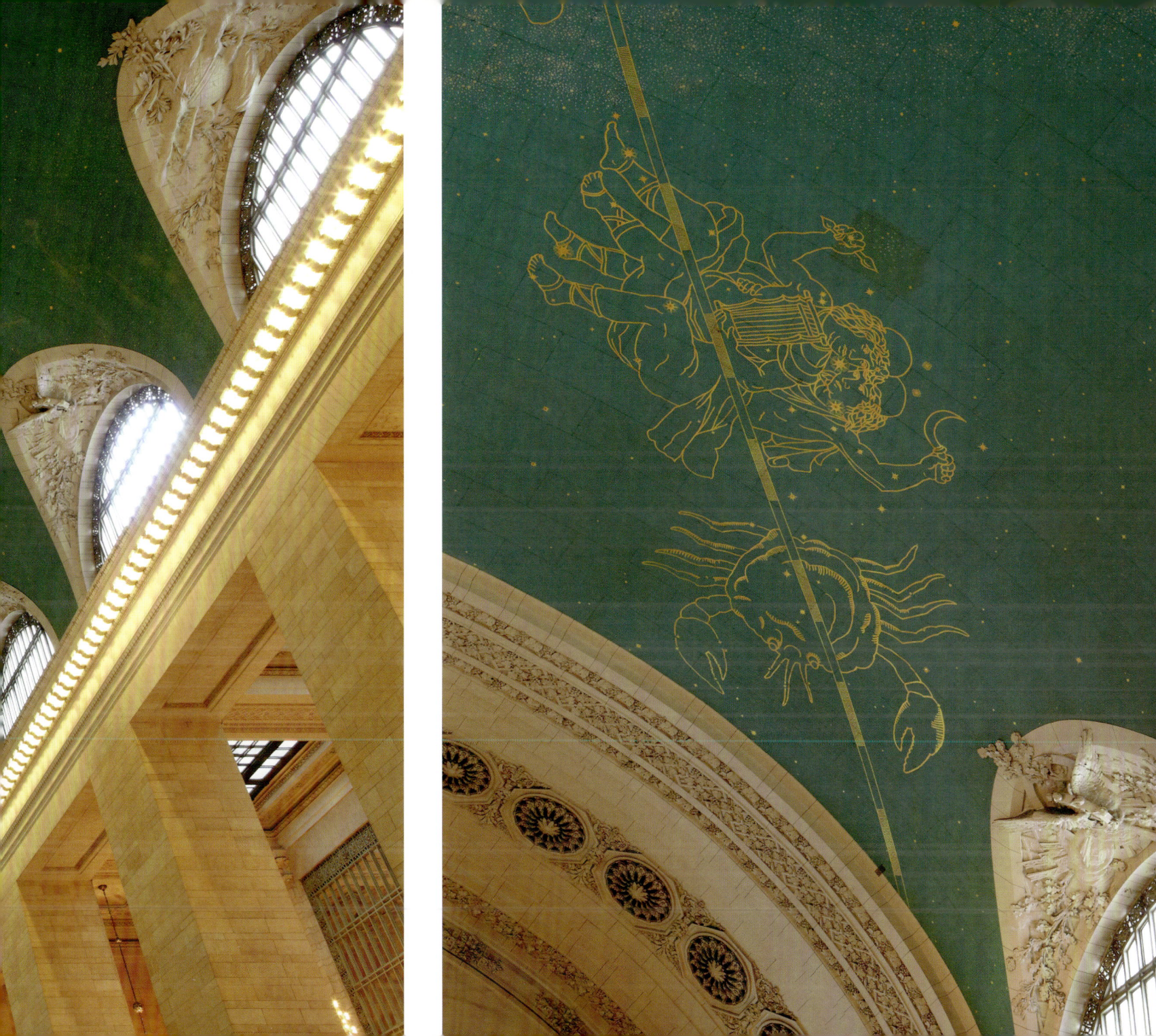

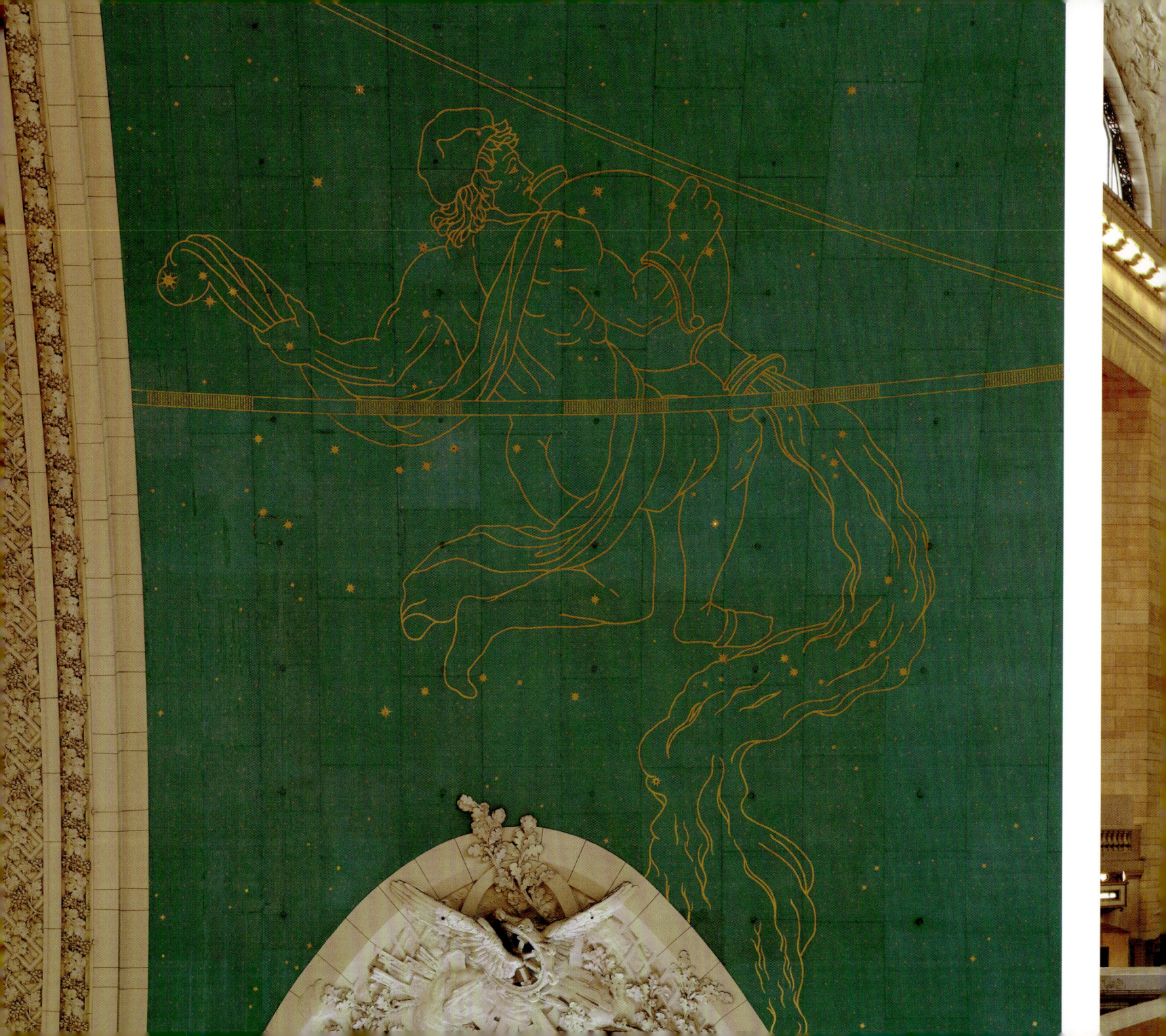

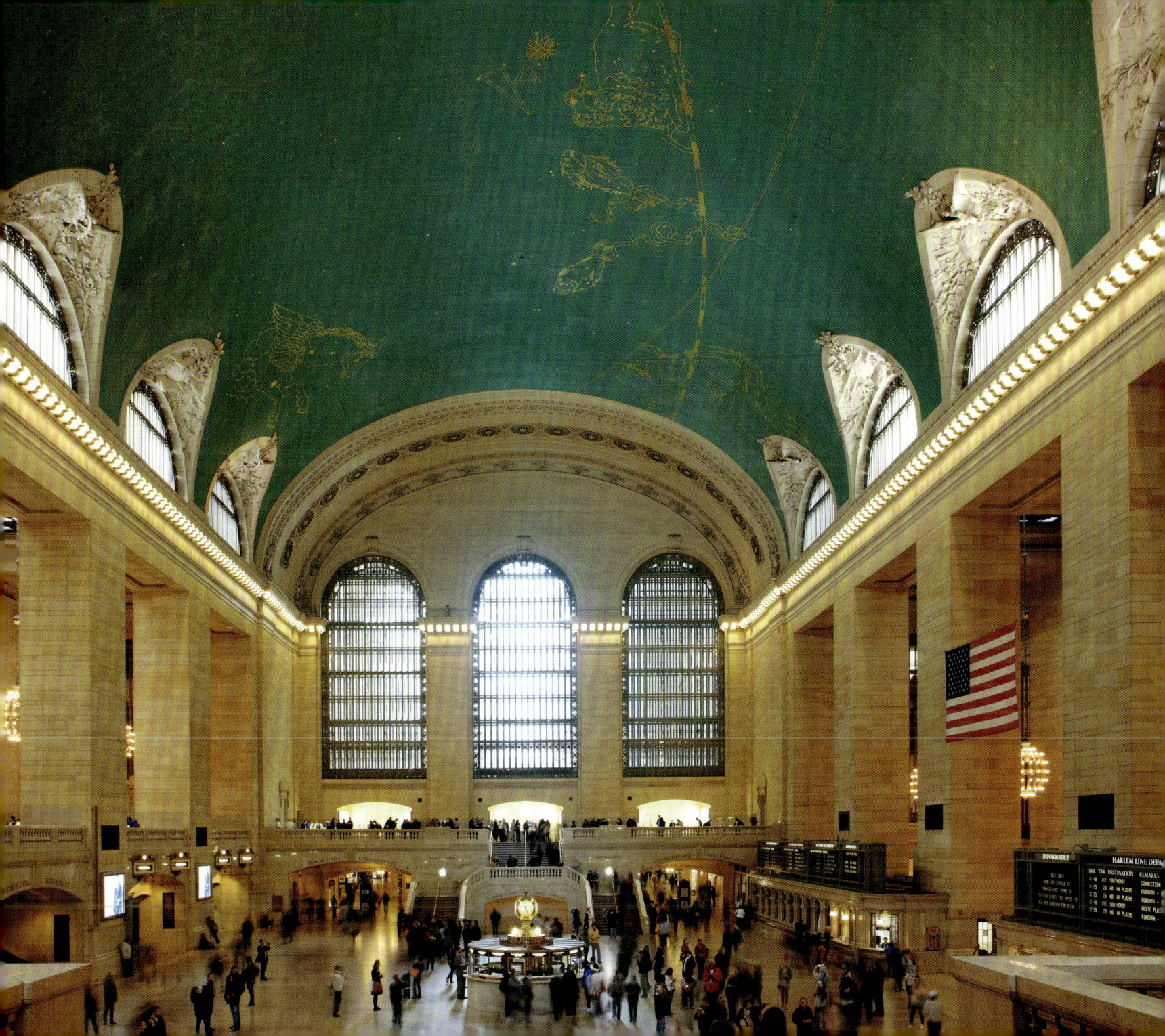

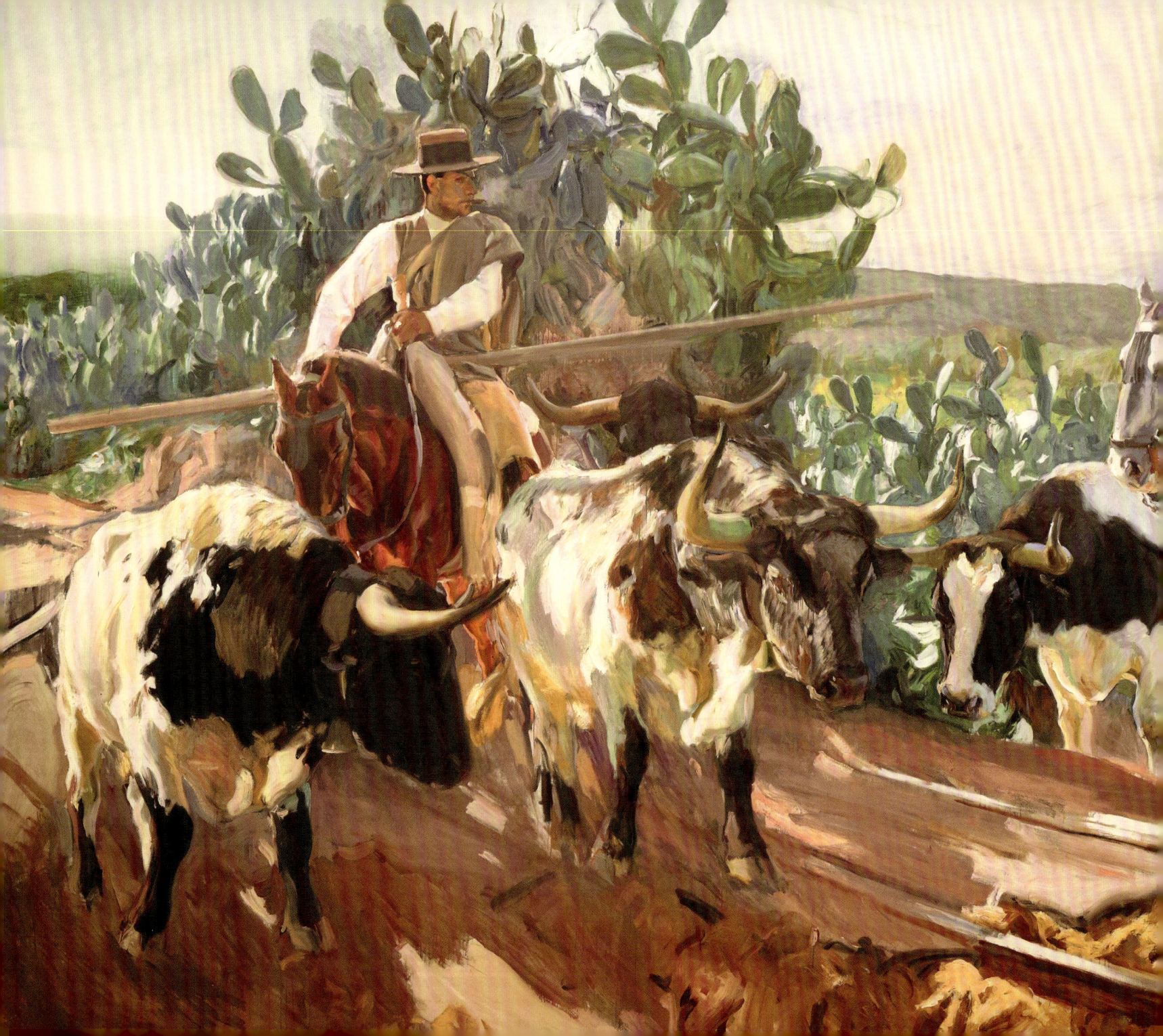

THE HISPANIC SOCIETY OF AMERICA

Anyone would be bedazzled by a billboard-sized mural entitled *Vision of Spain*, painted by the most brilliant painter they never heard of. It was painted a century ago and it cost the artist, Joaquín Sorolla y Bastida, his life.

Sorolla was a child prodigy, who, by fourteen years old, was studying under the finest artists in Valencia. At eighteen, he was copying the masters in the Museo del Prado in Madrid, and, at twenty-two, he won a grant to paint for four years at the Spanish Academy in Rome. As Sorolla matured as a painter, so did his choice of subjects. *Another Marguerite*, an oil of a fallen woman, earned him international acclaim. *Sad Inheritance*, a touching tableau of crippled children, won the Grand Prix and a medal of honor at the Universal Exhibition in Paris in 1900.

His work was a variant of Impressionism. A more precise definition would be Luminism, the painting of light. His brush danced across the canvas. The spontaneous energy, the pure delight of paint, was there in every energetic brushstroke. He painted more than thirty-five hundred paintings over the course of his lifetime.

Archer Milton Huntington, founder of the Hispanic Society of America, invited him to present his paintings in the inaugural exhibition of his new museum. Sorolla could not have asked for a better introduction to New York. In one month, 160,000 visitors came to see his work and of the 356 paintings in the show, 195 were sold.

In 1911, Huntington commissioned Sorolla to paint a series of oils for an installation at the Hispanic Society. The paintings were to be 12 feet high and 227 feet in length and depict the history of Spain. Sorolla had a different idea and proposed an ethnographic study of ten regions of Spain. It was an epic project. Sorolla had to hire a crew, scout locations, cast actors, acquire authentic costumes, do hundreds of preparatory sketches and small paintings, stage each painting, stretch a giant canvas, and paint it, only to move on to the next location.

It took nearly a decade to complete the series. The largest panel, *Castile*, is 46 feet long and took him nearly two years to paint. Sorolla captured the light, atmosphere, and energy of folk dancers, bullfighters, and fishermen of his idyllic youth. But by the time he finished, the regional details he lovingly re-created were, in real life, being neutralized by twentieth-century homogenization.

By 1917, Sorolla was exhausted and, in 1919, only months after finishing the last painting, he was felled by a stroke. He remained paralyzed, unable to work, until his death in 1923. He never lived to see *Visions of Spain* installed in the museum.

While the Hispanic Society underwent renovations from 2007 to 2010, *Visions of Spain* toured seven cities in Spain. More than two million people came to see Sorolla's work, making the exhibition the most attended art event in Spanish history.

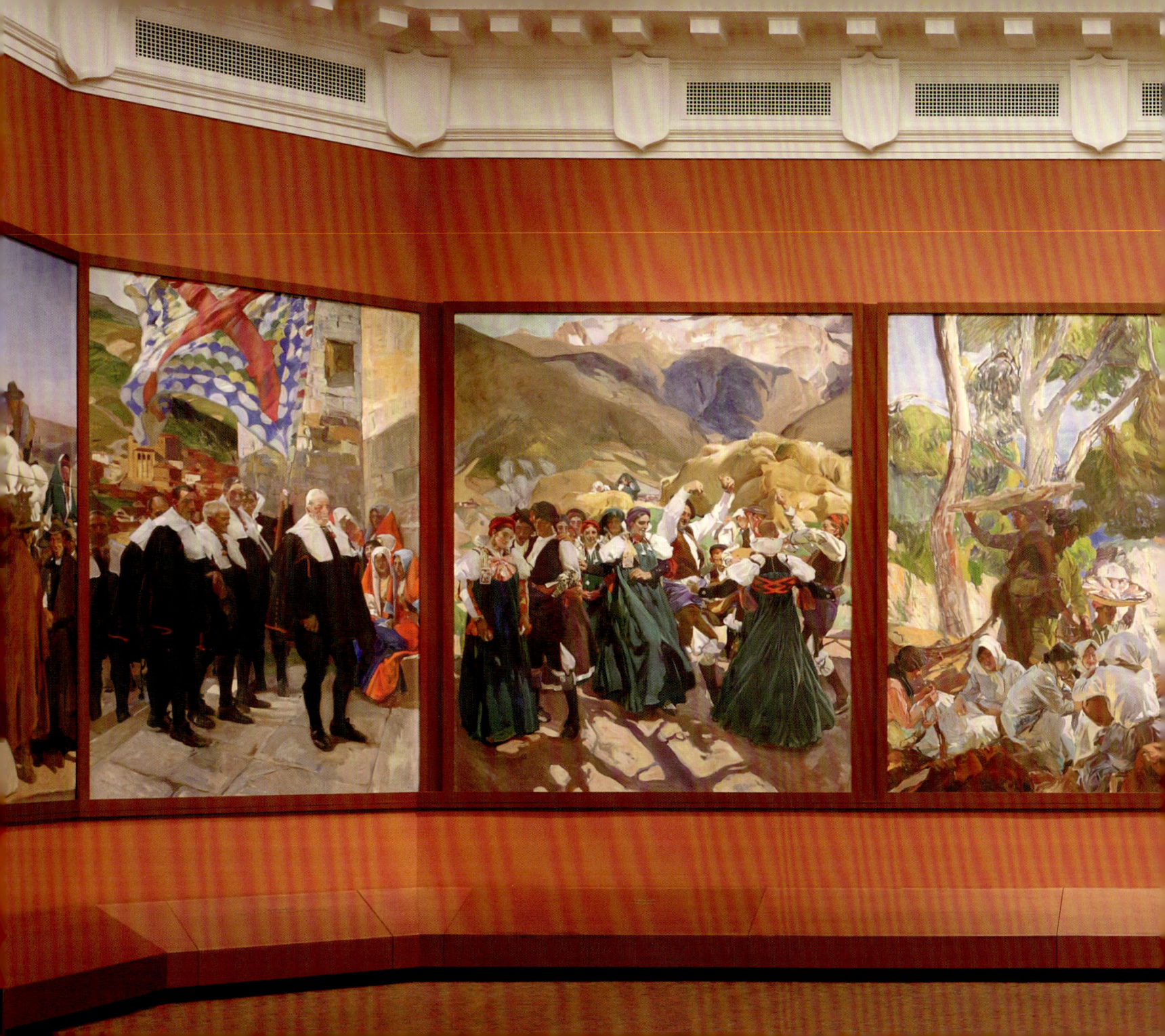

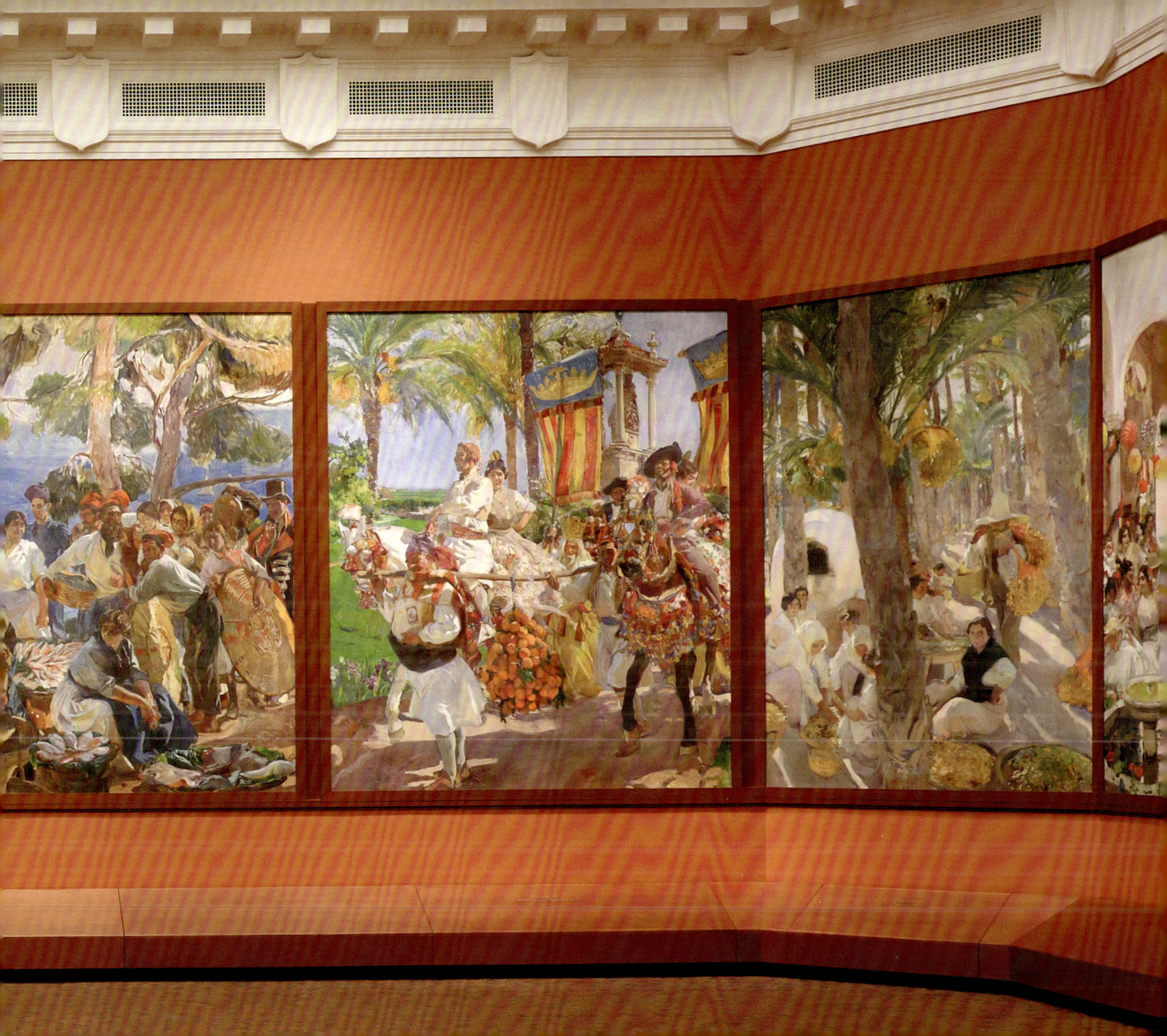

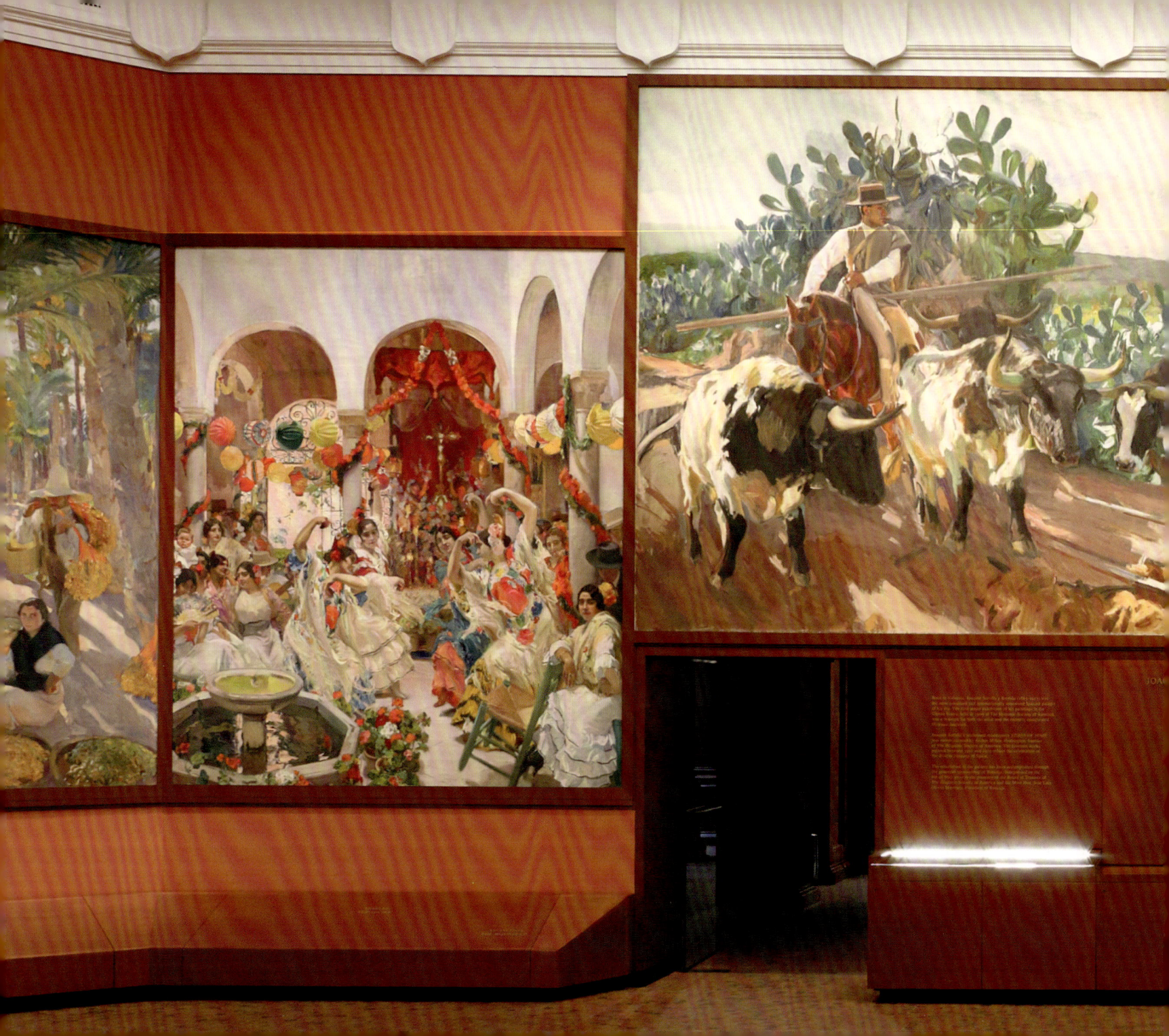

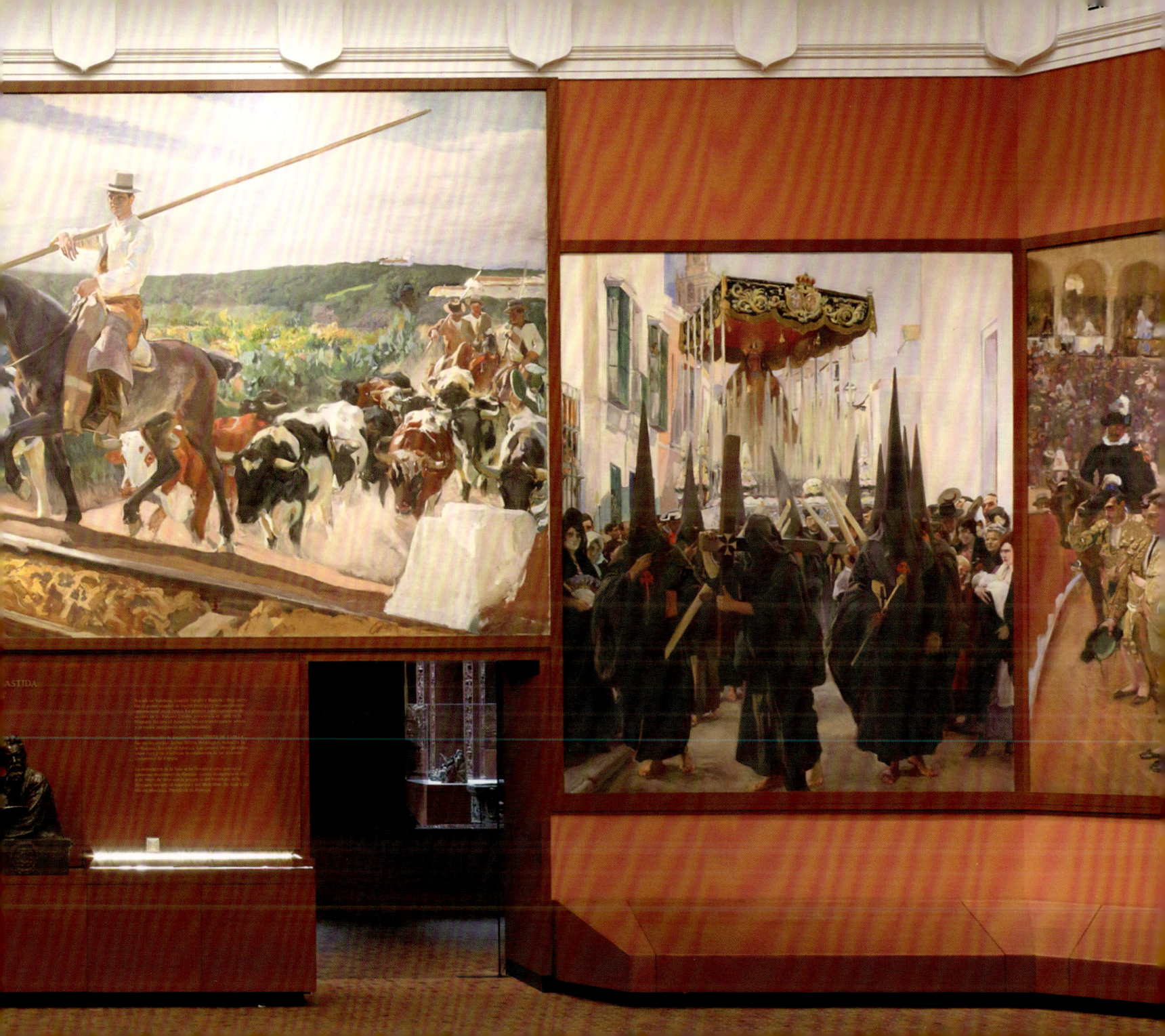

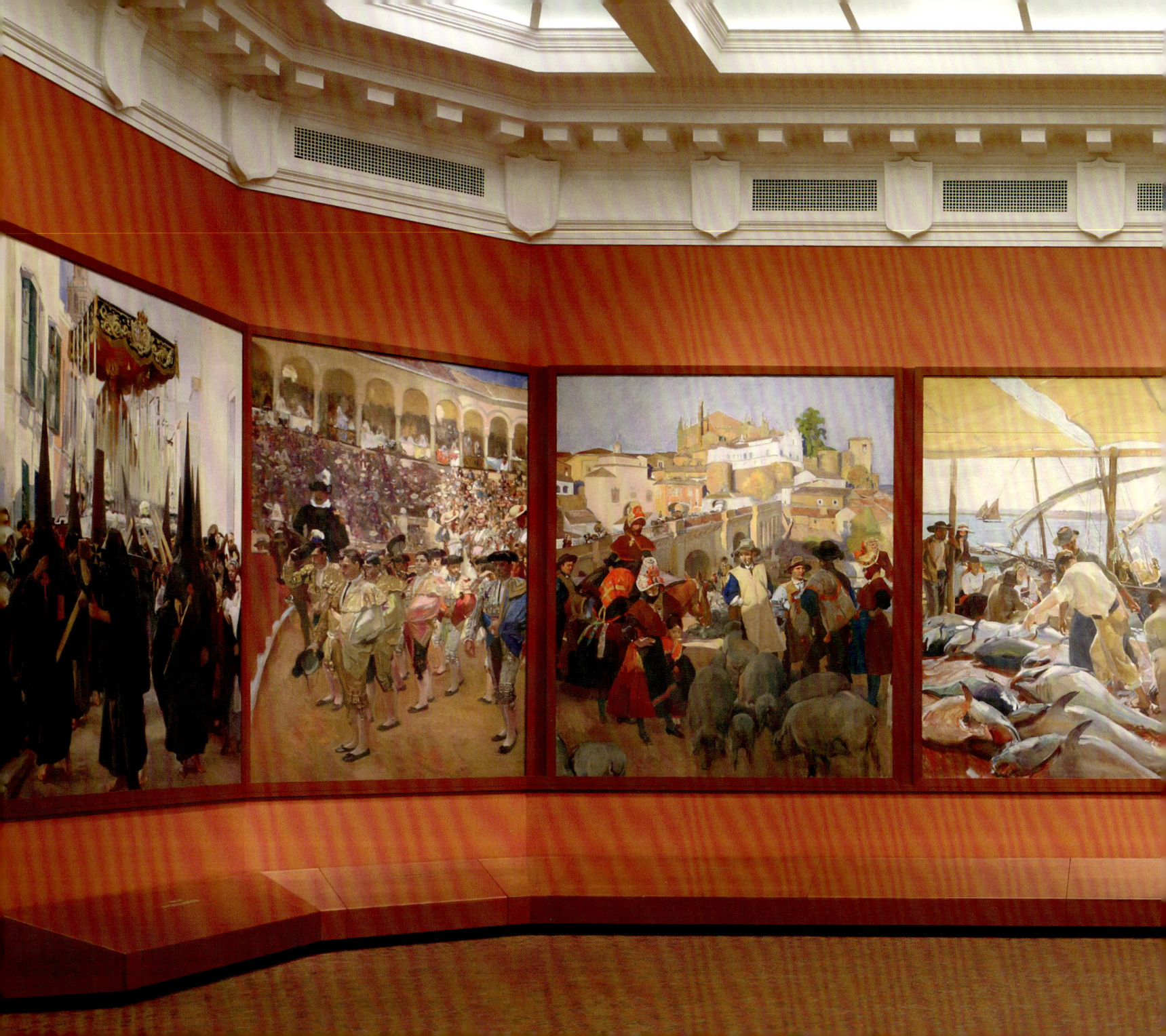

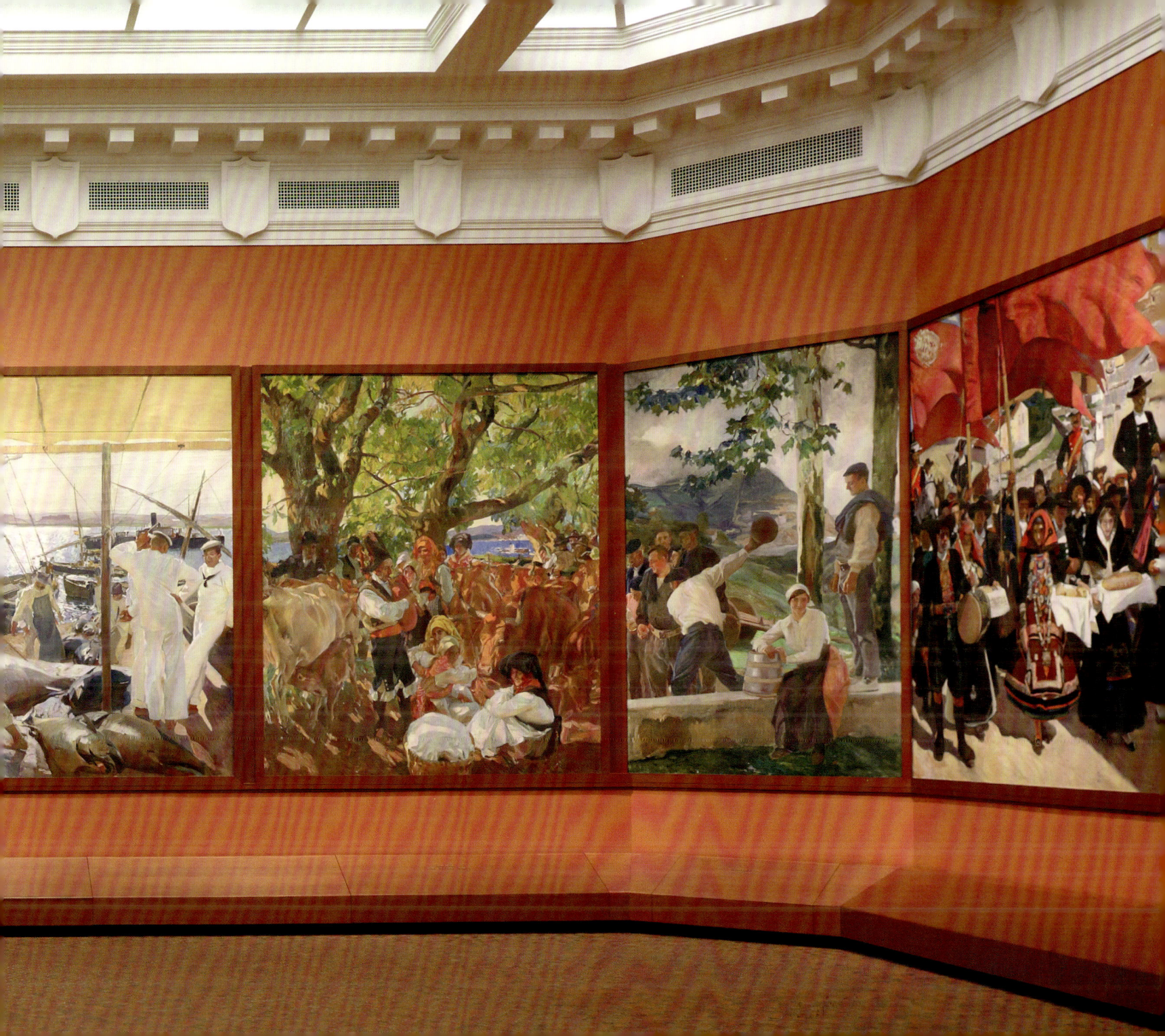

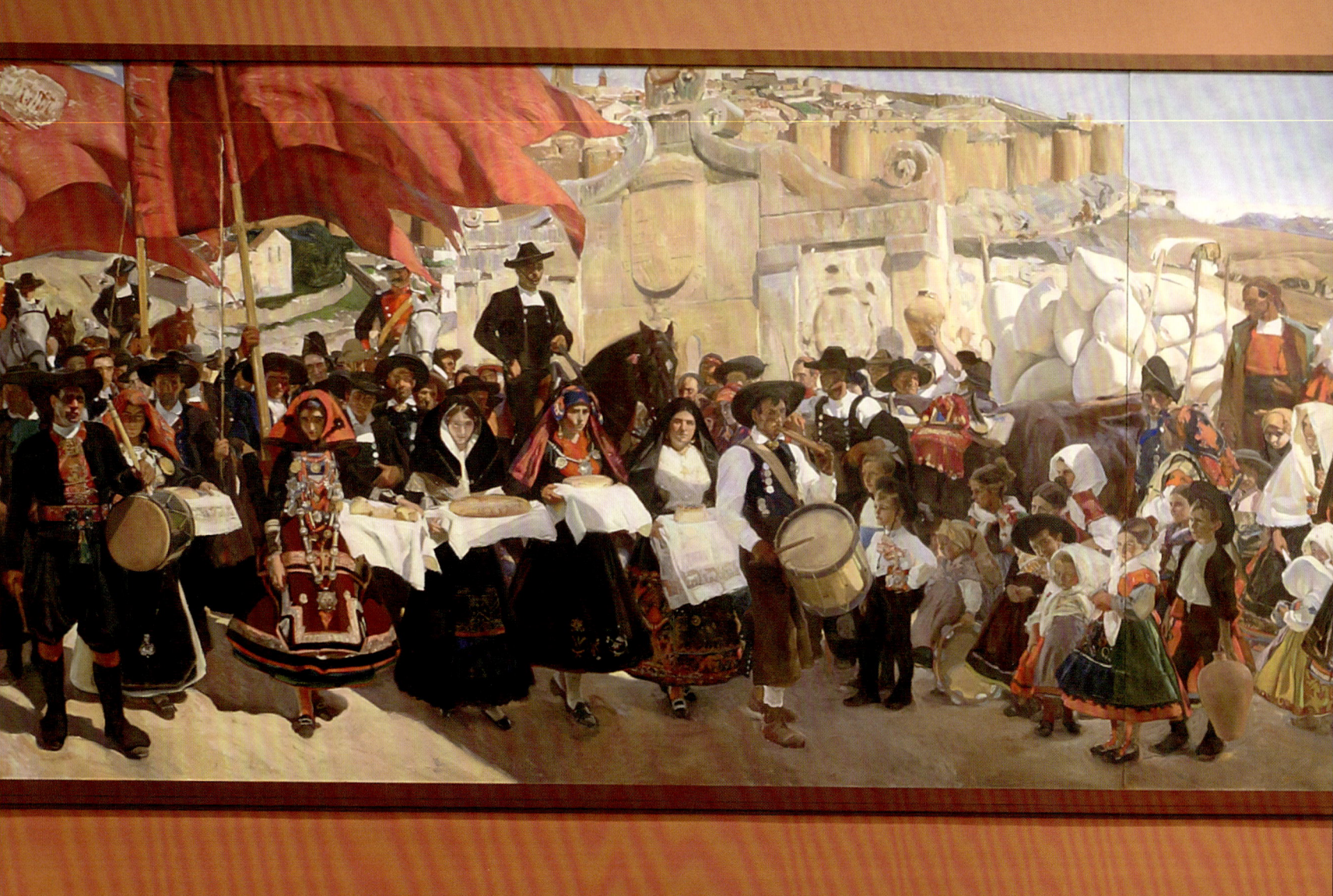

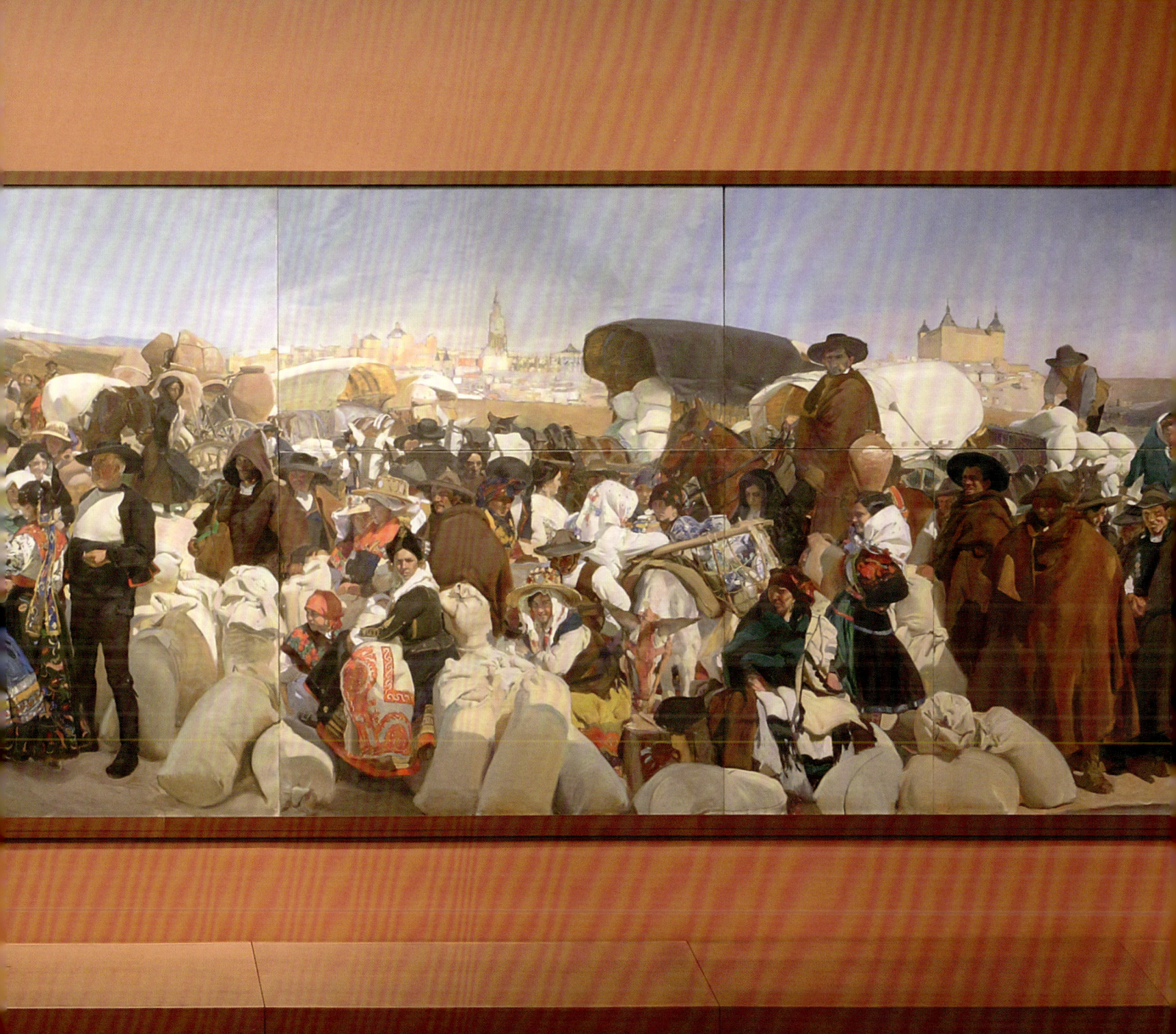

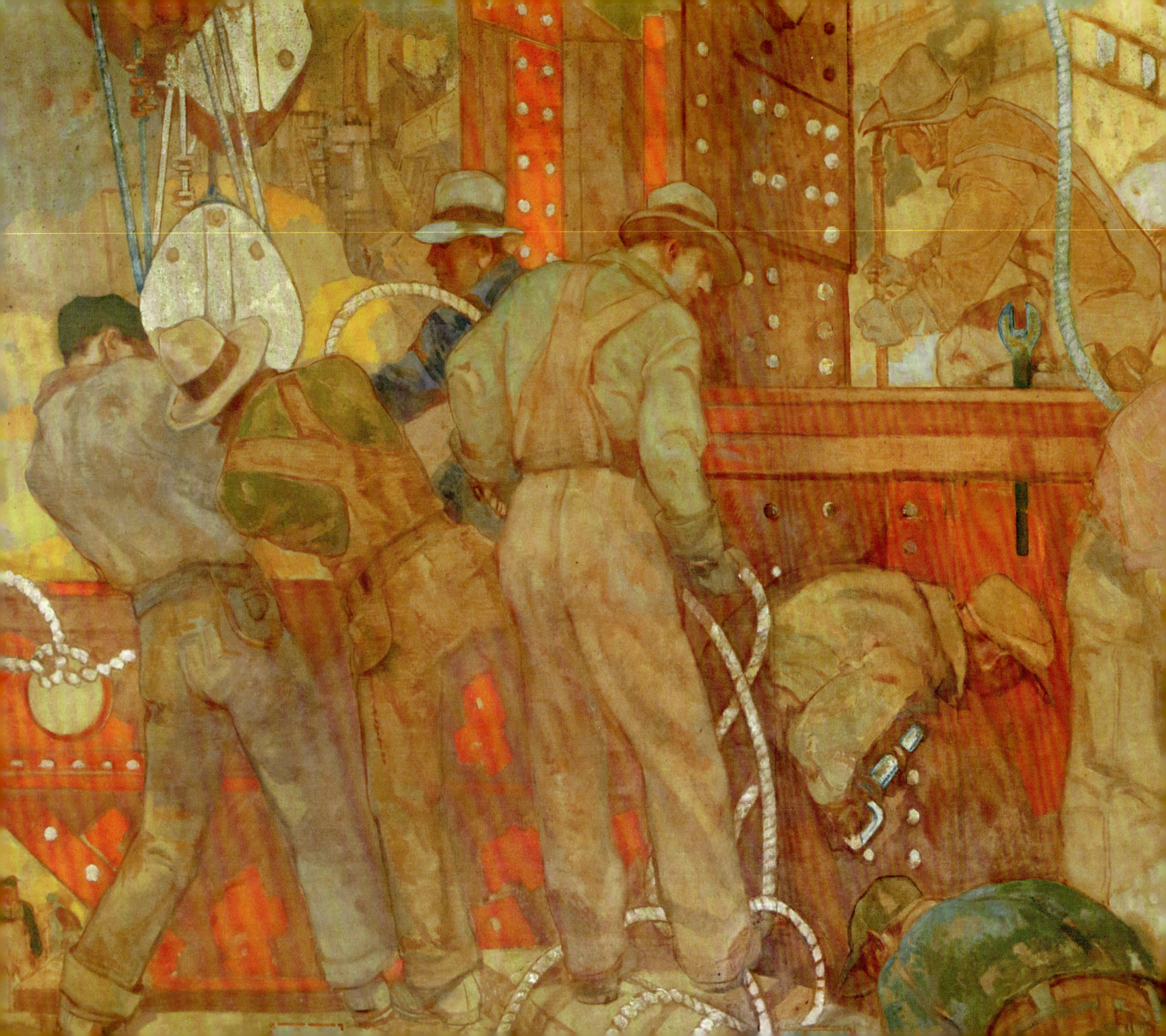

CHRYSLER BUILDING

Edward Trumbull, a descendant of one of Connecticut's oldest families, found his way from Stonington to the Art Students League in Manhattan, and in 1911 he moved to London, where he worked as an assistant for England's greatest mural painter, Sir Frank Brangwyn. Brangwyn was self-taught, and in his youth, he had worked for the artist and textile designer William Morris. The origins of Trumbull's richly decorative style can be traced back beyond Brangwyn to that original influence. Trumbull was the worthy protégé of Sir Frank but fell afoul of his mentor's strict religious and moral standards in a highly publicized scandal, which involved multiple marriages, an annulment, and an eventual self-deportation to Pittsburgh.

While in Pittsburgh, Trumbull painted murals for a variety of clients, including the Heinz Company. Returning to New York in 1920, he painted murals for the Oyster Bar and the concourse connecting Grand Central Terminal to the Graybar Building.

Then, in 1930, he was given the opportunity to paint a 76-by-110-foot mural on the lobby ceiling of the city's most impressive skyscraper–the Chrysler Building.

A brochure from the 1930s states that the mural, originally titled *Energy, Result, Workmanship, and Transportation* but later renamed *Transport and Human Endeavor*, represents "brawny man power, symbolic of the vitality and the force typical of our age. The power of the individual worker who labors with his hands, the muscled giant whose brain directs his boundless energy to the attainment of the triumphs of this mechanical era in that never-ending struggle to bend the elements to his will."

The mural is an illustration of Walter Chrysler's work ethic, the power of industrial America, being the strongest and the best, and the virtues of hard work and achievement. All of the technologies of the mid-twentieth century, including a radio, telephone, trains, ships, and multiple airplanes, the most impressive being an aluminum-leaf Ford Tri-Motor with a painted seven-foot wingspan, are robustly displayed in the incredibly elaborate painting. Planes, representing the worldwide reach of American technology, are shown along the mural's border, a highly stylized map of the world. Workers and craftsmen, modeled after the real-life men who built the Chrysler Building, are shown constructing the building. Trumbull signed the mural in two different places, and the initials "E.T." can be seen on a carpenter's level in one panel.

The rich Moroccan-marbled lobby has a unique triangular shape. Above the Lexington Avenue entrance is a portrait of the Chrysler Building from which radiate four incised tiers of inverted triangles. The final, and smallest *V*, above the lobby clock, portrays a man's muscular back surrounded by beautiful decorative patterns that would suggest a significant nod to Gustav Klimt and Art Nouveau.

A misguided attempt to modernize the lobby in the 1970s led to twenty-four recessed light fixtures being cut into the painting and the entire ceiling covered by a coat of polyurethane. The lights were so bright that the painting became impossible to see, and the polyurethane muddied the brilliant colors into a chocolate mush. Fortunately, in 1999, the building's new owners engaged EverGreene Architectural Arts to restore the mural to its original glory. The spotlights were removed and their holes filled, covered with canvas, and repainted. Once the polyurethane was cleaned away, the dazzling colors gleamed once again.

Upon completing the Chrysler Building mural, Trumbull was hired by the architects of Rockefeller Center as a creative advisor, and coordinated the overall aesthetics of the buildings' interiors, with the exception of Radio City Music Hall. Although he wasn't invited to paint murals himself, he was entrusted with selecting the artists whose work would adorn the lobby of 30 Rockefeller Plaza. One of the artists he lobbied for, and won, was his former mentor, Sir Frank Brangwyn.

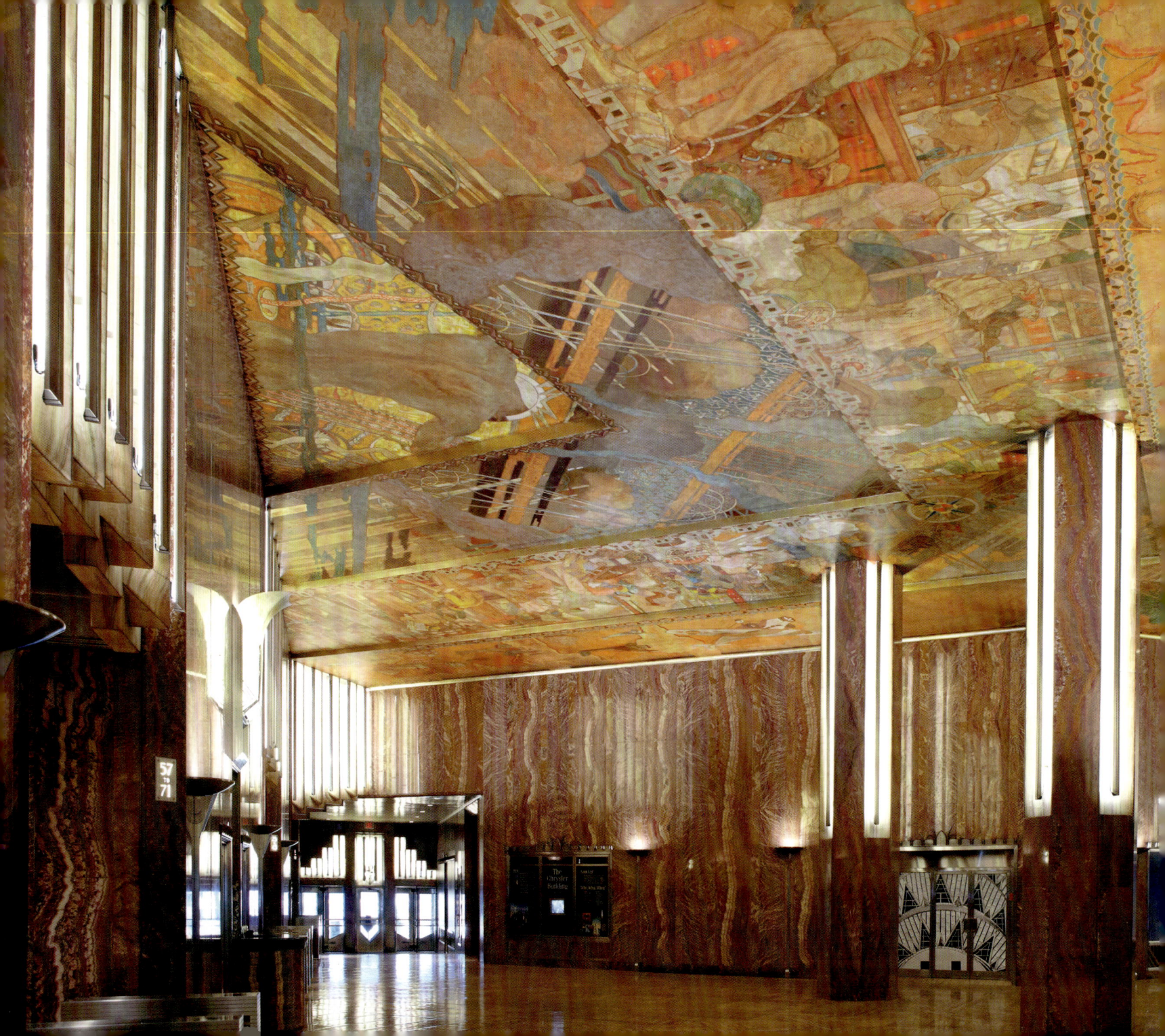

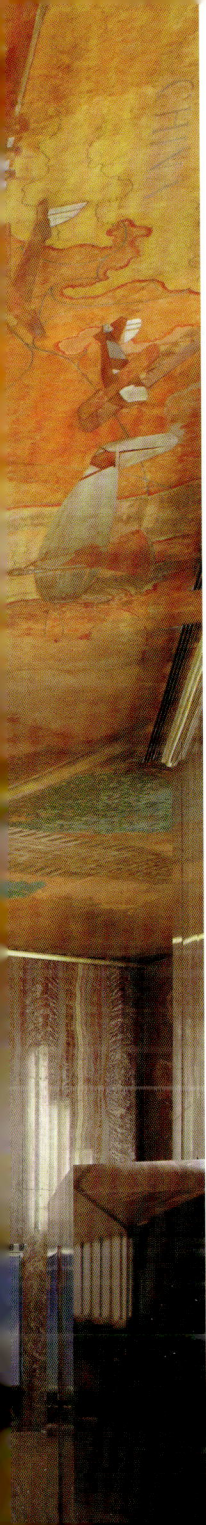

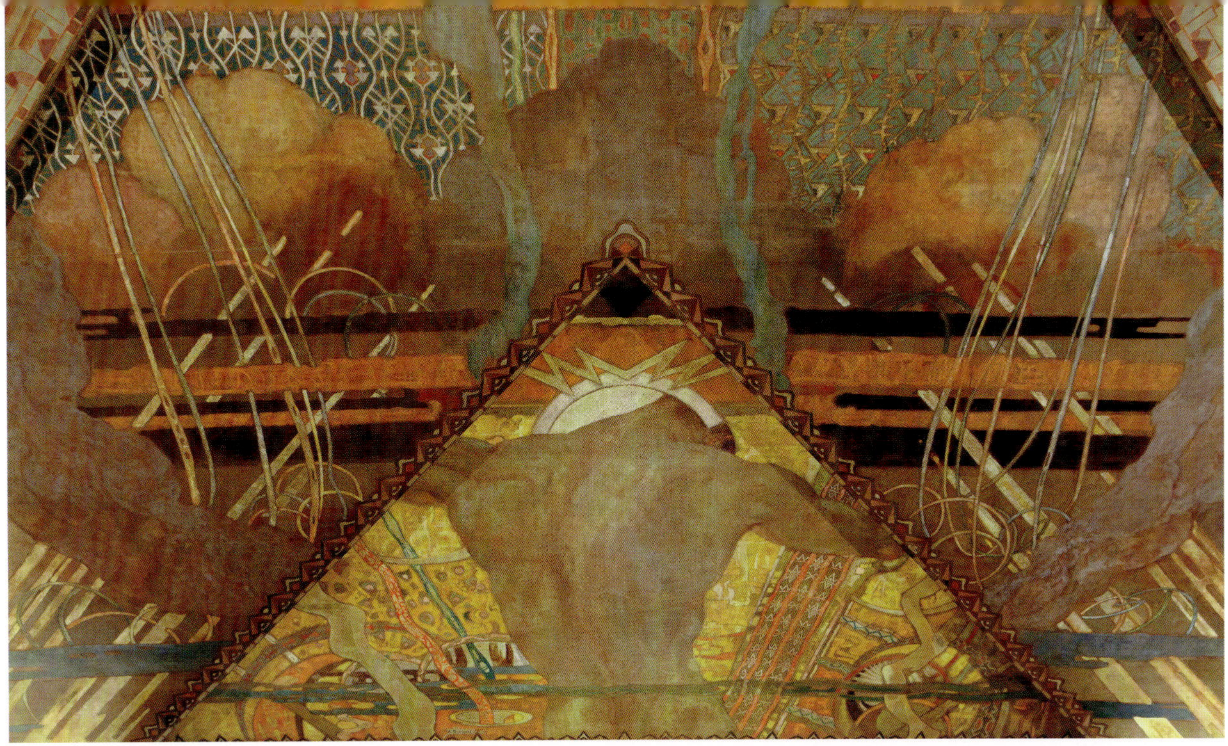

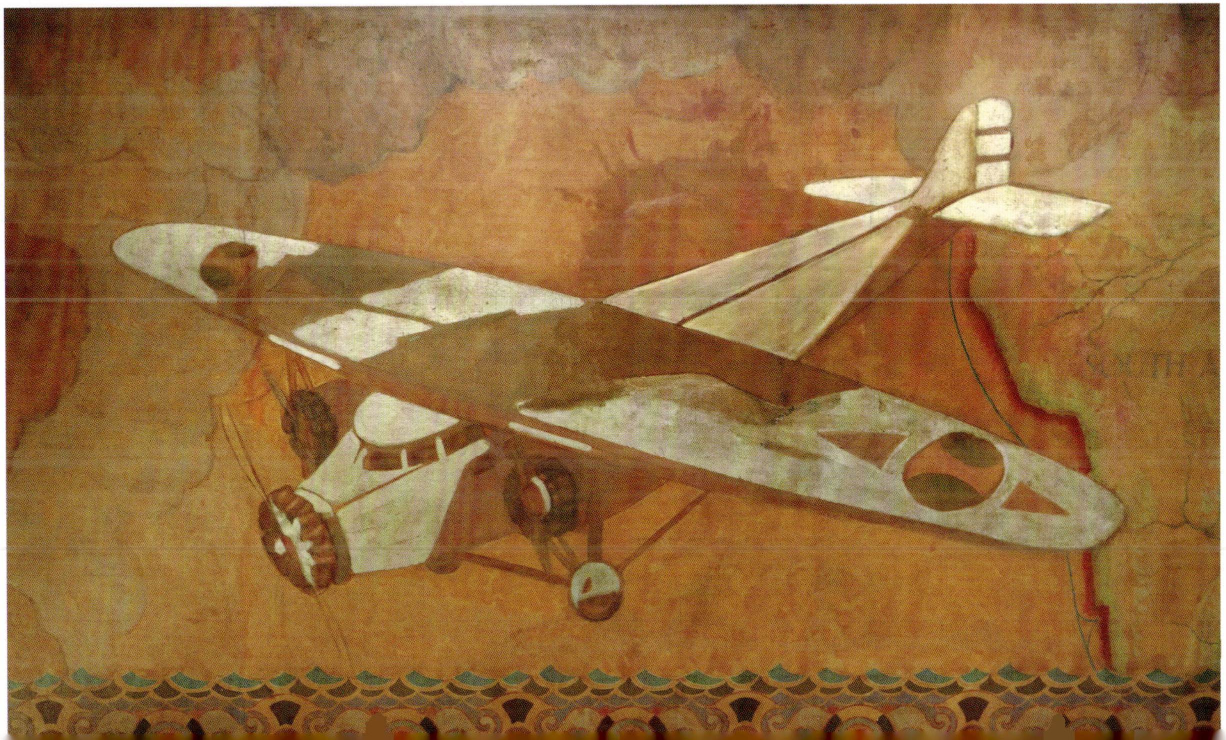

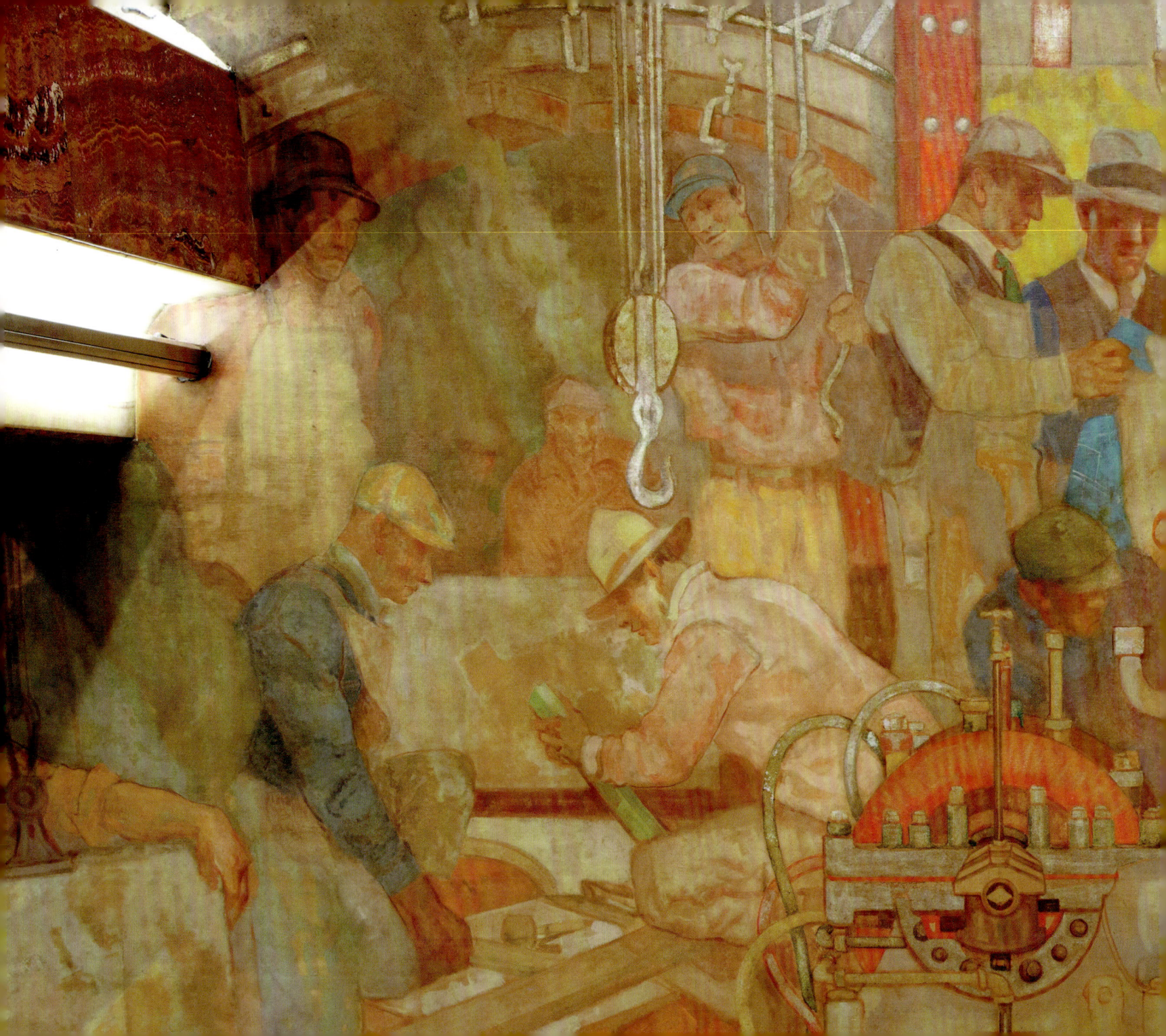

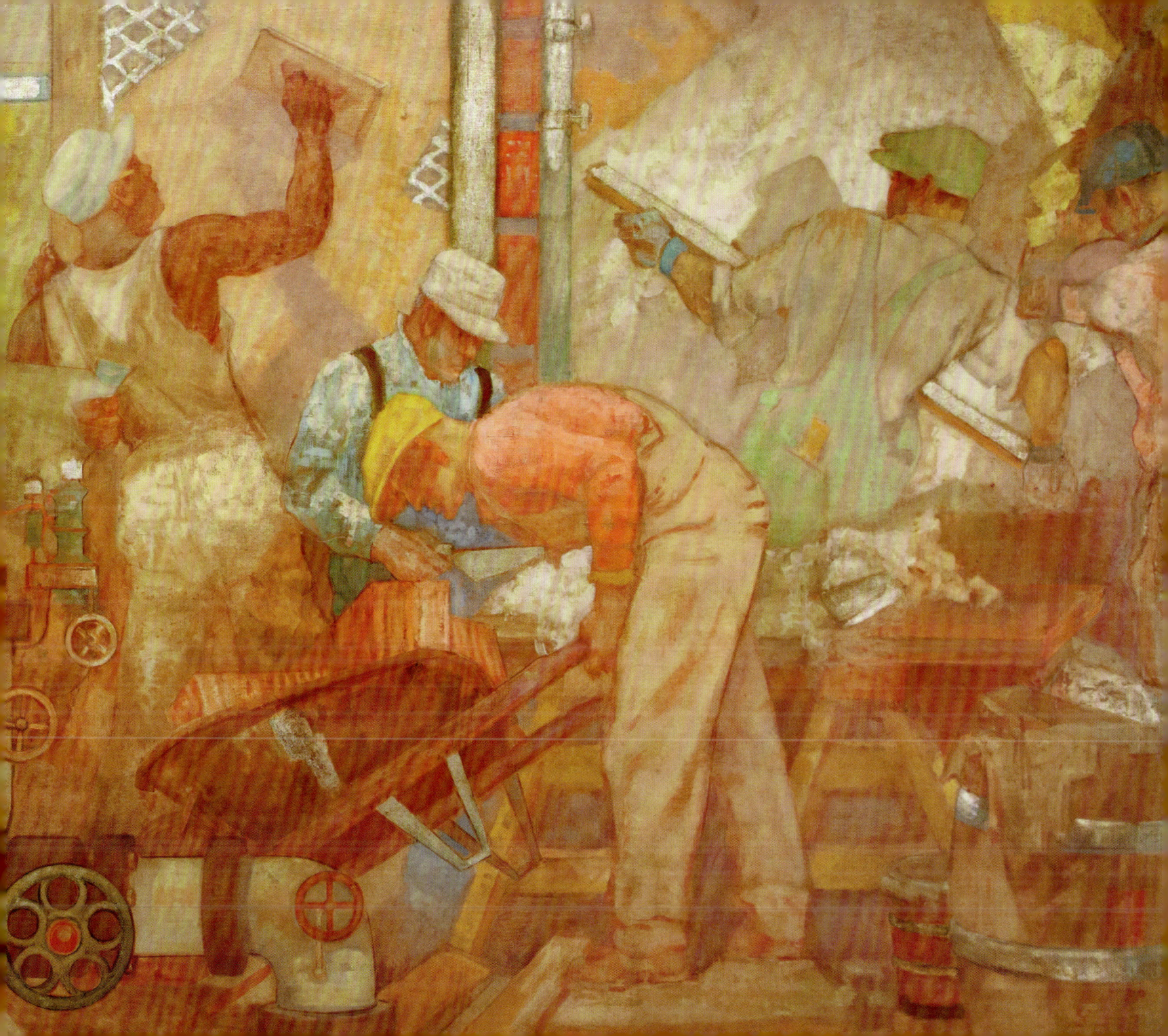

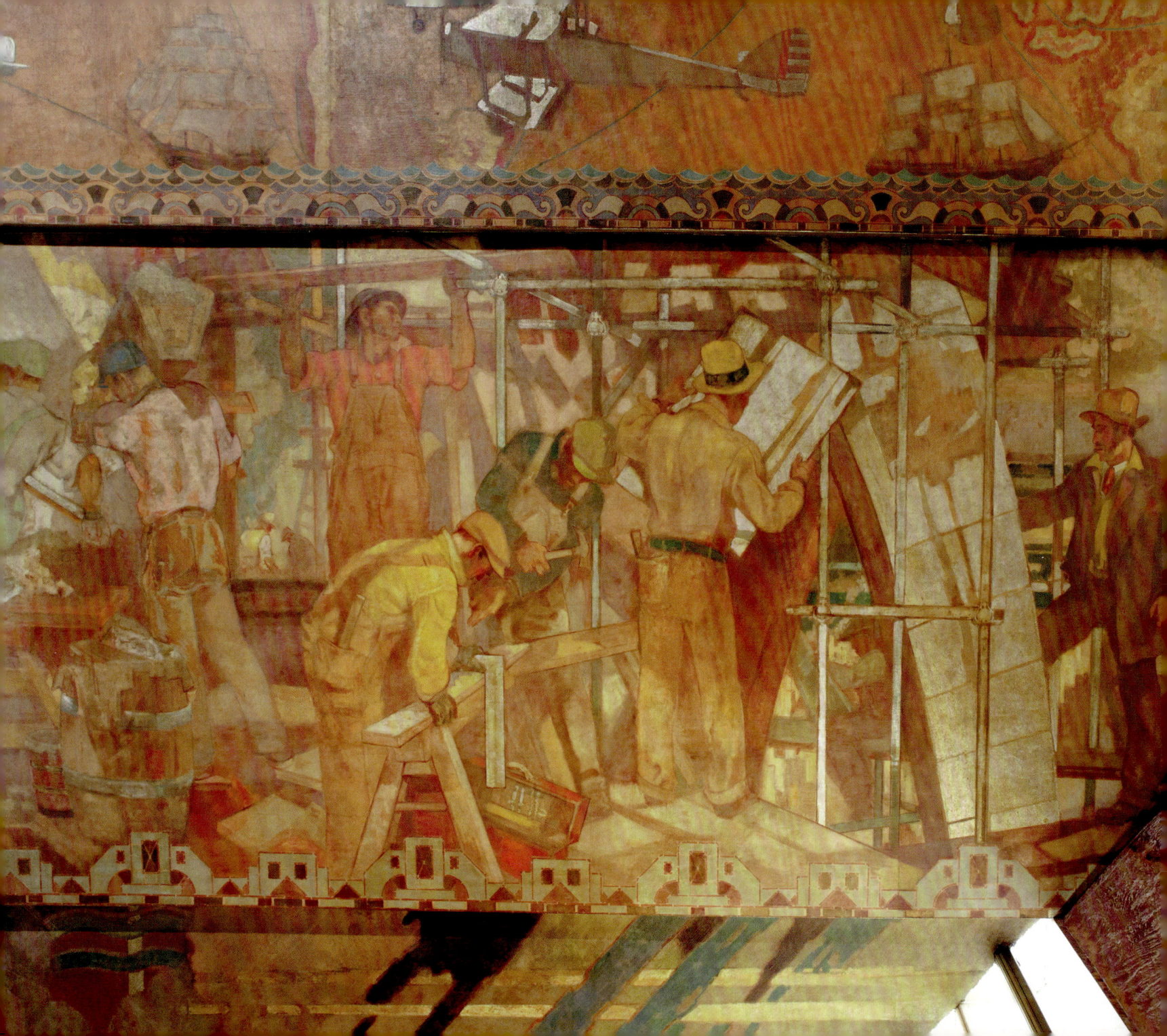

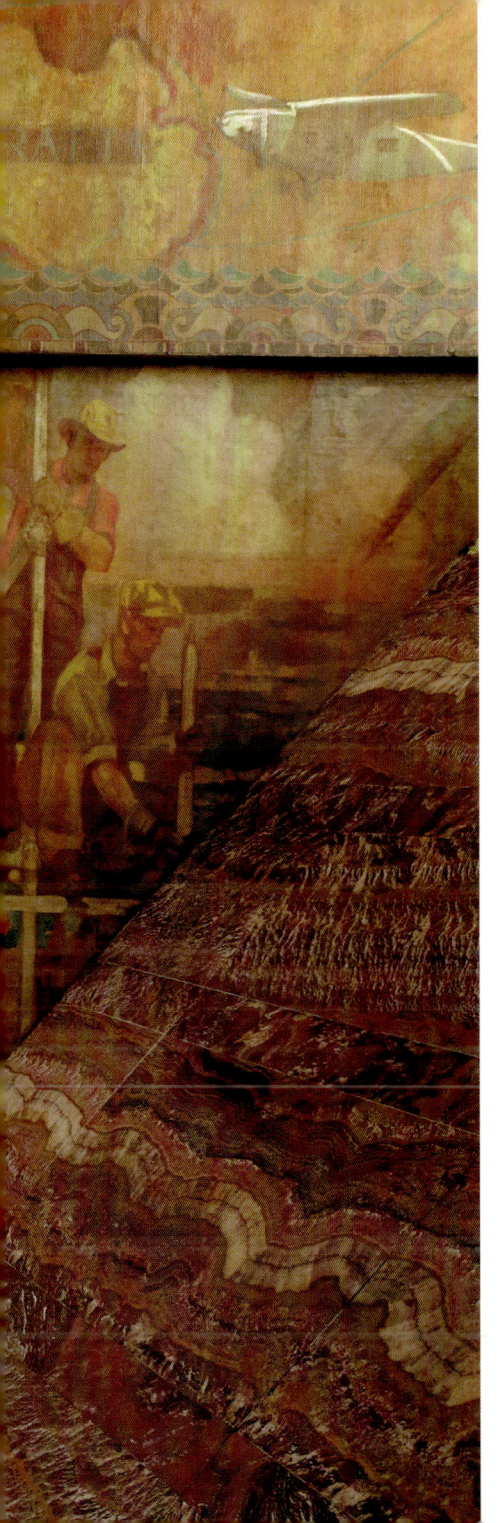

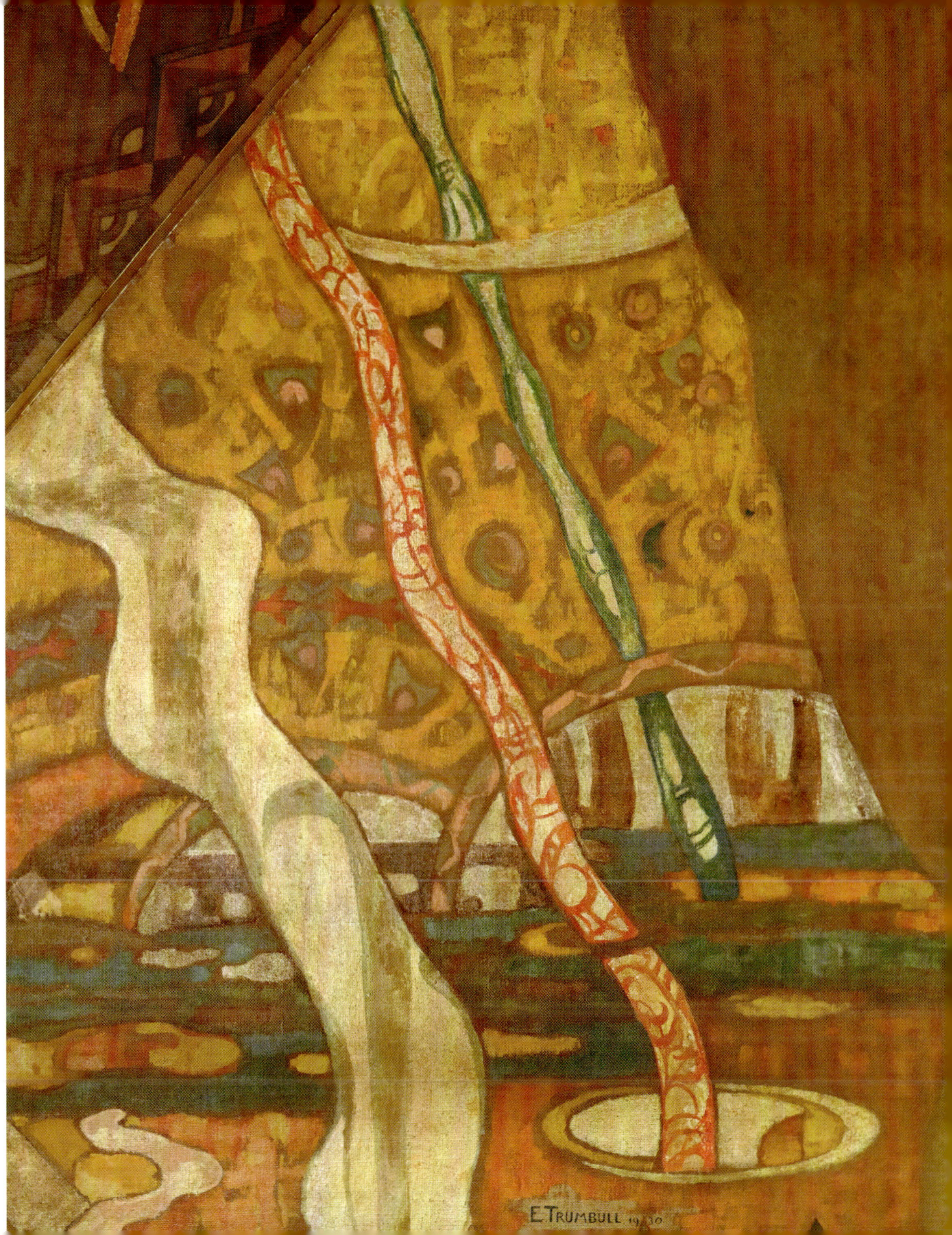

E.TRUMBULL 1930

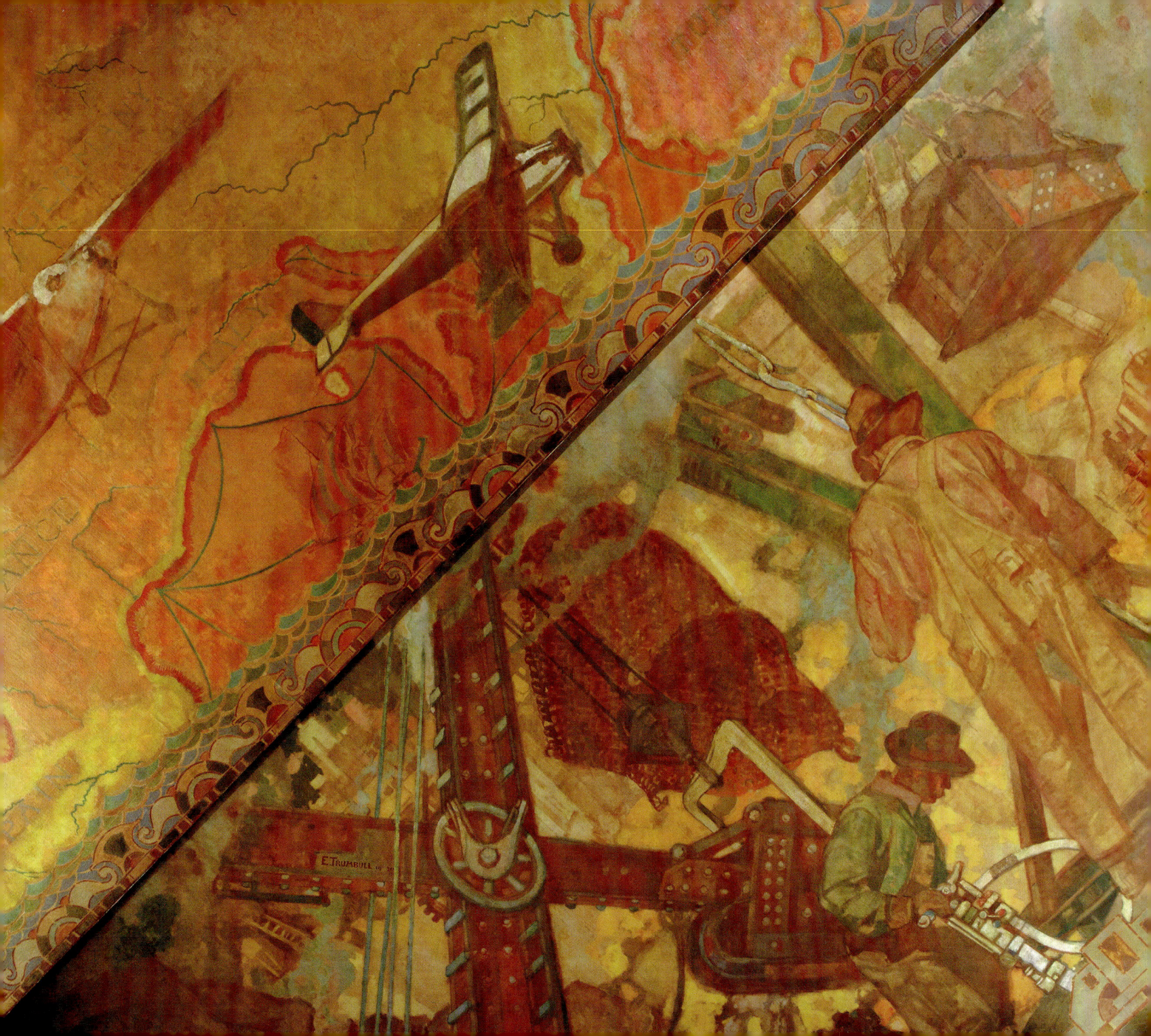

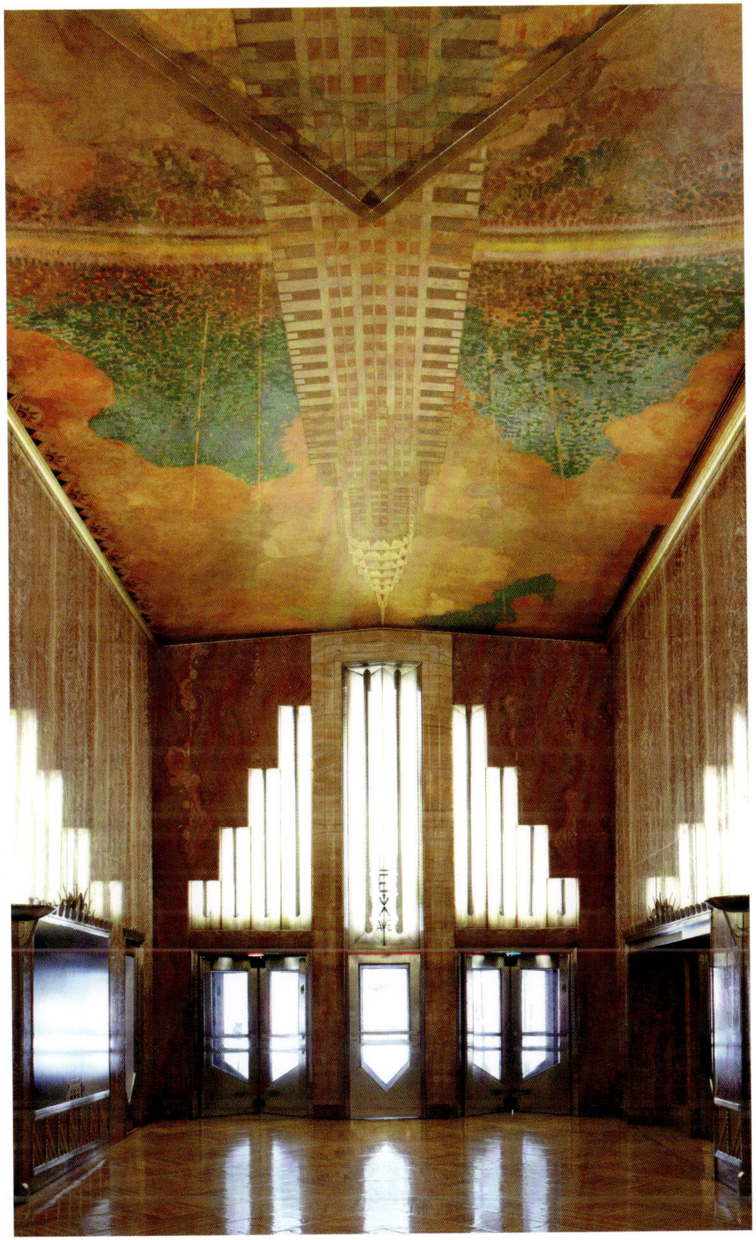

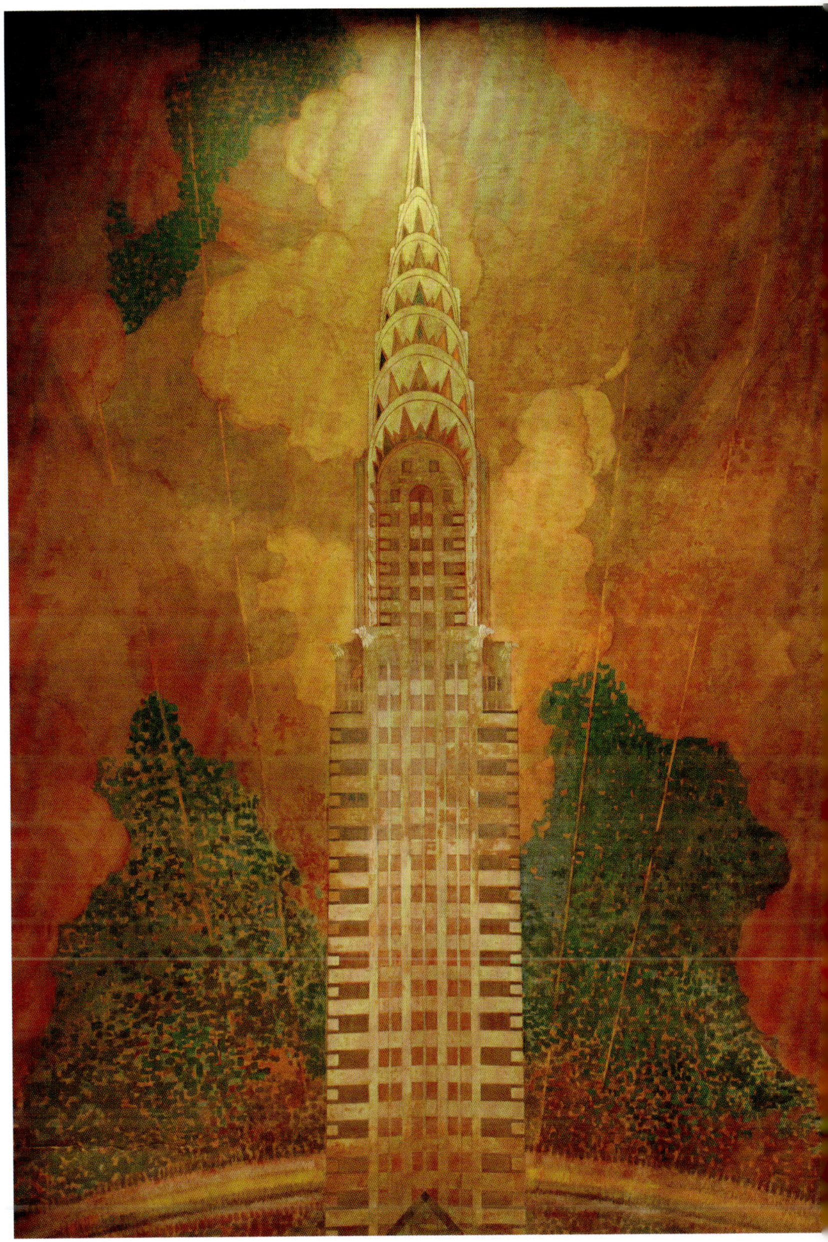

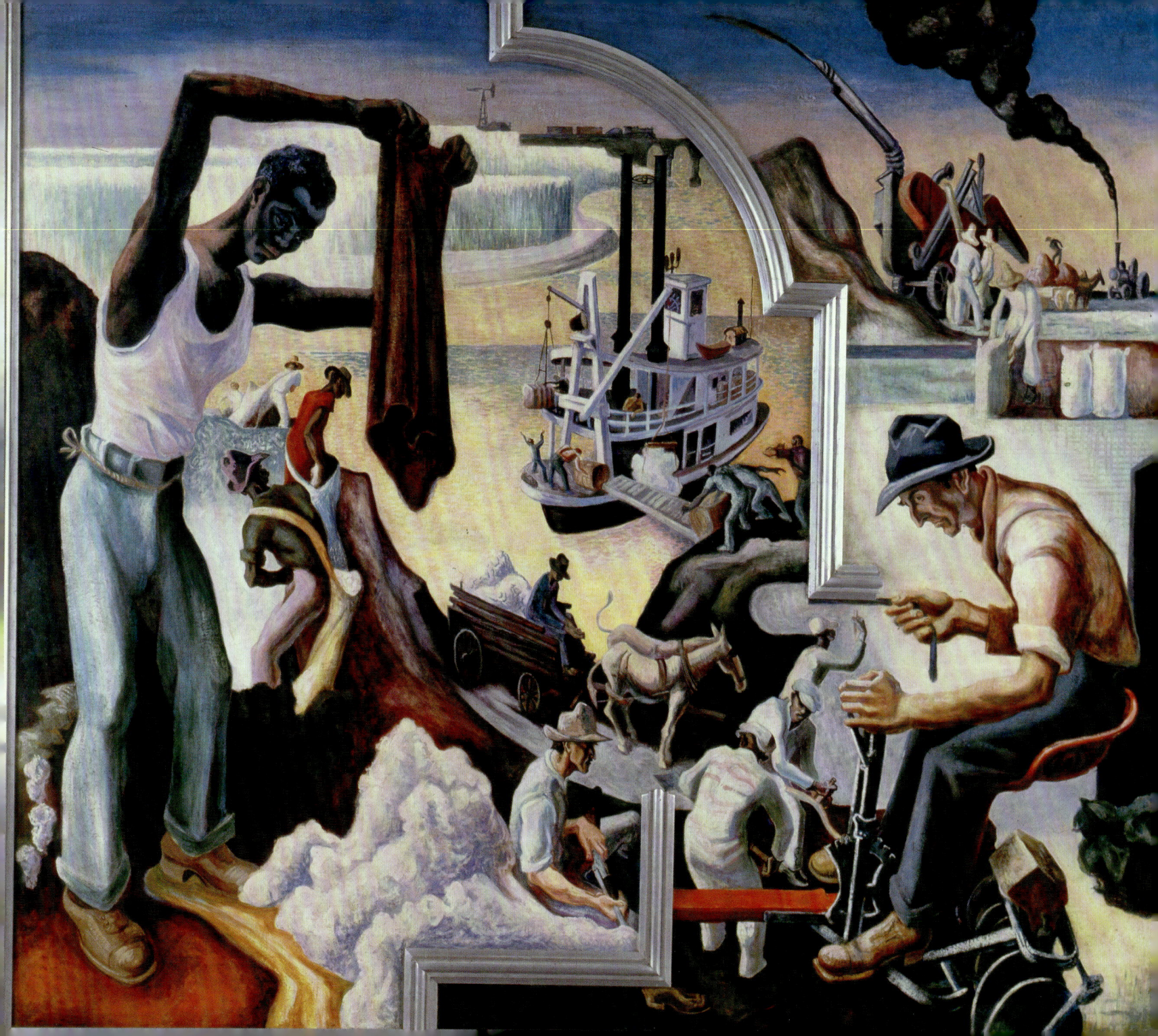

THE METROPOLITAN MUSEUM OF ART

It's hard to imagine anyone more midwestern than Missouri's Thomas Hart Benton. The great-nephew and namesake of the state's first senator, he was the first artist in his political family. In the late 1920s, Benton went roaming, Woody Guthrie style, to capture America with his pencil and sketchbook. He followed his pencil through the coal mines and sharecroppers' shanties of Appalachia, the cotton fields of the former Confederacy, the breadbasket farms of his native Midwest, and the oil fields of the Texas Panhandle. Though it wasn't planned, the hundreds of sketches and watercolor studies of pre-Depression America that he created along the way would become the basis for *America Today*, the mural that made him famous.

Historically, it is rare for an artist to get the opportunity to create a new mural. But rarer still are the times when commissions are offered to artists possessed with a sense of social destiny by patrons who are willing to support political expression. But such was the case in 1930, when Alvin Johnson, the founding president of the New School for Social Research, and his architect, Joseph Urban, wanted to embed the public spaces of their newly completed International Style building with permanent art.

Benton's wife, Rita, pressed Johnson to give her husband a mural to paint for the new building. Since Johnson had already given a commission to a foreigner, Mexican José Clemente Orozco, Rita thought a "real" American deserved a commission as well. Because the economy had collapsed a year before, there was no money to accompany the opportunity. Benton agreed to paint for free but, since he worked in the ancient technique of egg tempera, and eggs were expensive, he famously said to Johnson, "I'll paint you a picture if you finance the eggs."

Johnson had only one directive for Benton: paint what he considered to be the most powerful movement of his time. Benton, fascinated by the emergence of technology and its impact on the twentieth century, chose to show the explosion of human energy and technological power in America.

Though Benton's *America Today* often suffers from the popular misconception that it is about the Great Depression, it is in fact a populist exploration of the explosion of creativity, wealth, building, social change, and technology of the Jazz Age. "I wanted to show the energy and rush and confusion of American Life," he said about the mural in 1931.

Benton painted the different regions of America: *Deep South*, his beloved *Midwest*, and *The Changing West*. He also dealt with contemporary life in *City Activities with Dance Hall*, and *City Activities with Subway*. The last panels show the impact of *Coal* and *Steel*, as well as their resulting uses in *Instruments of Power* and *City Building*. The last panel, *Outreaching Hands*, was added as an afterthought, expressing Benton's leftist sentiments about silk-hatted capitalists.

Unlike fellow Grant Wood, who painted *American Gothic* and an idealized America, Benton preferred to explore the hard realities of life. The ten panels of this mural cycle are filled with energetic figures competing for attention. *America Today* is the visual equivalent of Aaron Copland's *Fanfare for the Common Man*. It is the poetry of Carl Sandburg and the spirit of Mark Twain in paint.

Benton had a very complicated and labor-intensive way of working. He would sketch, then sculpt clay models, set up lights around them, and then paint them, as if from life. It took six months to sculpt and another three months to paint the mural. But when the New School opened on New Year's Day in 1931, the original nine mural panels were completed and adorned a third-floor boardroom (the tenth panel was added later). In 1984, the New School sold the panels to what is now known as AXA Equitable, who installed them in two different lobbies over the thirty years. When the last location was closed, they were generously donated to the Metropolitan Museum of Art, where they will soon be on permanent display.

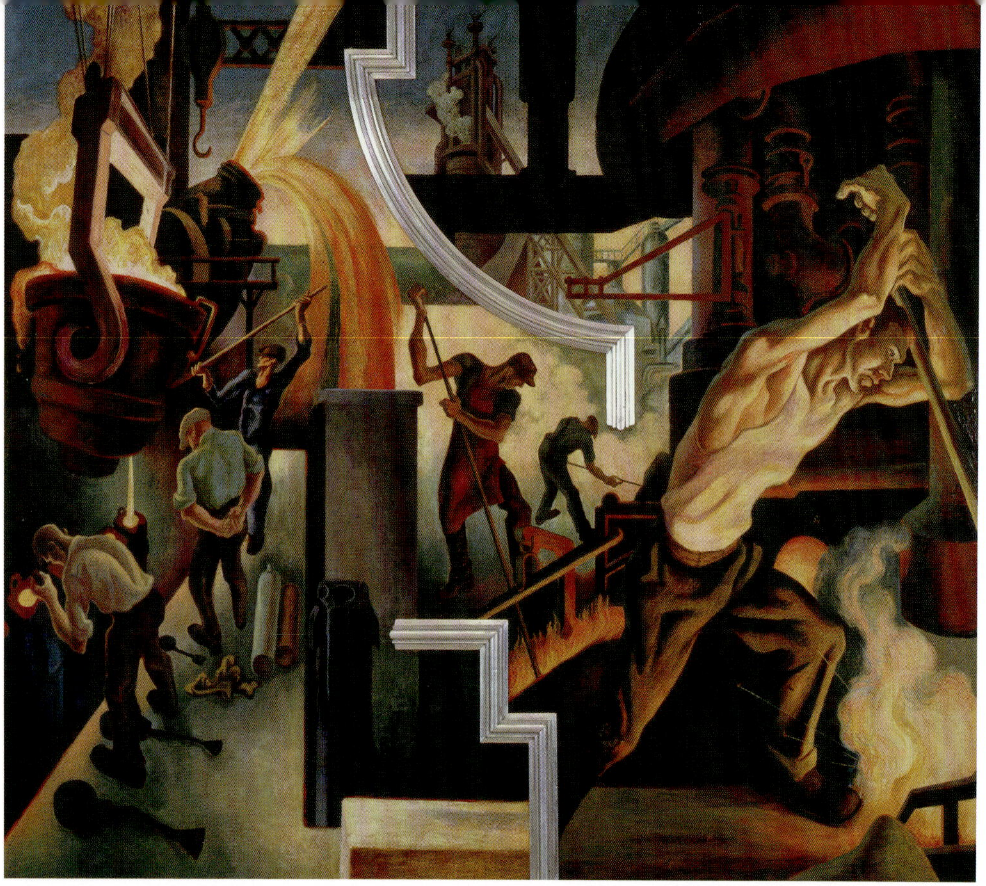

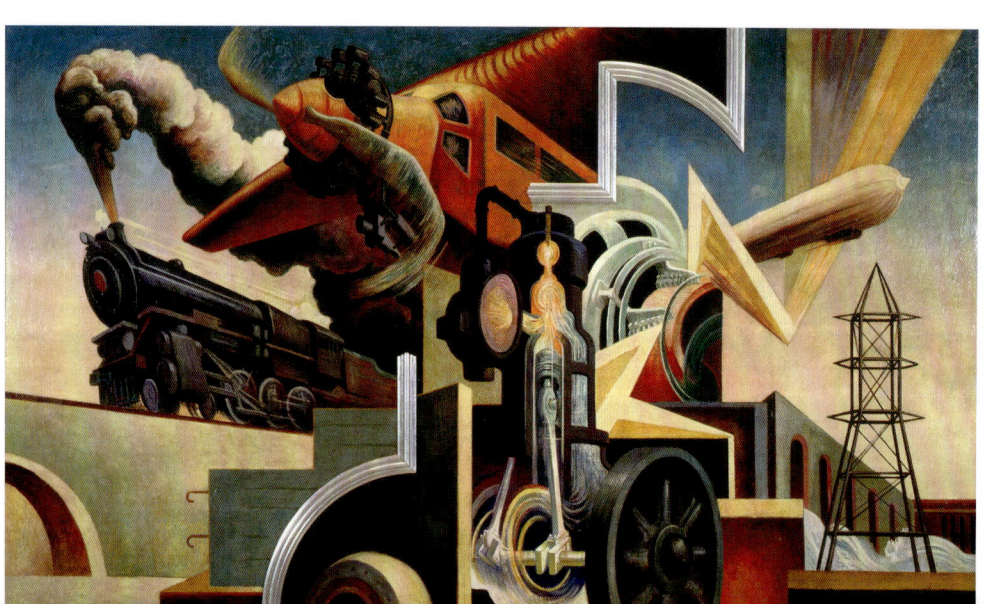
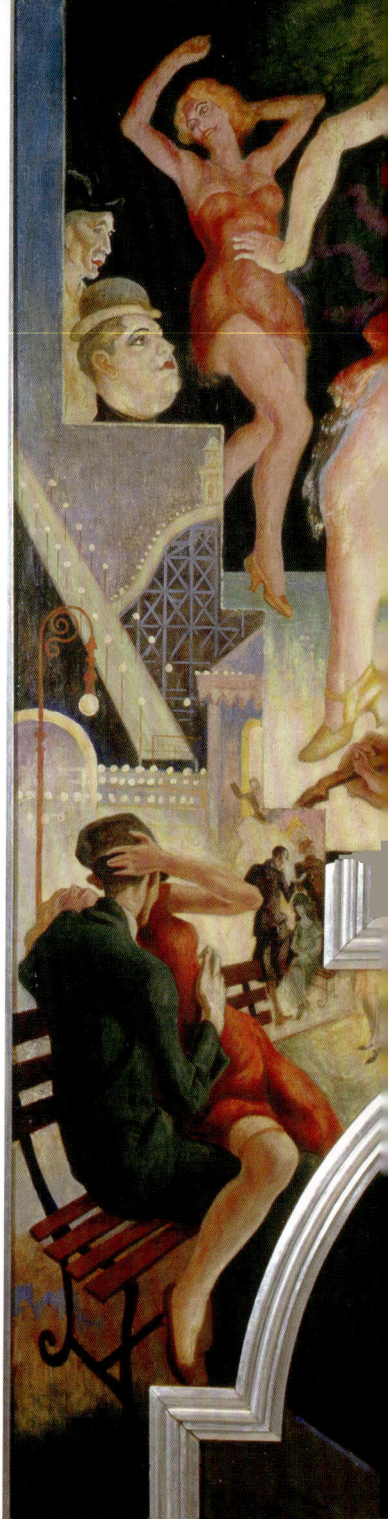

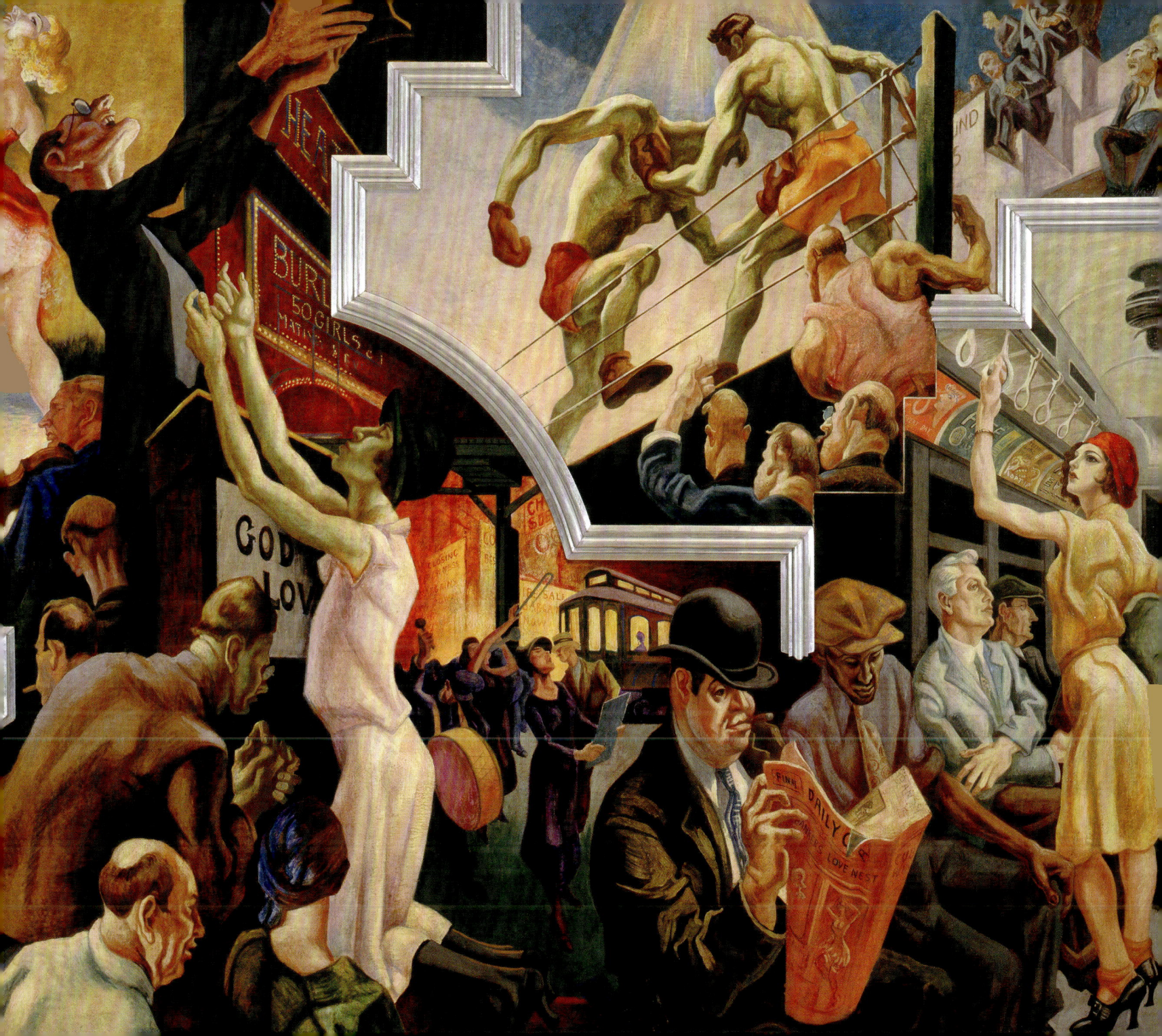

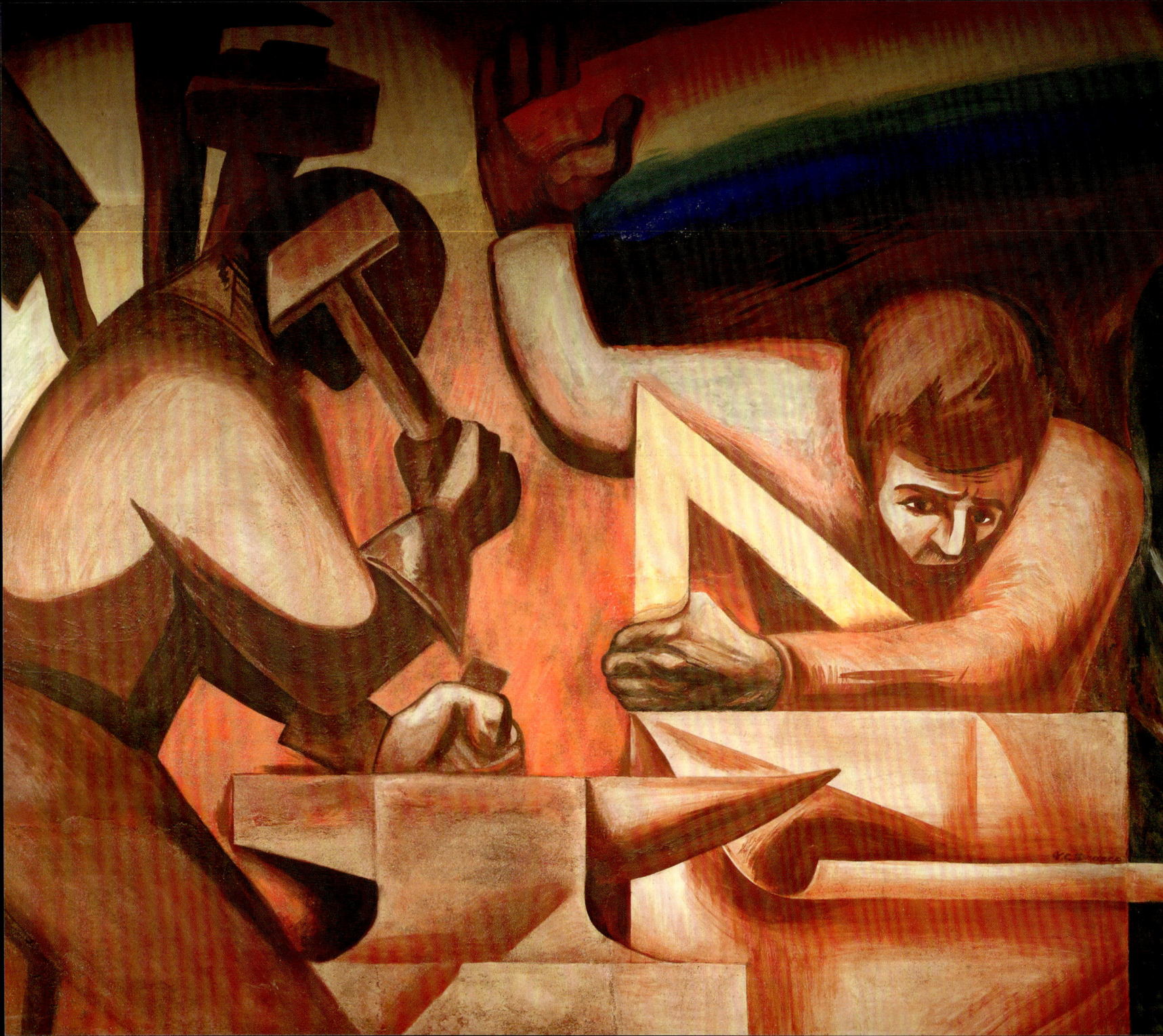

THE NEW SCHOOL

"What could have been my feeling when Orozco, the greatest mural painter of our time, proposed to contribute a mural? All I could say was, 'God bless you. Paint me the picture. Paint as you must. I assure you freedom.'" Such was the sentiment of Alvin Johnson, the founder of the New School for Social Research, when José Clemente Orozco offered to paint a mural in 1931 for only the cost of materials.

The life of José Clemente Orozco, who, along with David Alfaro Siqueiros and Diego Rivera, composed the triumvirate of Mexican mural's post-revolution renaissance, is one of the great, untold stories of twentieth century art. Orozco, who had his left hand amputated after a childhood fireworks accident and had a bad heart as a result of rheumatic fever, was unable to fight in the decade-long Mexican Revolution that claimed over a million lives and devastated millions more. But Orozco witnessed the carnage and cruelty of war, as well as the turbulent social upheaval left in its wake.

While Joseph Urban, the architect of the New School's building, wanted a painterly counterpoint to the severity of his International Style design, Johnson and his administration were looking for a visual expression of their liberal ideology. They all believed Orozco, who felt that the tempestuous social revolutions of the time were the energy that would drive the twentieth century into a modern age, was the right man.

As you approach the Orozco Room on the seventh floor, you are greeted by a mural, framed between two doors, entitled *Science, Labor, and Art*, presenting an artist, scientist, and laborer making their contributions.

As you enter the room, you are surrounded by *A Call for Revolution*, This four-walled mural cycle is based on a "Delphic Circle," a utopian organi-zation of intellectuals who believed in the goal of international peace and universal brotherhood.

On the east wall is the mural of national liberation, *Struggle in the Orient*. The white-collar workers are shackled and threatened in contrast to the Asian and African slaves who are rising up against their bondage. A British officer commands turbaned Indian Sikhs in red tunics who are participating in the oppression of their own people. They are confronting Indian national hero Mahatma Gandhi and poet and activist Sarojini Naidu. In *Table of Universal Brotherhood*, eleven men of different races and nationalities sit around a pristine white table upon which rests a blank book of peace waiting to be written. This painting is a harbinger of the United Nations. On the wall to the right is *Struggle in the Occident*, a tribute to the assassinated governor of the Mexican state of Yucatán, Felipe Carrillo Puerto. Sharing the panel is the Russian Revolution and the dominant figure of Vladimir Lenin, along with Stalin. His gray troops bristle with murderous bayonets. During the witch-hunts of the McCarthy era, the school hung a yellow curtain over Stalin's and Lenin's portraits. The last panel between the two doors, *Homecoming of the Worker of the New Day*, shows a laborer returning home. The fully laden table is the counterpoint of *Table of Universal Brotherhood* on the facing wall.

More than twenty thousand people came to view the murals in the first few months of their January 1931 inauguration. After triumphing in the States, Orozco returned to his homeland and painted major frescos in Mexico's greatest public buildings for the remainder of his life. Orozco's frescos in New York City turned out to be the only surviving examples of the twentieth-century pinnacle of Mexican public art.

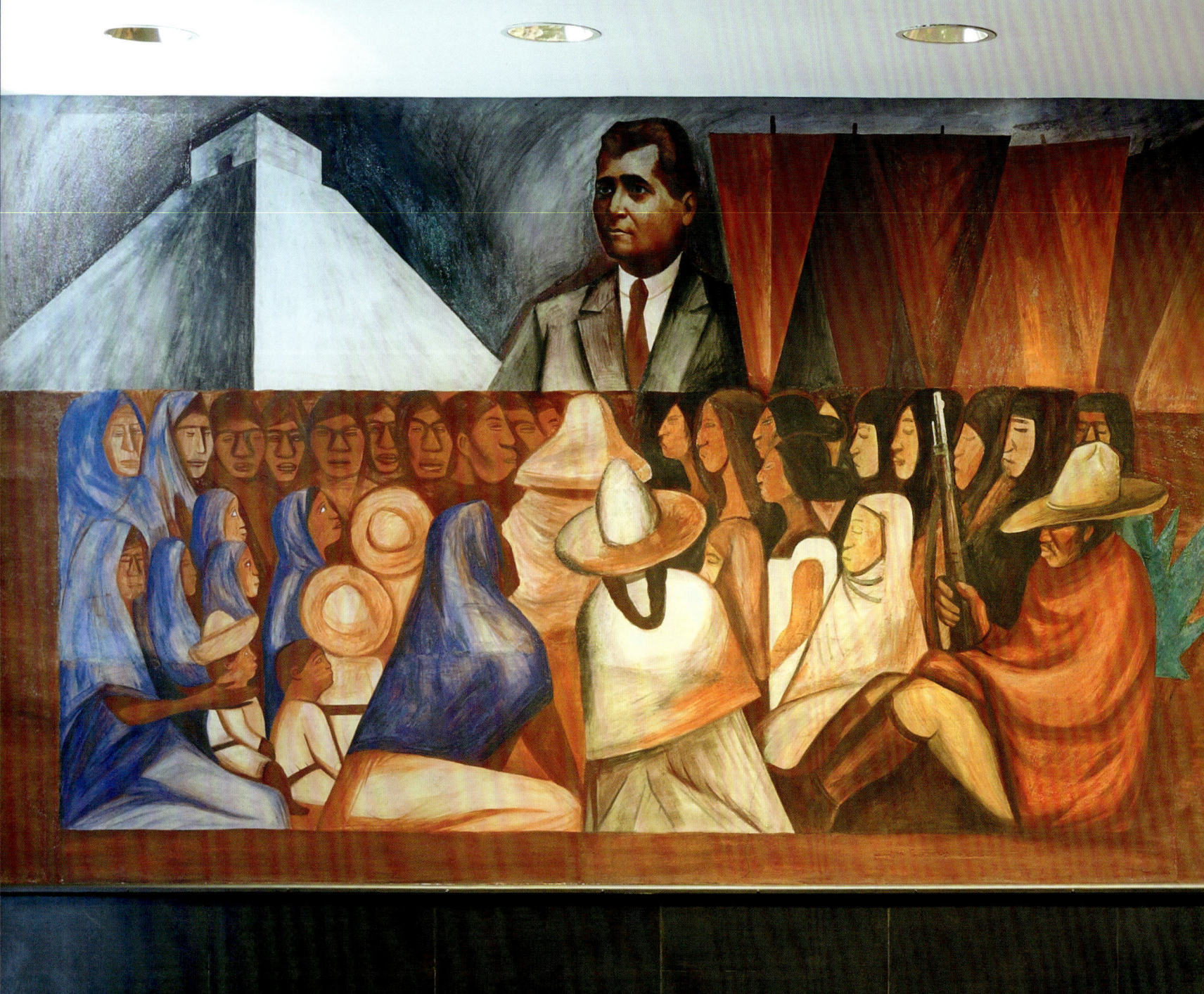

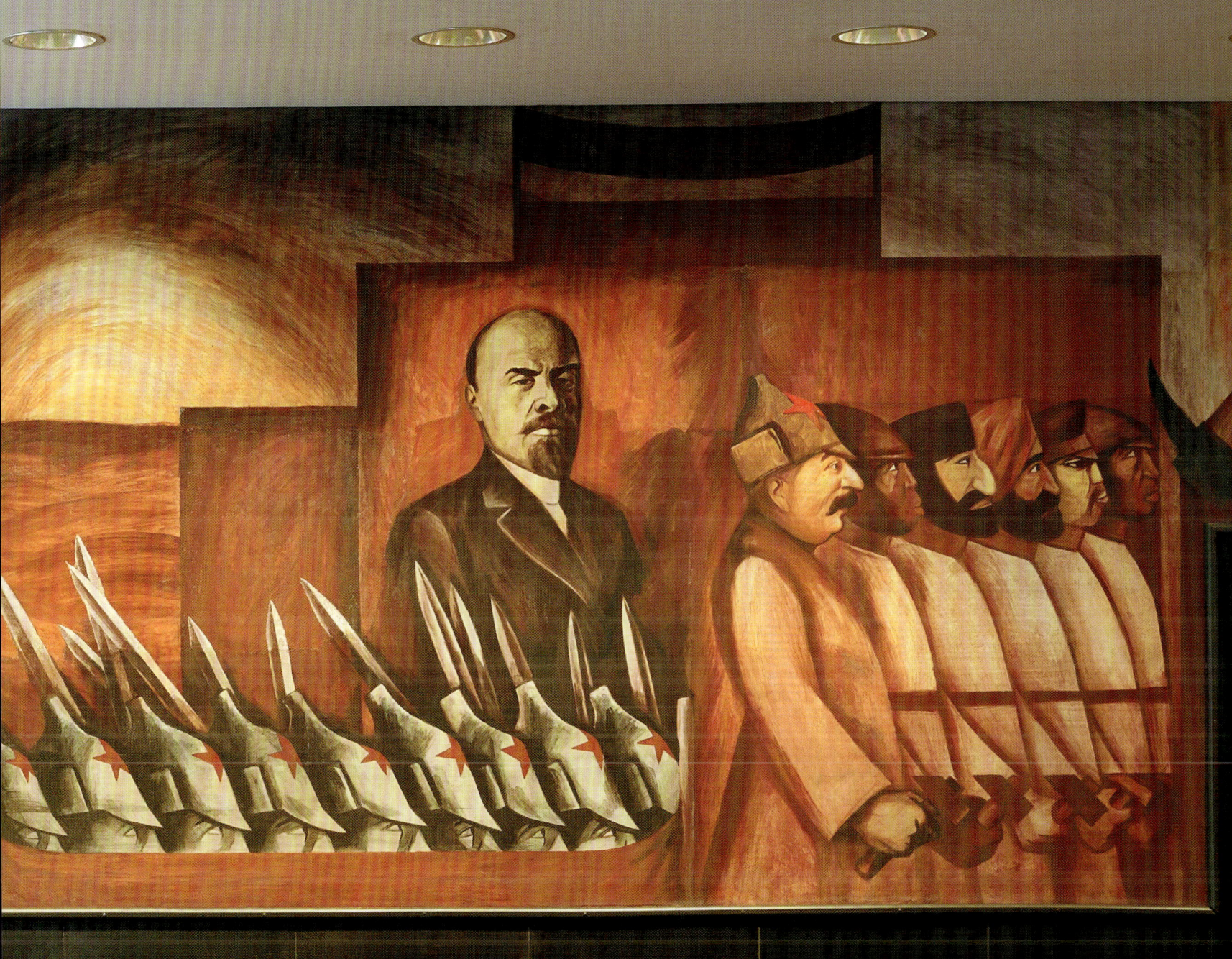

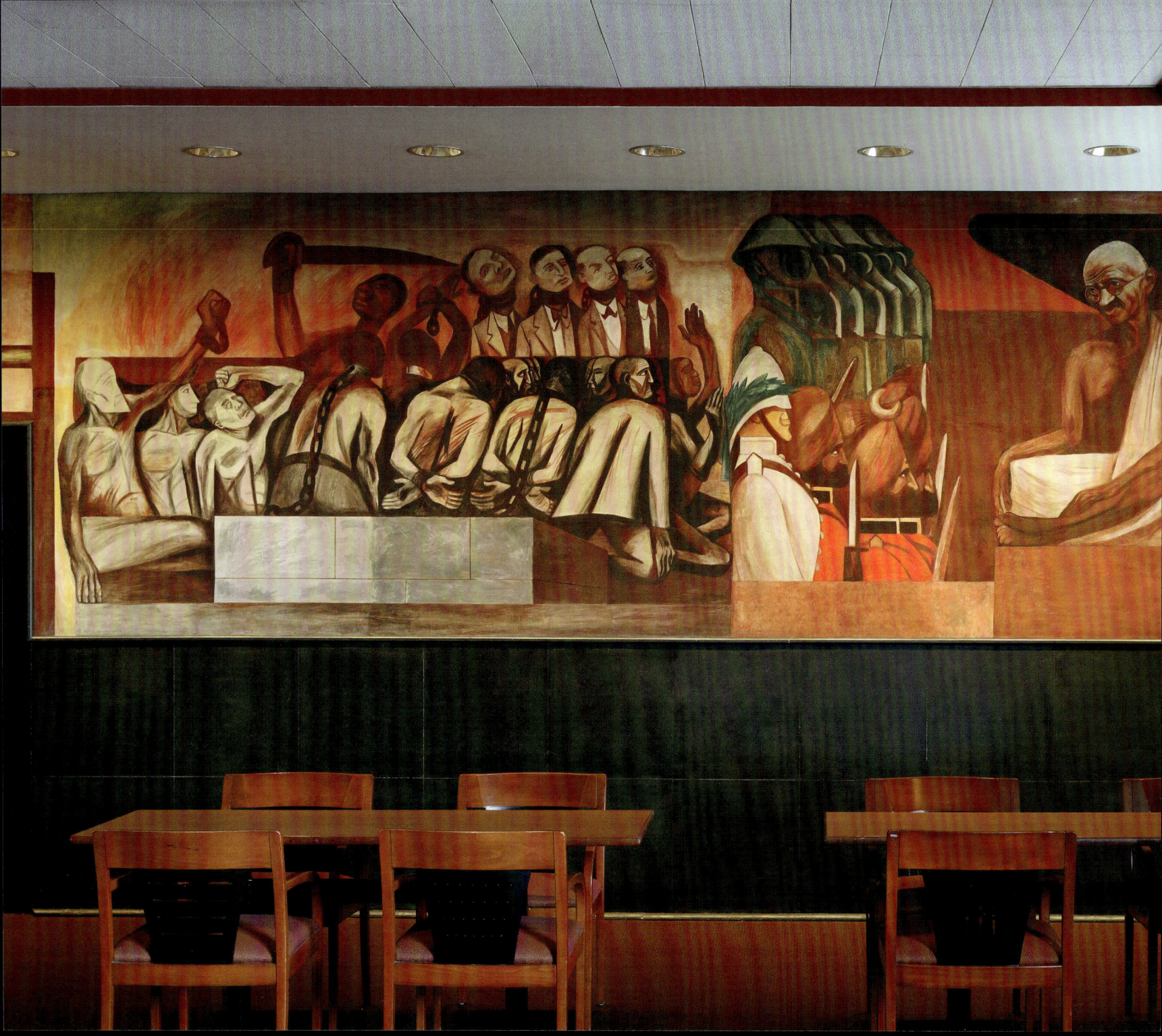

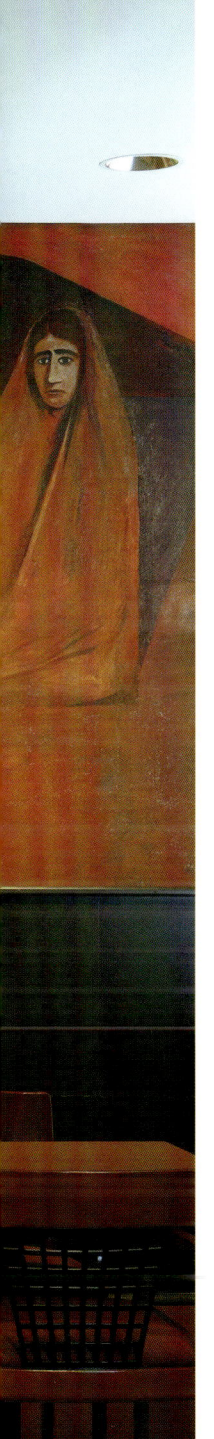

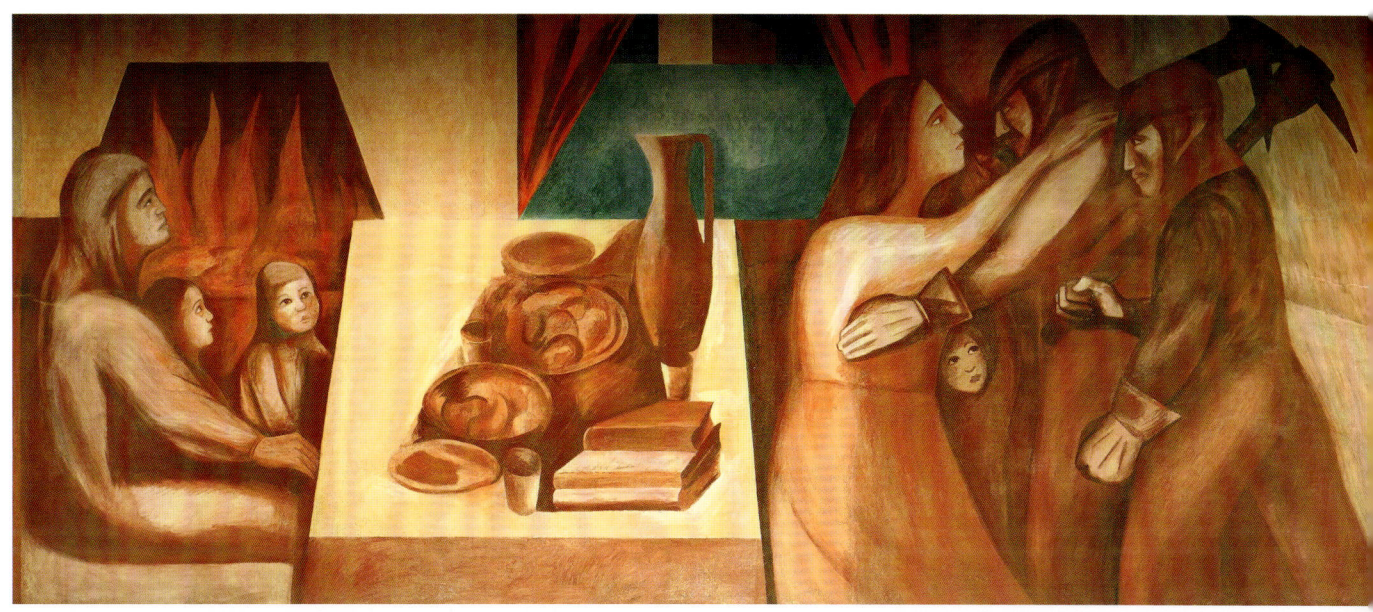

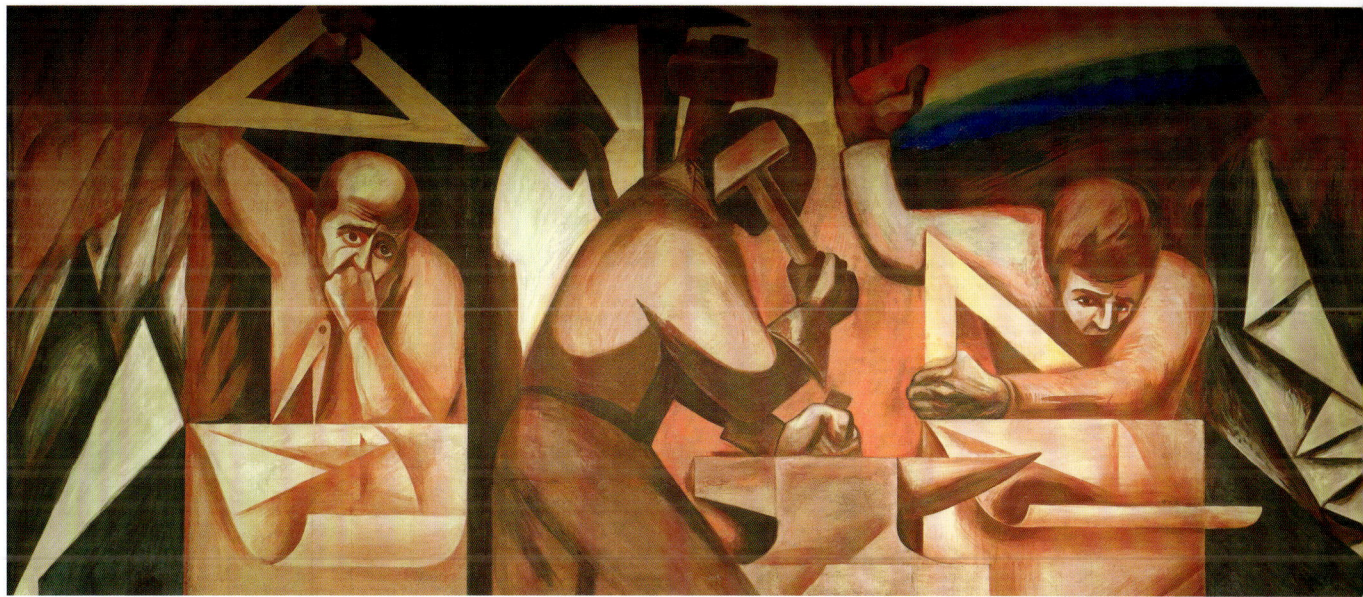

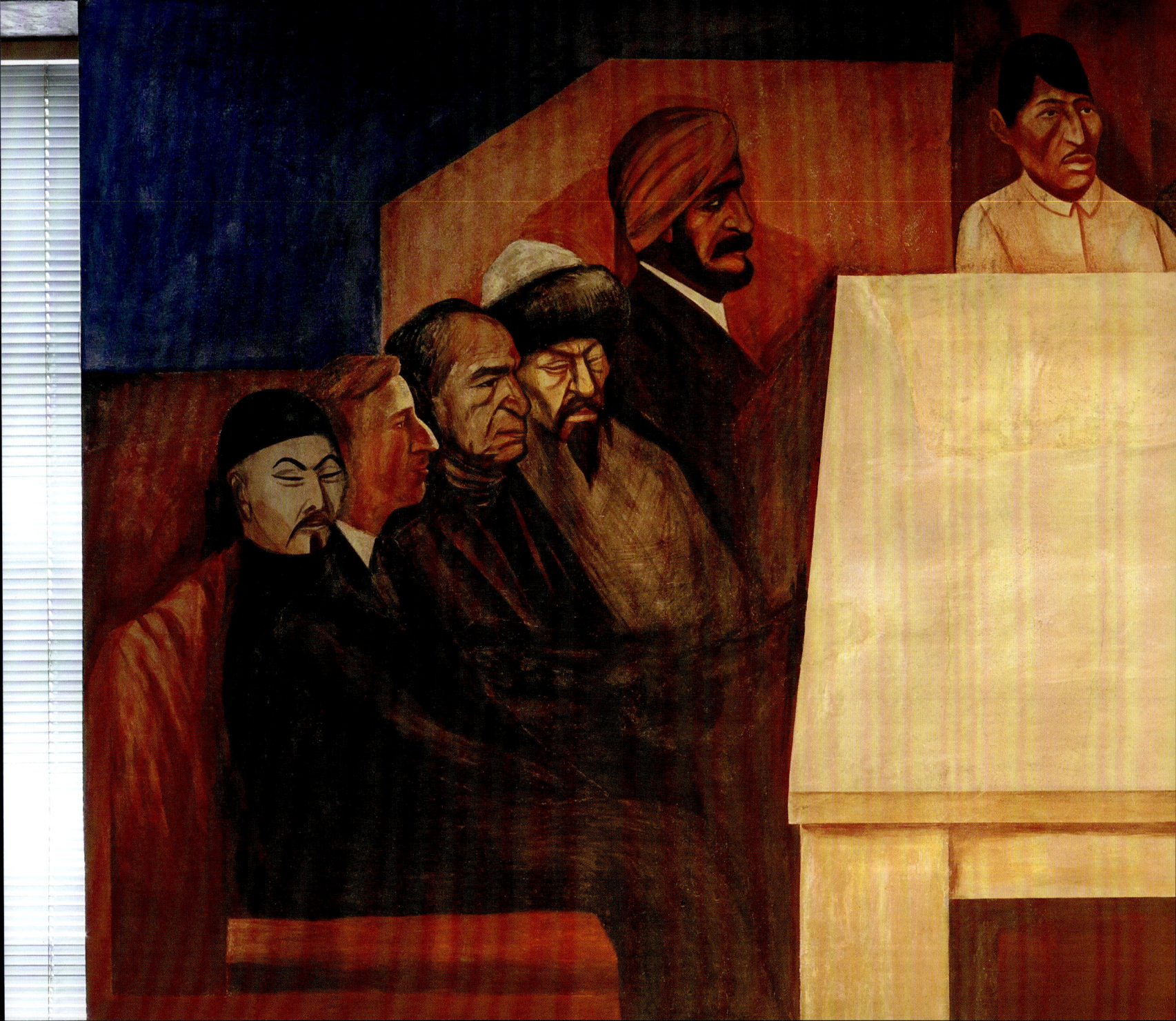

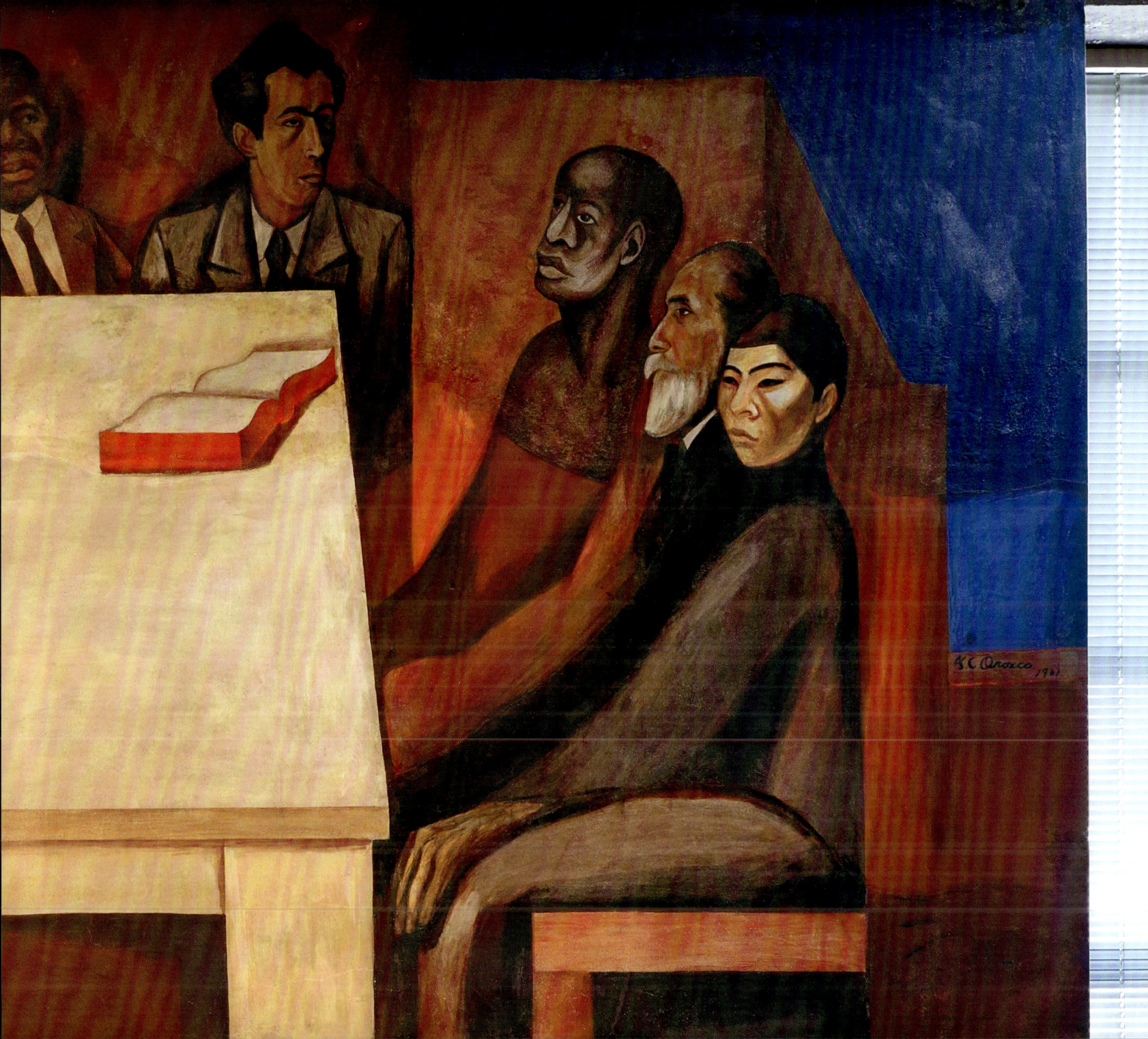

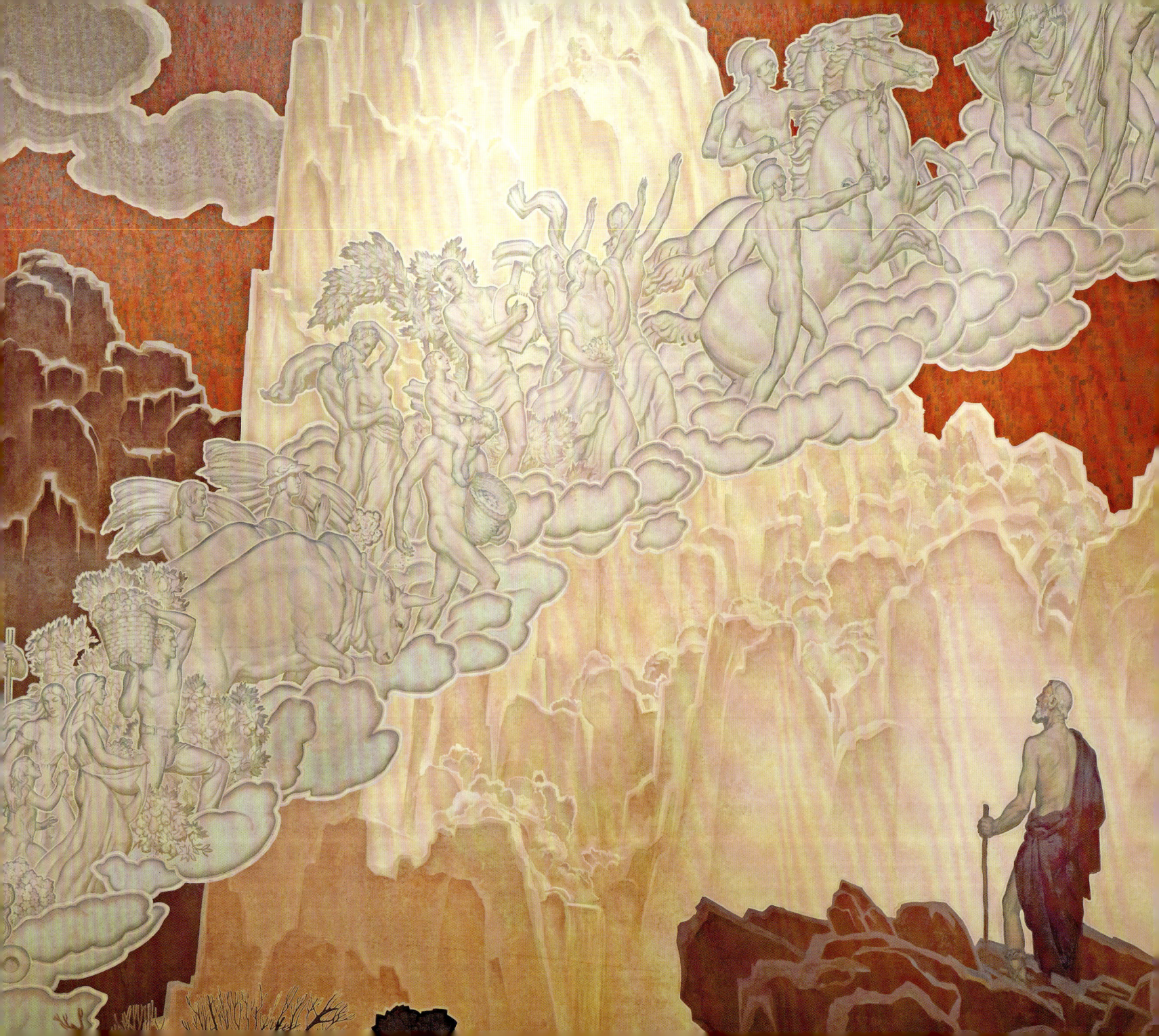

RADIO CITY MUSIC HALL

STUART DAVIS • YASUO KUNIYOSHI • EZRA WINTER

When Radio City Music Hall opened its Depression-defying doors in 1932, noted historian and urban critic Lewis Mumford called it "the sorriest failure of imagination and intelligence in modern American architecture." But the vision of its designer, Donald Deskey, a passionate devotee of Art Deco, changed the course of American interior design.

Deskey, charged with commissioning artists to create murals for the building, assigned Michigan native Ezra Winter the largest and most impressive commission: the space above the main lobby's sweeping grand staircase. Winter was as handsome as a silent-screen idol and monomaniacal in his ambition to become an art star. He was such a successful muralist that he was able to spend the Roaring Twenties in a vast two-story-high studio in the attic of Grand Central Terminal, which also served as party central during Prohibition. And even three years after the stock market crash, Winter had never been busier. Shortly before his forty-sixth birthday, he got the Radio City commission. To have enough room to paint the 40-by-60-foot mural, Winter rented the court of the Pastime Indoor Tennis Club in Long Island City. It was there, for six months during the spring and summer of 1932, that he and a team of assistants painted *Quest for the Fountain of Eternal Youth*, a painting based on a Native American legend from the area around Oregon.

In the painting, a solitary old man stands upon a cropping of rock looking across the chasm of time watching the procession of life. Perhaps it is Winter himself, who could never make the leap from decorative painter to serious artist, standing there watching the art world he wanted so much to be a part of passing him by. Critics ridiculed the painting. They said the painting lacked the energy and modernity of the other murals in Radio City, notably Stuart Davis's *Men without Women*, located in the men's lounge, or Diego Rivera's doomed *Man at the Crossroads*, across the street at Rockefeller Center. On April 6, 1949, Winter left his magnificent 8,000-square-foot Bauhaus home-studio in Connecticut, walked into the woods, and shot himself. Though he left no note, the melancholy metaphor of apartness and the doomed search for beauty in *Quest for the Fountain of Eternal Youth* may give clues to the torment within that brought him to that sad ending.

Originally, Georgia O'Keeffe was to have painted the mural in the ladies' lounge on the mezzanine. At that time, her paintings, due to the stewardship of her husband, Alfred Stieglitz, were selling for $5,000 when a Picasso could be had for $300. But O'Keeffe longed to do a large-scale mural and signed the contract with Deskey for a $1,500 fee. Stieglitz objected, claiming that knowledge of her painting a bathroom for a pittance would damage her reputation and drive down the prices for her paintings. The contract rescinded, O'Keeffe was hospitalized for two months with a nervous breakdown. O'Keeffe was replaced with Japanese painter Yasuo Kuniyoshi, known as "Yas." For his approach, Yas picked up on O'Keeffe's original flower theme and painted a sensuous, East-meets-West garden of botanicals softly painted with Rousseau-like foliage against a background of soft salmon pinks and blues. The mural was poorly covered with a South Pacific–esque repainting during a misguided 1986 restoration, but it was restored once again in 1999. Rather than strip away the over-painting to uncover what lay underneath and risk irreversible damage to the original work, the decision was made, by EverGreene Architectural Arts' Yohannes Aynalem, to paint it over once again—but this time in a faithful replication of the original. Perhaps one day, restoration techniques that allow a resurrection of the deeply hidden original will be devised.

In the meantime, we, or at least half of Radio City Music Hall's audience, can enjoy an informed, perfectly executed reproduction of Kuniyoshi's painting.

Stuart Davis was the most artful–and the least arty–American painters of his time. He was a Pop artist before there was Pop. After losing his teaching job at the Art Students League, he was delighted, in 1932, when he was chosen to paint a mural for Radio City Music Hall. Because it was to be installed in the main men's lounge, he chose to populate his 10-by-17-foot abstract composition with masculine symbols of recreation. The result is such a beautifully composed work that Picasso used a newspaper photograph of it in planning the forms for his masterpiece *Guernica*. Davis originally entitled his painting *Mural*, but the committee who had chosen him retitled it *Men without Women*, after a Hemingway short-story collection. When it was gifted to the Museum of Modern Art in 1975, it was first changed back to *Mural* and finally to *Untitled*. After the 1999 renovation, MoMA lent *Mural/Men without Women/Untitled* back to Radio City Music Hall be reinstalled in its original location. Today, both sexes may enjoy the murals located in the lobby and their respective lounges.

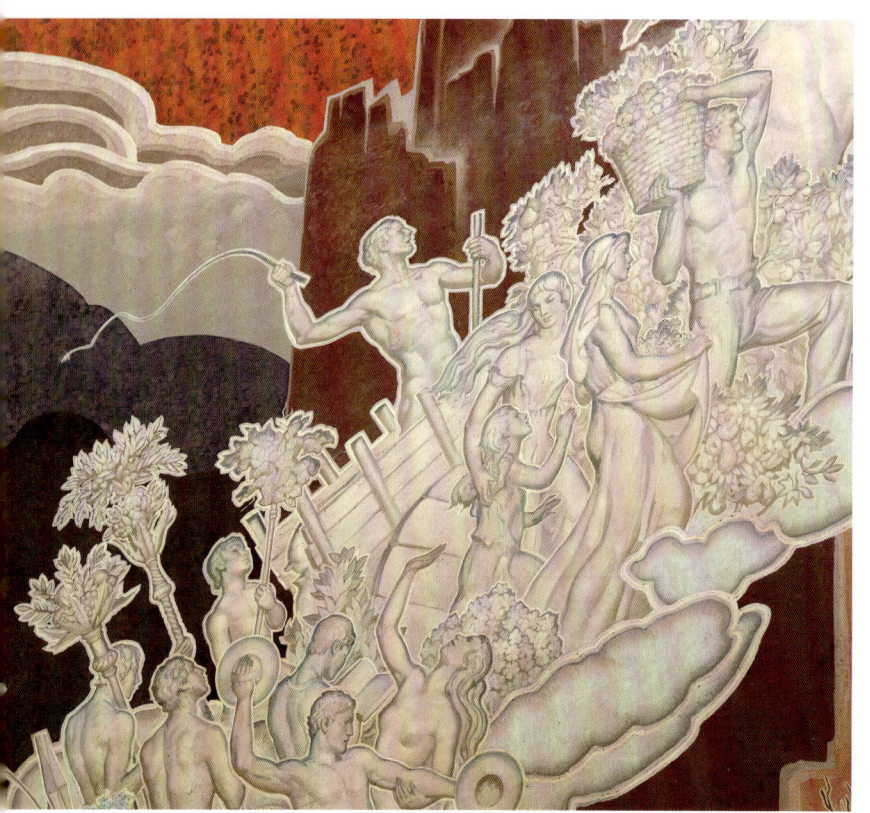

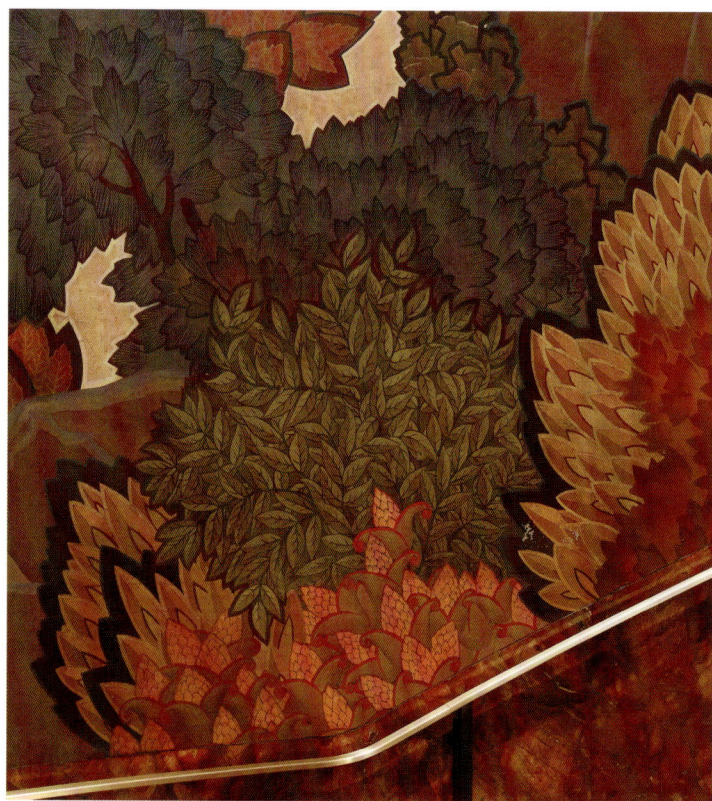

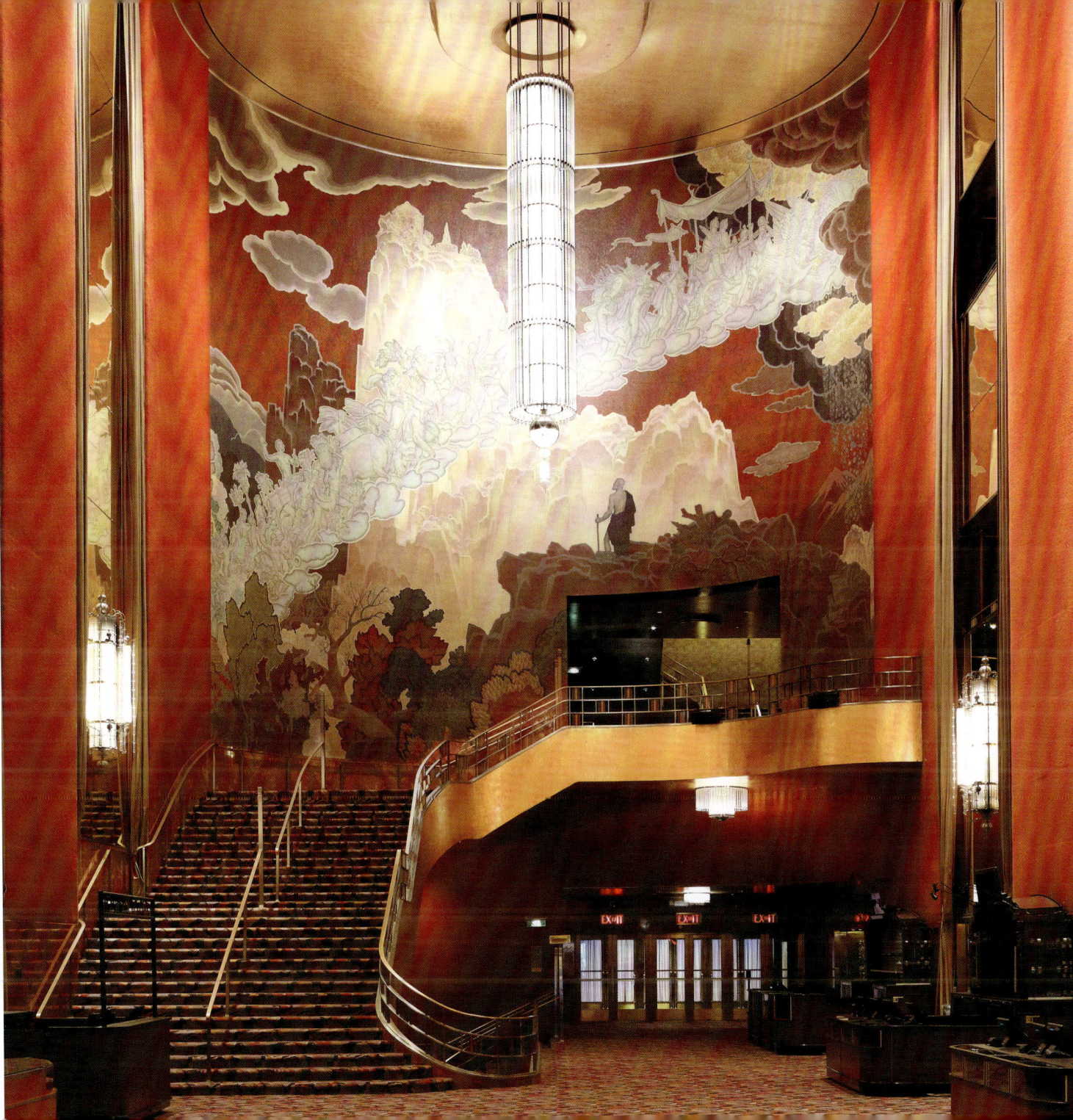

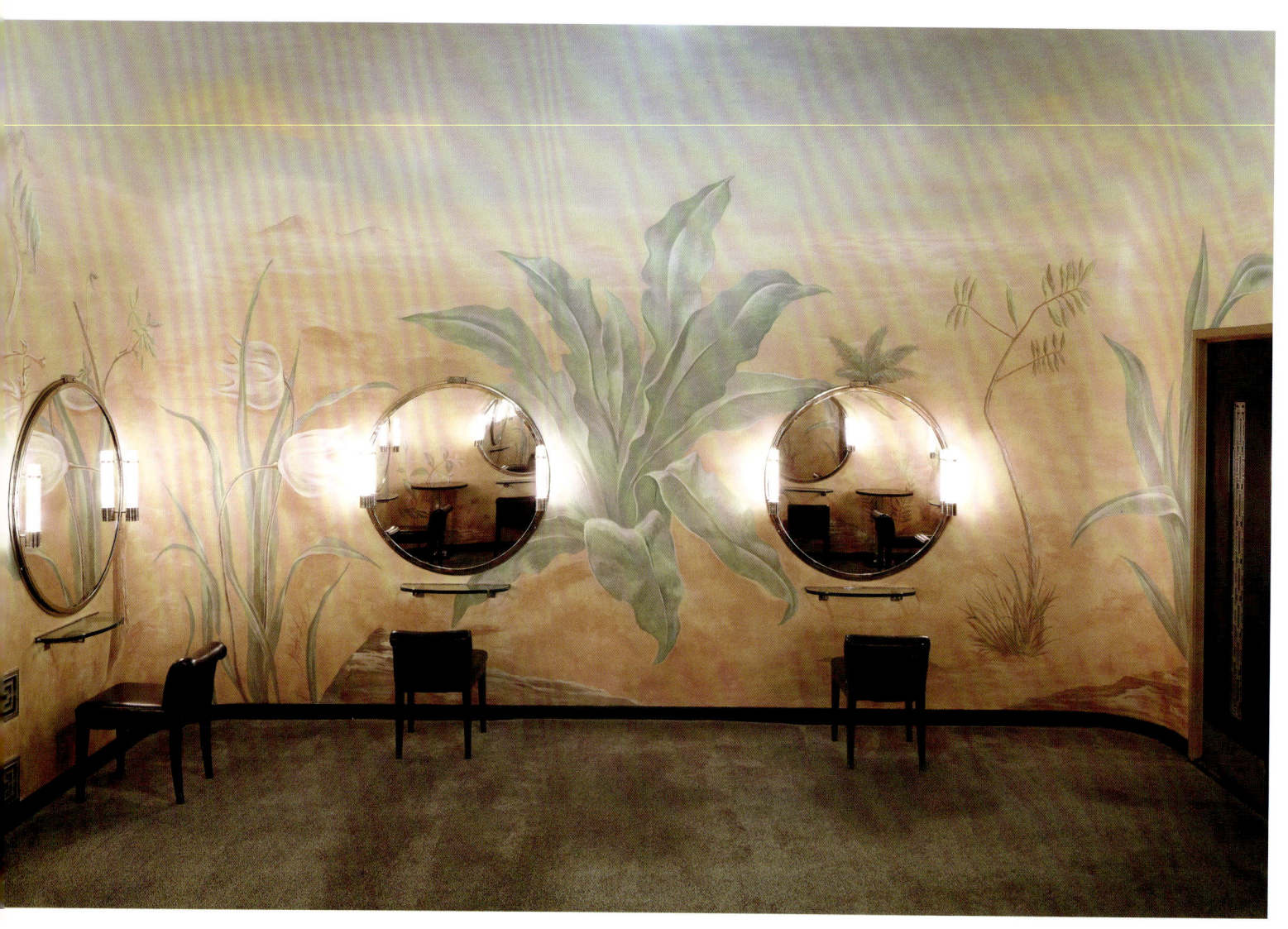

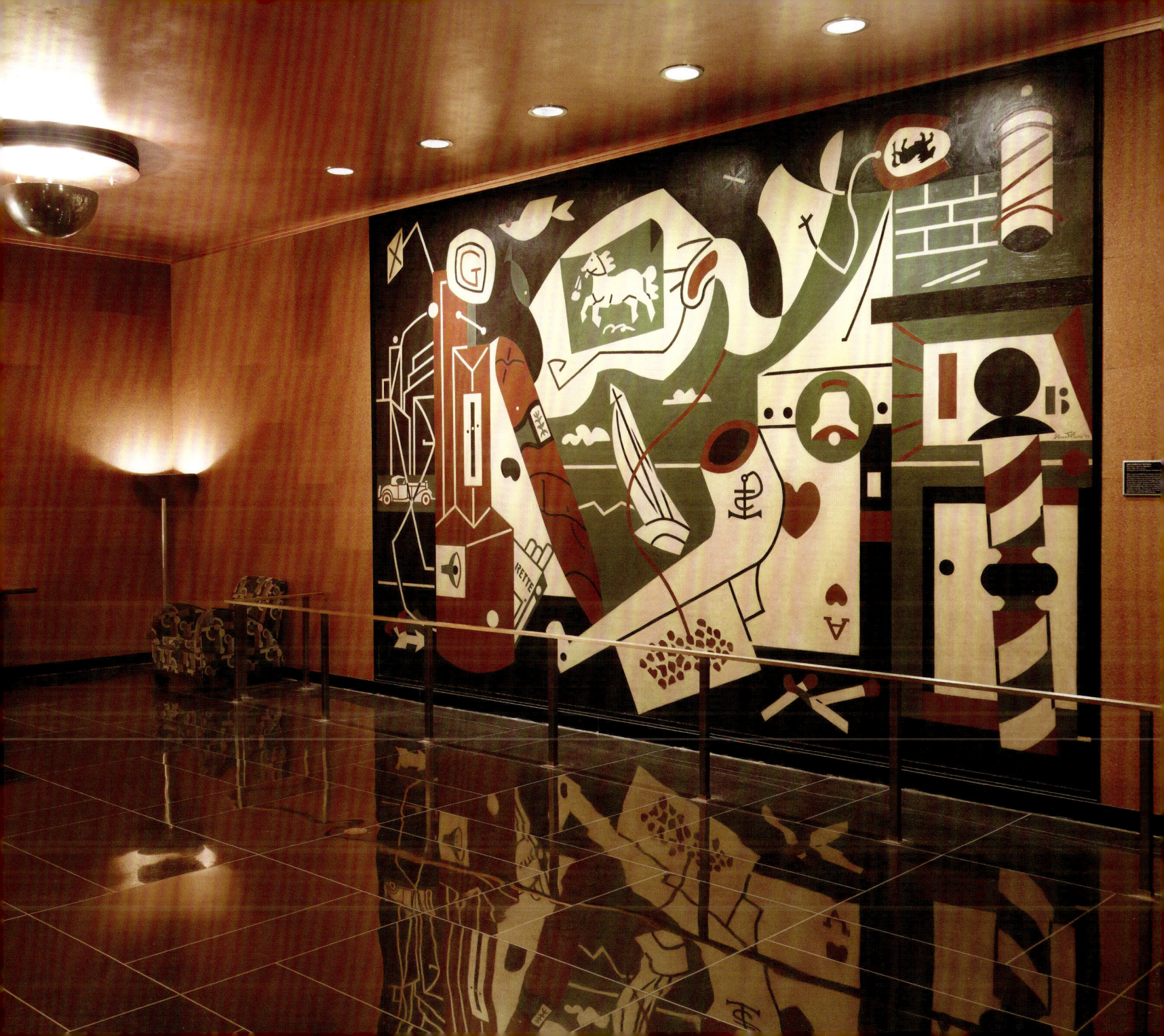

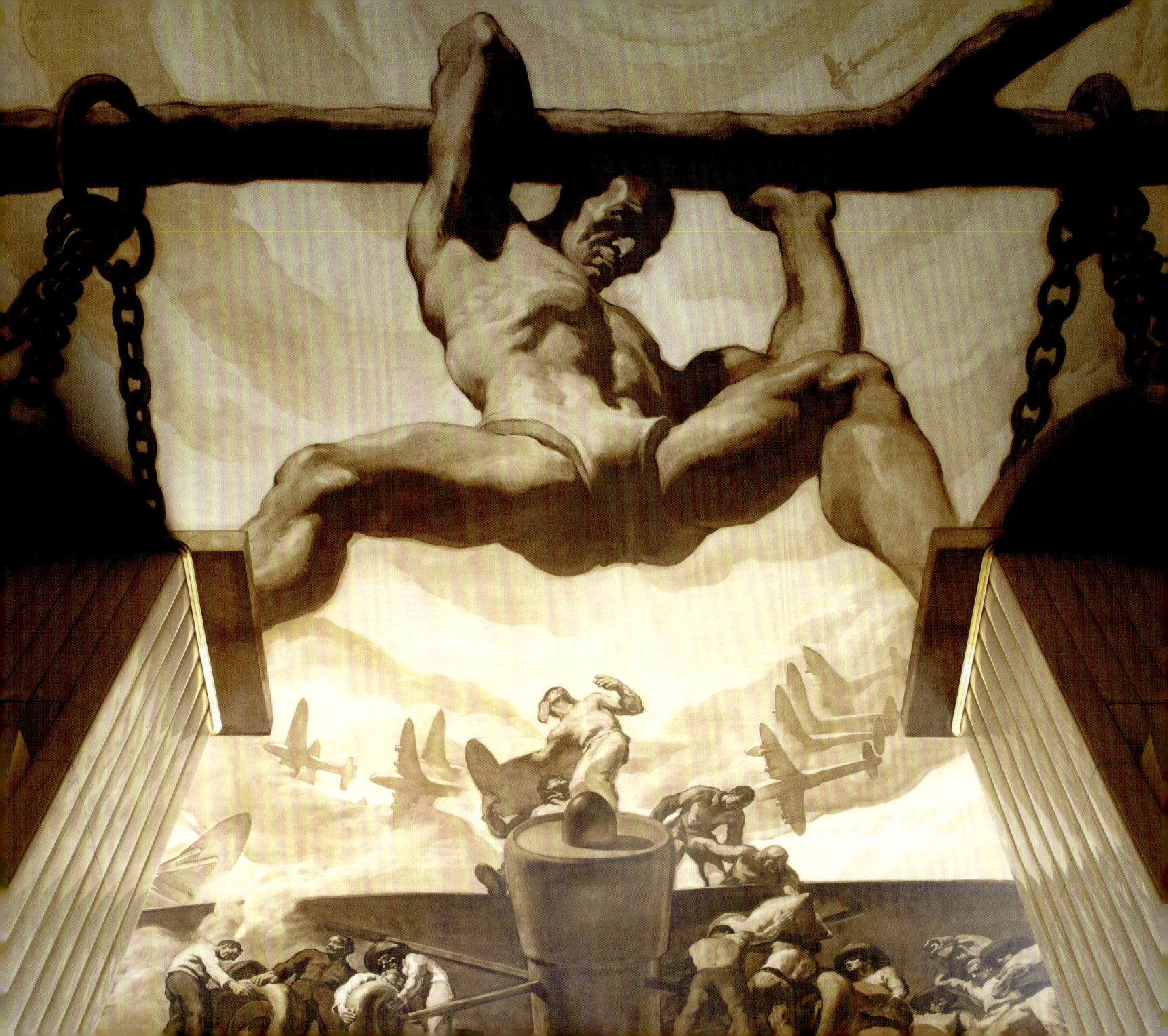

ROCKEFELLER CENTER

SIR FRANK BRANGWYN • JOSÉ MARÍA SERT

In the studio, an artist may follow his or her own impulses, mind, and heart. It is up to the marketplace to then either accept or reject the artist's creation. The muralist, however, must be able to adjust his or her vision to the dictates of the client and the public, without losing his or her integrity. On May 9, 1933, Diego Rivera climbed down the scaffold in Rockefeller Center for the last time. His patron, Nelson Rockefeller, had fired him because he had refused to remove the portrait of Vladimir Lenin from the mural he was painting for the lobby of the RCA building at Rockefeller Center. Uniformed security guards escorted him from the building, and the mural was covered from view.

Edward Trumbull, who had just painted the ceiling murals in the lobby of the Chrysler Building, had already been retained by the Rockefeller Center architects to be the overall coordinator for their murals. He had recommended Sir Frank Brangwyn and José María Sert to paint the murals flanking Rivera's masterpiece. Trumbull was directing every aspect of their projects: materials, ground color, themes, method of painting (chiaroscuro), and a severely limited palette of black, white, and gray. But the ferociously independent Rivera had not been able to abide such restrictions. Rivera considered the other painters vastly inferior to him and had to be coaxed to share the lobby space with them. Rivera demanded complete artistic freedom, insisting that he paint in true fresco, embedding paint directly in wet plaster, rather than working in a studio as Brangwyn and Sert had been doing.

The lobby's theme was to be a hopeful celebration of science and man's harnessing of nature. At the start of the project, Rockefeller and the architects had agreed that the art should show "Man at the Crossroads Looking with Hope and High Vision to the Choosing of a New and Better Future." But Rivera wanted his panel to show ". . . the Workers arriving at a true understanding of their rights regarding the means of production. It will show the Workers of the Cities and the Country inheriting the Earth." After he and Rockefeller failed to compromise on their respective visions, he descended the scaffolding and never returned. In his final letter to Rockefeller, Rivera wrote, "Rather than mutilate the conception, I should prefer the physical destruction of the concept in its entirety, but preserving, at least its integrity." The painting remained covered until February 9, 1934, when, without any fanfare or publicity, workmen demolished the mural with hammers, picks, and chisels, and carted it away in wheelbarrows.

Nobody was happier about this turn of events than José María Sert. He detested Rivera, and with him literally swept away, Sert had the opportunity to paint on arguably the most important wall in New York, if not America. Sert's 1,000-square-foot painting, *American Progress*, which replaced Rivera's fresco, is an allegorical scene of mankind building America. Rockefeller Center rises out of the mist as a symbol of the ultimate fusion of ideals and industry. (Sert knew how to keep a patron happy.) Overhead is a 5,000-square-foot mural, *Time*, grandiloquently trumpeting the lofty ideals that sought to elevate what could have been just another office building to a higher nobility. A powerful vortex of clouds and energy seem to serve mankind's airplanes circling upward toward a limitless destiny. The dominant element is the Colossus straddling the two main pillars with a great log from which scales are suspended, representing the past and the future.

In the north corridor are four murals, which, according to a 1933 press release ". . . express man's new mastery of the material universe, through his power, his will, his imagination and his genius. These are: 1. The painful labor of former ages conquered by the creative intelligence of the machine. 2. The pest and the epidemics of yesterday conquered by scientific inventions. 3. Ancient slavery conquered by the human will. 4. The combined faculties of man, applied to the quest for human happiness, which are strong enough to suppress war."

Brangwyn wanted his four panels in the south corridor to show "Man, in His Search for Truth and Happiness, Must Learn to Accept the Fundamental Teachings of Christ." Unfortunately for him, Rockefeller preferred to keep religion separate from the marketplace. Trumbull traveled to England where the paintings were being created, to try to get Brangwyn to modify his religiosity, in particular the figure of Christ in the Sermon on the Mount panel. Brangwyn was nearly as intractable as Rivera, but they compromised. Christ would have his back turned from the audience.

Though there will always be conflicts between the muralist and their client, occasionally, the conflict results in the creation of murals like those in Rockefeller Center, art that enriches the multitudes that pass by it day after day, year after year, generation after generation.

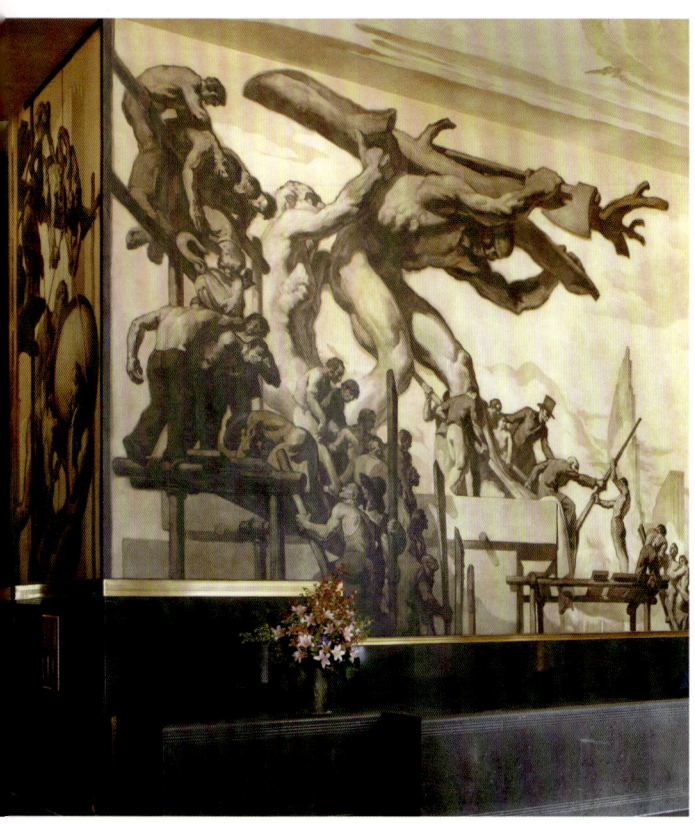

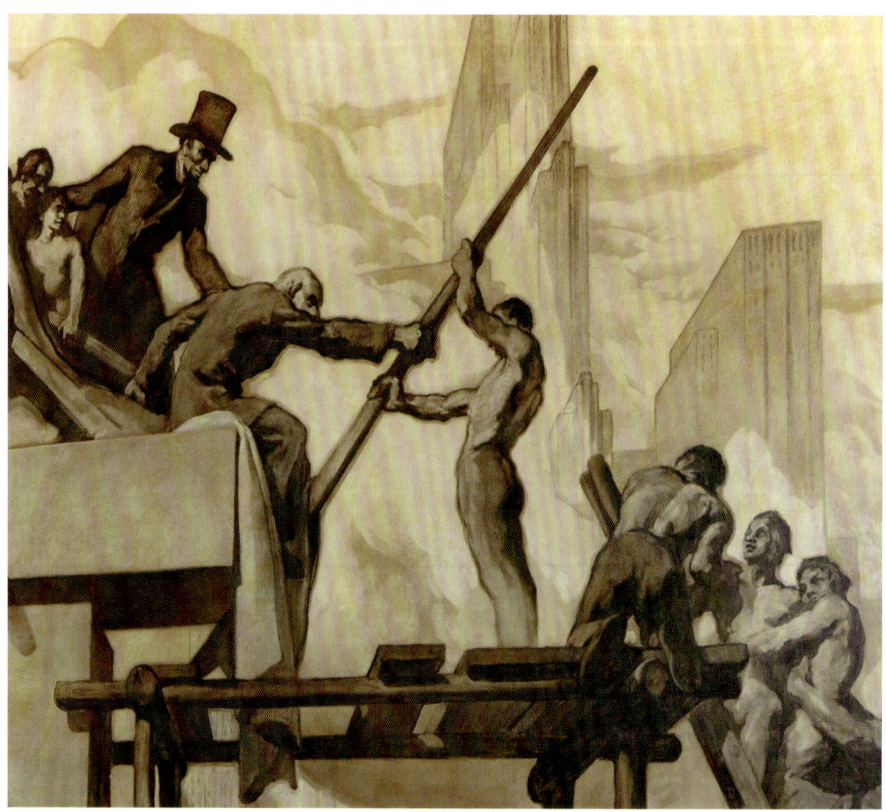

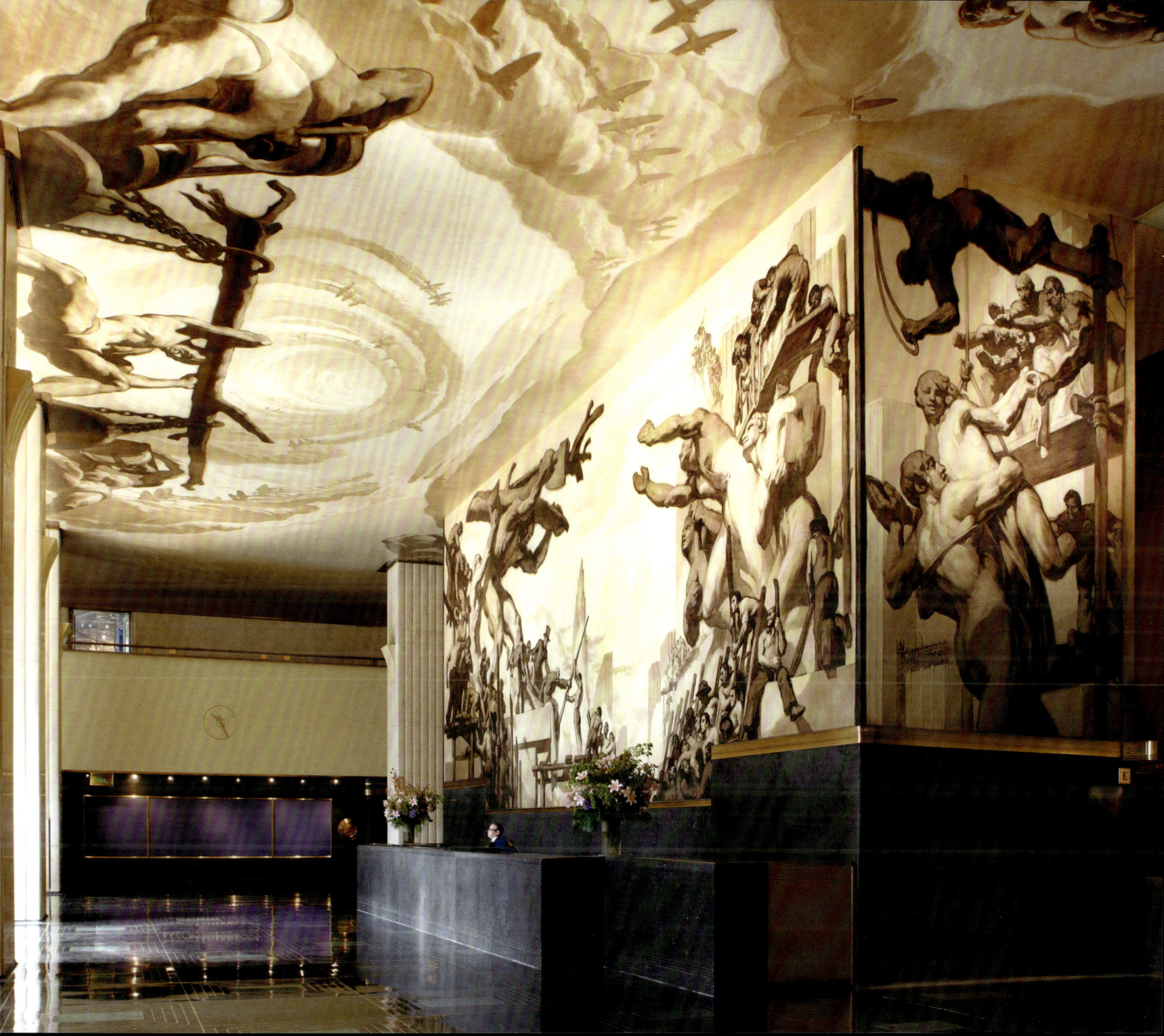

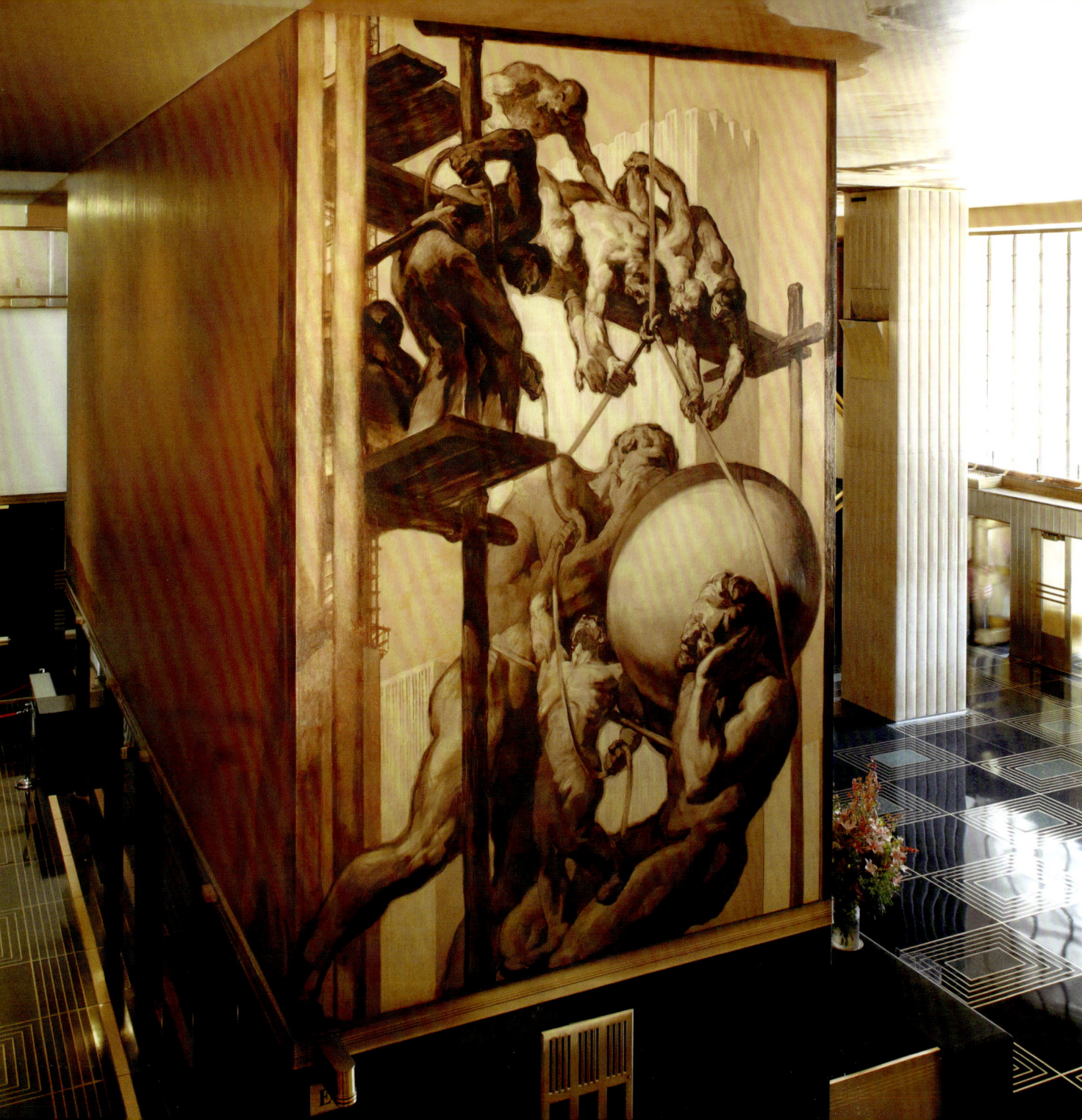

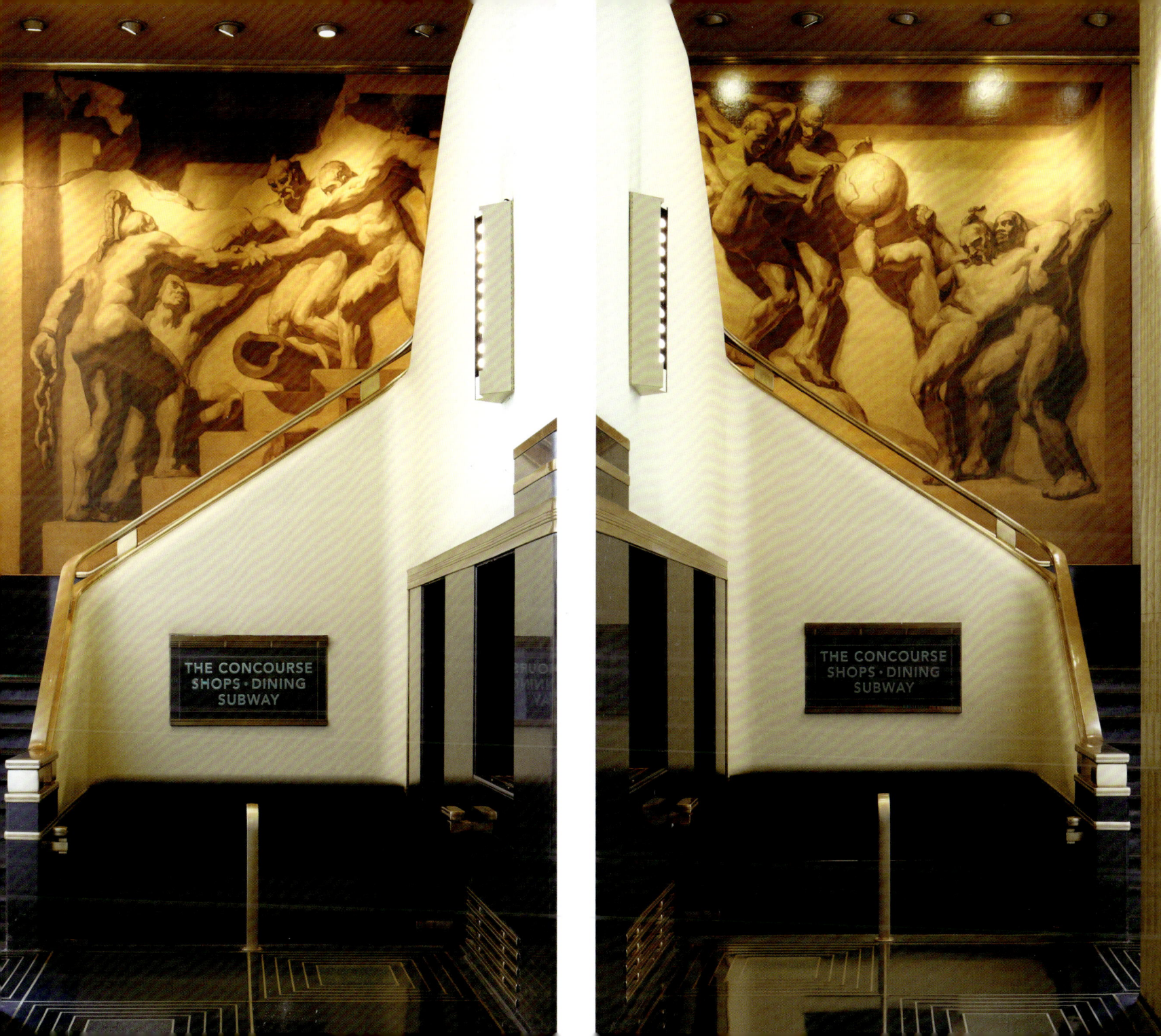

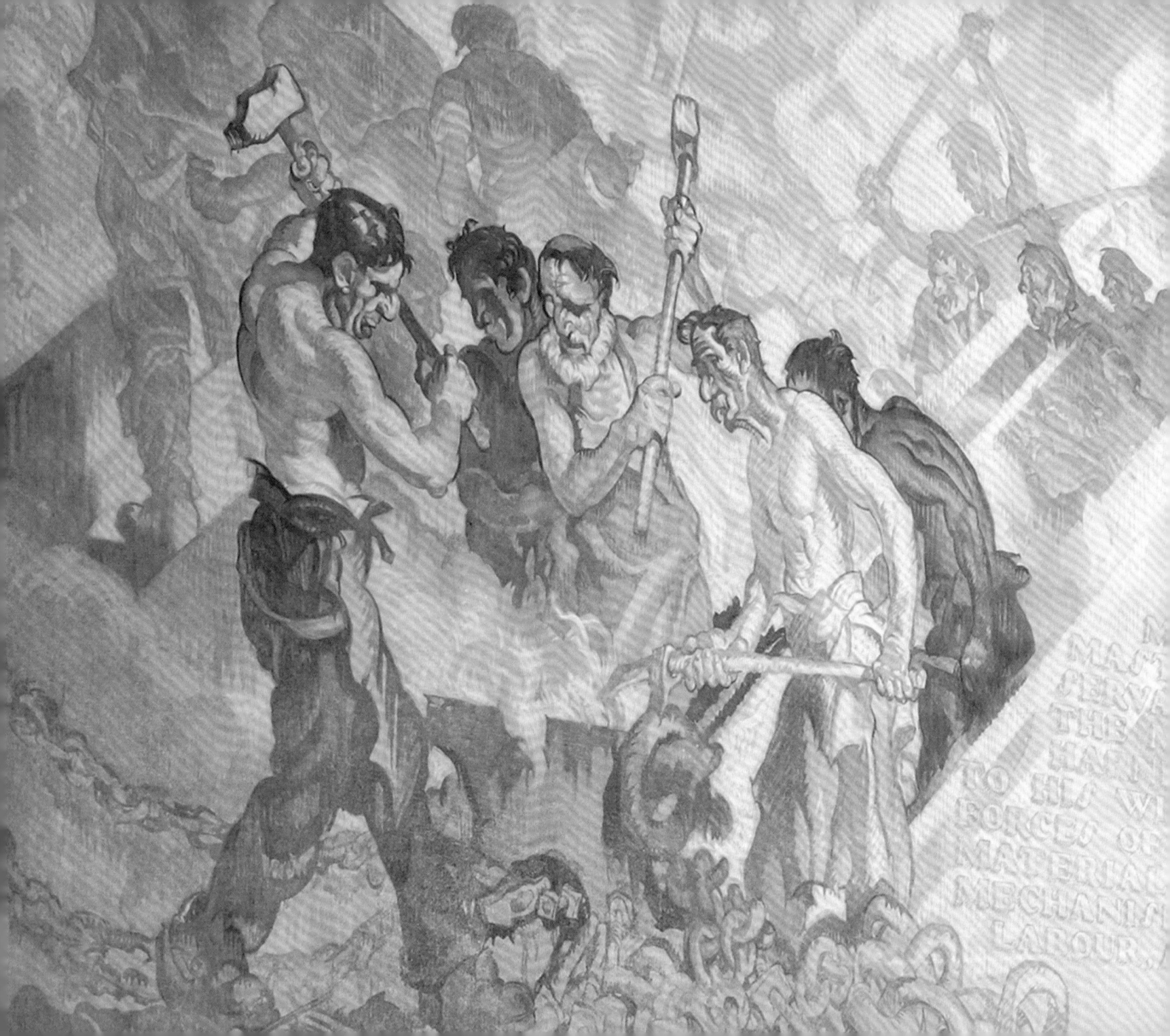

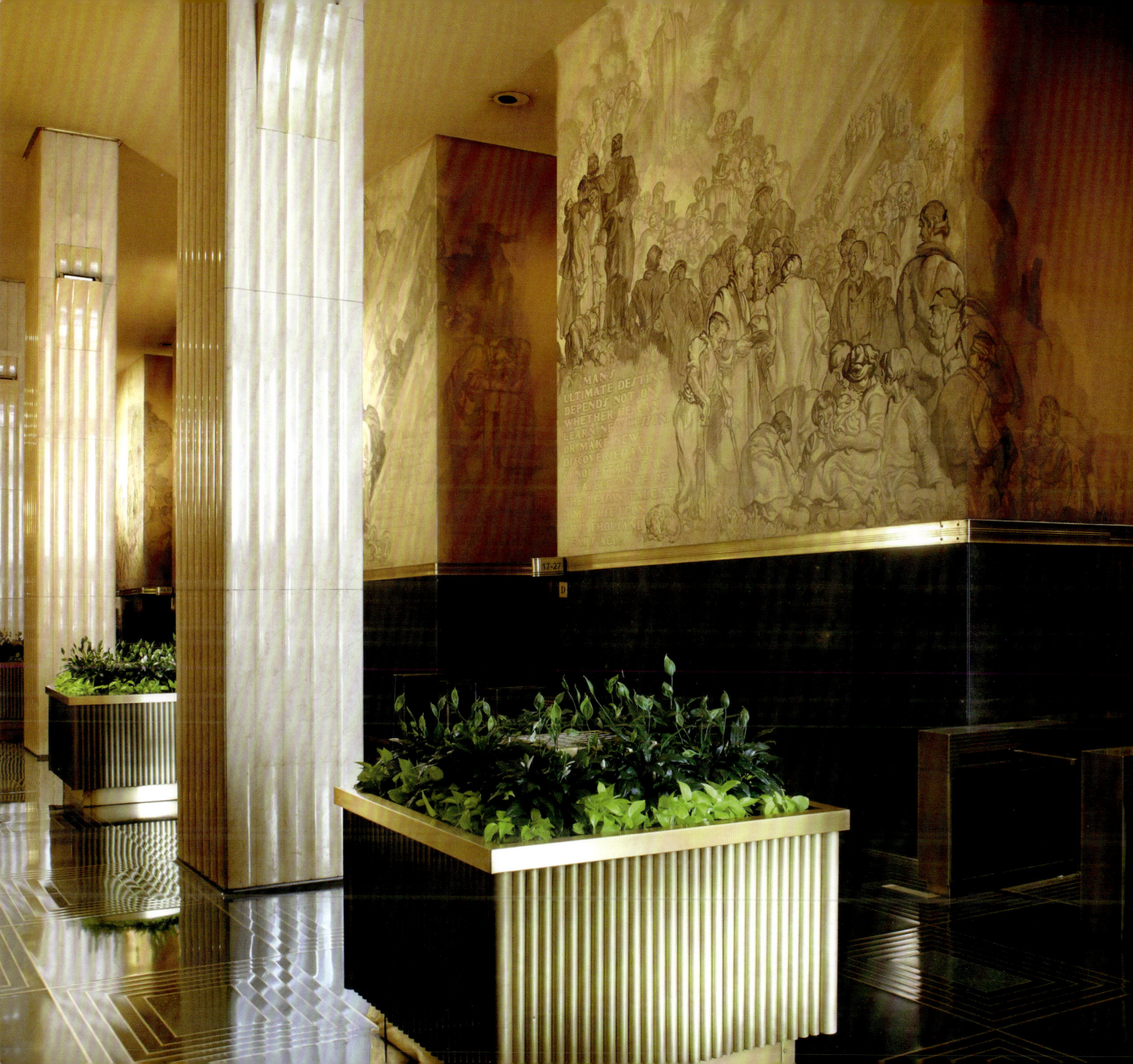

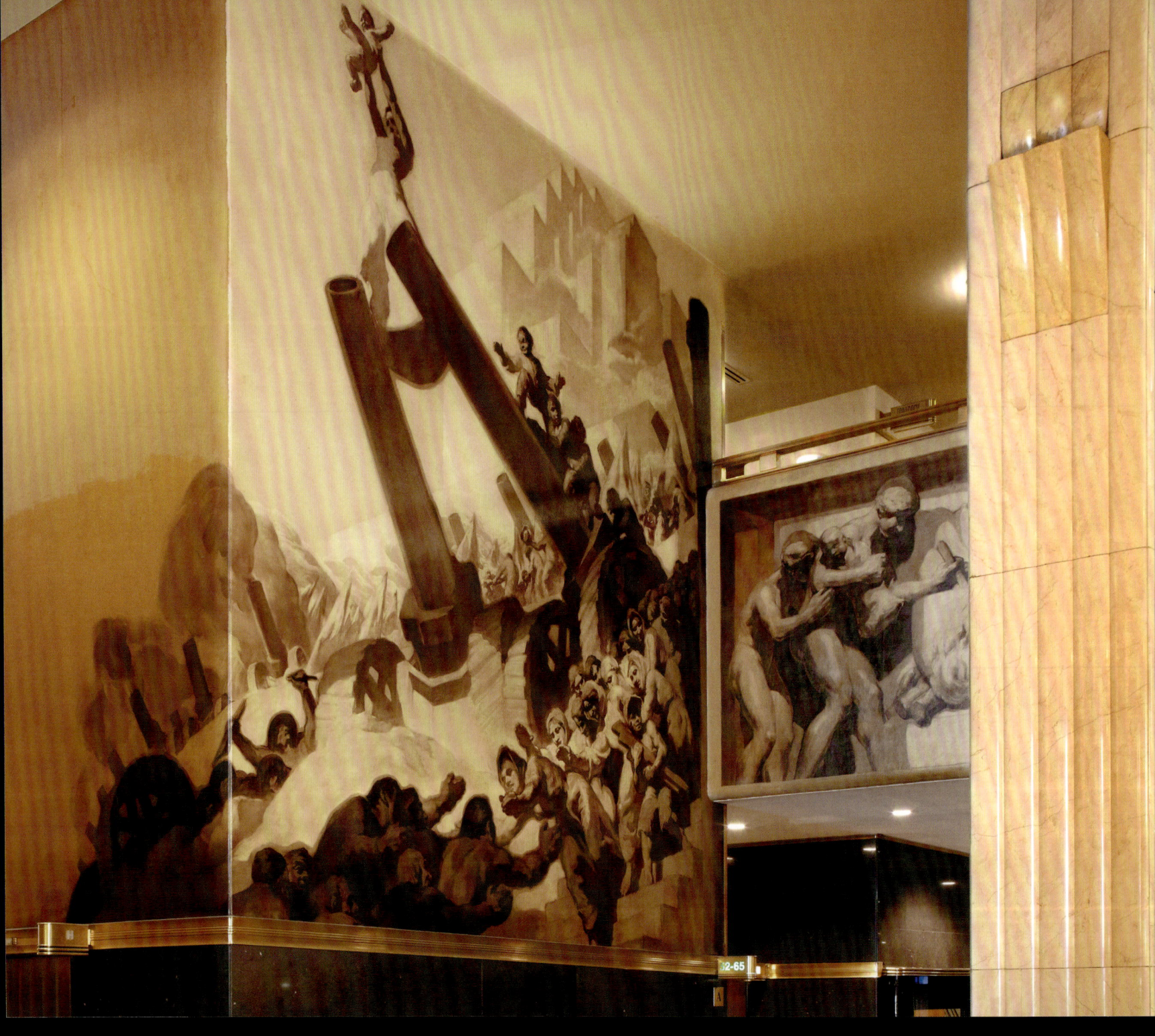

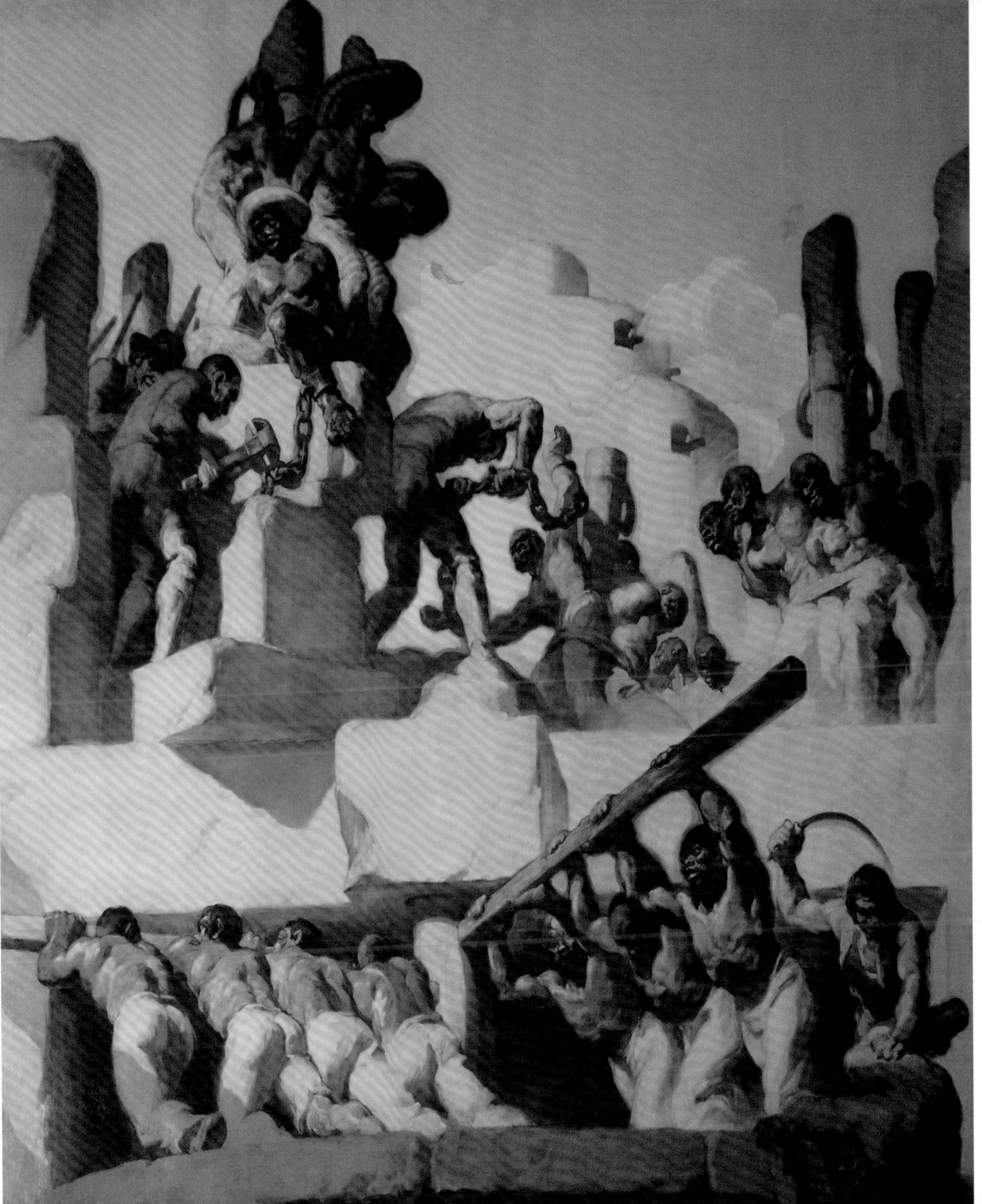

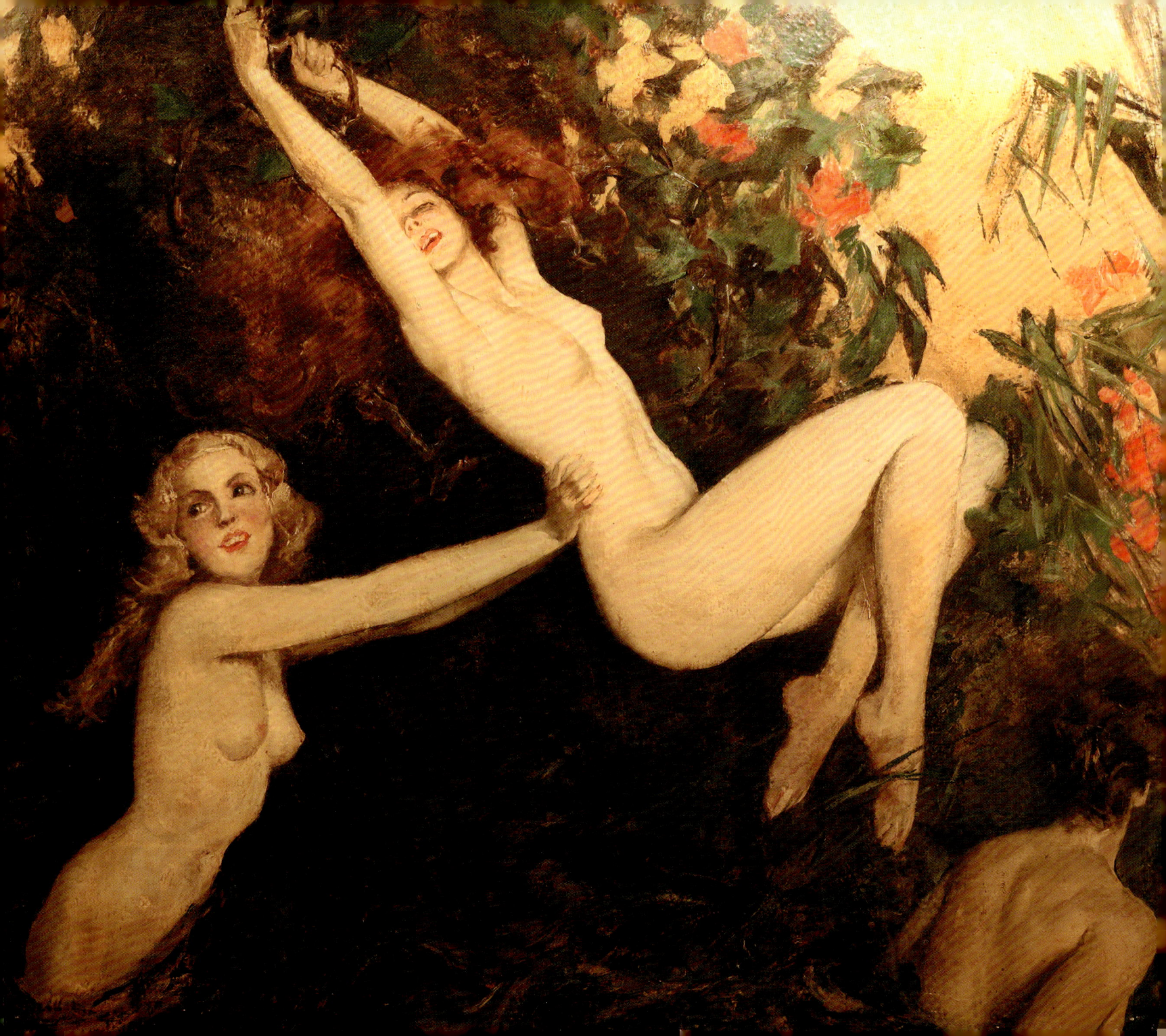

CAFÉ DES ARTISTES

For more than ninety years, the Café des Artistes has hosted almost anyone you can imagine, including Fiorello La Guardia, Leonard Bernstein, Scott and Zelda Fitzgerald, Isadora Duncan, Marcel Duchamp, George Balanchine, Norman Rockwell, the Duke and Duchess of Windsor, Cole Porter, Rudolph Valentino, Rudolph Nureyev, and, of course, the man who made it famous, Howard Chandler Christy. But the early twentieth century was the era when the center of America's art world could be found at the Hotel des Artistes, a cooperative apartment building located at 1 West 67th Street in Manhattan. Each apartment had 22-foot ceilings, mezzanine floors, a balcony, and enormous glass walls that flooded the workspaces with the most precious and elusive commodity for an artist in New York—light! One of the first residents was the most celebrated artist of the Jazz Age, Howard Chandler Christy, who bought an apartment in 1915 and lived there until his death in 1952.

Christy, who grew up in rural Ohio, moved to New York at sixteen to study at the Art Students League under famed painter and teacher William Merritt Chase. He began illustrating books and magazines in 1895 and, in 1898, was sent by *Scribner's Magazine* to cover the Spanish-American War with Teddy Roosevelt and his Rough Riders as a war illustrator.

After chronicling the atrocities of war, Christy returned to New York. Young, handsome, and talented, he was the toast of New York, marrying Maybelle Thompson, a debutante who became his favorite model and muse for the "Christy Girl," his version of the "Gibson Girl." One of the most famous Christy Girls was created for a World War I recruitment poster, adorably dressed in a U.S. Navy uniform, with the tag line, "Gee!! I wish I were a MAN. I'd join the NAVY."

All the artists living at the Hotel des Artistes gathered for meals, drinks, and socializing at the ground-floor Café des Artistes. It was a genteel, cozy bistro in the "English Ordinary" style and, though the residents loved it, the café was in danger of closing during the Depression. Christy approached the café's owner, Frank China, with a proposition. In exchange for a fee of two thousand dollars, he would paint murals of nude young women that would boost business and save the café. China accepted the offer, and Christy painted the first series of six paintings in 1934 and a second series of six in 1942.

In 1975, the café's then-owner, Romeo Sterlini, decided the twelve paintings were his property and, as such, wanted to take them with him before selling the café to its next owner, George Lang. Eventually a settlement was reached. The café retained *Tarzan*, *Fall*, *Spring*, *Parrot Girl*, *The Swing Girl*, *Ponce de León*, and *The Fountain of Youth*, while Sterlini spirited away *Snow Girl*, *Reclining Lady*, *Day Dream*, *The Leopard Girl*, and *Winter and Summer*, forever depriving the rest of us the pleasure of enjoying the complete suite intact. Their whereabouts are unknown.

Of the remaining paintings, we can see Christy's celebration of sensuality, youth, and beauty. Luscious naked wood nymphs cavort, dance, swim, and swing in glades and forests surrounded by rainbows, leaves, and flowers—a sybarite's vision of heaven.

The centerpiece of this erotic visual symphony is *The Fountain of Youth*, Christy's lush vision of eight sleek-hipped beauties in a pond with water falling gently from a fountain beneath a rainbow. *Parrot Girl* features Christy's mistress Elise Ford standing between two enormous bright-red parrots. Another panel shows Ponce de León and his conquistadors arriving in Florida. De León offers his sword to girls who look more like Elise Ford clones than Seminoles. The other paintings are of young maidens swinging, lying around on the grass, dancing, or hanging out with a WASPy, grape-bearing Tarzan wearing nothing but a leopard-skin loincloth. All of the women are young, flawless, and unselfconsciously naked—with no other desire than delighting our eyes.

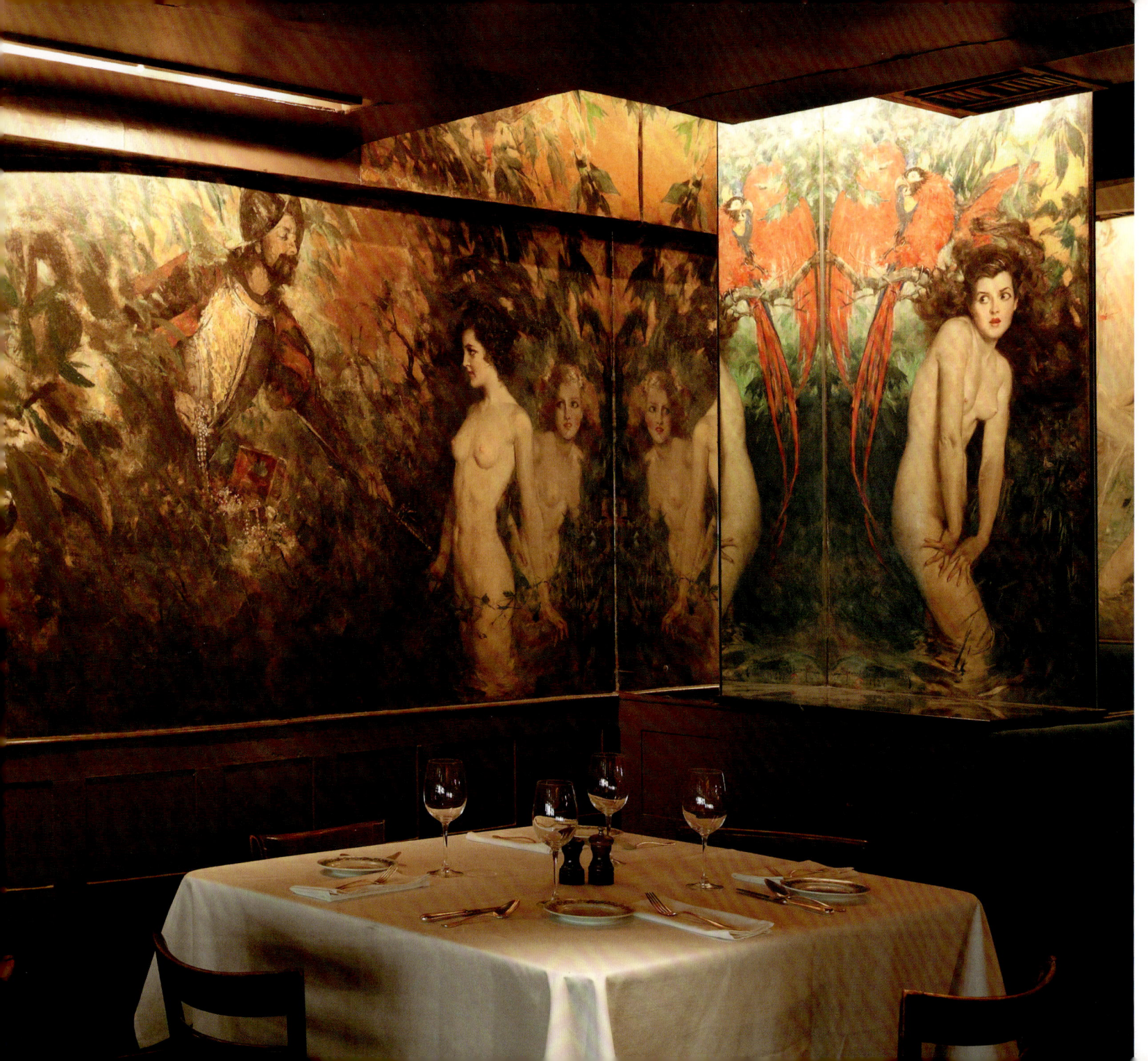

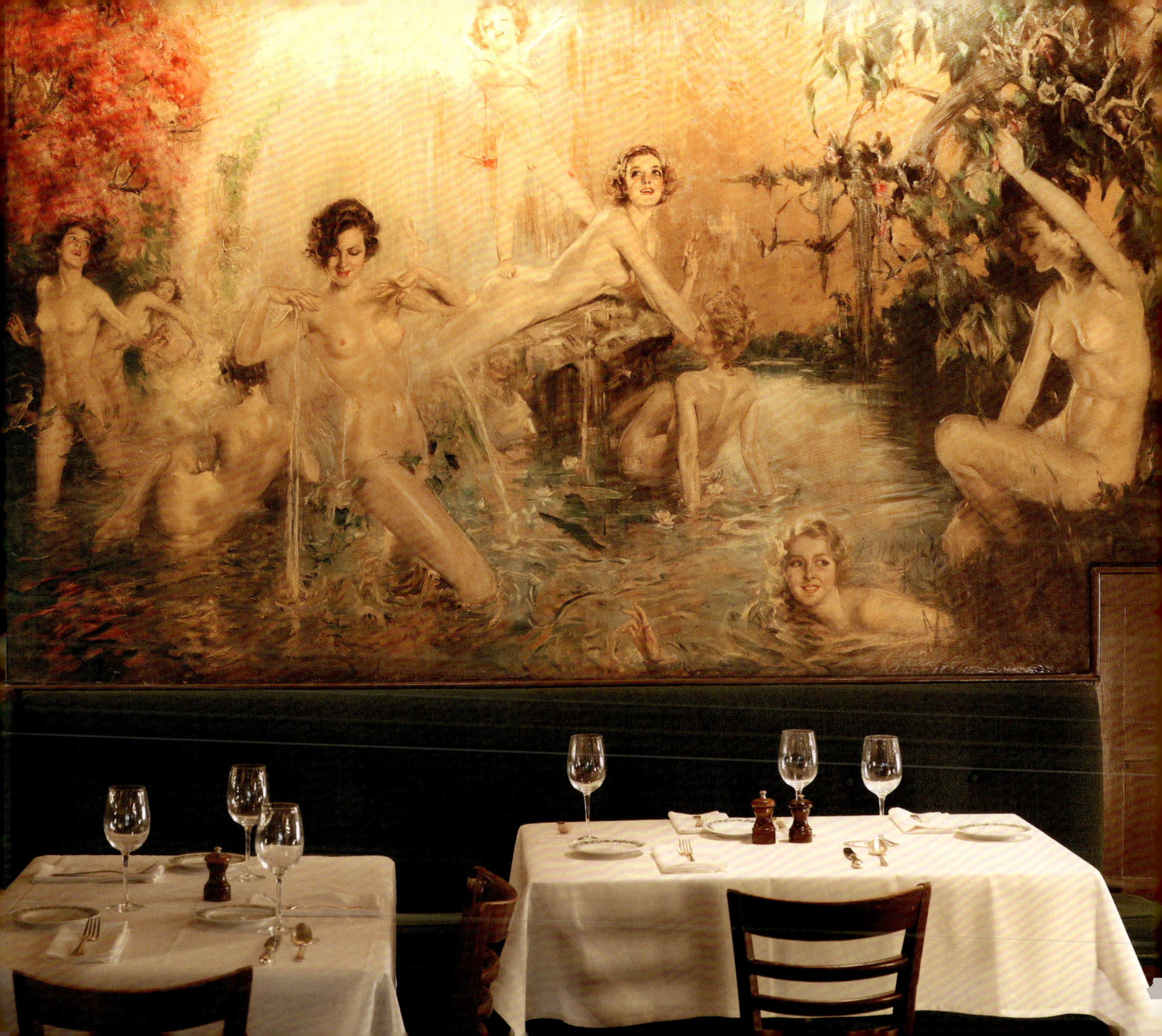

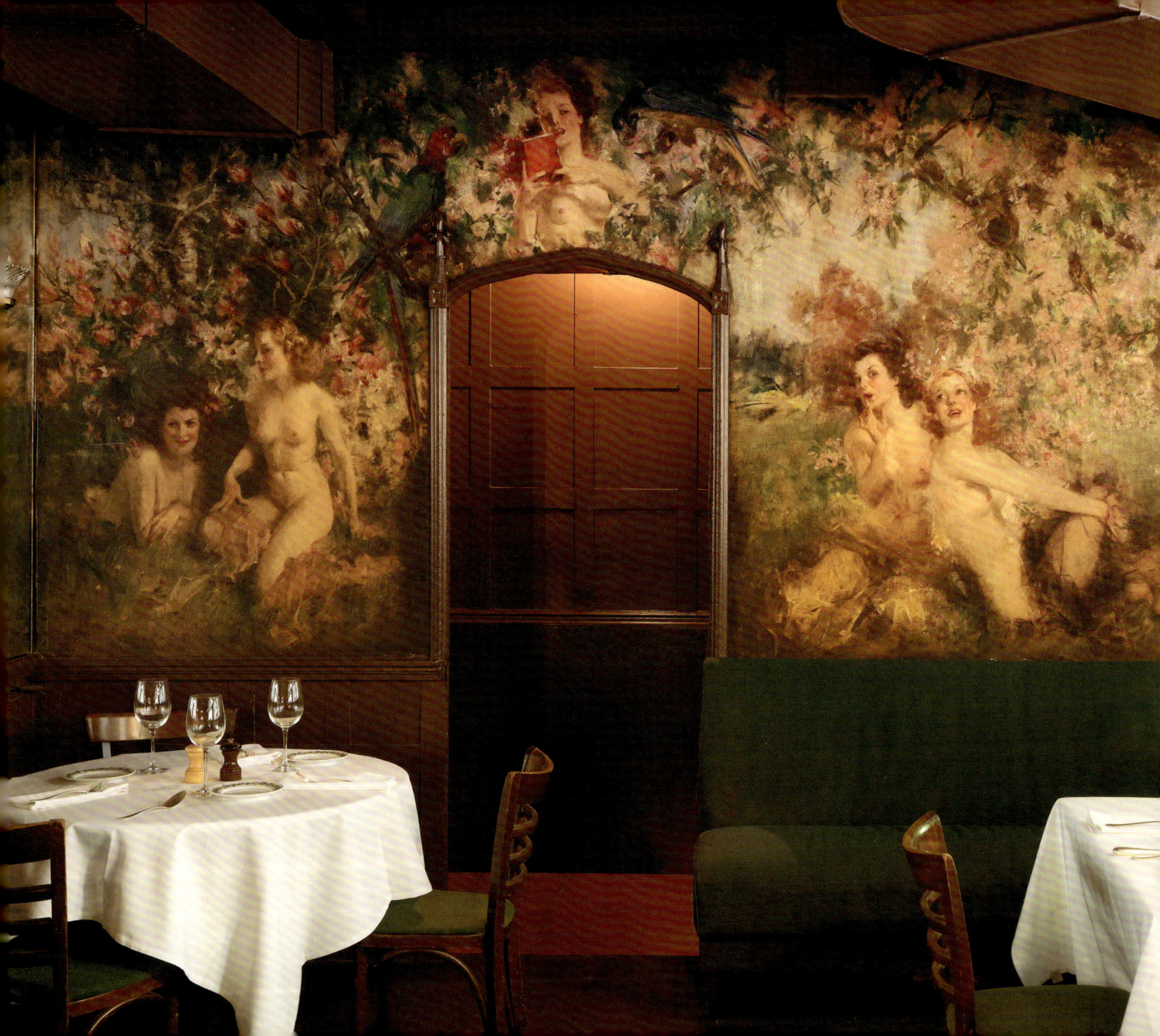

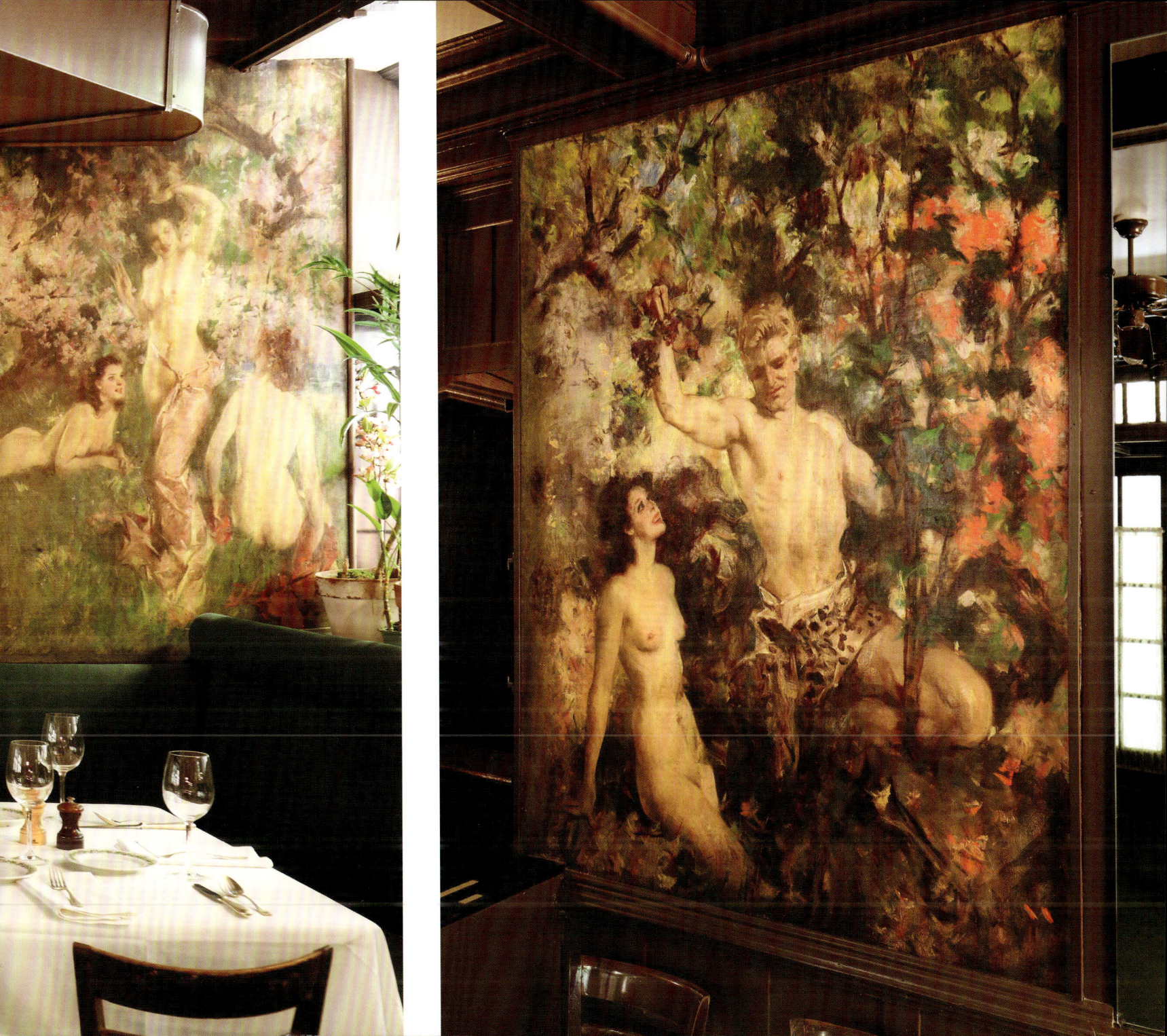

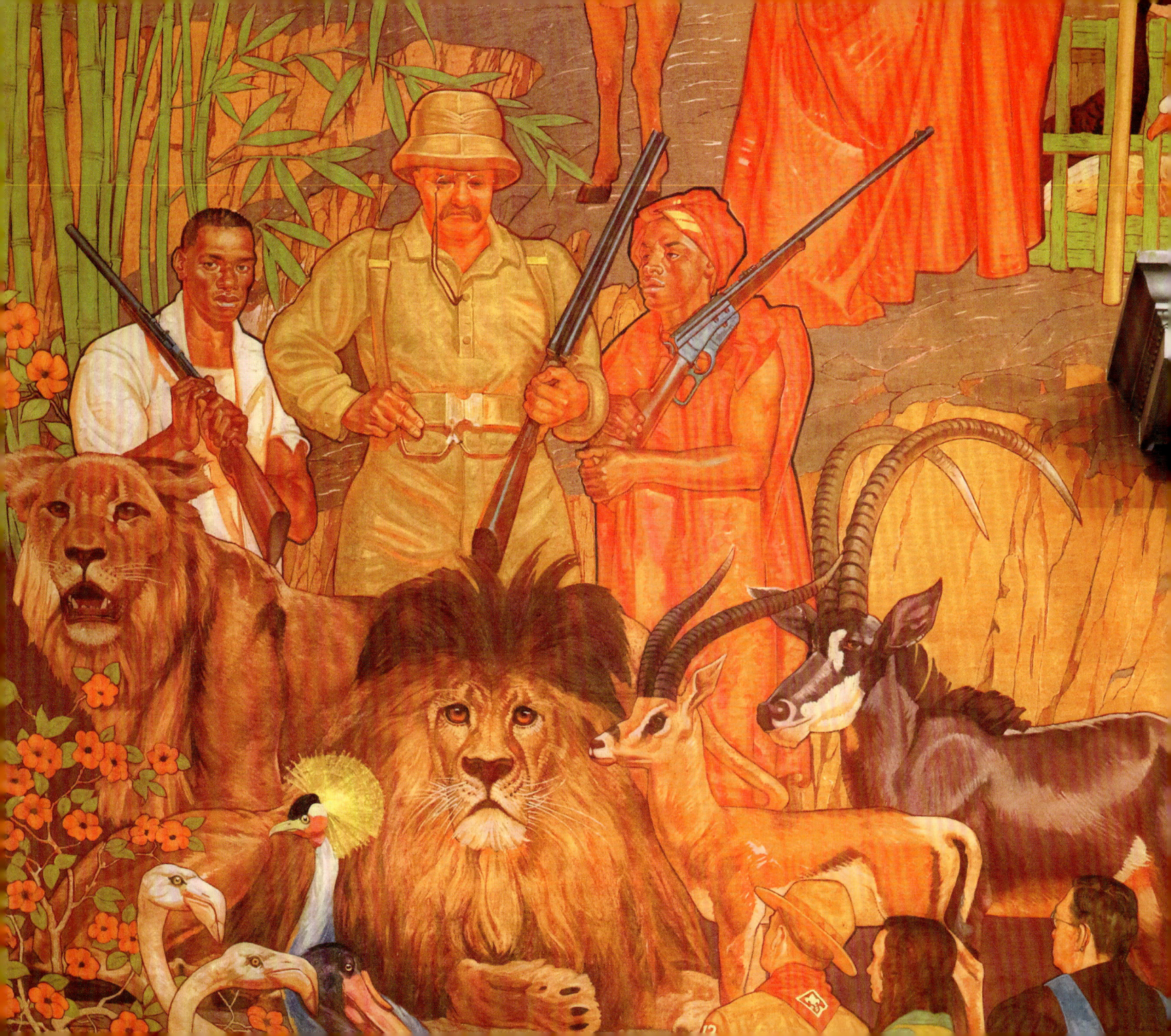

AMERICAN MUSEUM OF NATURAL HISTORY

200 Central Park West, Manhattan • WILLIAM ANDREW MACKAY

In March of 1933, just fourteen years after the death of Teddy Roosevelt, the American Museum of Natural History asked for submissions from artists interested in painting a suite of murals to memorialize his life. The jury received twenty-five anonymous sketches and unanimously chose the one belonging to William Andrew Mackay.

Mackay was born in Philadelphia in 1878 and studied art at City College in New York, the American Academy in Rome, and the Académie Julian in Paris. After his formal education, he assisted muralists Robert Lewis Reid, Francis "Frank" Davis Millet, and Elmer E. Garnsey.

During the World War I, Mackay applied his highly evolved color theories to the esoteric field of warship camouflage, proving that ships painted like pointillist paintings with red, green, and violet splotches would appear to "melt into sea and sky." The application of his ideas as chief camoufleur for the Second District of New York, Newport, and Cape May proved highly effective for merchant ships, but the U.S. Navy preferred to stick with a more manly battleship gray—examples of which can still be found on the bottoms of the world's oceans.

Mackay was tasked to pay homage to the extraordinary life of the late president, a man whose impact and legend were so large that his face had been carved on Mount Rushmore. His innumerable accomplishments as police commissioner, president, steward of the land, Rough Rider, and diplomat, notwithstanding, it probably didn't hurt that the museum's 1869 charter had been signed in his father's living room and his cousin currently resided in the White House.

Mackay used two hundred reference books in preparation for his initial designs and executed them with the help of three young assistants, Joseph Nussdorf, Clifford Young, and John Sitton, in a vast studio at the Metropolitan Opera House. There, often on a platform suspended in an eighty-foot well, amid the backdrops for *Lohengrin* and *Faust*, Mackay and his assistants painted an orange-red-ochre picture-book fantasy of Roosevelt's life replete with images of African animals, Genghis Khan, Buddha, a Captain Hook–like pirate, Japanese warriors, resplendent African tribesmen, and, of course, Roosevelt himself, again and again. Mackay was a stickler for accuracy and had experts advising him on everything from Mayan and Aztec civilizations to the building of the Panama Canal to the ceremonial gown of the first emperor of Japan. The murals were finished in April 1935.

Each of the three murals occupies an alcove 34 feet high and 62 feet wide, including the adjacent panels. Mackay was paid $60,000, which, in today's dollars, would be somewhere in the upscale neighborhood of $1 million. The 2010–2012 restoration of the murals ran $2.5 million.

In the west wall's bay, surrounding the entrance to the Akeley Hall of African Mammals, the painting illustrates Roosevelt's African expeditions in 1909 and 1910. The brilliantly colored confection depicts the Maasai and Kikuyu tribesmen of Africa and an intricate interweaving of flora and fauna—all the creatures you would hope to see on such an adventure: flamingos, zebras, an elephant, a leopard, a Nubian lion, an elephant (being captured by native hunters with shields and spears), giraffes, and Roosevelt depicted as the Great White Hunter. He and his group killed more than eleven thousand animals. Those that were not eaten were brought back to the United States to become part of exhibits both at the American Museum of Natural History and the Smithsonian Institution, the primary funder of the expeditions. In the mural, Roosevelt's son Kermit, dressed as a scout and standing beside a native wearing a lion skin and supporting the seal of the Smithsonian Institution.

To the left of the dueling barosaurus and allosaurus, partially hidden by massive pillars, is a mural on the south wall's bay celebrating the 1905 Treaty of Portsmouth, an event negotiated by Roosevelt that ended the Russo-Japanese War

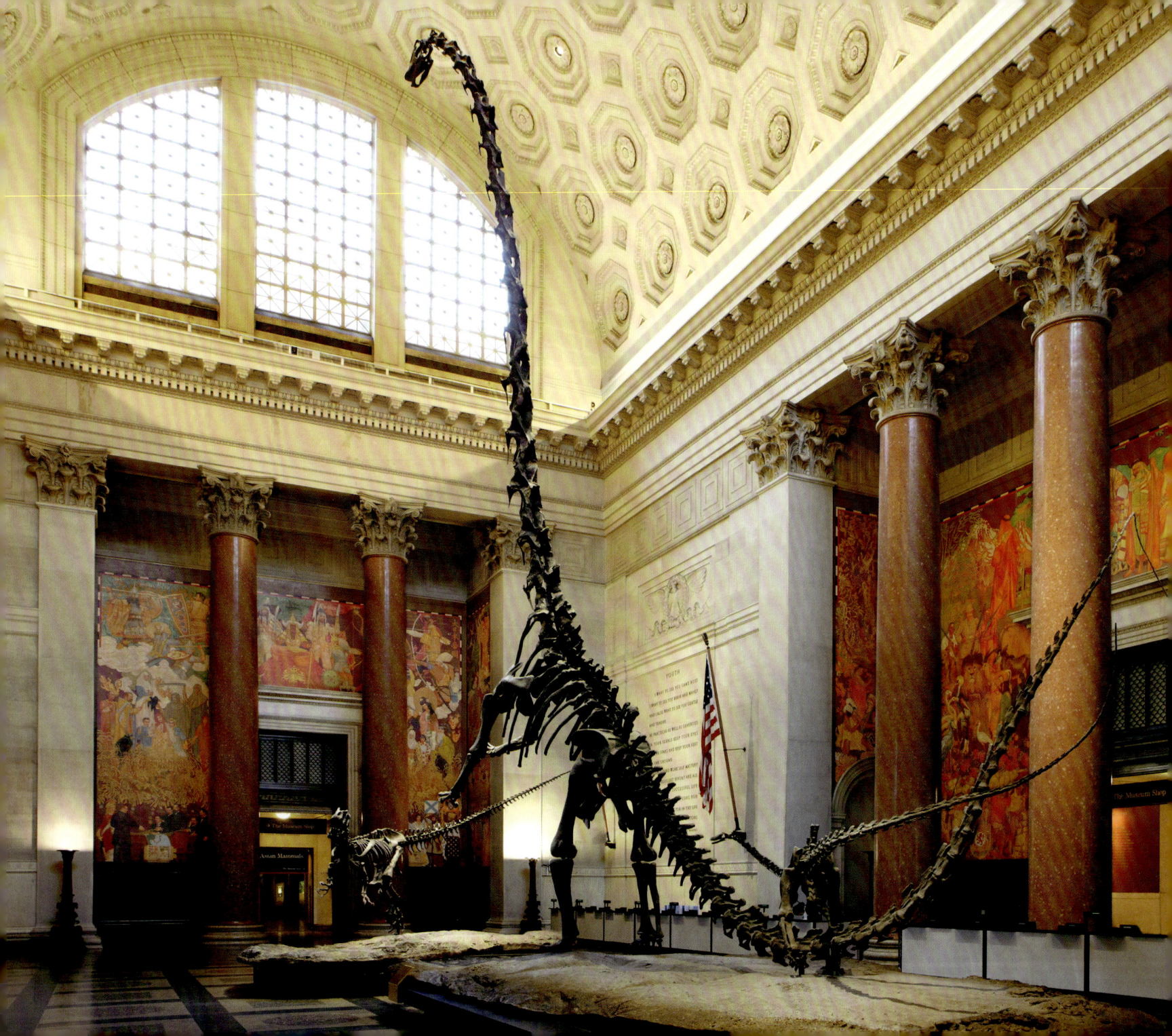

and won him the Nobel Peace Prize. The rich, symbolic imagery in the mural includes the histories and legends of Russia and Japan and an intricate interplay of folklore and historical figures.

The north bay's mural portrays the building of the Panama Canal. Against a backdrop of massive earthmoving equipment, Roosevelt confers with Chief Engineer John F. Stevens. An officer of the medical corps, holding a test tube, represents army doctors, including Major Walter Reed, whose theory about the mosquito's role in the spread of yellow fever allowed them to eradicate the disease in the Canal Zone within months. Also included is the Great Seal of the United States with the inscription, "Work on Panama Canal started May 4th, 1904, by President Theodore Roosevelt. The land divided, the world united. Completed 1914." On the far right is a scene from Roosevelt's last journey, an extremely arduous, nine-hundred-mile expedition in 1914 to map Brazil's River of Doubt. After nearly perishing from an infected leg injury and tropical fever, which afflicted him the rest of his life, he wrote to a friend, "The Brazilian wilderness stole away ten years of my life." In honor of his efforts, the River of Doubt was renamed Rio Roosevelt or Rio Téodoro.

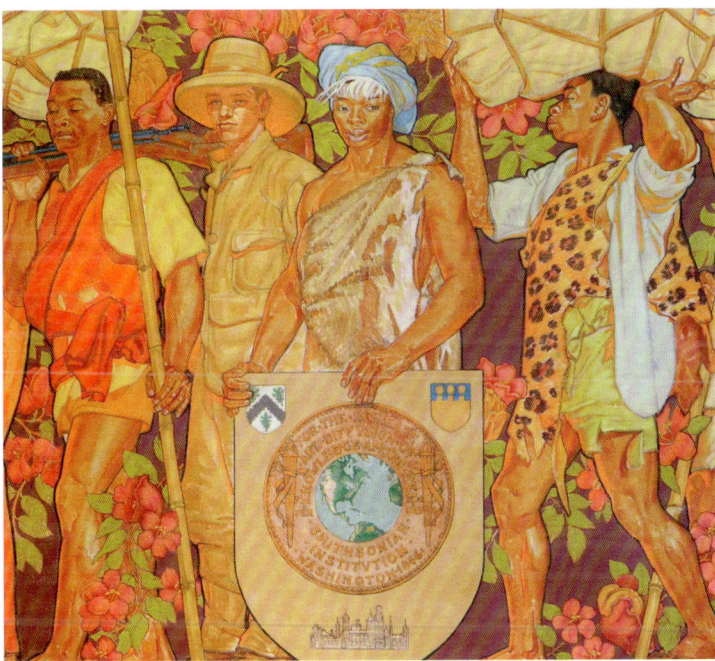

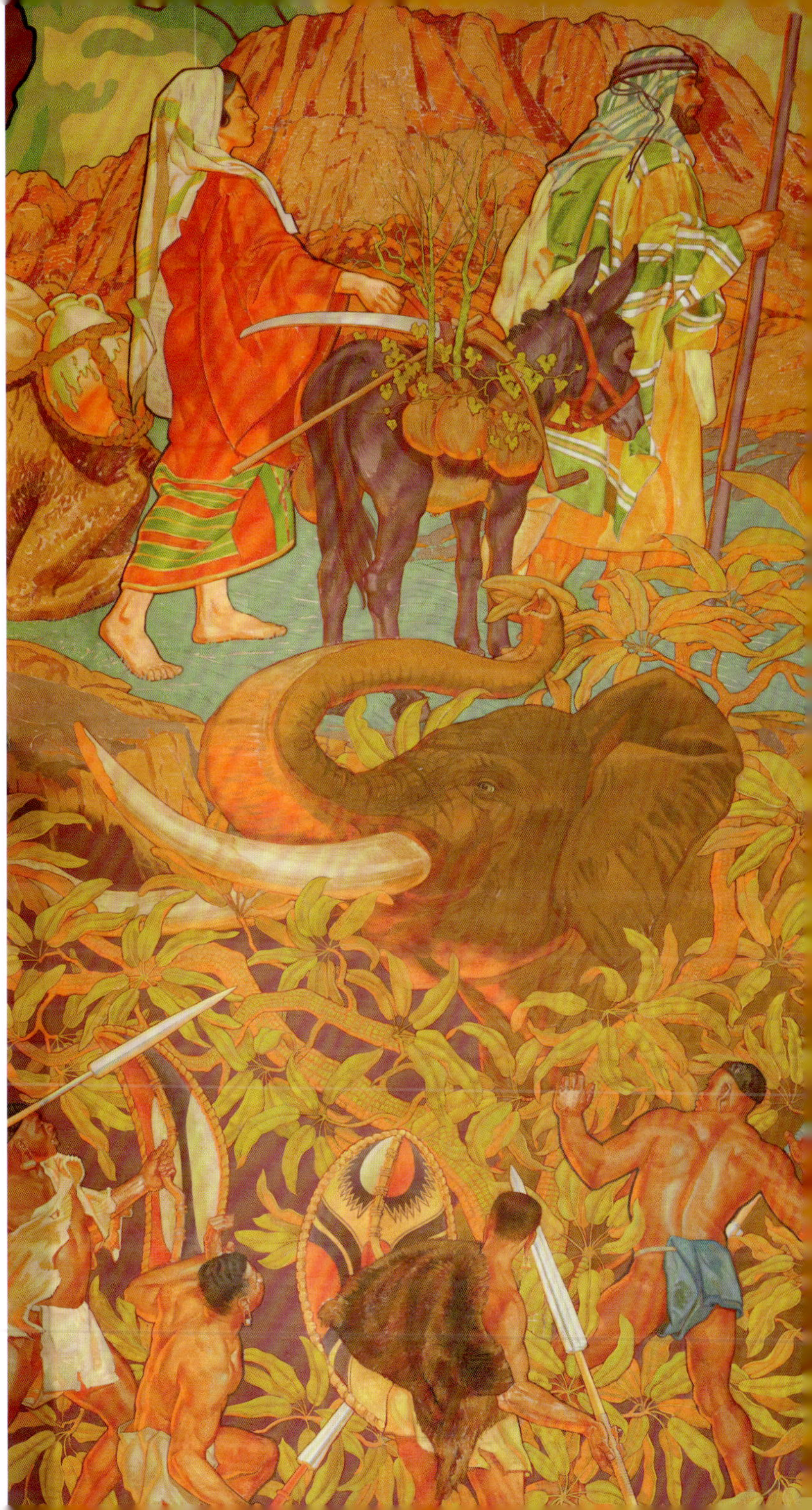

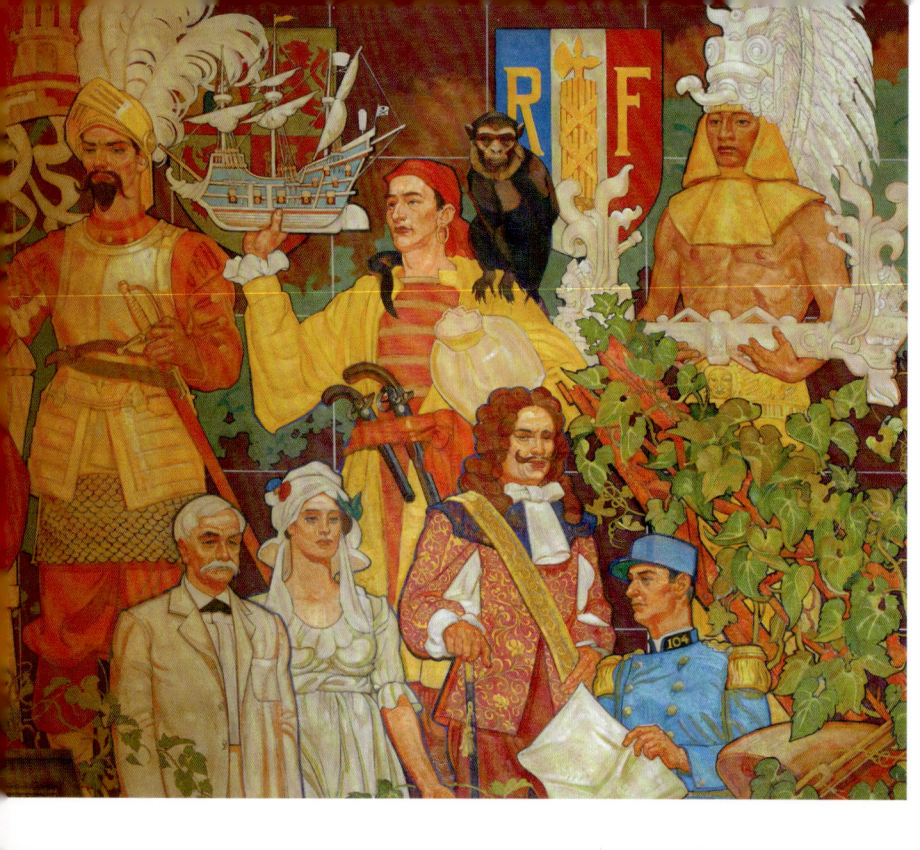

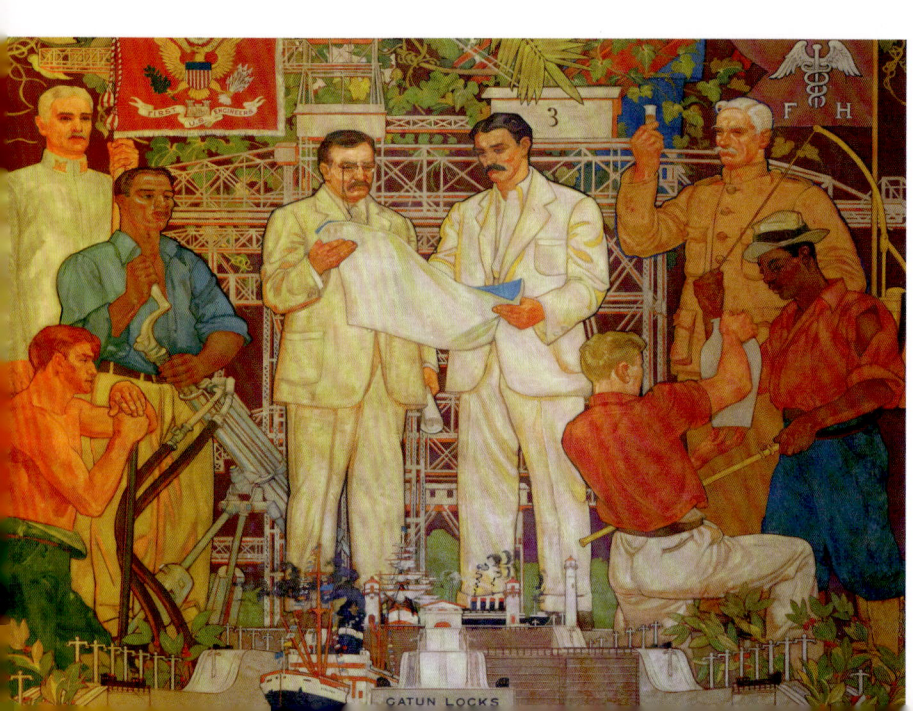

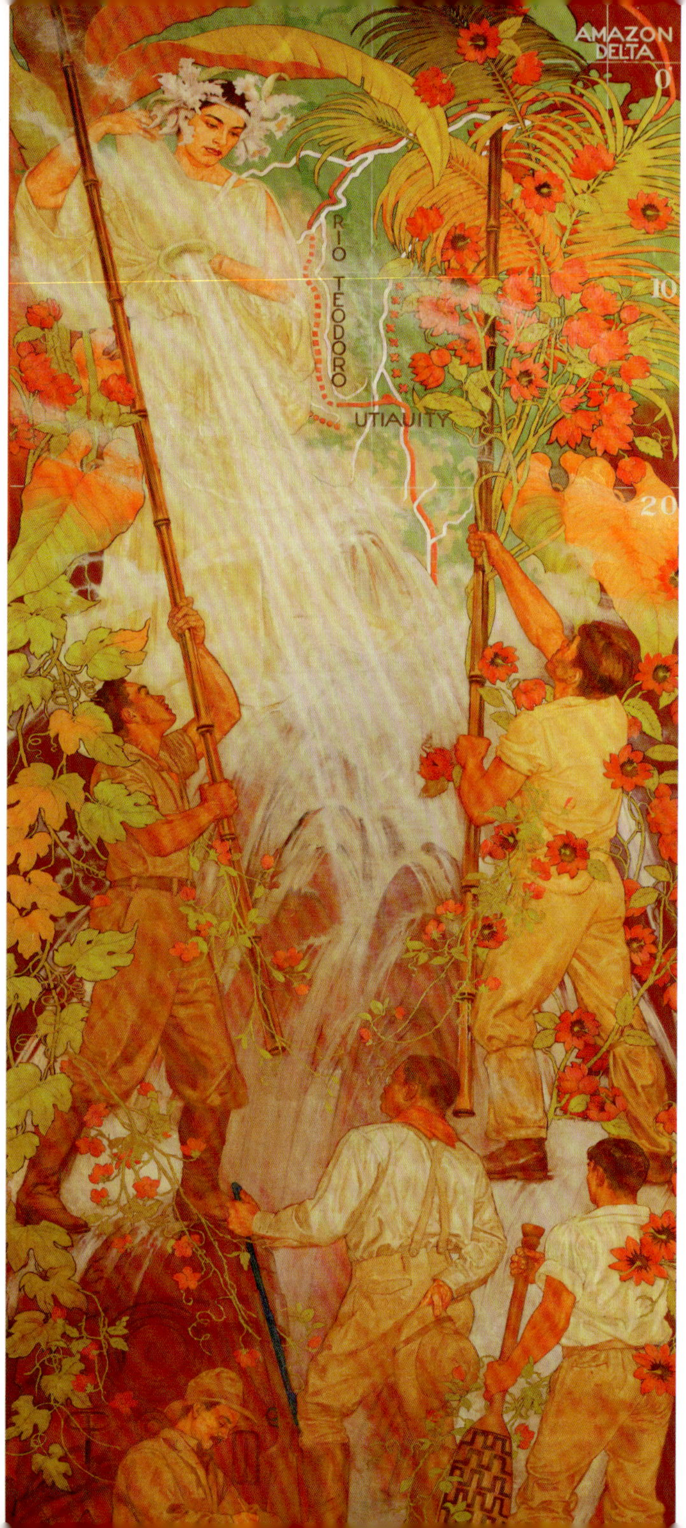

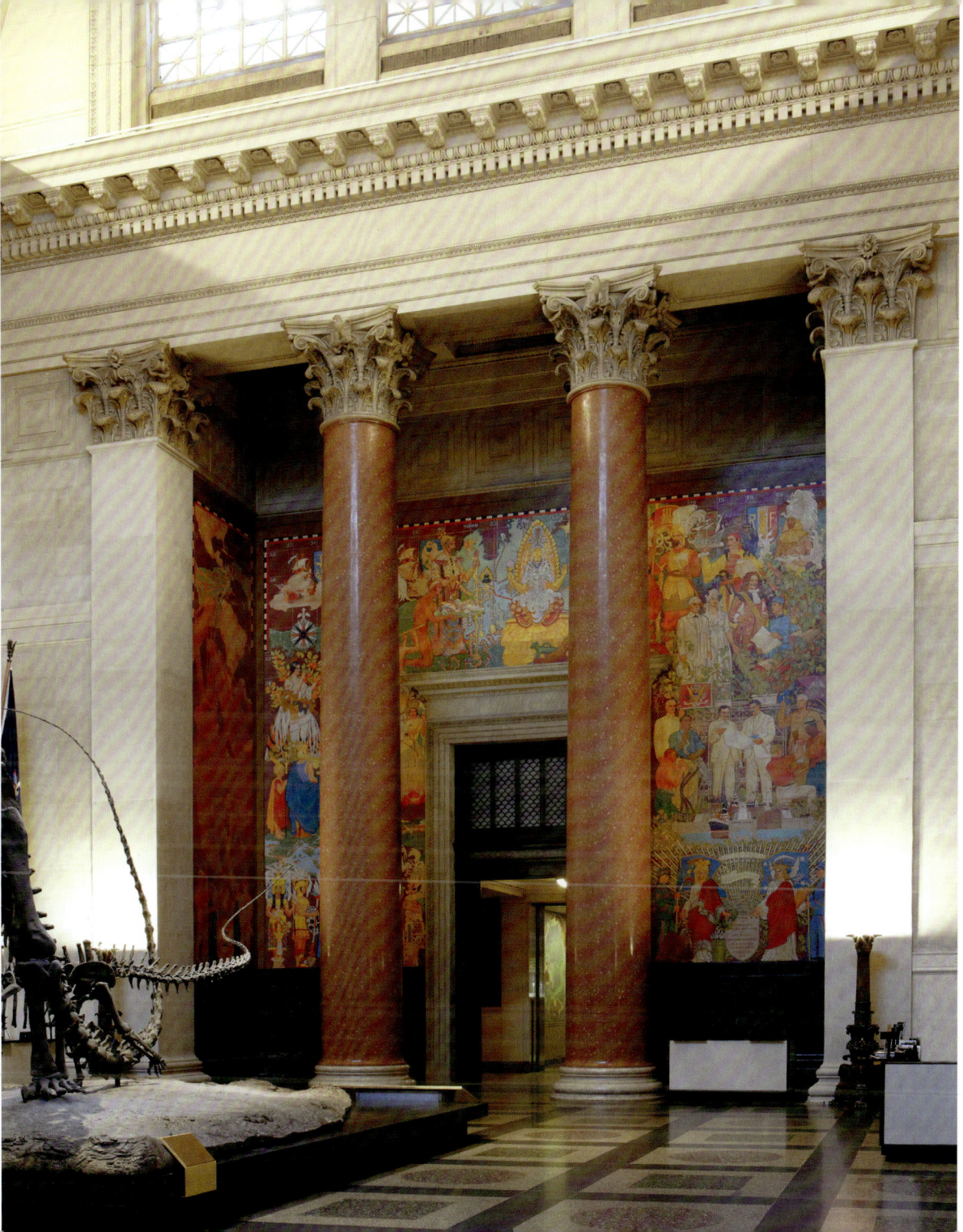

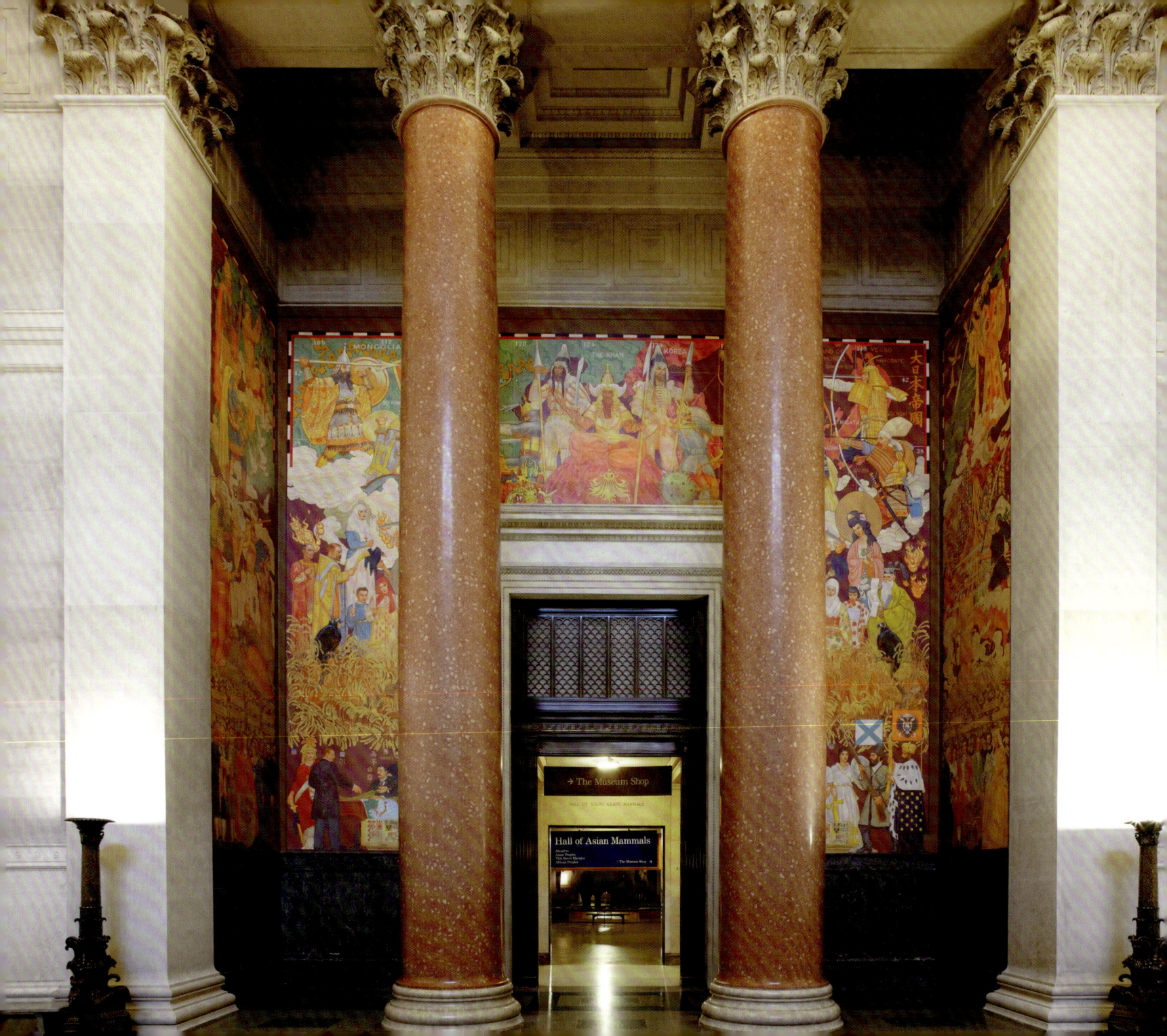

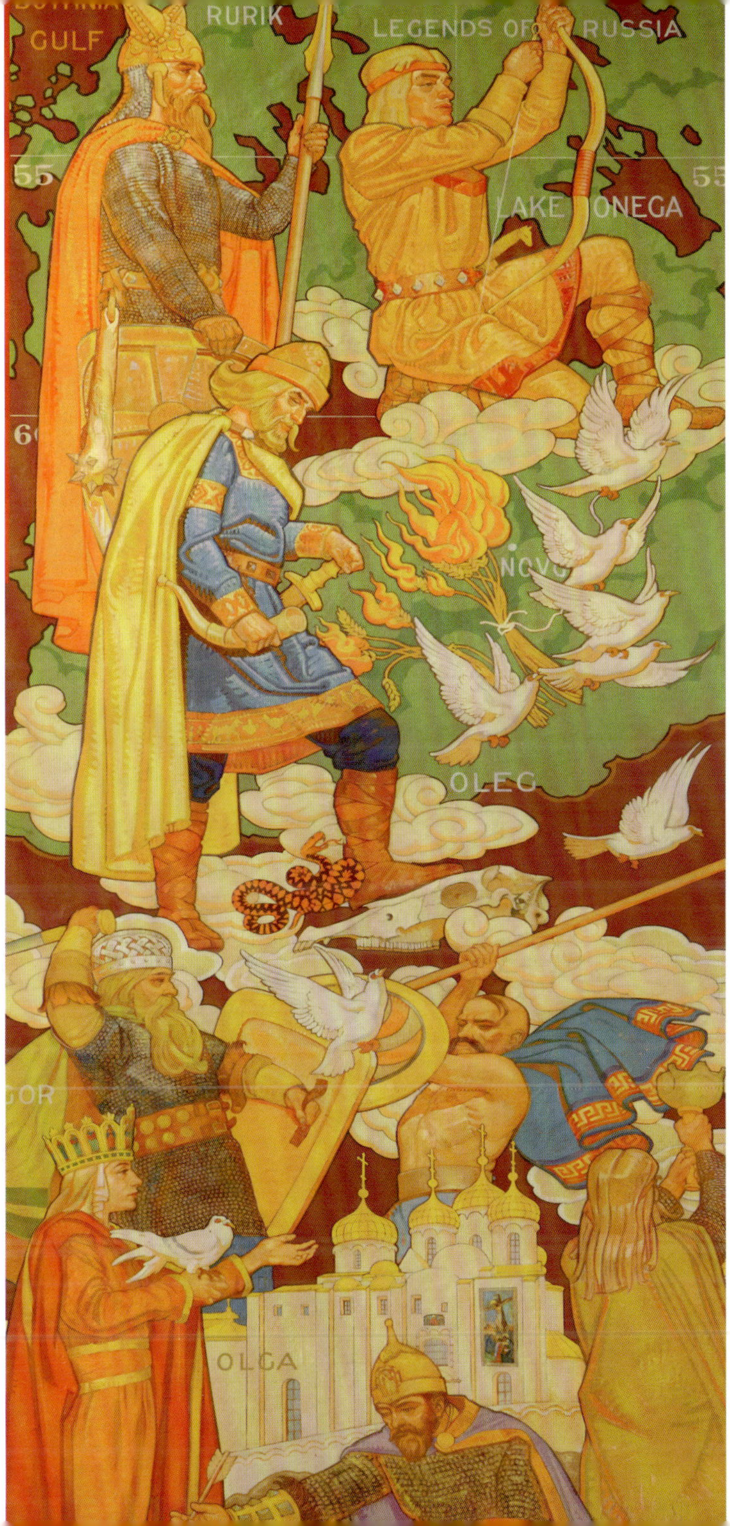

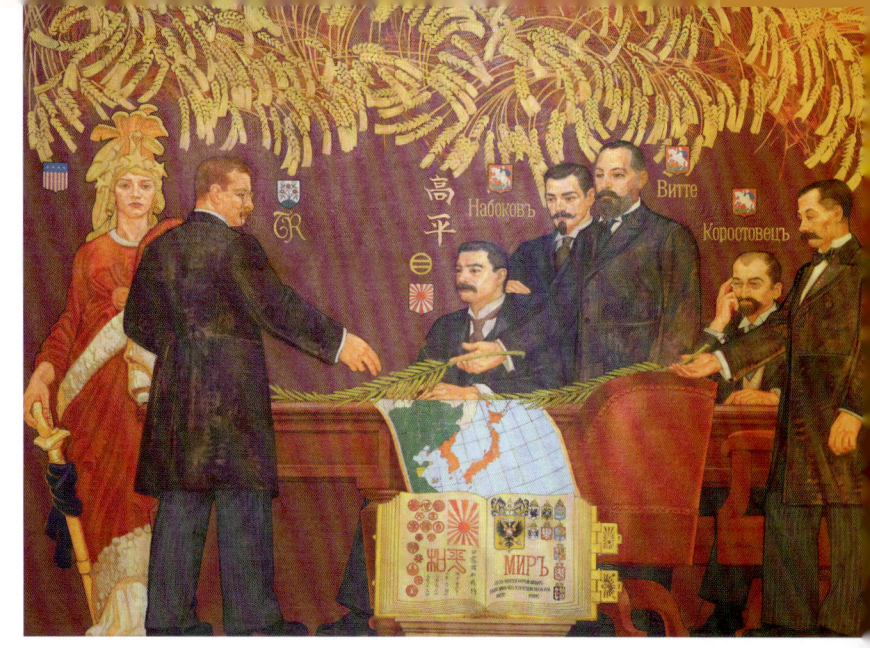
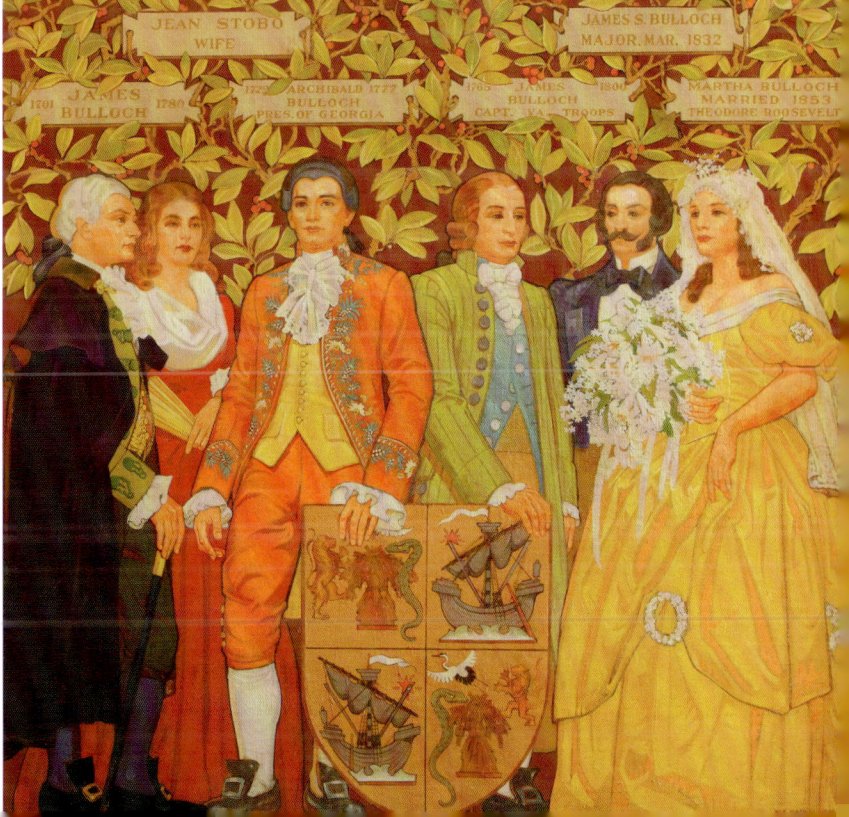

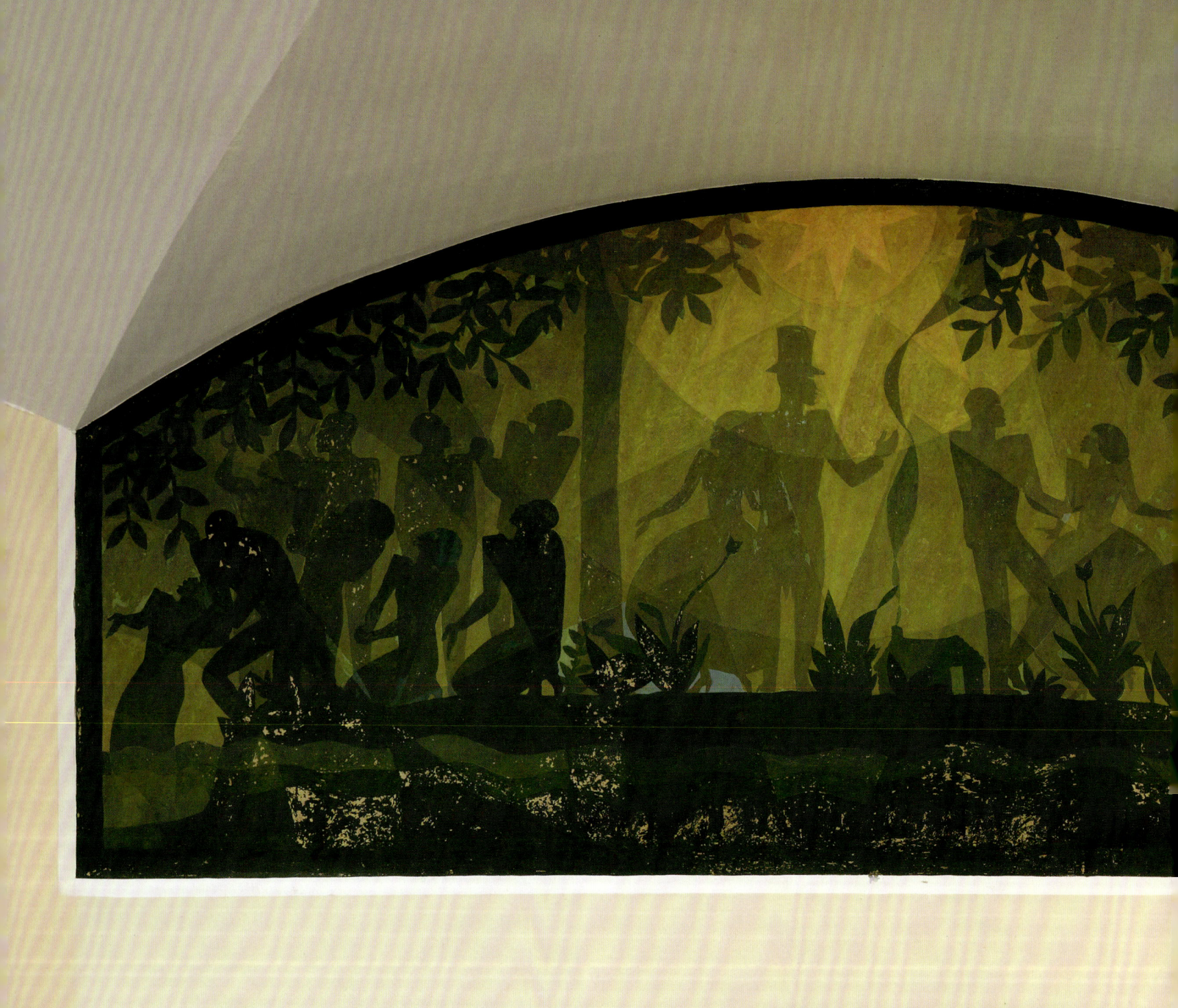

HARLEM YMCA

180 West 135th Street, Manhattan

AARON DOUGLAS

In the mid-1920s, Aaron Douglas from Topeka, Kansas, became the foremost visual artist and force behind the cultural flourishing known as the Harlem Renaissance. Through his paintings, murals, and book illustrations, he created the most commanding visual legacy of that movement, prompting philosopher and writer Alain Locke to call him the "father of Black American art."

Douglas studied under Winold Reiss, who helped him develop his American Modernist style, a fusion of jazz, African imagery, and social themes, all inspired with a Deco sensibility. Douglas, who collaborated with Langston Hughes, Claude McKay, and Wallace Thurman, is widely regarded as having fundamentally changed the way the world regarded African American art and artists.

Until he formed the Harlem Artist Guild, very little Works Progress Administration (WPA) money was available to African Americans. As its first president, he aggressively—and successfully—lobbied the WPA for capital to help African American artists gain employment and recognition. Another program, the Public Works of Art Project (PWAP), funded two of Douglas's best-known murals; *Aspects of Negro Life: From Slavery to Reconstruction*, four panels painted for the New York Public Library (now the Schomburg Center for Research in Black Culture) and the *Evolution of Negro Dance*, painted in 1935 for the Harlem YMCA.

Douglas's *Evolution of Negro Dance* is a lyrical ode to dance. Set into a vaulted arch, it is a brilliant ambiguity of jungle and nightclub. Geometric dancing figures emerge from the mist and from beneath leafy branches. The central character, in top hat and tails, is crisscrossed by theatrical rays of limelight. To one side, is a woman in a bell-shaped skirt; to the other, a man in a bowler hat playing a banjo. The dynamic composition vibrates with musical energy.

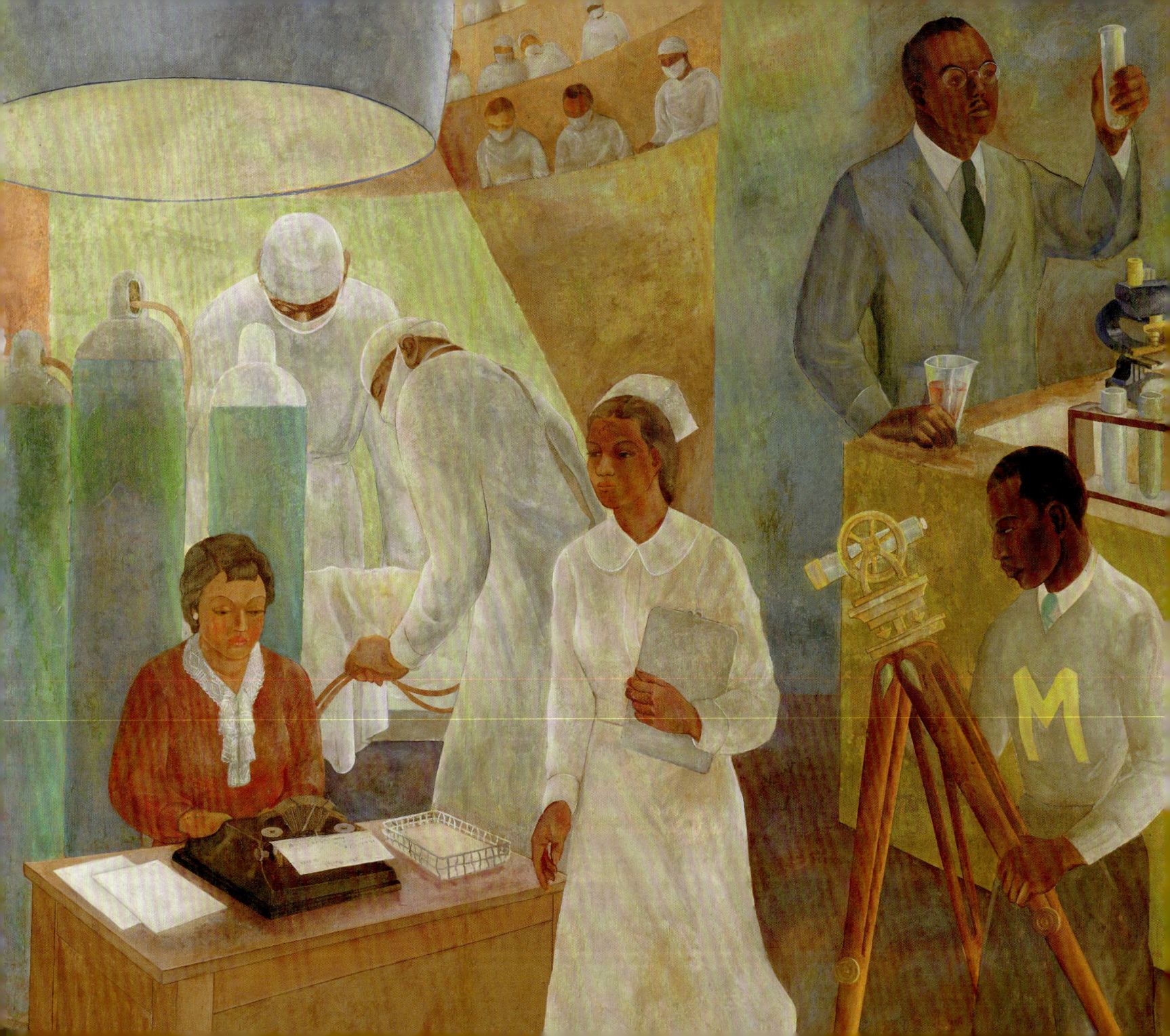

HARLEM HOSPITAL

506 Lenox Avenue, Manhattan

CHARLES ALSTON • ALFRED D. CRIMI • VERTIS HAYES • GEORGETTE SEABROOKE

When African American artist Charles Alston was denied work, he lobbied the WPA on the behalf of all African American artists. As a result, four painters were commissioned to create murals for the Harlem Hospital in 1935. Three of them, Charles Alston, Georgette Seabrooke, and Vertis Hayes, were African American; the fourth was a Sicilian immigrant, Alfred D. Crimi.

Though the official art jury of the Federal Art Project approved the proposed sketches, the hospital's white superintendent, Lawrence T. Dermody, only accepted Crimi's, saying the work of the three African Americans contained "too much Negro subject matter," as the Harlem Artists Guild summarized his rejection comments in a sharply worded–and highly publicized–statement. In an effort to fight for the right of Alston, Seabrooke, and Hayes to paint the murals, this guild statement and letters of protest were sent to everyone from Fiorello La Guardia to President Franklin Roosevelt. Ultimately, the three artists won the right to paint their murals.

Charles Alston was one of the most influential and popular artists of the Harlem Renaissance. His bronze bust of Martin Luther King, Jr., became the first representation of an African American in the White House and now rests in President Obama's Oval Office. For the hospital mural, Alston painted a diptych, *Magic in Medicine*, which deals with African folk medicine, and *Modern Medicine*, which was designed, as Alston said when asked about the painting in 1940, "to show the different races working together on the same basis with an absolute lack of discrimination." The scene depicts the fathers of modern medicine, including Louis Pasteur and Louis T. Wright, who championed the murals, in a modern operating room.

At seventeen, Georgette Seabrooke was the youngest artist, and only woman, chosen. Her *Recreation in Harlem* is a 108-square-foot oil-on-plaster snapshot. Two women chat through an open window, a mailman makes his rounds, a couple dances, a children's choir sings, and everyone enjoys a warm summer day. The administrators balked at Seabrooke's African American-centric composition, stalling not only the mural's completion, but her graduation from Cooper Union. Seabrooke broke the stalemate by adding eight white characters, but in her own way. Five of the eight face away from us, and the other three are racially ambiguous.

Vertis Hayes was only twenty-five when he was chosen to paint his *Pursuit of Happiness*, an eight-panel mural in the corridor of the New Nurses Residence. The work depicts African American history, from eighteenth-century Africa to slavery, freedom, and life in the rural American South and industrialized North.

In preparation for his *Modern Surgery and Anesthesia* mural, Alfred D. Crimi was granted research access at the Kings County Hospital. He was struck by, and endeavored to represent, the "constant interaction of eyes and hands" between the surgeons, as he described in his autobiography, *A Look Back–A Step Forward: My Life Story* (Center for Migration Stories of New York, 1988).

Harlem Hospital's 2005 expansion and restoration project restored all four murals. Three panels of *Pursuit of Happiness* were digitized and reprinted on 429 panes of glass, forming a massive replica of the painting on the 13,000-square-foot, five-story, city-block-long exterior wall facing Lenox Avenue. As a light box, Hayes's painting is visible in daylight and, illuminated by interior lights, glows luminously at night. This wonderful work is now visible to, and emblematic of, the city at large. Mural Pavilion is dedicated to the permanent display of these wonderful paintings and their place in the history of Harlem.

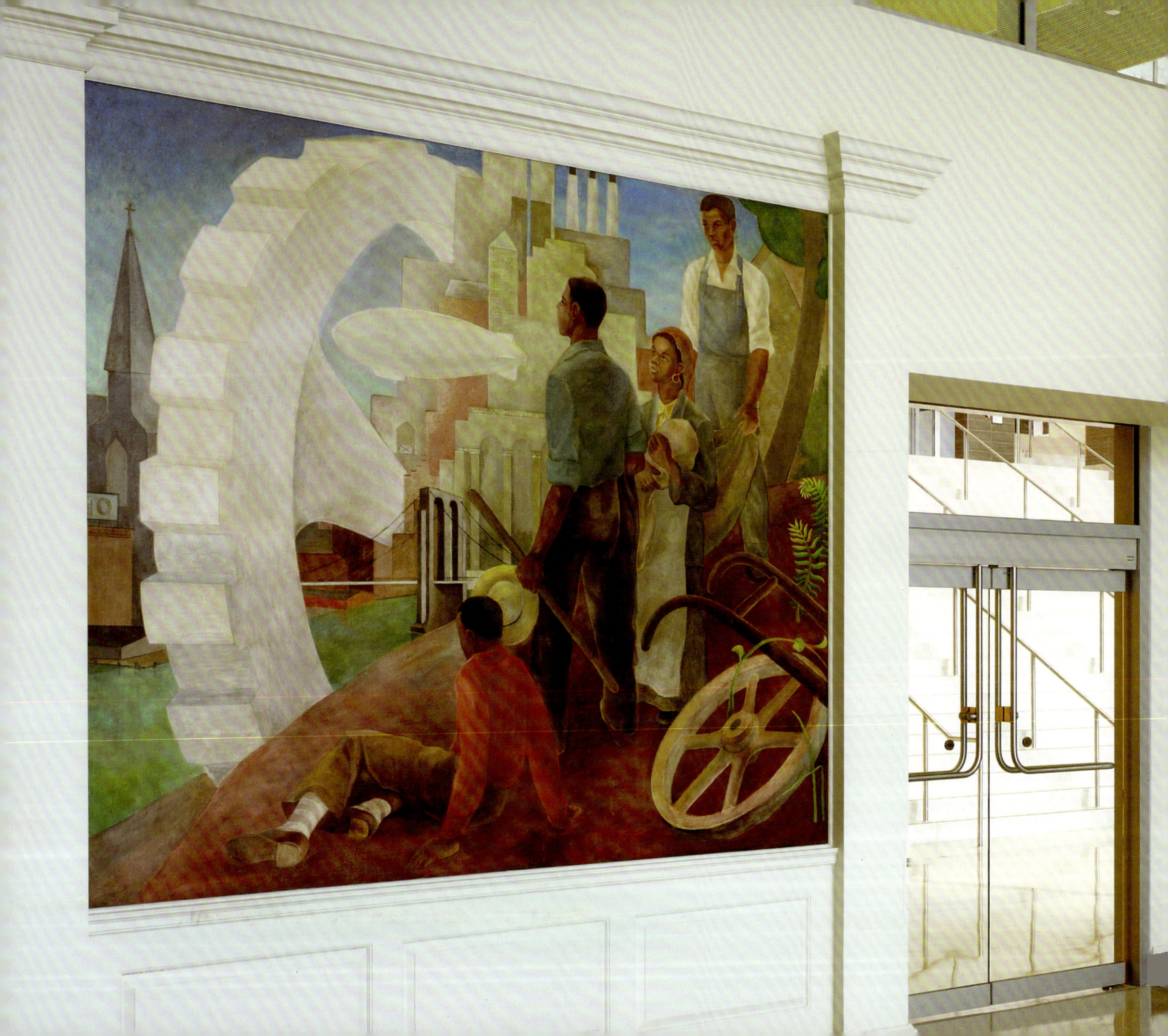

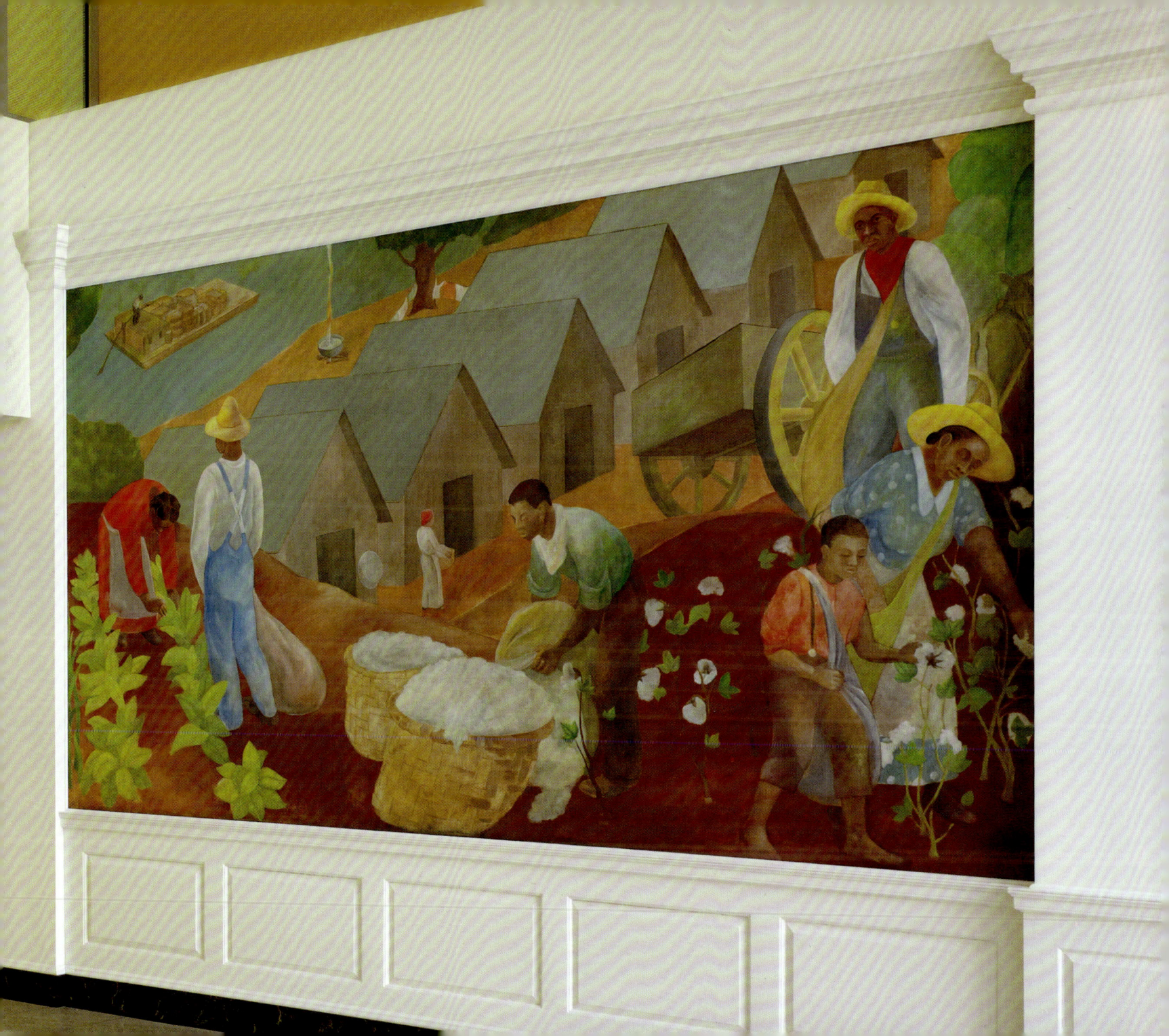

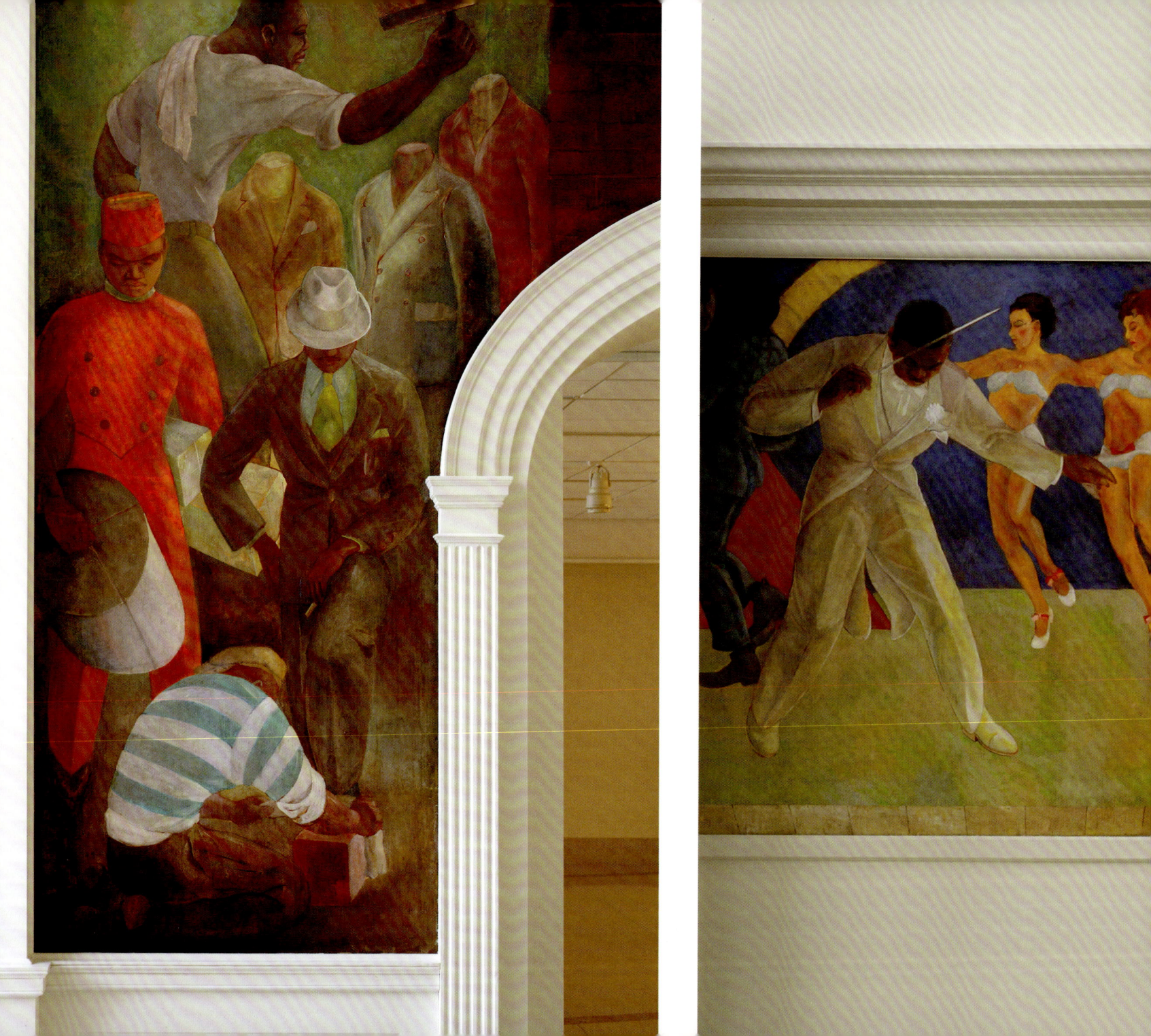

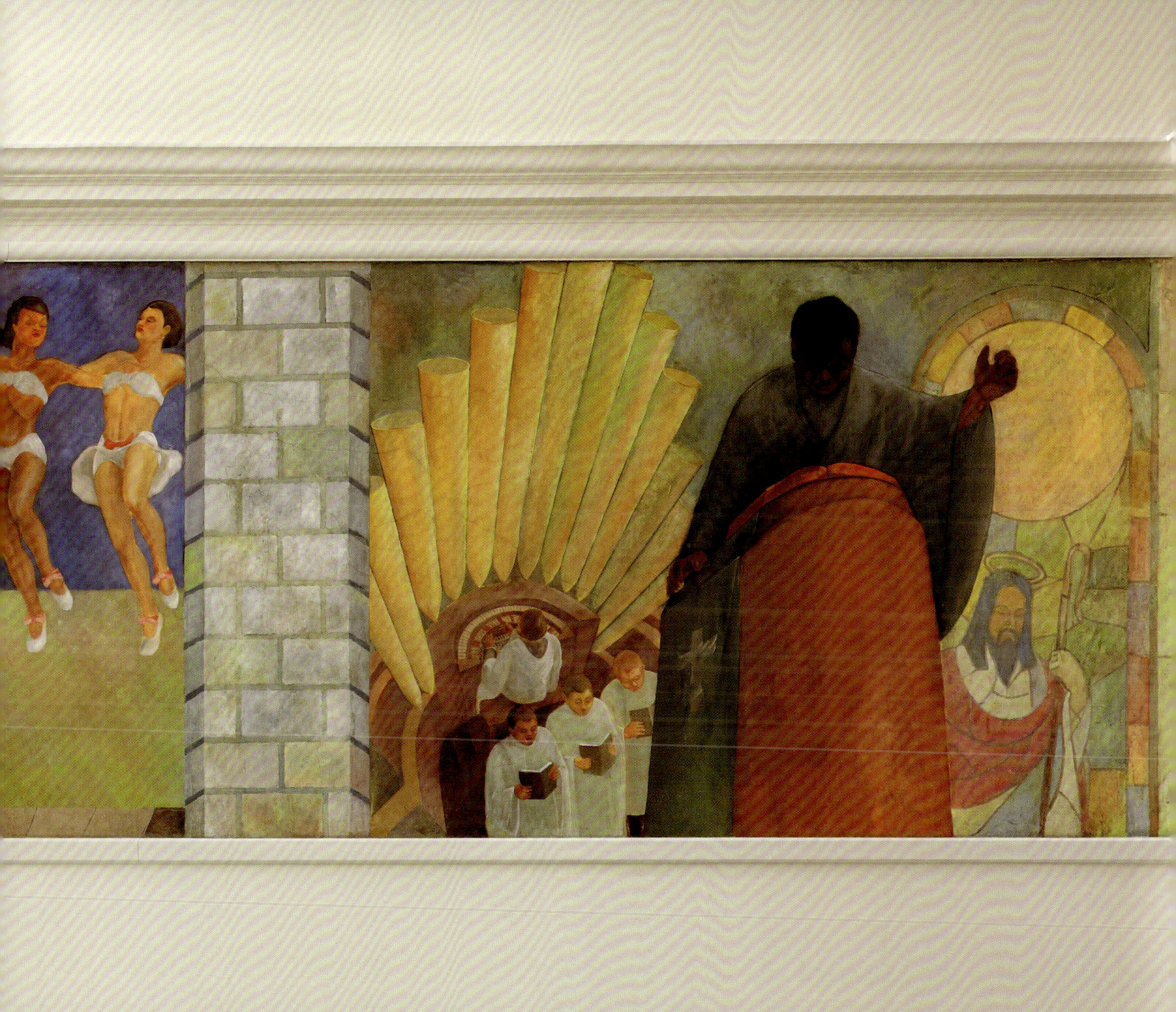

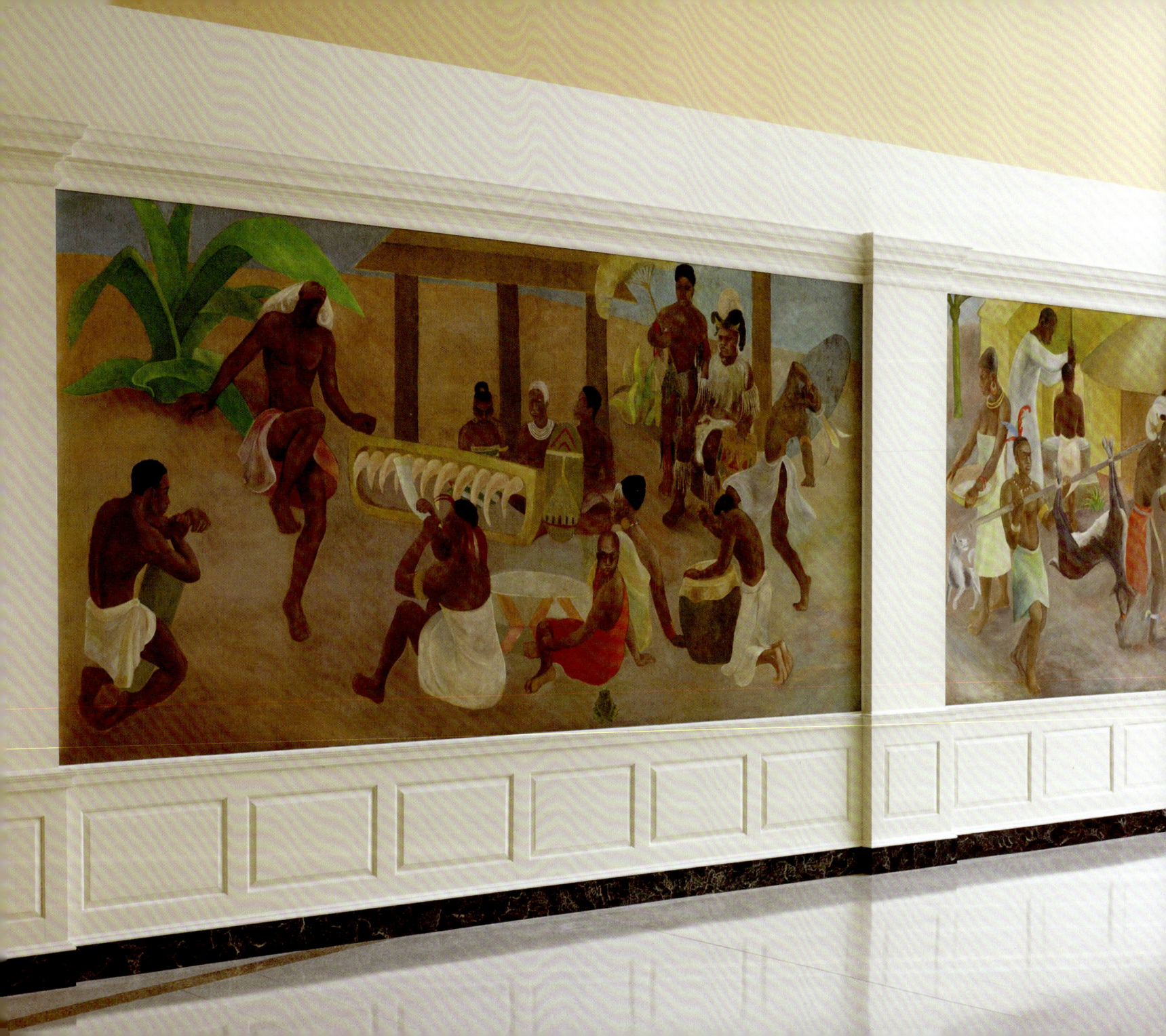

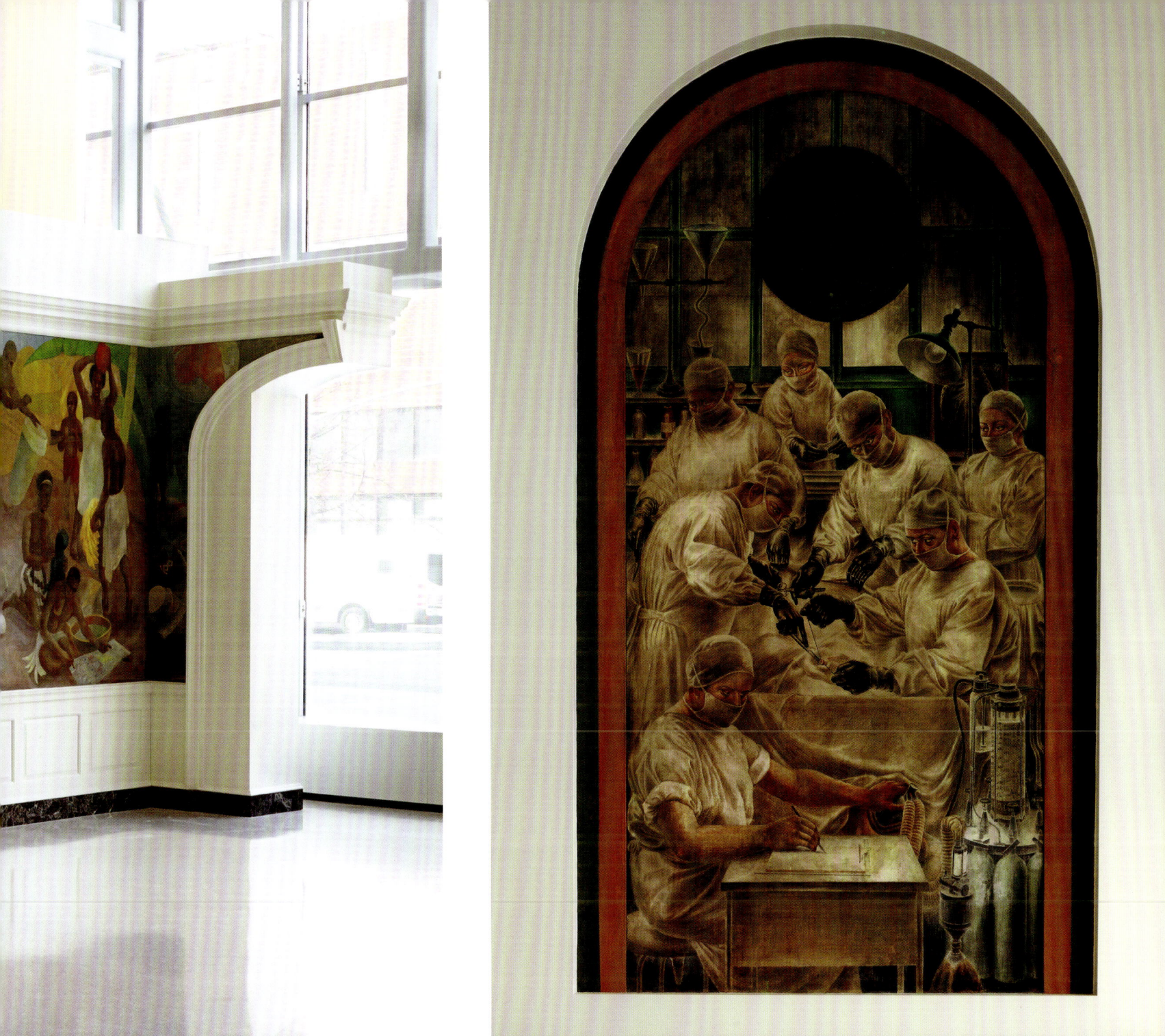

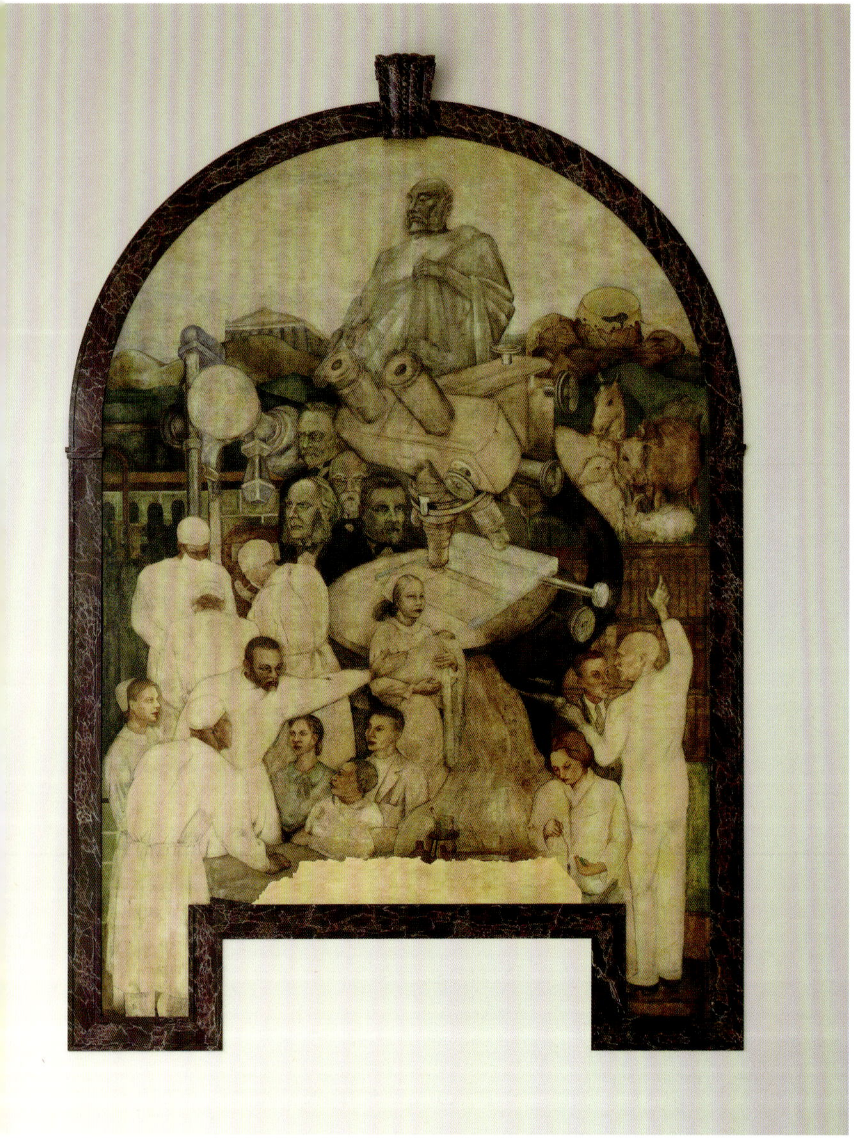

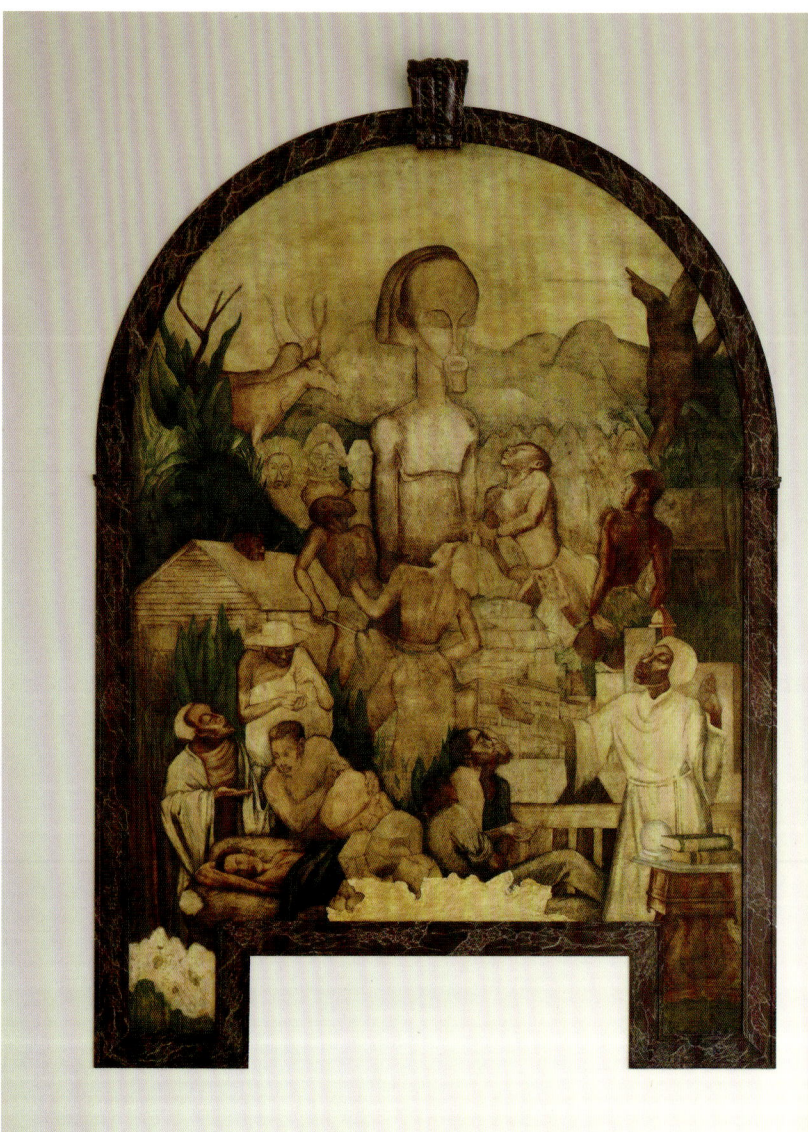

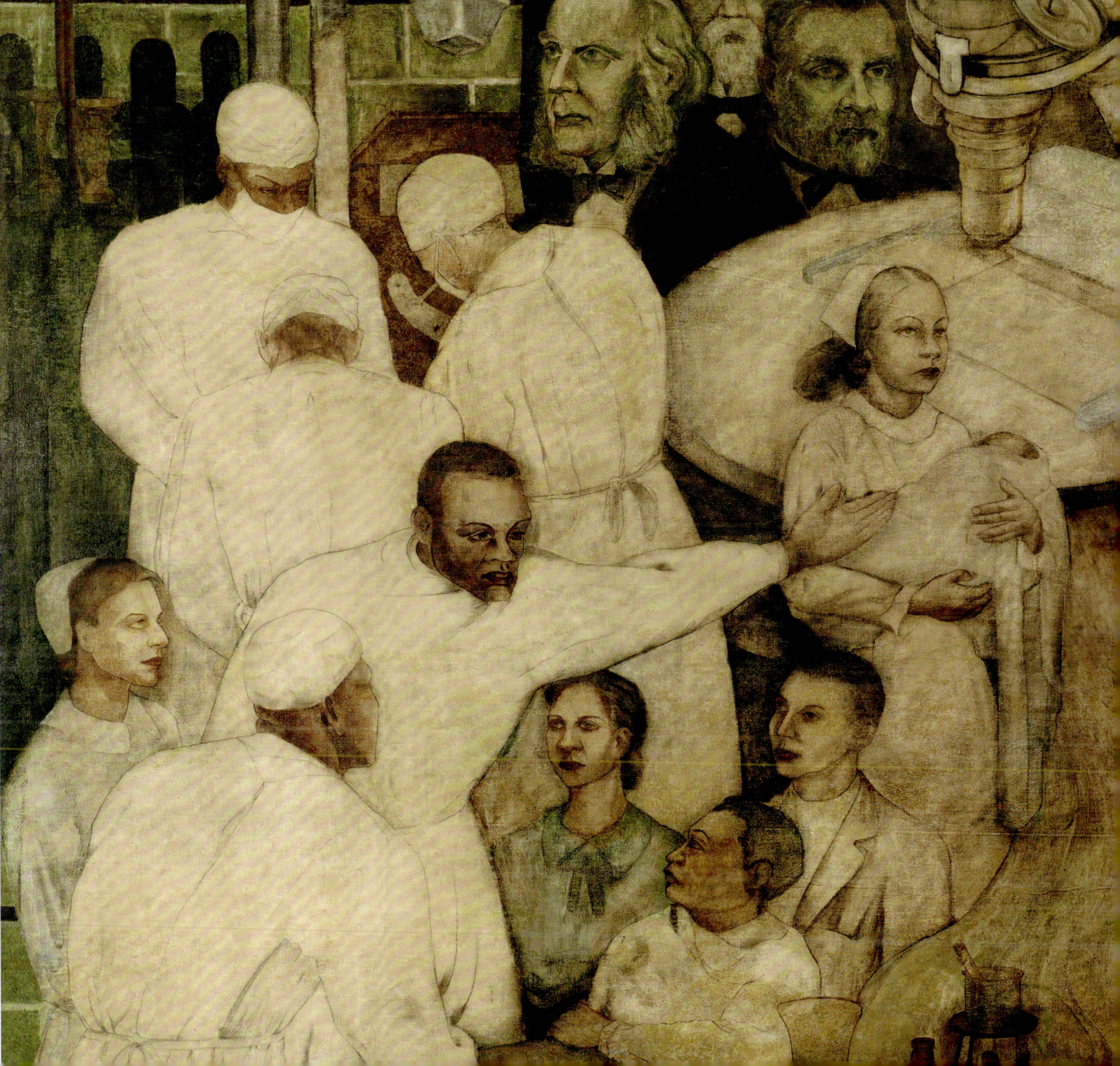

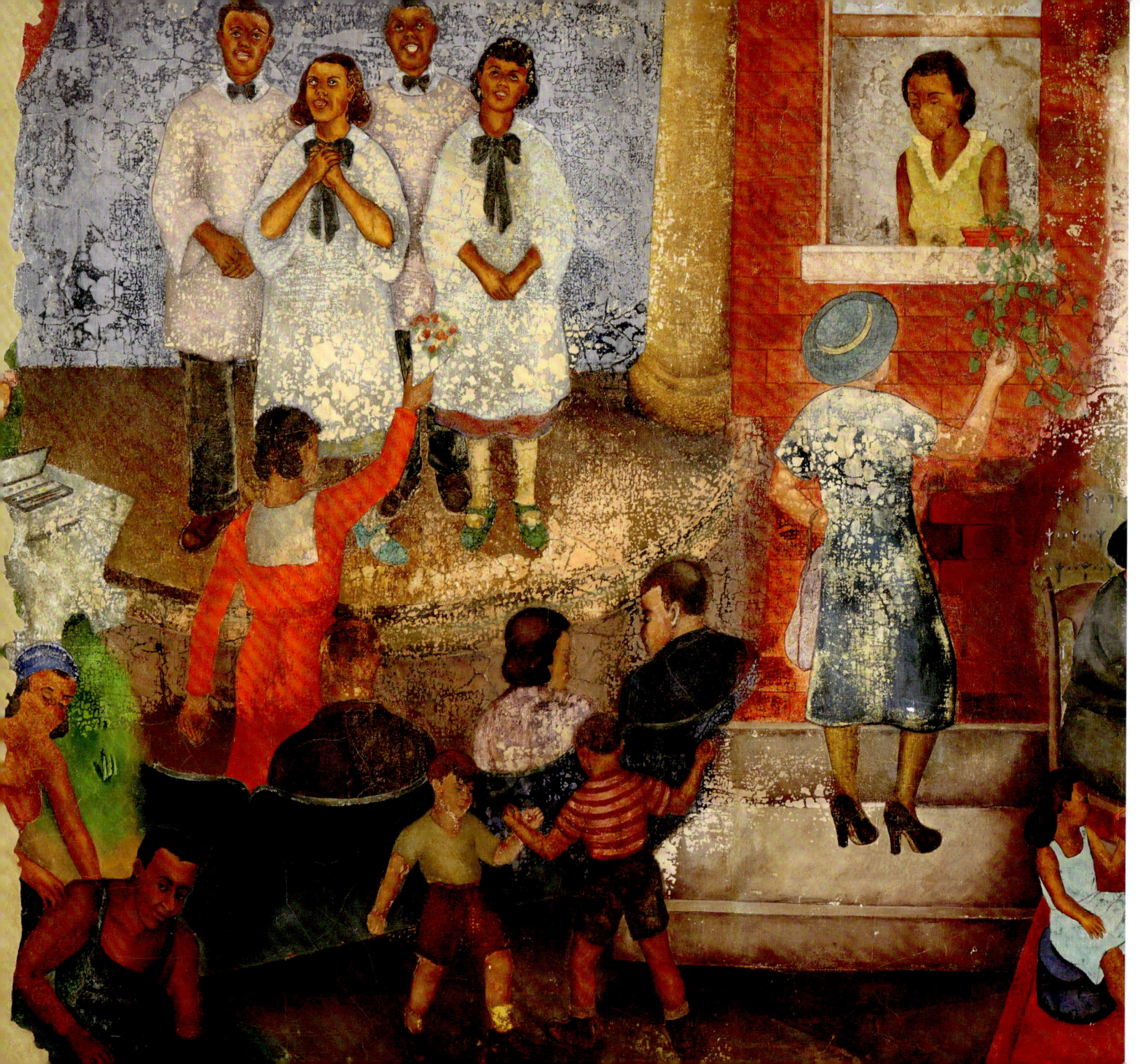

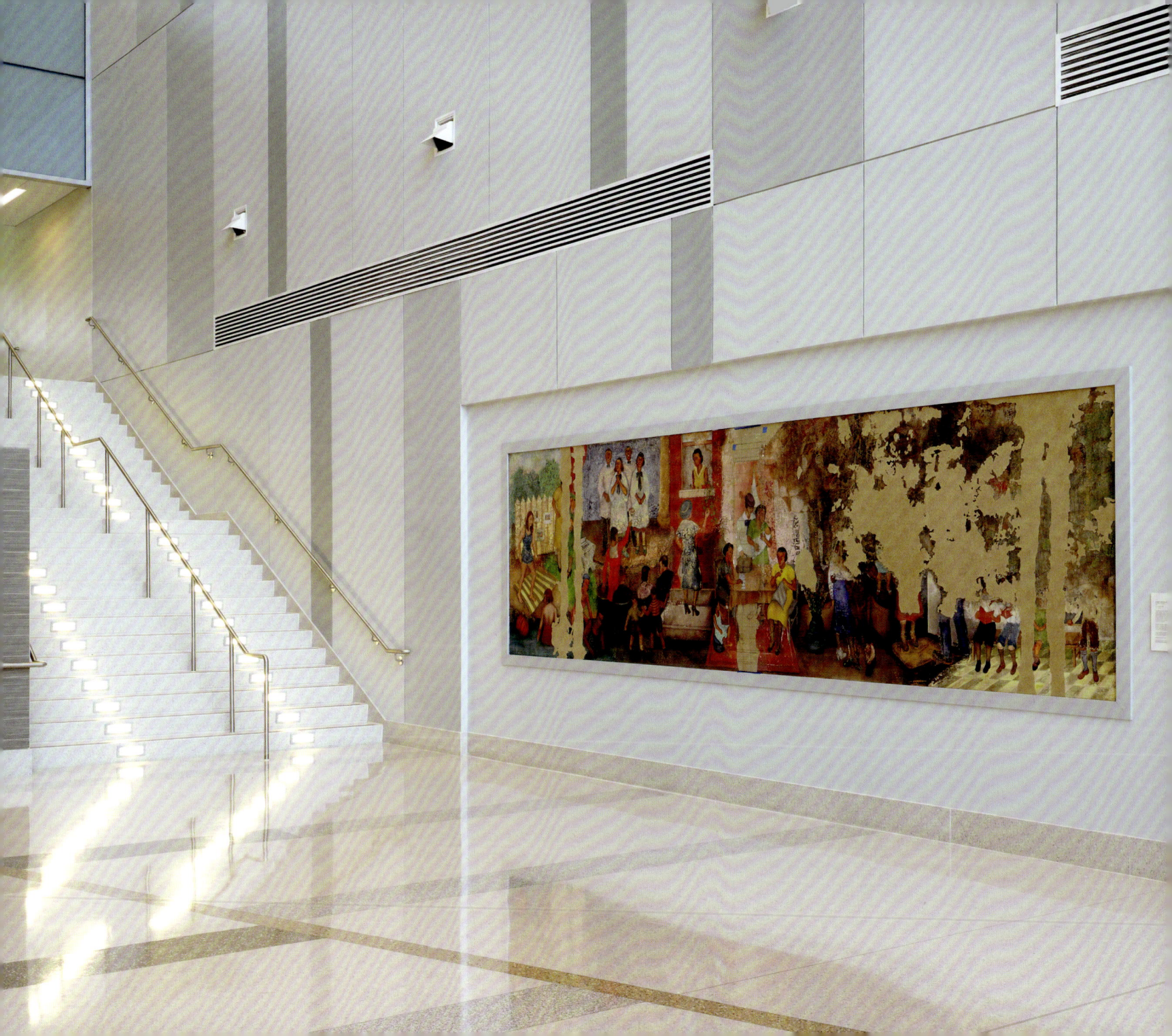

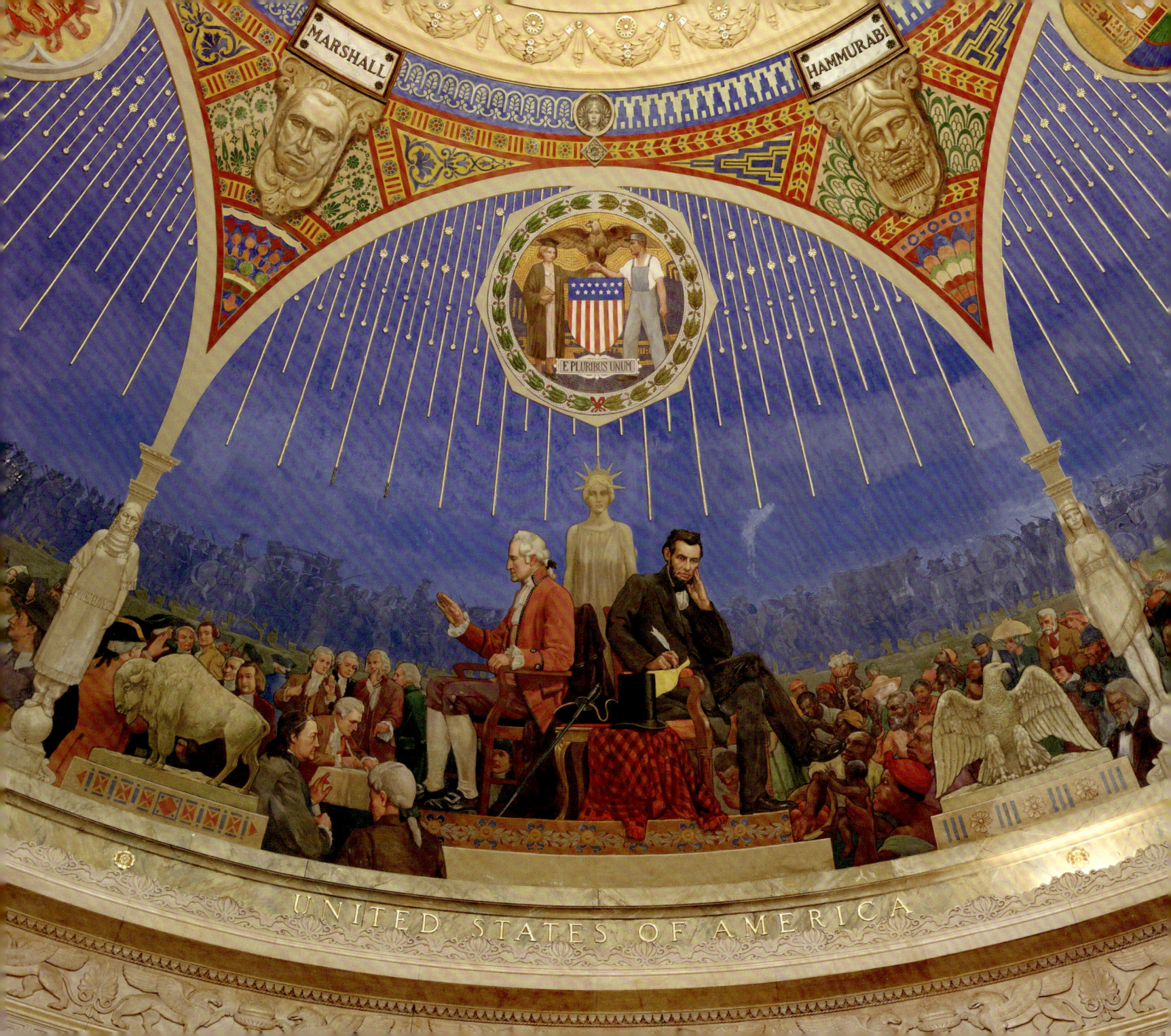

MARSHALL   HAMMURABI

E PLURIBUS UNUM

UNITED STATES OF AMERICA

NYS SUPREME COURT

JOHN EDWARD JACKSON · ATTILIO PUSTERLA · ROBERT RYLAND
ANDREW THOMAS SCHWARTZ · WINTHROP DUTHIE TURNEY

Guy Lowell, the quintessential gentleman architect of the American Renaissance, designed the Neoclassical New York County Supreme Courthouse, with its magnificent portico, massive columns, and 100-foot-wide flight of thirty-two steps. Fans of *Law and Order* have seen those steps more times than most lawyers have.

Though he had approved artist Attilio Pusterla's sketches for his plans to paint the murals and opulent decorative embellishments for the interior of the building in 1927, the Great Depression postponed them until the Public Works of Art Project (PWAP) funded the project in 1934.

Pusterla was born in Milan, Italy, in 1862. He broke with the classic tradition of studio painting to become a leader of the "Sunlight Revolutionaries," preferring to paint outside in nature. After immigrating to America at the turn of the century, he established himself as a significant mural painter. He and Lowell had previously collaborated in 1915 for the murals in a Gatsby-esque mansion on Long Island's Gold Coast.

In the foyer of 60 Centre Street, now a backdrop to the metal detectors and security screening, Pusterla designed the walls and ceiling with beautifully executed concepts dealing with the administrations of justice, inspired by the paintings in the Palazzo Madama in Rome. But when you visit the courthouse, after you have placed your personal items on the conveyer belt, look overhead to a panel in the barrel vaulted ceiling. You'll see, not a Roman holding the spear of justice, but a naked woman holding a mirror and a bit of juicy New York history—the blonde who posed for that painting played a part in the downfall of New York's most colorful mayor ever, Jimmy Walker. During Prohibition, Walker loved cruising around in his silver Duesenberg in the company of showgirls, visiting the best of New York's speakeasies, several of which he owned. In the middle of his second term, Walker fell in love with Betty Compton, a *Ziegfeld Follies* showgirl, and was charged with accepting in excess of a million dollars in bribes. Facing indictment, he resigned under pressure from Governor Franklin D. Roosevelt, left his wife, and sailed to Europe with Betty. But before his downfall, while he still had strings to pull, Walker immortalized his affection for Miss Compton by having Pusterla incorporate her naked body into his painting. Behind her is a figure representing justice and, prophetically, a fleeing, naked man seeking cover.

In the center of the building is the spectacular Rotunda, 200 feet in circumference and rising 75 feet to a cupola 30 feet in height and 20 feet across. Pusterla painted the 30-foot high dome of the Rotunda with a stunning mural entitled *The History of Law*. The six lunettes incorporate three hundred human figures and depict the most important developments in the history of law from Assyrian times to the mid-nineteenth century. The classical, delicately painted work was the pinnacle of Pusterla's artistic career. He painted his masterpiece, with a team of assistants, directly on plaster. The work was completed in 1936 at a cost of $20,000.

If you are ever called to jury duty at 60 Centre Street, you will be sent to either room 448 or room 452. If you're assigned to Room 448, bring a good book. The room is decorated with eleven tediously painted copies of old prints of early New York by Robert Ryland. But if you end up in room 452, you're in luck. Here, Pusterla and his team of painters, John Edwin Jackson, Andrew Thomas Schwartz, and Winthrop Duthie Turney, turned out a gorgeous collection of paintings celebrating New York

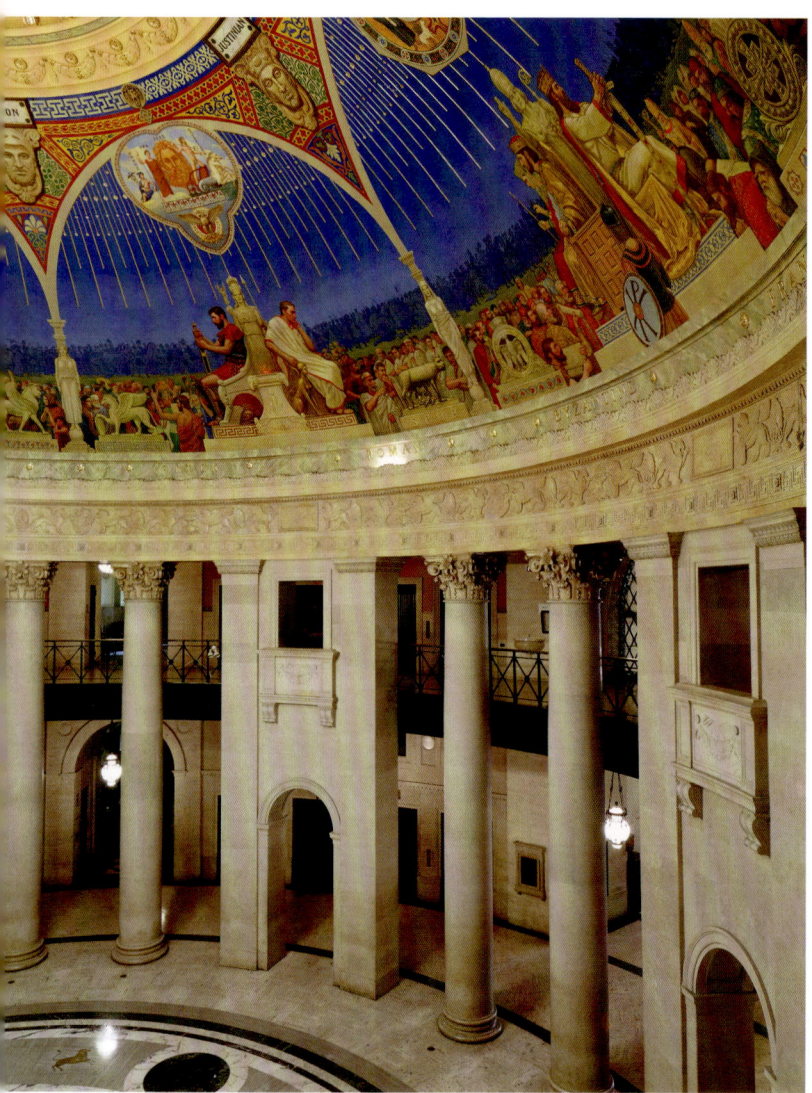

in the 1930s. Pusterla completely shifted gears from the rigid decorative discipline in the Rotunda and trotted out a sunlit revolutionary approach. The predominant panel is a panoramic view of New York City harbor, complete with a tugboat, the Staten Island ferry, and the Statue of Liberty. One of the most charming visions of New York of that time to be seen anywhere, Mayor David Dinkins used it for his Christmas card in 1991.

On the opposite wall is an equally charming painting by John Edwin Jackson, of Midtown Manhattan, showing the Empire State Building and the Chrysler Building as seen from Brooklyn. Sharing that same wall is a painting by Winthrop Duthie Turney, of Riverside Drive and the Hudson River. As a subtle backdrop to the dominant paintings in the room are six sepia visions of New York City by Andrew Thomas Schwartz. He painted Wall Street, Columbia University, the Woolworth Building, the Public Library on Fifth Avenue, Rockefeller Center, and the Brooklyn Bridge with a dark and shadowy delicacy. They provide the perfect counterpoint and a subtle complement to the storybook colors of the three larger panels.

Lowell was only fifty-six when he died on February 4, 1927, only a few days before the dedication of the building that had taken him eight years to build. The other painters who participated in the decoration of the courthouse were neither art stars nor visionaries and are, as a result, all but forgotten. Very little has been written about their lives, or their other art. But it was they who, during those few short years during the middle of the Depression, a time when bread lines lined the sidewalks and despair colored the streets, gifted New York City with a beauty that continues to outlast any economic turmoil or social crisis.

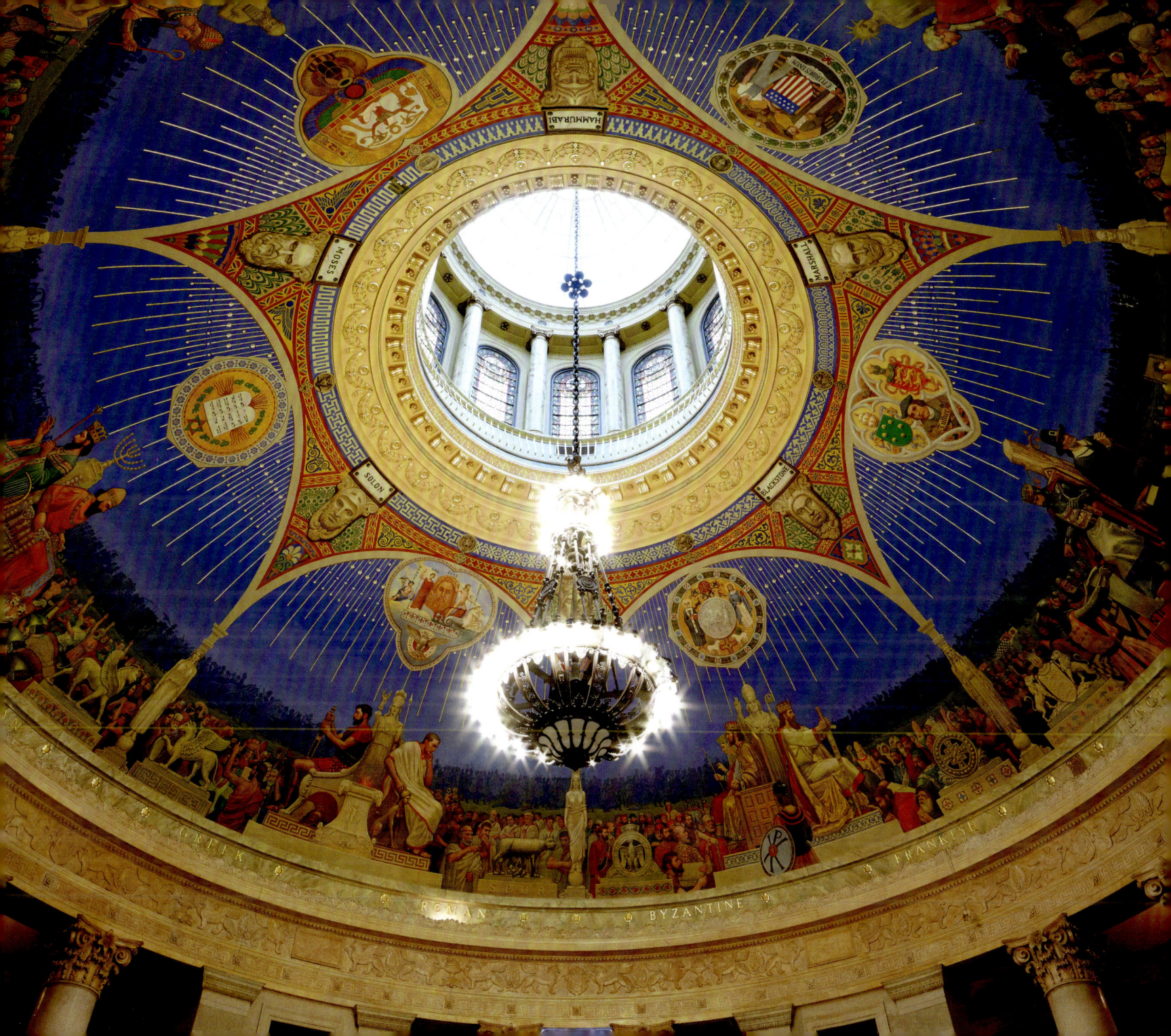

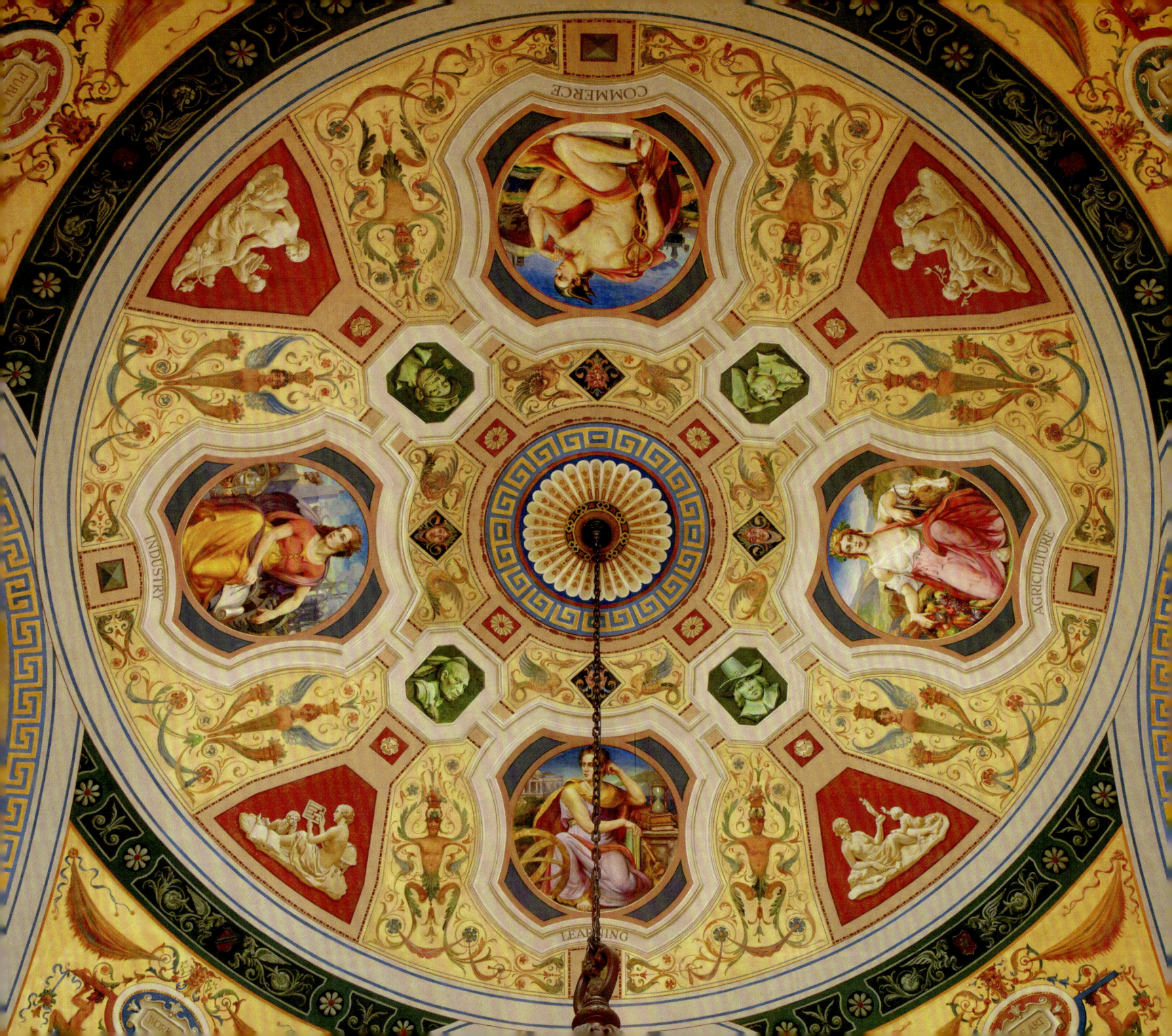

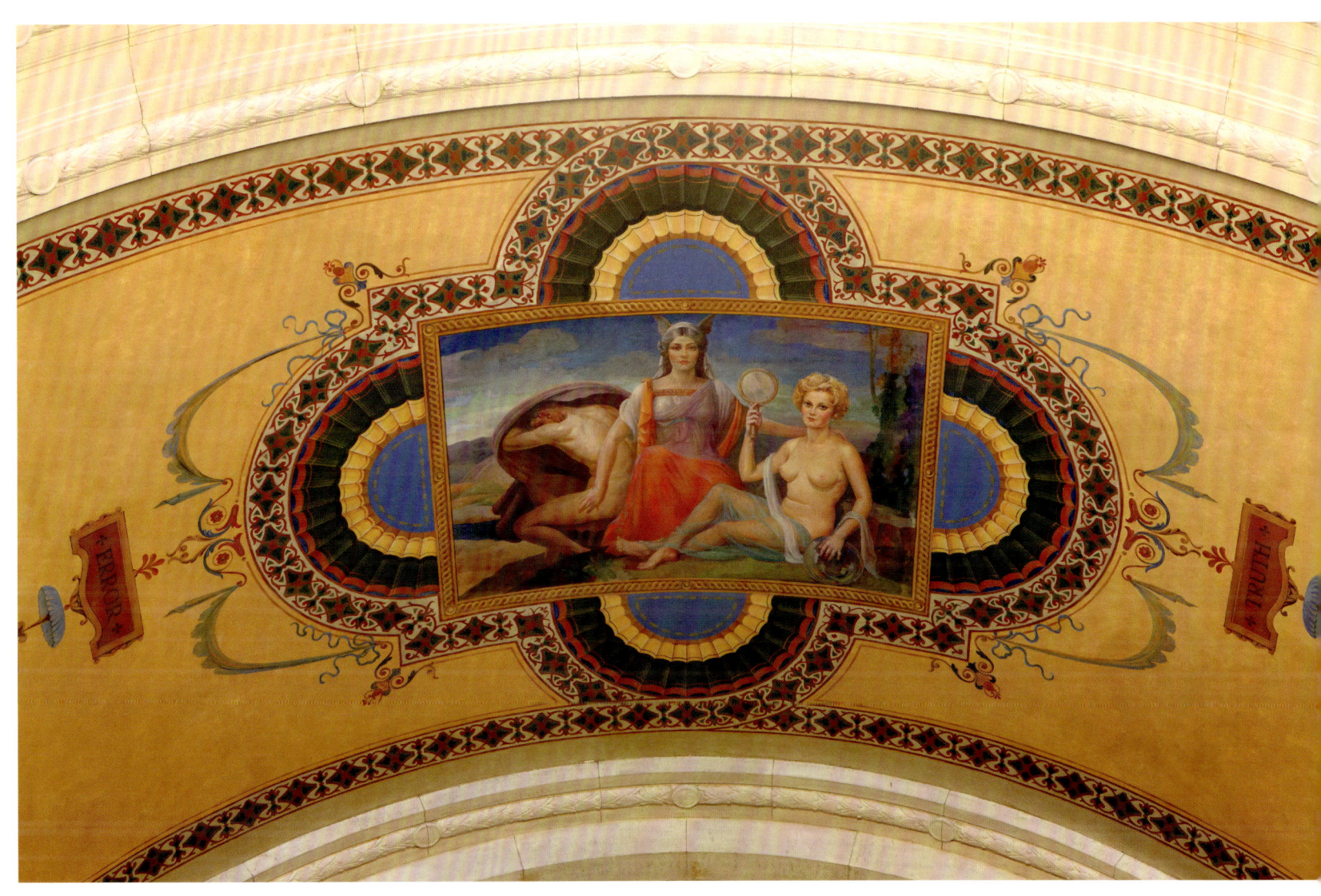

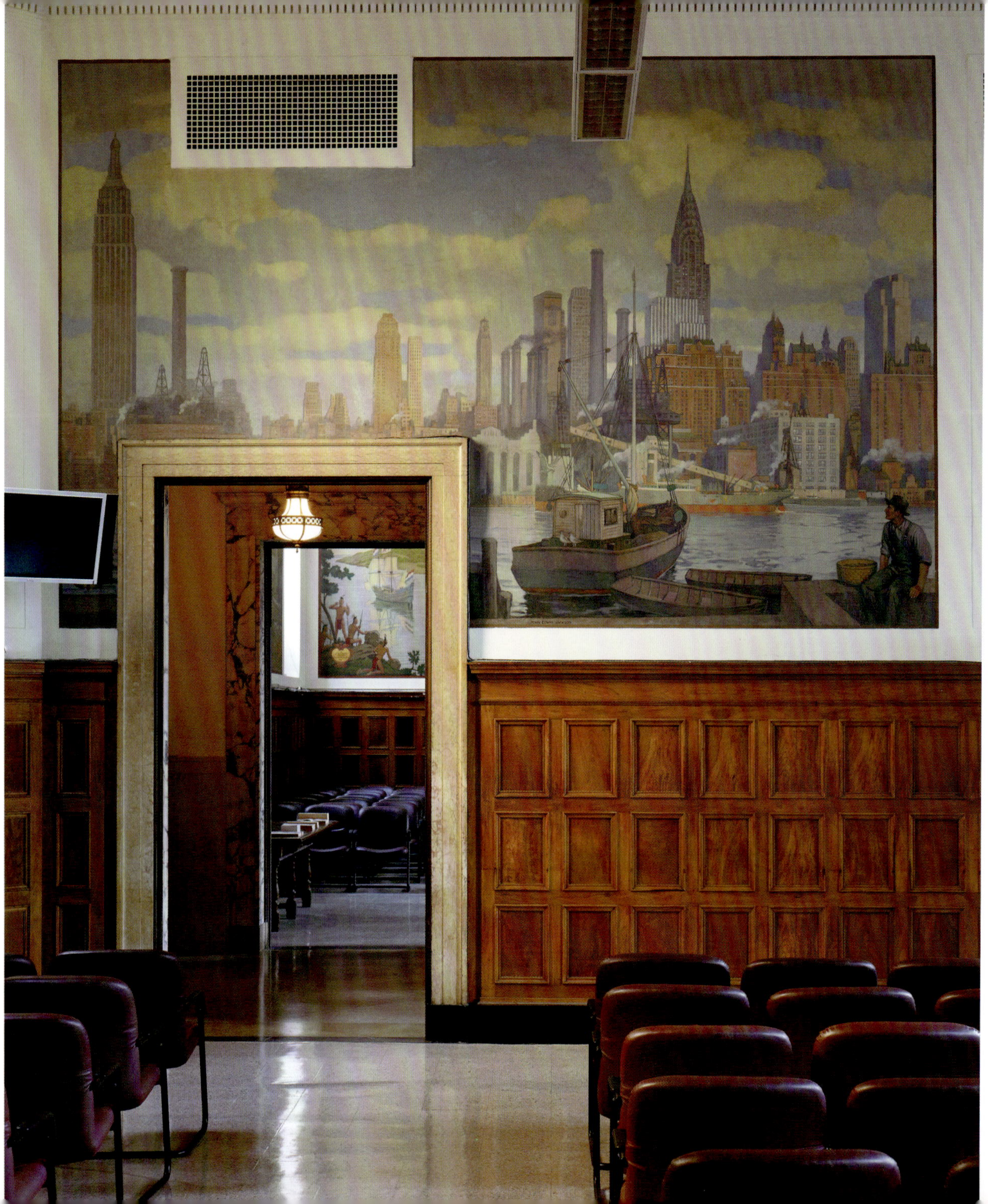

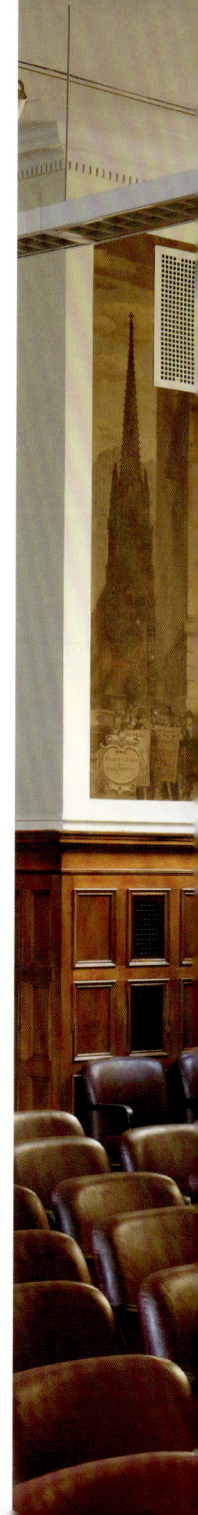

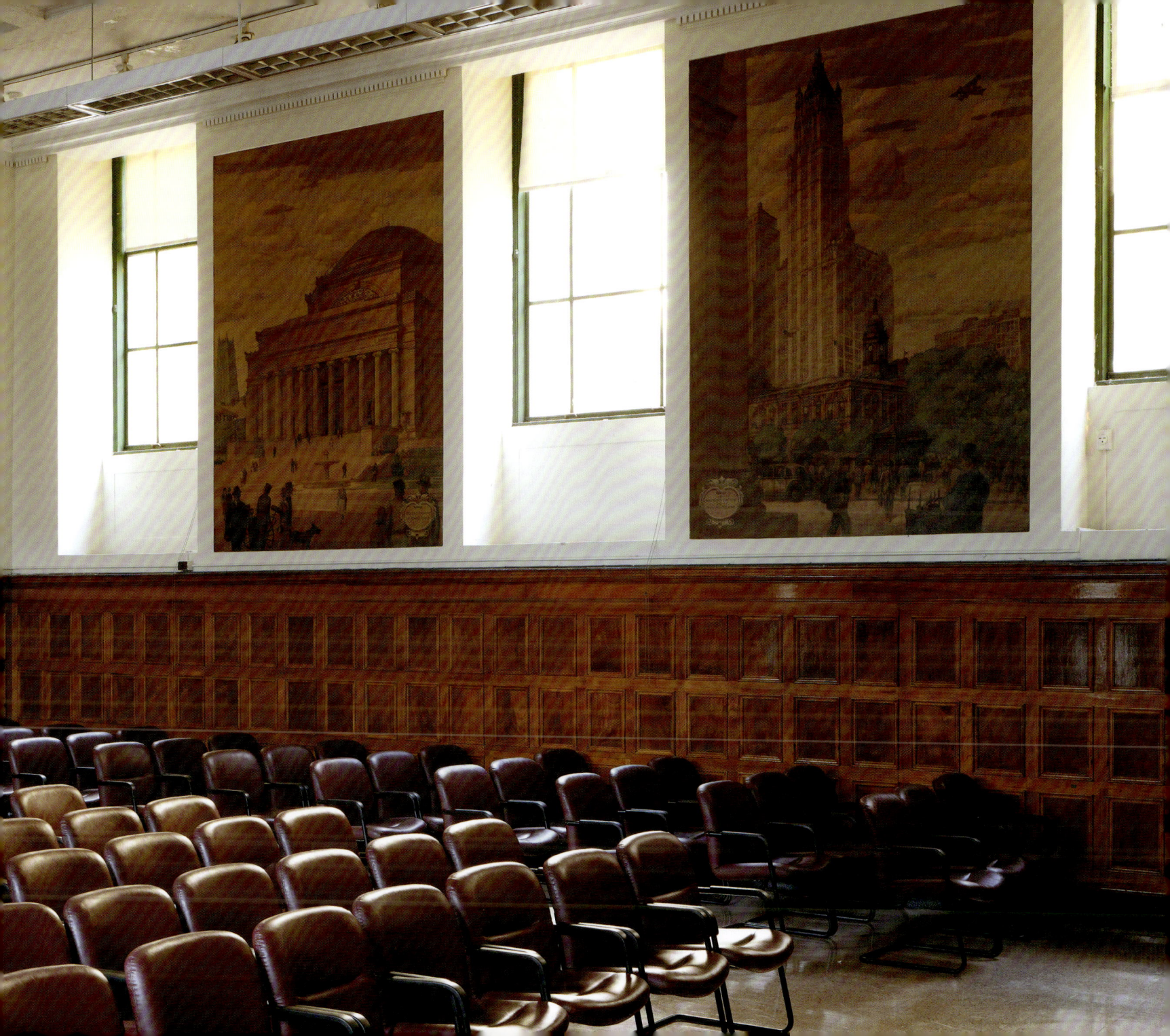

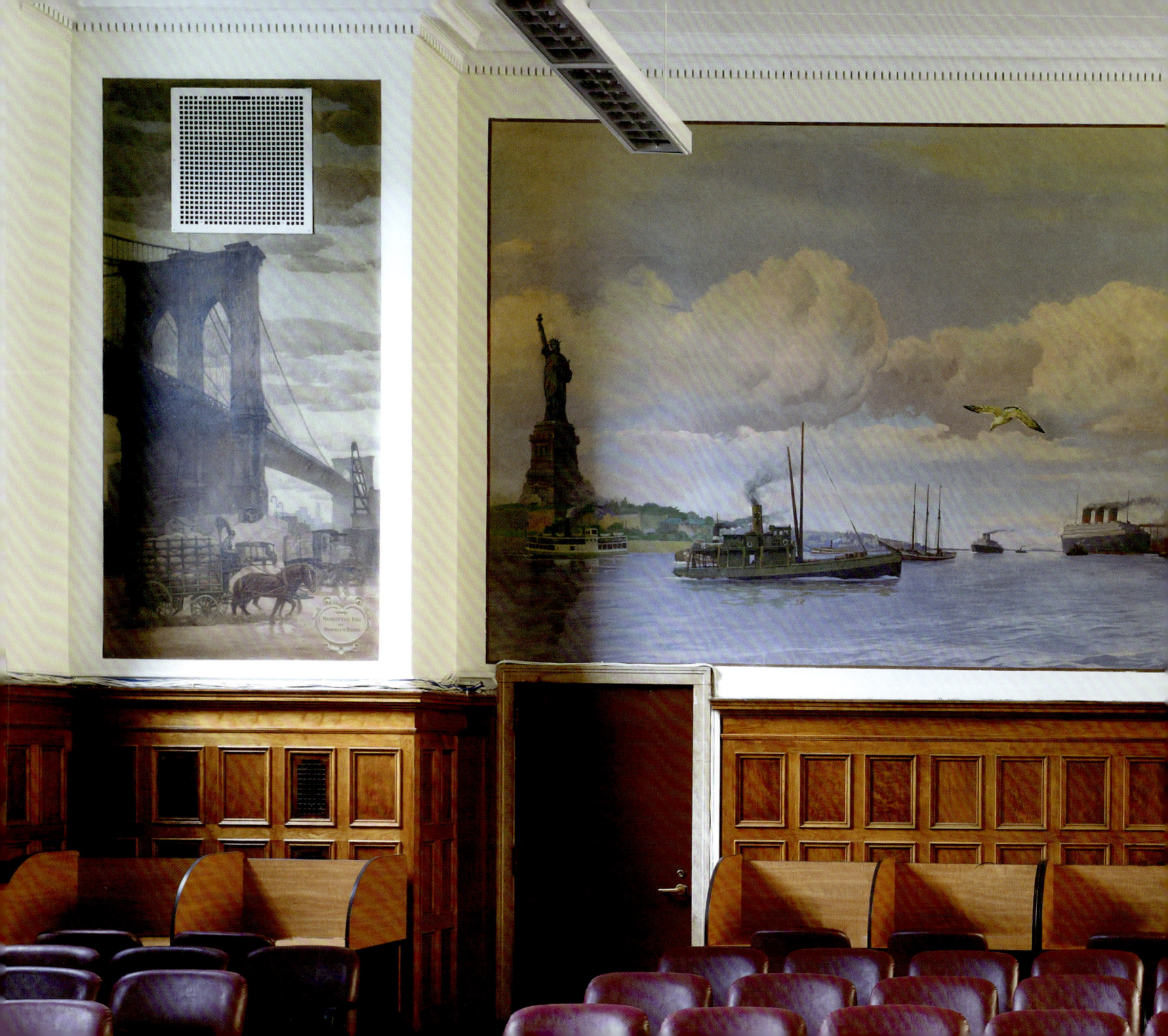

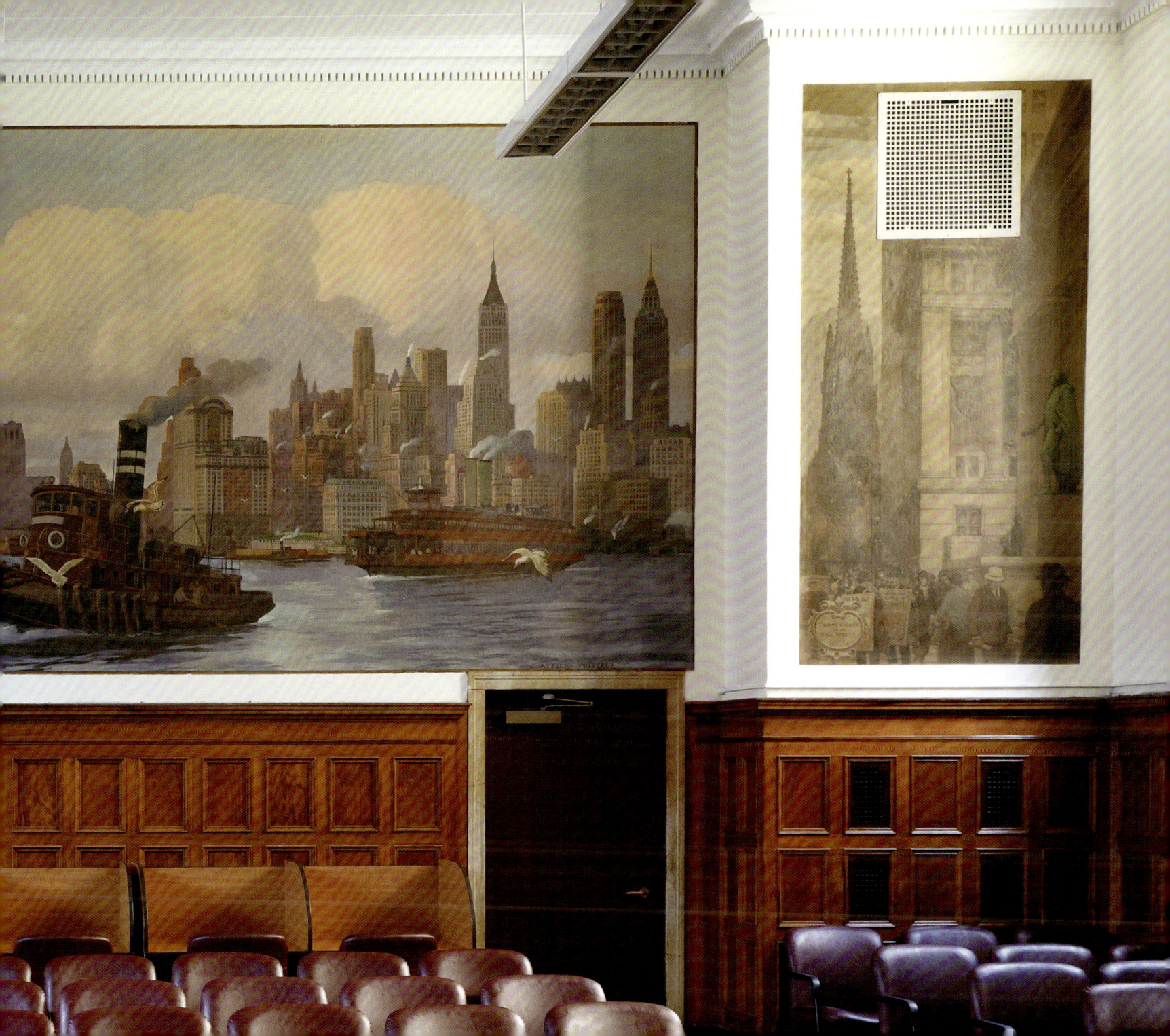

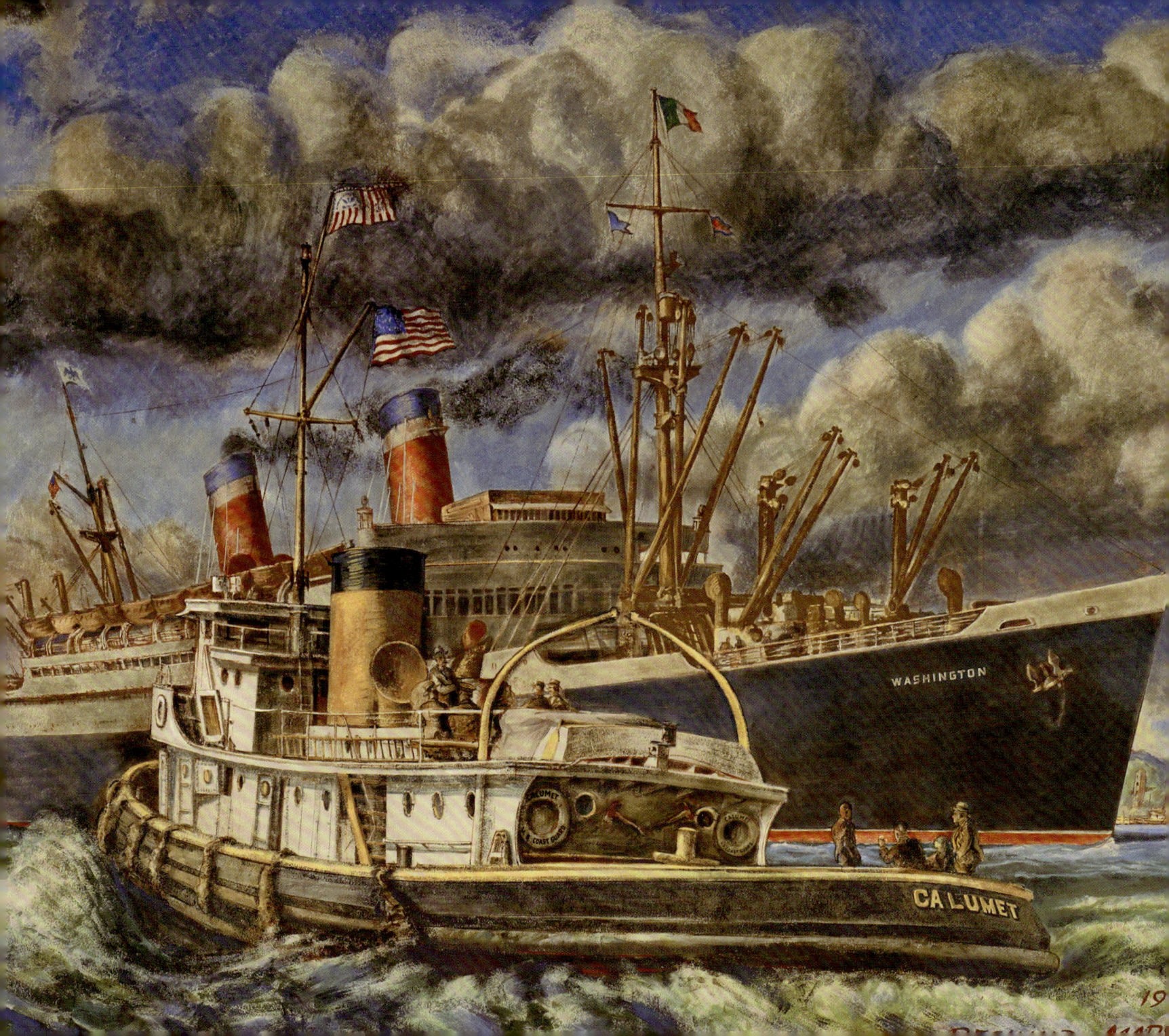

ALEXANDER HAMILTON
U.S. CUSTOM HOUSE

1 Bowling Green, Manhattan • REGINALD MARSH

Reginald Marsh had no interest in painting the bourgeois world of his own background. Born to wealthy expatriate artists in Paris, he returned to the United States and studied at the Art Students League in New York. Encouraged by teacher and artist John Sloan, Marsh, along with Thomas Hart Benton, George Bellows, and Edward Hopper, became part of the Ashcan School, a movement that rebelled against the romanticism of early twentieth-century American Impressionism. They painted the unbeautiful reality of daily life in the poor neighborhoods of New York.

Marsh's voyeur's eye was captivated by the inelegant visual possibilities of tawdry burlesque stages, the seedy pathos of the Bowery, and the summer surge of sexual energy at Coney Island and its sideshow grotesques. When stymied by an easel painting, Marsh would set out from his Union Square studio to sketch on the Bowery or, when the weather turned inhospitable, in the burlesque theaters on Irving Place. He loved New York and New Yorkers. He rambled the urban landscape with a handful of Waterman fountain pens loaded with India ink and a handmade sketchbook, capturing everything that tempted his covetous eye. As William Hogarth was to London and Honoré Daumier to Paris, so was Reginald Marsh to New York.

But of all the treats to be savored in the visual smorgasbord of New York City, he loved the harbor most of all. The slender island of Manhattan wore a bristling necklace of piers and docks that jutted out into the harobors of the East River and the Hudson River. Ships and tugboats kept a tempo of orchestrated frenzy as the bounty of the world flowed in and out of the city. There, at the foot of "Steamship Row," as Broadway was called because of all the shipping companies in the area, the Department of the Treasury built the Alexander Hamilton U.S. Custom House, designed by Cass Gilbert.

There, in the center of the second floor, Gilbert designed a stunning marble-lined elliptical rotunda lit by a 140-ton skylight. Enormous sculpted classical moldings, designed to embrace murals, decorated the double-height room. Unfortunately, the project had gone so far over budget because of the excesses of Gilbert's flamboyant artistic freedom that the murals could not be commissioned. The walls would remain blank for thirty years.

During the Great Depression, the Works Progress Administration (WPA; later the Works Projects Administration) and the Treasury Relief Art Project (TRAP) were commissioning unemployed artists to decorate government buildings. It was a perfect time to fulfill Cass's vision of his rotunda. In 1937, Reginald Marsh was commissioned to paint the maritime murals in the U.S. Custom House. Marsh was used to doing little sketches on paper that could fit in his pocket and painting small oils in his studio. The prospect of painting eight enormous panels and eight smaller paintings 30 feet in the air was a daunting one. He employed eight assistants who worked with him fourteen hours a day, seven days a week, for ninety straight days. Marsh was paid the same rate as an assistant clerk in the Treasury, ninety cents an hour. His final fee for seventeen hundred hours of work was $1,560.

Marsh chose two grand passenger ships, the *Queen Mary* and the *Normandie*, as his subjects. The mural cycle's story begins with the Lightship *Ambrose* encountering an ocean liner at sea to escort the giant ship through the shipping channel's entrance into the harbor. Once safely in the harbor, the ship takes on the Sandy Hook pilot, who assumes control of the ship to steer it to its berth.

In the next panel, the harbor tug *Calumet* approaches the ship in the channel off Staten Island. Next, a tug meets the ship with government officials, who come aboard. There is an aerial view of the ship passing under the view of

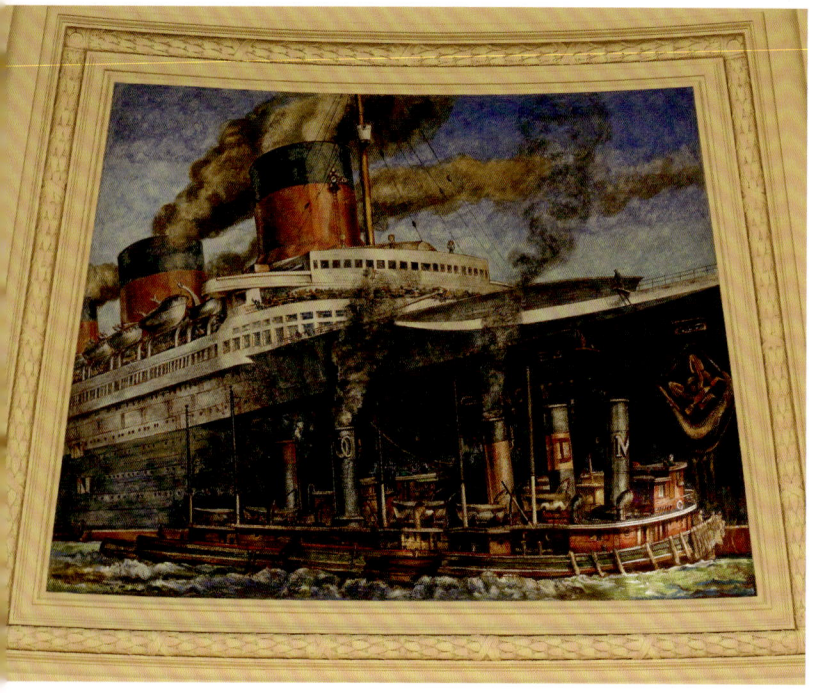

the Statue of Liberty with Lower Manhattan in the background. Once the ship has docked, the paparazzi are shooting, filming, and interviewing a movie star (said to be Greta Garbo).

Finally the tugboats bully the S.S. *Normandie* into her berth on the west side of Manhattan. In the final panel, the ship disgorges its cargo and passengers with an intricate web of gangways, rigging, and webbing.

Ambassador Joseph P. Kennedy, who was chairman of the U.S. Maritime Commission, attempted to coerce Marsh into changing the ships' names to the names of American ships. Marsh, always polite and affable, declined but did agree to "smudge the names . . . a bit." In between the large panels are eight trompe l'oeil paintings of famous navigators including Amerigo Vespucci, Henry Hudson, and Christopher Columbus.

Ambassador Joseph P. Kennedy, who was Chairman of the U.S. Maritime Commission, attempted to persuade Marsh to change the names of the ships to those from America. Ever the diplomat himself, Marsh declined to change the names, but in the spirit of compromise, did agree to "smudge the names . . . a bit"

The murals were completed on December 27, 1937. In 1968, the U.S. Customs Service moved to the World Trade Center and, by 1972, Gilbert's building was abandoned, sealed off, and neglected for twenty-five years until Senator Patrick Daniel Moynihan waged the battle for its preservation. Senator Moynihan, a long-serving and staunch advocate for New Yorkers and the preservation of New York heritage, fought to keep the murals. As a result of Senator Moynihan's heroic effort, the building, and Frederick Marsh's murals, will survive as long as there is a New York and people who love the city and its history.

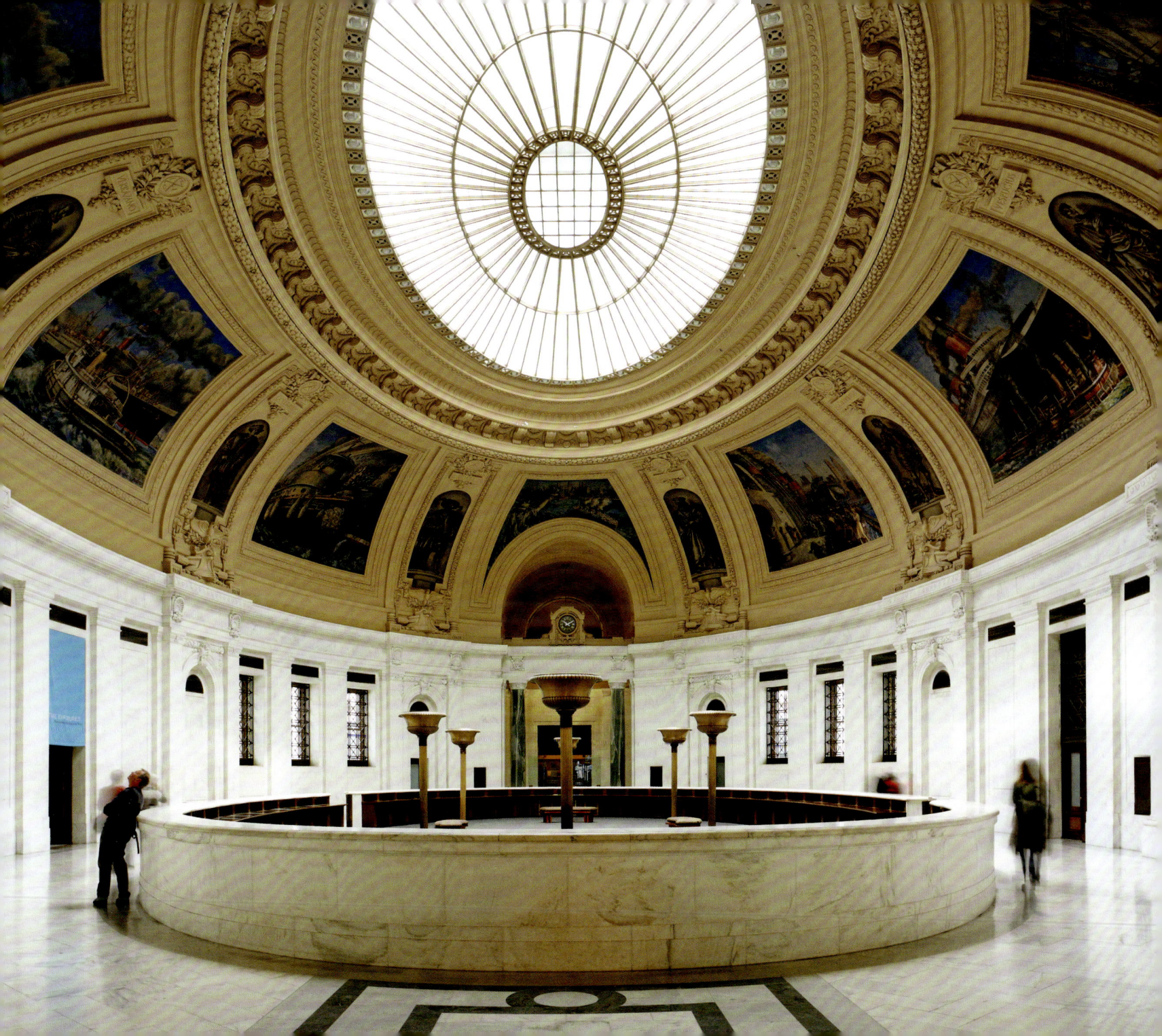

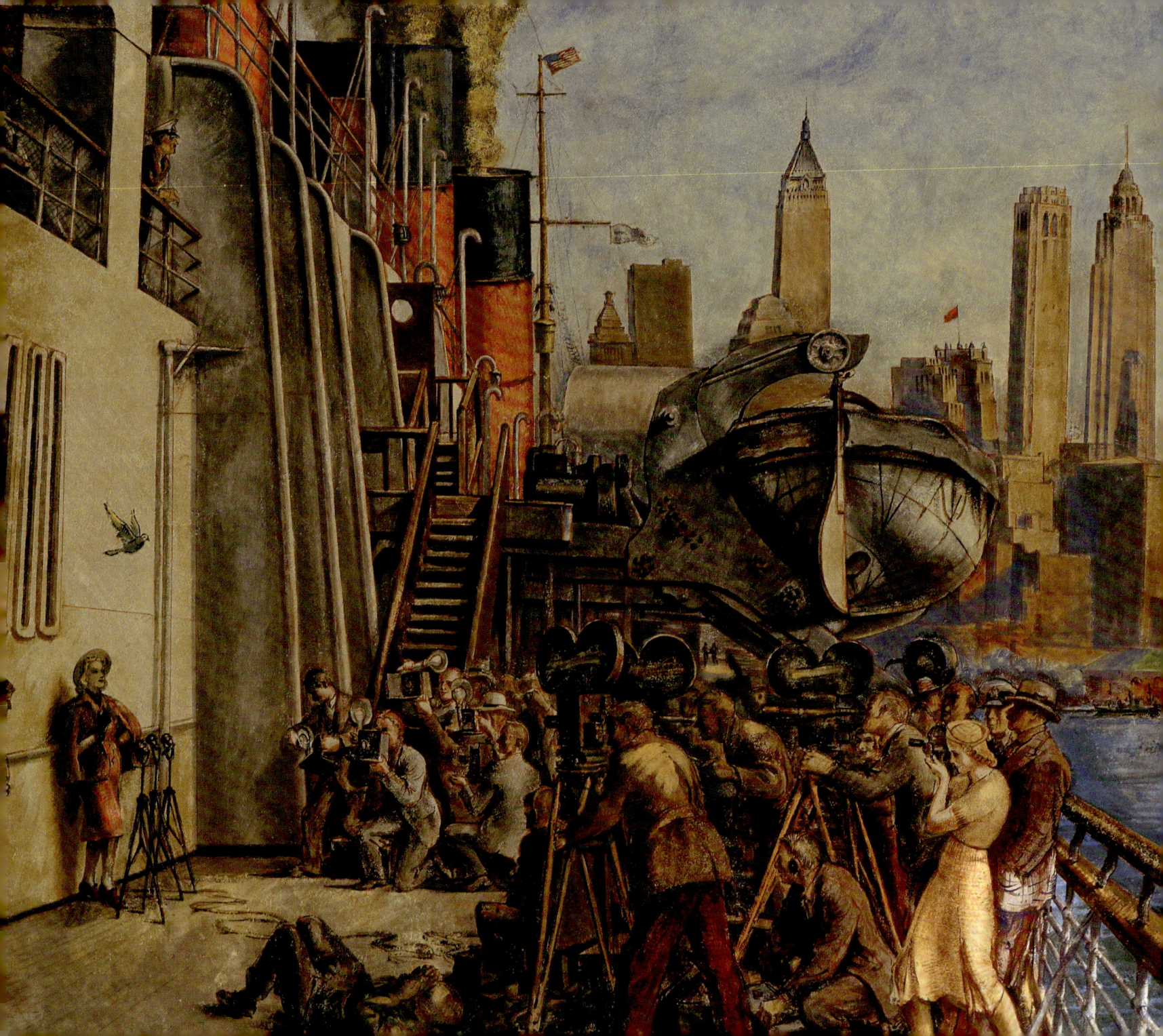

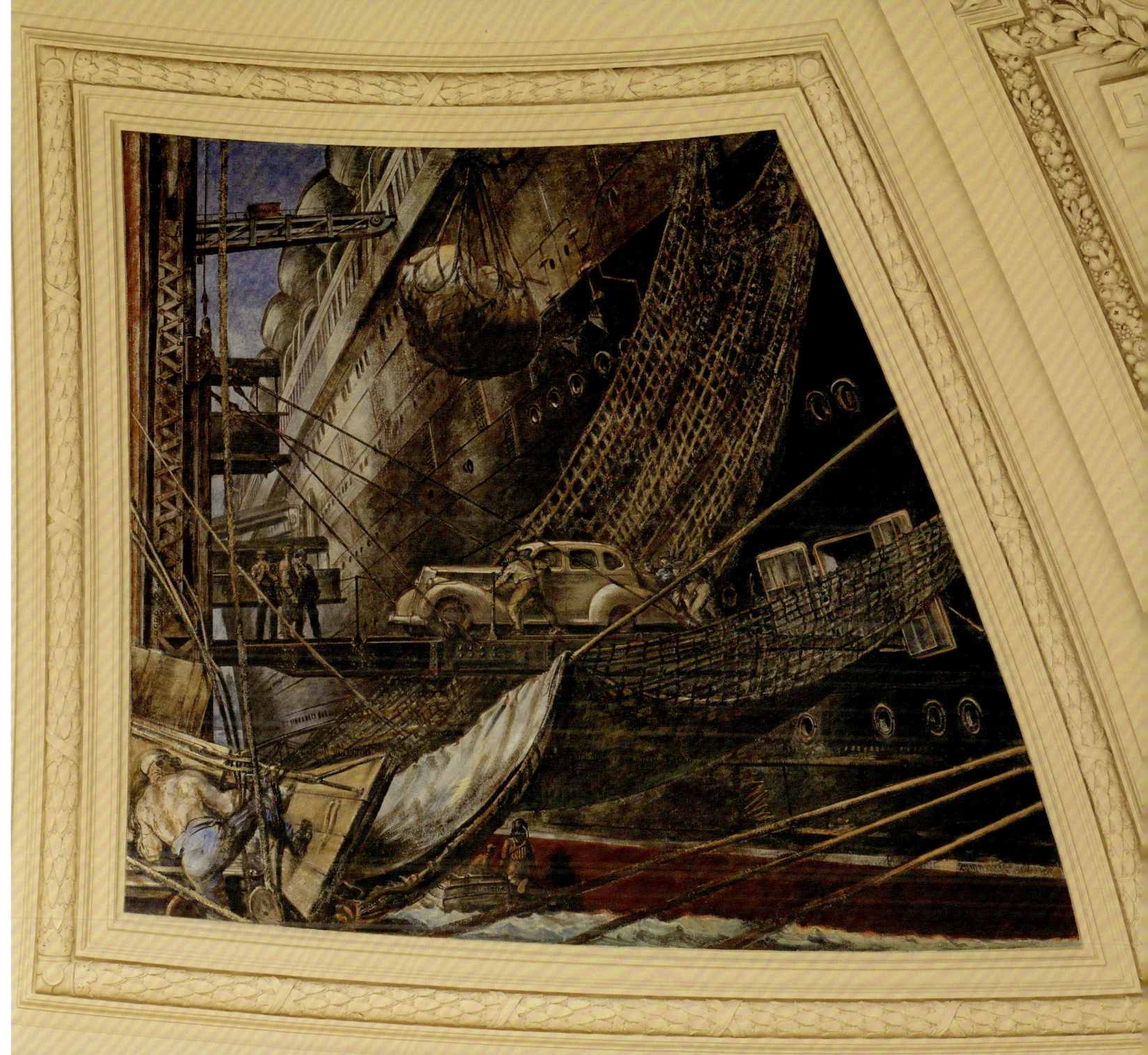

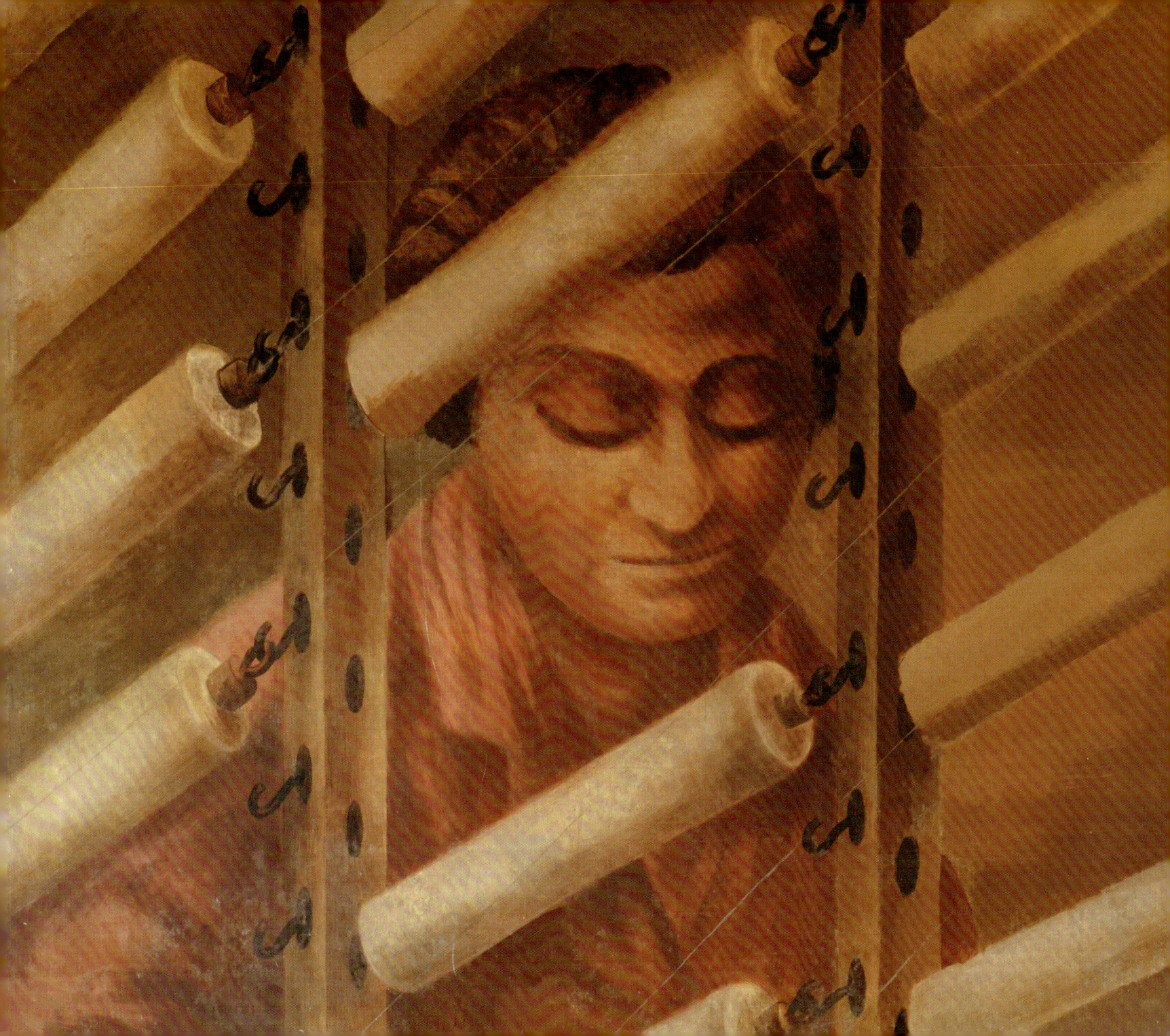

BRONX GENERAL POST OFFICE

558 Grand Concourse, The Bronx • BEN SHAHN

When Ben Shahn assisted Diego Rivera on his doomed Rockefeller Center murals in 1933, he witnessed the ramifications of intransigence. Once Rivera spurned his patron's request to alter his mural, he was left with only a self-congratulatory flush of artistic integrity and the sight of his glorious mural reduced to rubble. So, in 1938, when Shahn brought down the wrath of prominent members of the Catholic Church, the Holy Name Society, and the Knights of Columbus by placing Walt Whitman's ". . . to recast poems, churches, art (Recast, maybe discard them, end them—maybe their work is done, who knows?) . . ." into his Works Progress Administration proposal for the Bronx General Post Office mural, he judiciously substituted a few lines from a more benign Whitman poem.

The quote from "As I Walk These Broad, Majestic Days" appears in the first major panel of the mural cycle, being read by Whitman himself:

"For we support all, fuse all,
After the rest is done and gone, we remain;
There is no final reliance but upon us;
Democracy rests finally upon us, (I, my brethren, begin it,)
And our visions sweep through eternity."

Ben Shahn's journey to the Bronx began in Lithuania, when his father was exiled to Siberia for revolutionary activities. That persecution led to his family's migration to Brooklyn in 1906 and a lifelong dedication to the underdog.

He explored the ideas of injustice and persecution in his twenty-three gouache paintings based on the trial and execution of two immigrants, *The Passion of Sacco and Vanzetti*. These paintings brought him to the attention of Diego Rivera, who hired him and his future wife, artist and photojournalist Bernarda Bryson, to work on the *Man at the Crossroads* mural for Rockefeller Center.

One day, Shahn's studio partner, famed photographer Walker Evans, gave him a camera and instructions on how to use it as he dashed out the door: "Use f/9 for the bright side of the street, f/4.5 for the shady side!" Armed with that basic information and daily practice, Shahn became such a credible photographer that, in 1935, he was chosen by the Farm Security Administration (FSA), along with Evans and Dorothea Lange, to photograph Depression-era workers in the Deep South. He and Bryson traveled for three months shooting cotton pickers, sharecroppers, and textile workers. The images from that trip became the basis for the Bronx General Post Office murals.

Shahn and Bryson sketched the cartoons for the murals, a thirteen-panel panorama, inspired by Walt Whitman. Entitled *Resources of America*, it was to be a celebration of the nobility of the American worker and a document of the production of raw materials and their transformation into consumable goods. The paintings portray white and black workers as solid women and heroic men with powerfully muscular physiques. These are not poor and huddled masses, but industrious, purposeful, hardworking people. The cool, neutral grays of the marble floors and walls of the post office provide the perfect background for Shahn's earthy, rust-tawny palette.

The center panel of the triptych on the north wall shows Whitman, looking more like Karl Marx than the poet, reading his poem aloud to the proletariat. The flanking panels are of miners.

To the right of the triptych is a panel of a man working in a factory with a pneumatic drill. Next is a man in a field, staring intently at the blueprint in his hands as huge girders behind him transport electricity. To his right, a farmer is pitching hay. His solid back and shoulders seem to be formed by a life spent in the fields rhythmically repeating the same motions season after season. The next panel is a plain-faced, impassive woman in a textile factory behind multiple spools of thread. On the short wall are two paintings; The most poignant image in the cycle shows a modern African American man picking cotton in much the same way as his slave ancestors would have, and its companion panel, two men loading baled cotton onto trucks. They, unlike the field hand, stand tall.

Next is a man in a textile factory. Spools of thread appear to stretch back deep into the building behind him. The next panel, positioned directly across from one showing a single farmer, features a group of twentieth-century farmers working a threshing machine. The following panel celebrates a Tennessee Valley Authority (TVA) hydroelectric dam; a worker toils high above on the dam. On the opposite wall, the companion piece shows an engineer controlling the transfer of the electrical energy. Completing the cycle is a steel worker surrounded by the fruits of his labor.

Years after his paintings were completed, Shahn returned to this post office, where a service-crew foreman approached him. In a 1944 interview, Shahn recalled the man asking him, "You the guy who did these pictures?" Shahn told the interviewer, "I said yes, and asked him how he liked them. 'Not particularly,' the foreman said, 'but I'm sure glad you put all these guys in overalls up on the walls. It helped me organize the building crew. Made 'em think they were important.'"

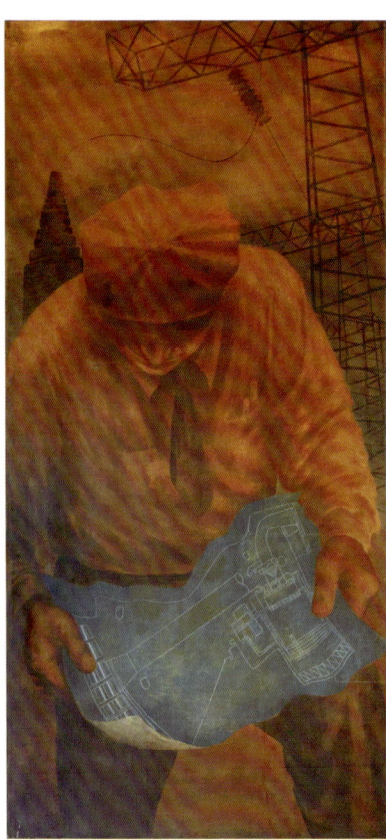
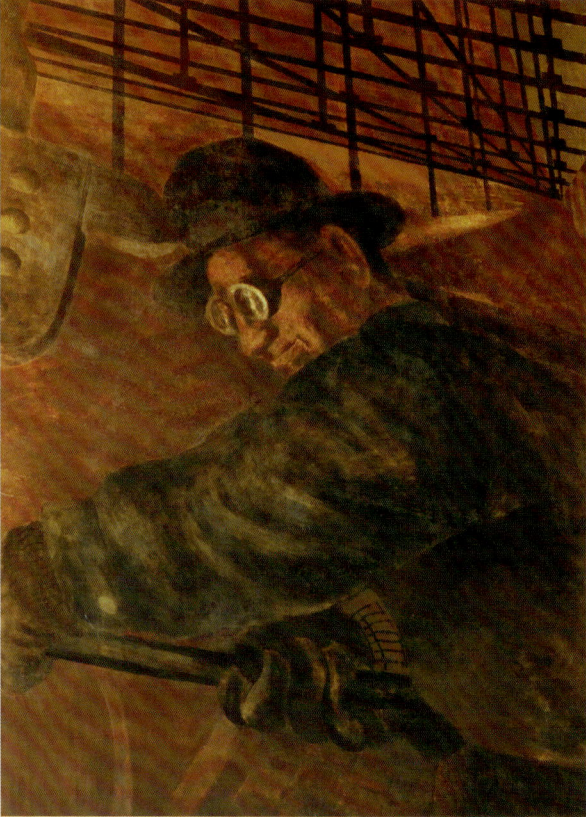
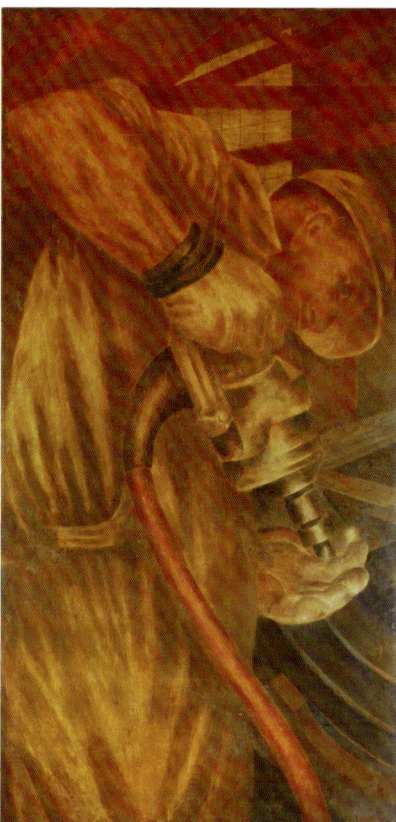

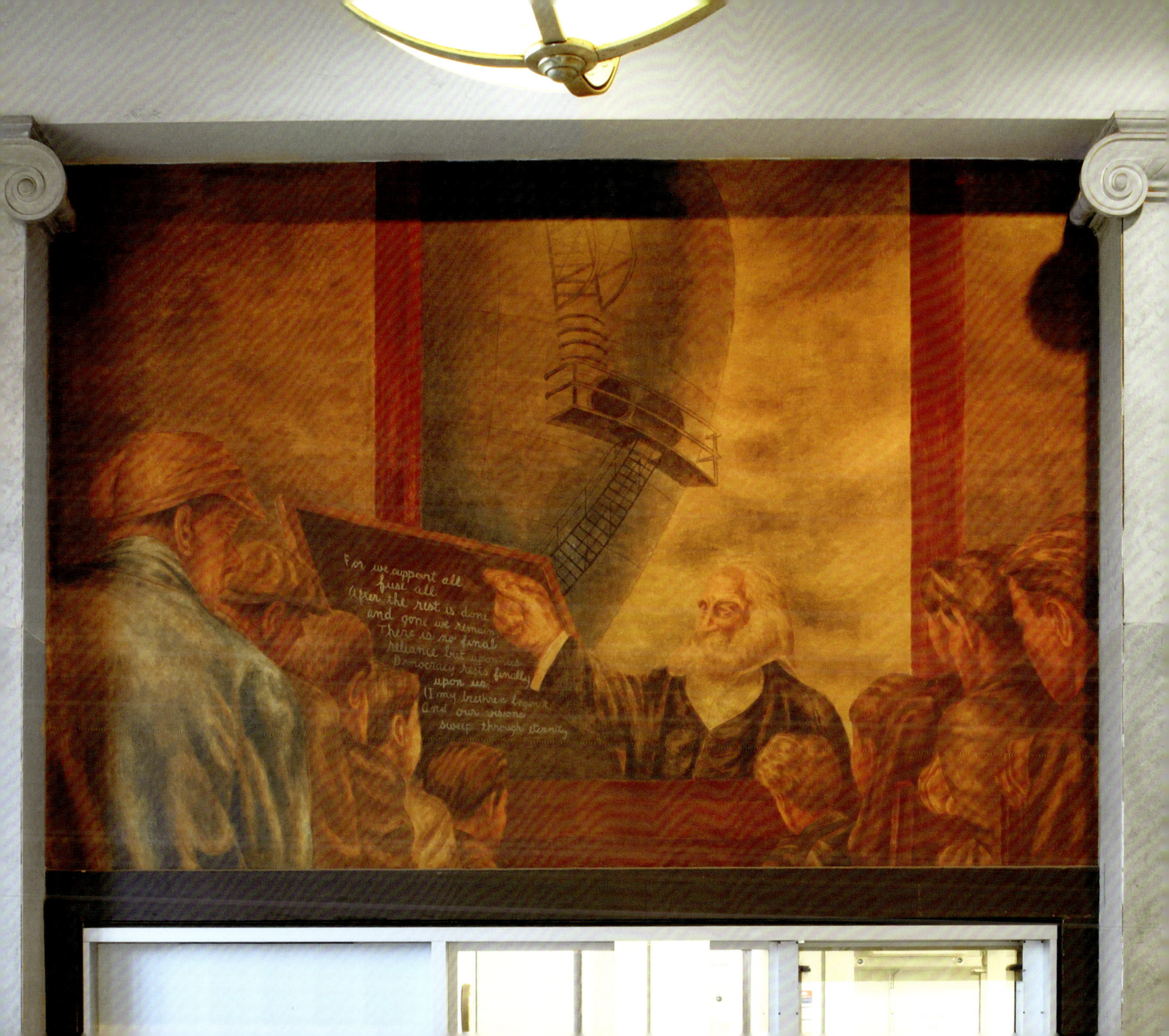

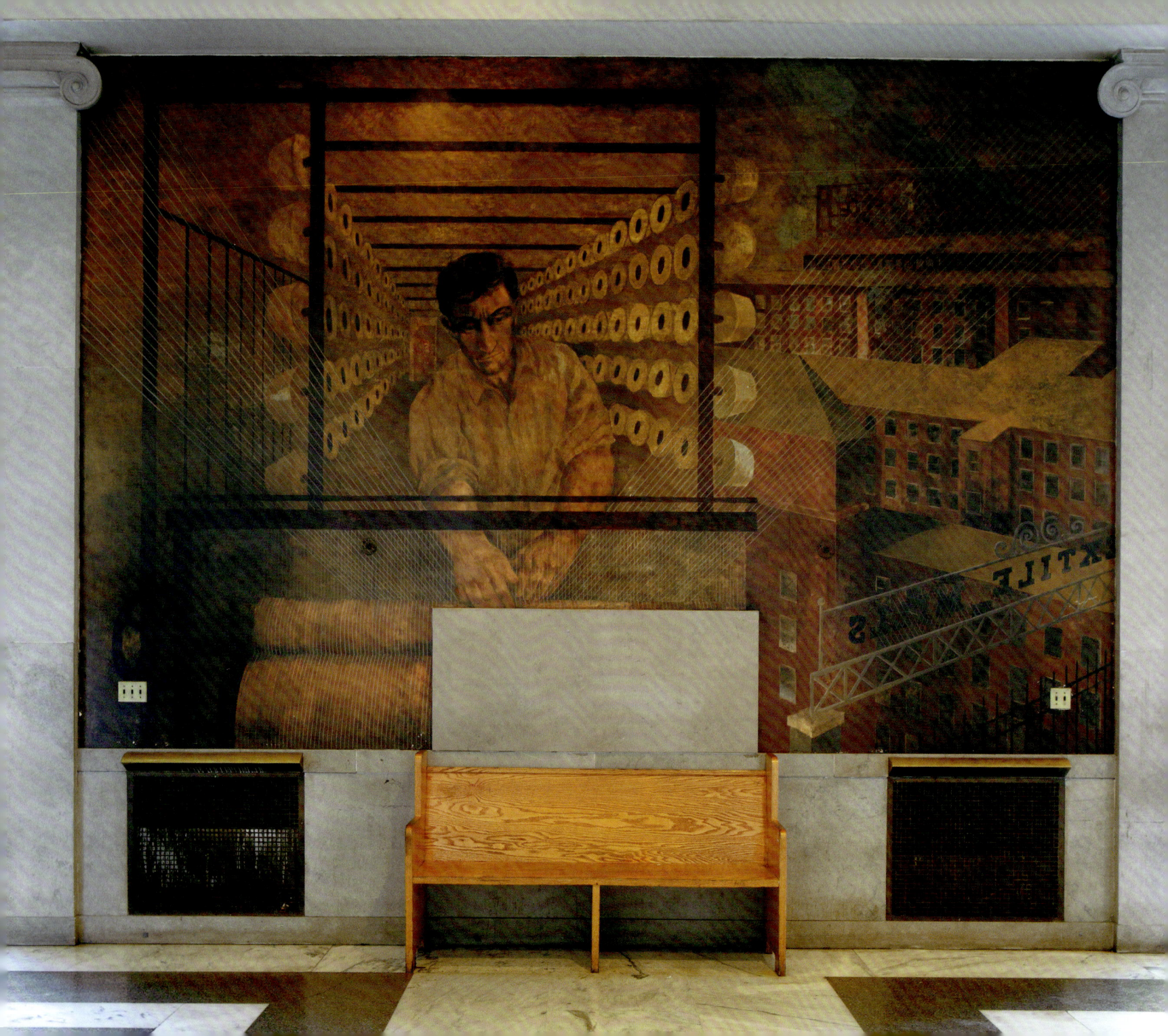

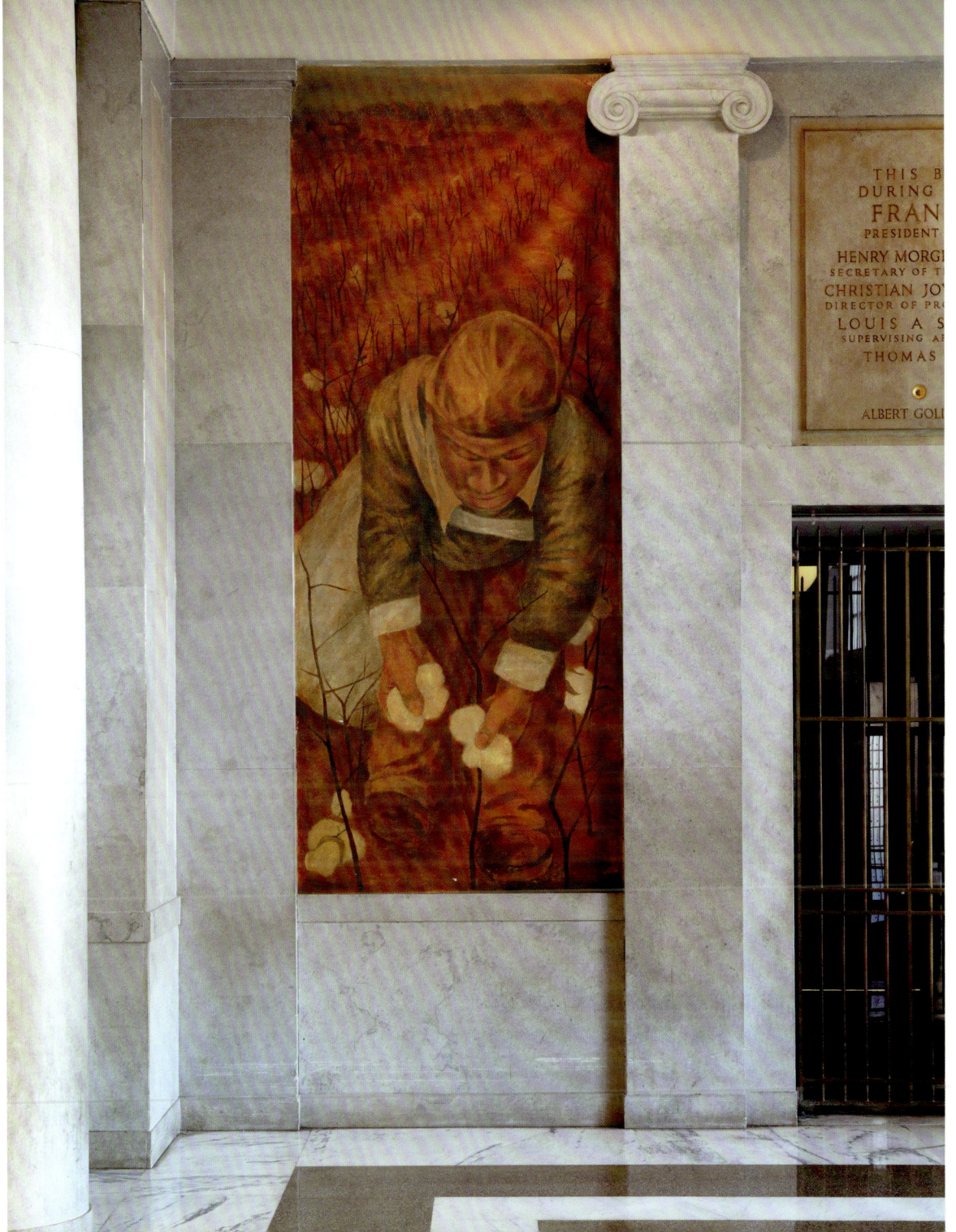

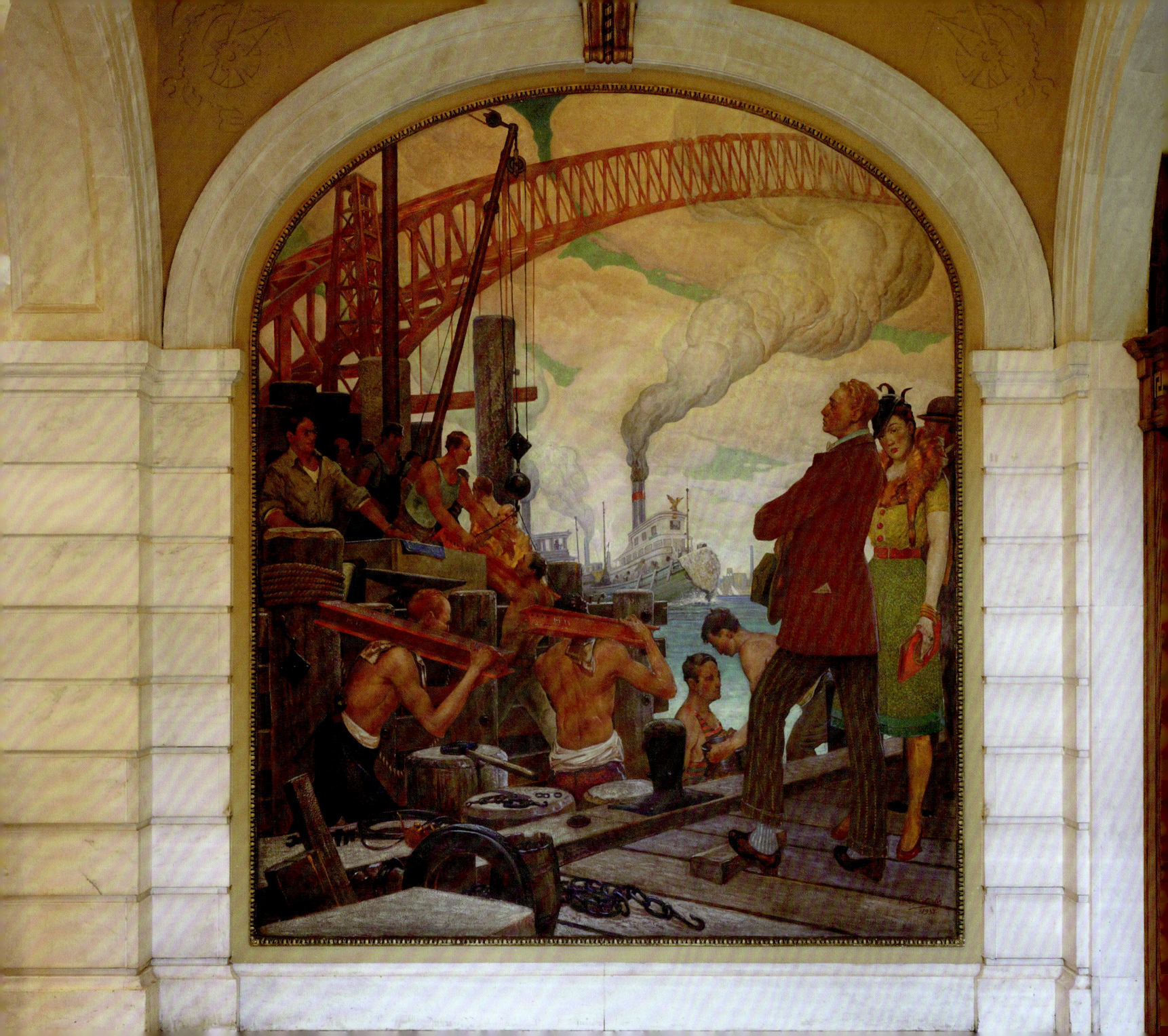

STATEN ISLAND BOROUGH HALL

10 Richmond Terrace, Staten Island • FREDERICK CHARLES STAHR

At the end of the nineteenth century, when Frederick Charles Stahr was a boy growing up on Staten Island, it was nothing more than sixty square miles of farmlands with a smattering of villages. But when he returned home just before World War I, after studying painting in Munich and the Academy of Design in Rome, Staten Island had become a borough of New York City.

Richmond Borough Hall, now called Staten Island Borough Hall, was constructed on the mythical site of Henry Hudson's 1609 disembarkation. The building was designed in the fashionable French Renaissance style by the architectural firm Carrère and Hastings. John Carrère promised his fellow Staten Island native a commission for the new building: a suite of murals commemorating the history of Staten Island. Carrère designed thirteen arched niches, each 13 feet high by 6 and half feet wide, on the main floor to accommodate the paintings. But, by the time of the building's completion in 1906, there was no money left, and the niches remained blank for three decades. In 1936, Stahr approached the WPA for assistance. They agreed to fund the project and, thirty years late, the work began. Stahr was given a studio office on the third floor of the building. For the next two years, he created the oil paintings on canvas, which were then brought downstairs and cemented in place as he went along.

Painted in an idealized swashbuckling, storybook style, the series of paintings begins with the 1524 discovery of the island by Giovanni da Verrazzano and goes on to tell the myths we've all agreed upon, or what is called history. Next is a panel of Henry Hudson, arriving on a Dutch ship in 1609 and giving the island a Dutch name, "Staaten Eylandt," to satisfy his investors. The next two panels depict the native Lenape tribe and the first invasion of the colonial real estate developers. Rather than showing the slaughter and mayhem that resulted, Stahr depicts the Lenape as stoic and cooperative as they exchange their valuable furs for cheap Dutch trinkets. As the suite progresses, the French Huguenot farmers gradually dominate the island. The next panel shows the British Admiral Richard Howe taking charge of the island and the building of Fort Hill. The next painting shows the only attempt at a peace conference during the Revolutionary War, between Admiral Howe and a contingent of writers and signers of the Declaration of Independence, including Benjamin Franklin and John Adams.

Next is a painting commemorating the exaggeratedly named Battle of St. Andrew's. Eventually, the yoke of British repression was thrown off, and the Redcoats left the island. The departing British ships in the center of the composition divide the crowd watching their parting into two symbolic groups. On the left is a couple waving a very enthusiastic good-bye, but on the right is a more somber group not at all thrilled about the end of British rule. The ninth painting jumps thirty years to the War of 1812 and the erecting of Forts Richmond and Tompkins. The tenth panel shows a stagecoach stopping at the Black Horse Tavern on its way to Richmond. This painting is dated 1937, which was three years after the tavern was demolished to make room for a wider Richmond road, so it is perhaps Stahr's attempt to preserve a bit of history. The next painting depicts the 1907 fire that destroyed the Hotel Castleton, which, during the nineteenth century, was run by freed black men. The twelfth painting is a confusing disruption of the chronological order of the paintings, taking us back to the creation of the first Clifton-to-Tottenville railroad in 1860. The last painting, completed in 1938, shows the building of the Bayonne Bridge sometime between 1928 and 1931. Even though the bridge was finished well before Stahr painted it, he chose to show it in the middle of construction. The snappily dressed blond man was the span's designer, Othmar Ammann, who also designed ten more New York bridges, including the George Washington and Verrazano-Narrows.

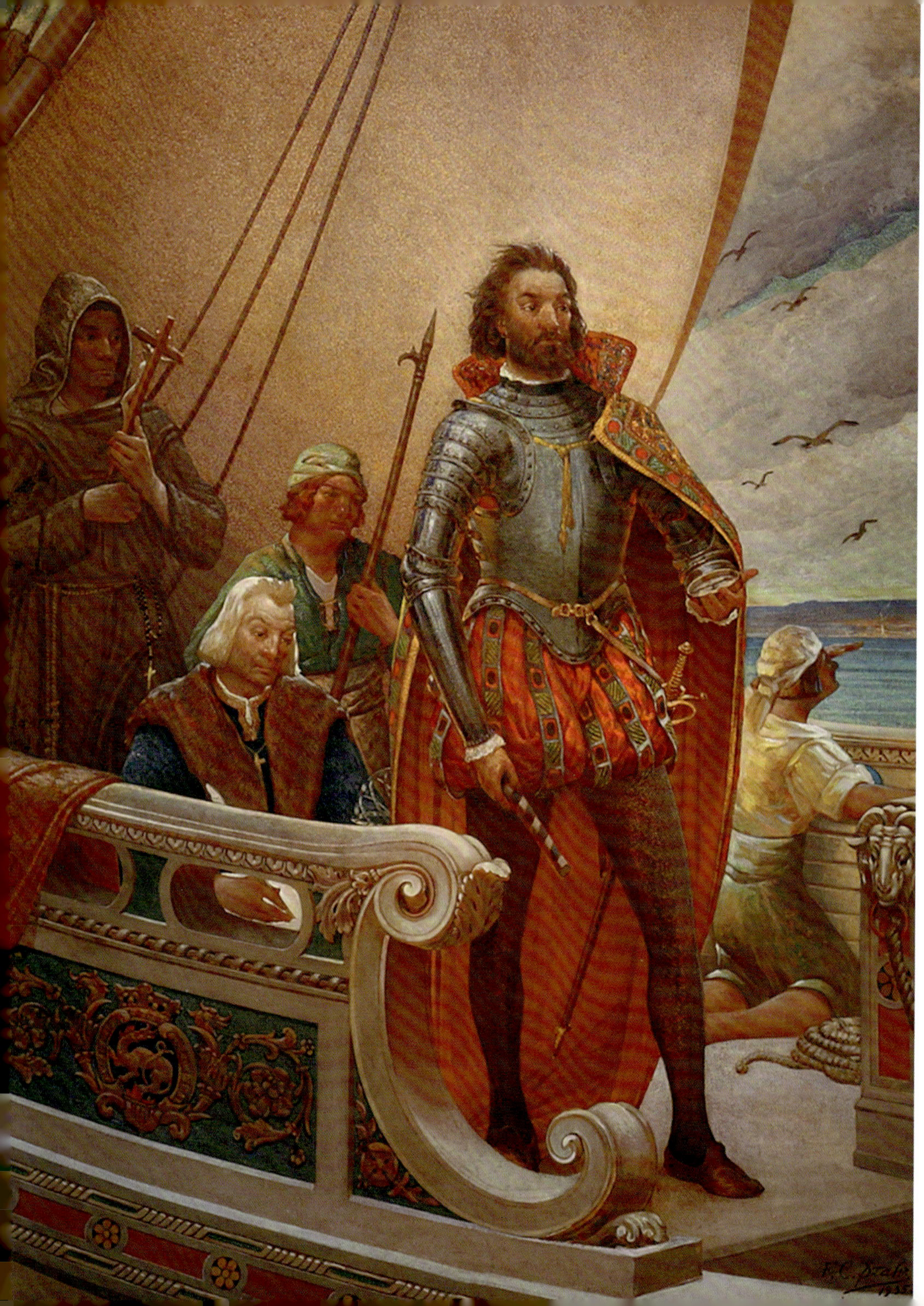
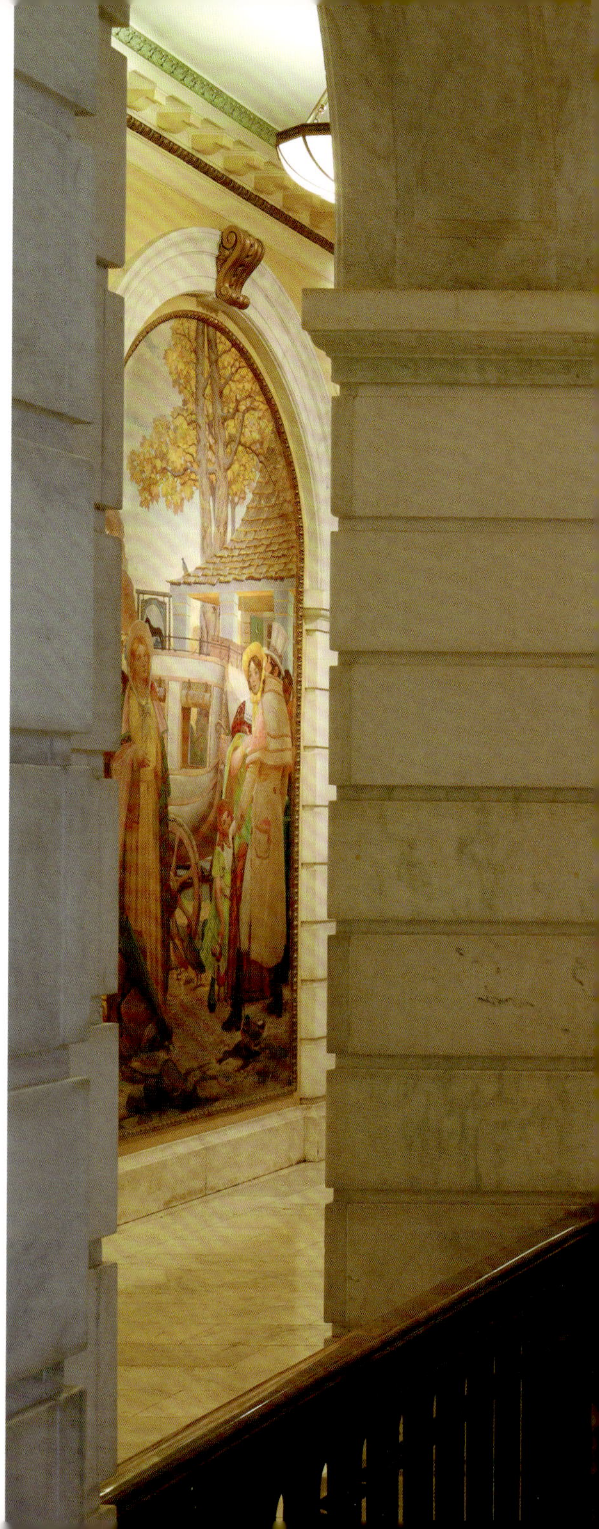

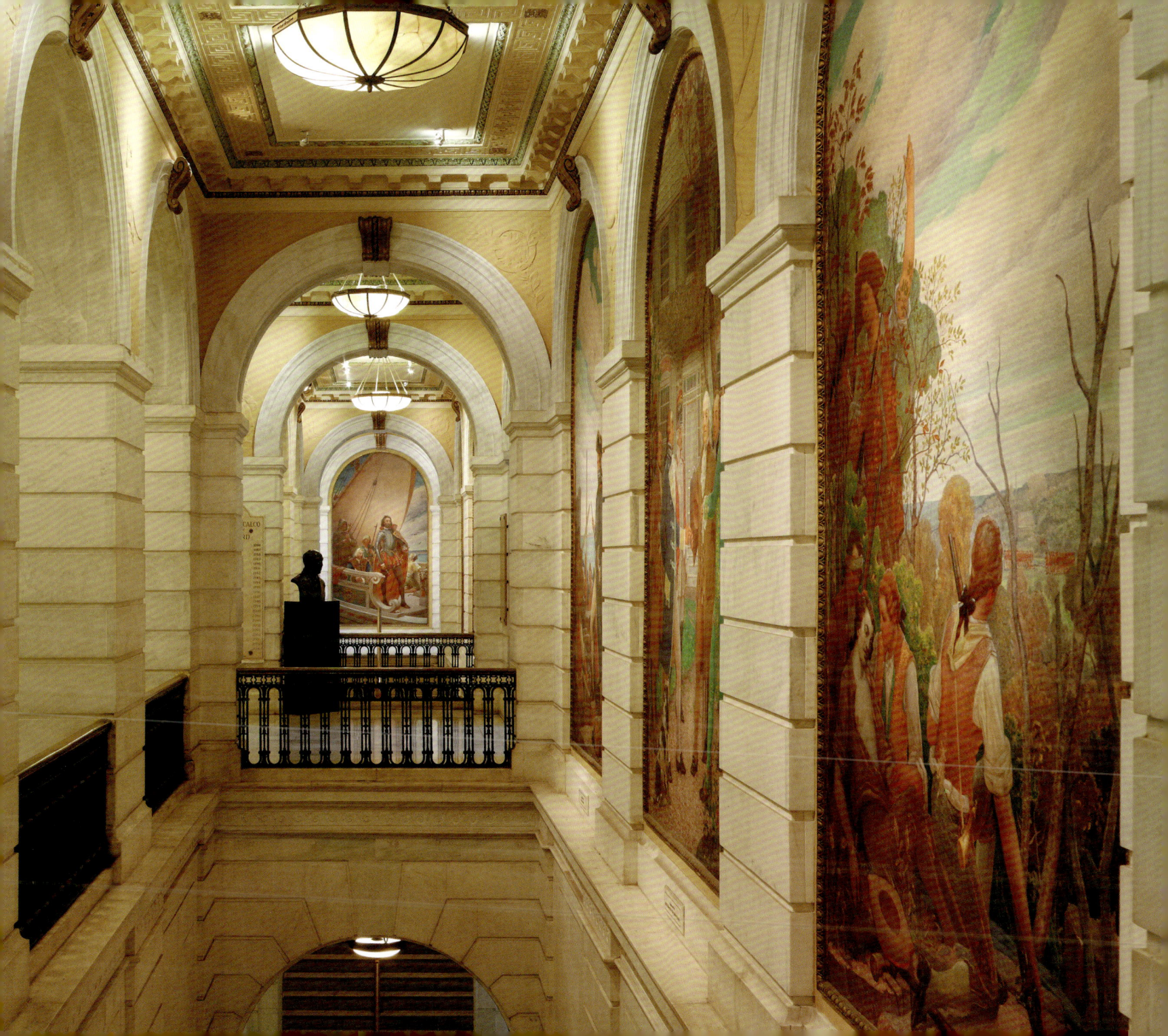

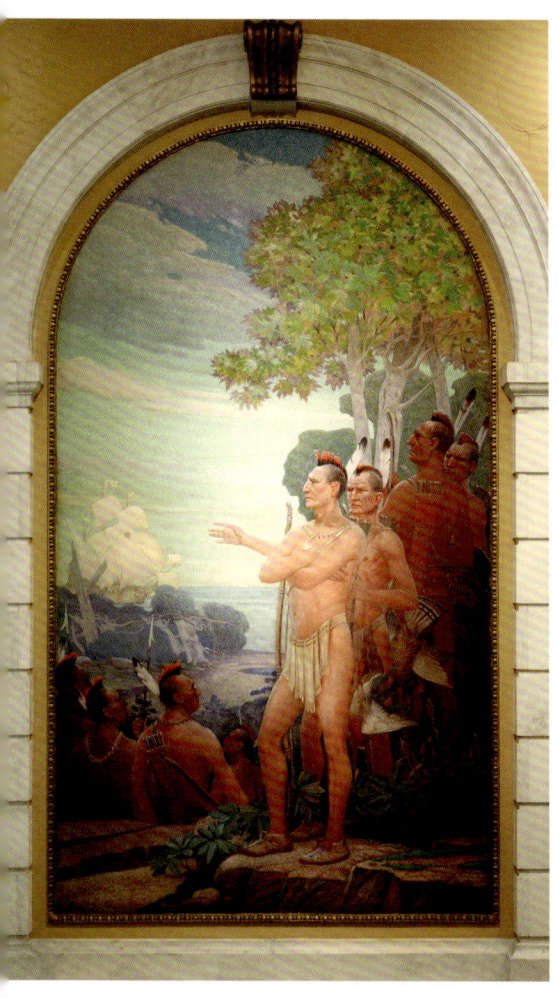
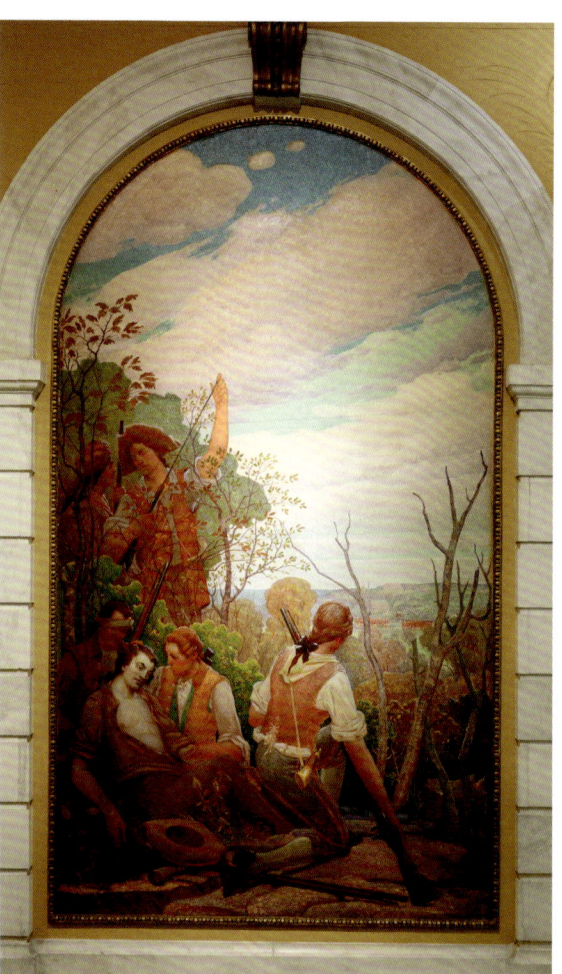
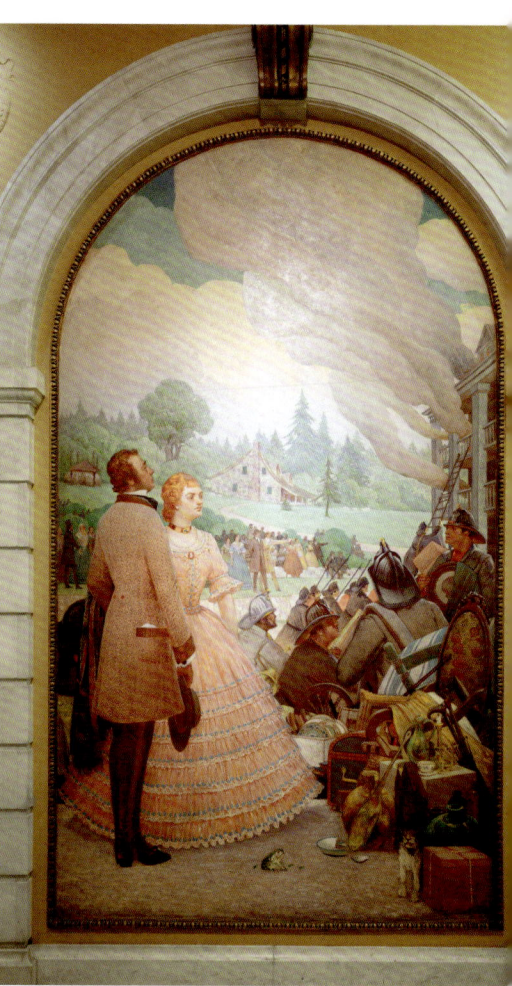

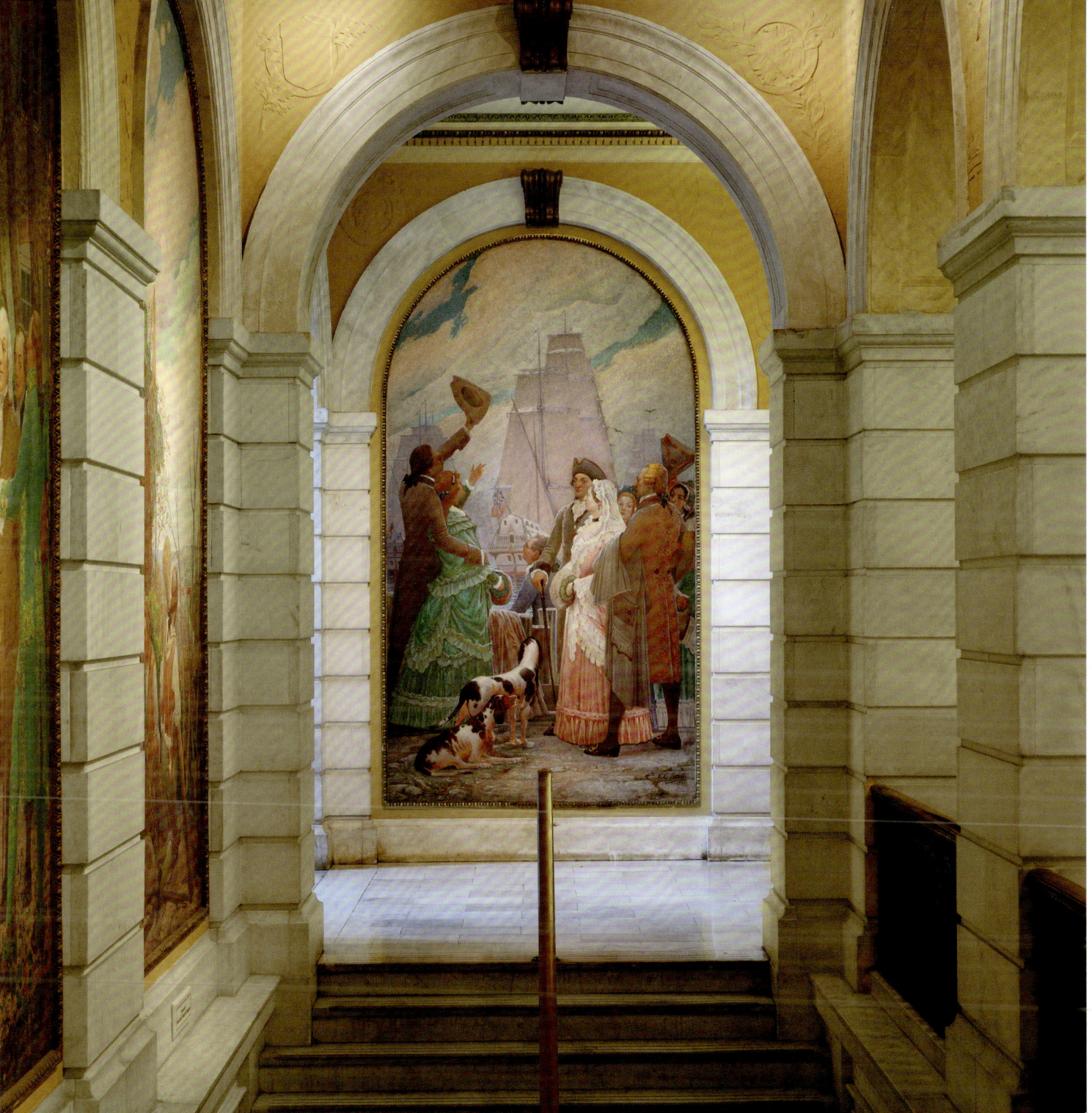

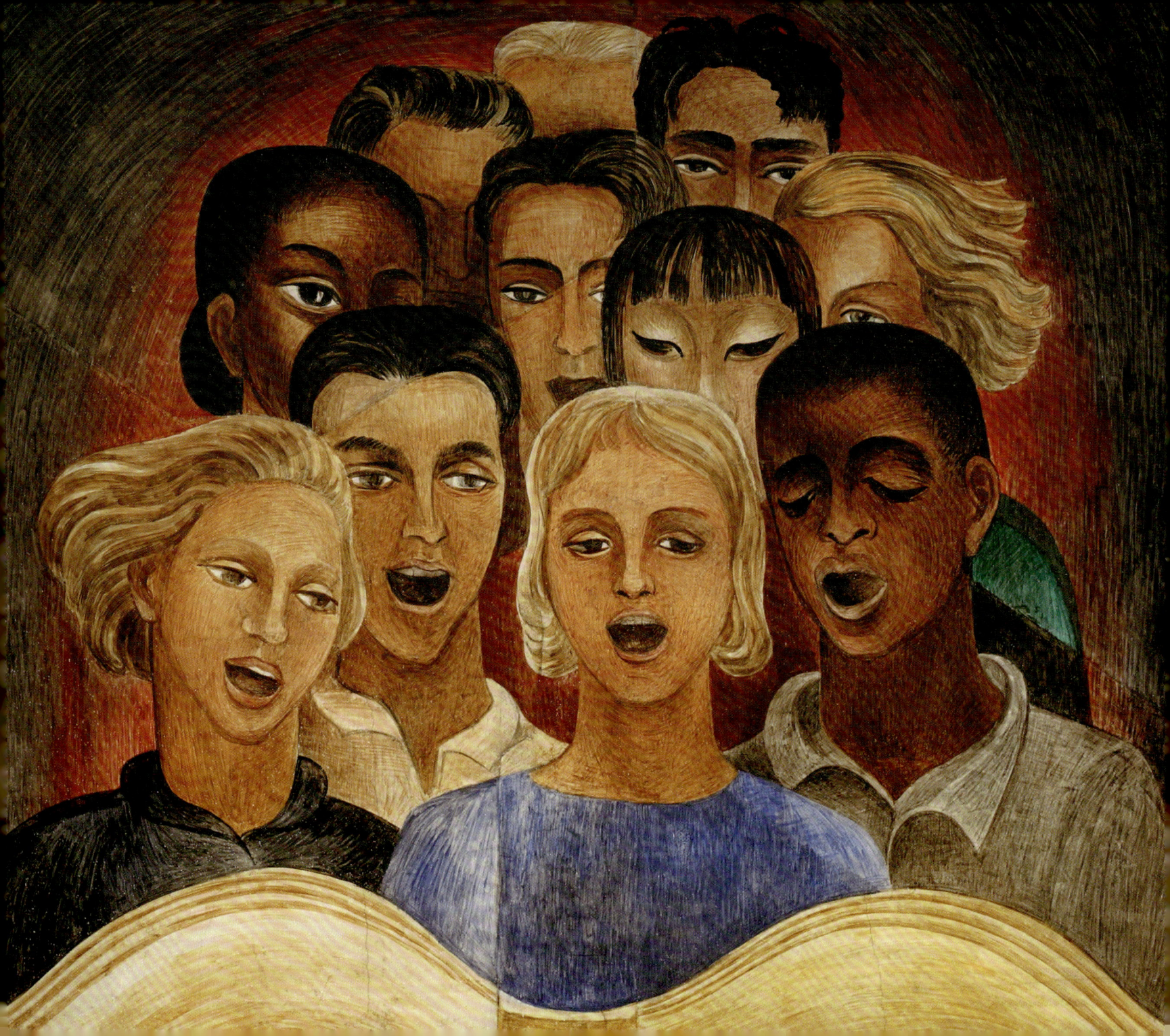

GEORGE WASHINGTON HIGH SCHOOL

Following in the Social Realism movement championed by her mentor, Diego Rivera, Lucienne Bloch, along with her husband Steve "Dimi" Dimitroff, created more than fifty murals from 1935 to 1939. But it was a moment on May 8, 1933, for which she is best remembered.

Bloch was assisting Rivera on his fresco, *Man at the Crossroads*, in the great hall of 30 Rockefeller Plaza. Rivera, a devoted Communist, included a portrait of Vladimir Lenin in the composition. Nelson Rockefeller ordered him to remove it, but Rivera refused. Rockefeller decreed that no photographs of what he viewed as the desecration of his property would be allowed. Security guards, armed with revolvers, sealed off the lobby. Their standoff was front-page news, and on that day, Bloch had concealed a Leica camera in her voluminous overalls. Accompanying Lucienne that day were Rivera's wife, Frida Kahlo, and Dimi, his chief fresco plasterer. Each had a part to play. Frida was to distract the guards while Bloch, pretending to prepare for the day's work, would secretly photograph the mural. Dimi was to make excessive noise to cover the sound of the Leica's clicking shutter. She photographed the sole visual record of Rivera's masterpiece. Rockefeller's forces had underestimated the courage and resolve of a tiny twenty-four-year-old woman. Eventually the mural, in an act of cultural vandalism, was demolished. But, with Bloch's photographs as reference, Rivera re-created the painting in Mexico City's Palacio de Bellas Artes—proving that the pen is mightier than the sword and the brush more enduring than the pickaxe.

Bloch painted murals throughout New York City: one in the Madison House on the Lower East Side, *The Cycle of a Woman's Life* for the Manhattan Women's House of Detention's segregated black prisoners recreation room, one in the New York Workers School, and a mural for the Swiss Pavilion at the 1939 World's Fair.

The Evolution of Music, painted in 1938 for the music room of George Washington High School in Manhattan, is her only surviving New York mural.

Bloch was the Geneva-born daughter of the classical composer and photographer Ernest Bloch. After her father became the director of the San Francisco Conservatory of Music, her mother moved the children to Paris. There, her artistic genius flowered during her studies at l'École des Beaux-Arts. She studied sculpture and became so accomplished in working with glass that Frank Lloyd Wright invited her to teach at Taliesin East. It was about that same time when she met Diego Rivera.

Some years later, when she painted *The Evolution of Music*, Bloch had developed her own aesthetic vision. Her faith in music's potential to eclipse ethnic, religious, and racial differences provides the mural with a richness and depth. The work is organized according to Jay Hambidge's theory of dynamic symmetry, in which the symmetry of classical art and nature can be quantified and mathematically applied to create visual harmony in painting. The triangles and rectangles in her composition create their own music.

In 1991, through the Municipal Art Society's Adopt-A-Mural program, the singer Madonna and Agnes Gund, then president of the Museum of Modern Art, paid for the restoration of the mural. At the rededication, Bloch spoke about her painting:

"When I came into the room for the first time, I asked myself, 'What in music is visual?' I went to the library, and while there I suddenly realized that music is composed of sound waves. So I made an oscillating pattern to run through the whole fresco and tie it together. That's visual. I decided to put in instruments representing music from all over the world. My father, Ernest Bloch, was a composer, and he used to give us children records so that we could learn about music from Arab countries, from Polynesia . . . everywhere. My sister became fascinated by medieval European music, and, because of her interest, she learned to play the lute. So I painted her over there in the medieval section with her instrument. Then comes the modern orchestra, with the prima-donna conductor, all the lights trained on his beautiful hair. That's [Leopold] Stokowski. Next to this you see the composer writing music in the dark. That's my father. Then come a group of black hands clapping, just the way you see them back there in the African section, but with white gloves on—jazz. It ends up with barbed wire. Remember, this was 1938, and Hitler was in power. I saw war coming and showed it. But I had a little bit of optimism, and on top of a wire I put one bird."

After finishing the music mural, she and Dimi moved back to his hometown of Flint, Michigan, where he worked as a union organizer and she taught art at the Flint Institute of Arts.

Lucienne Bloch was my first art teacher.

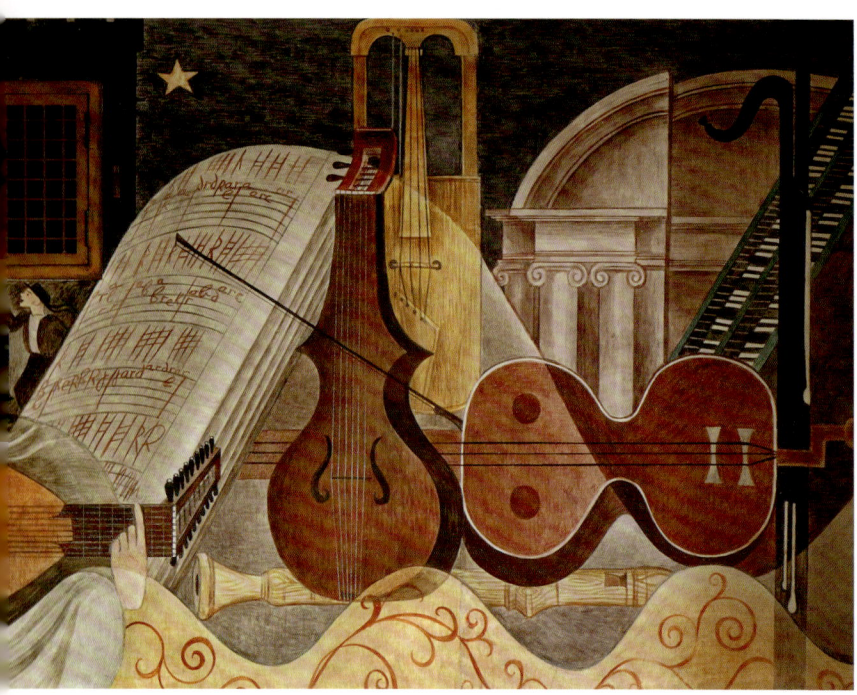

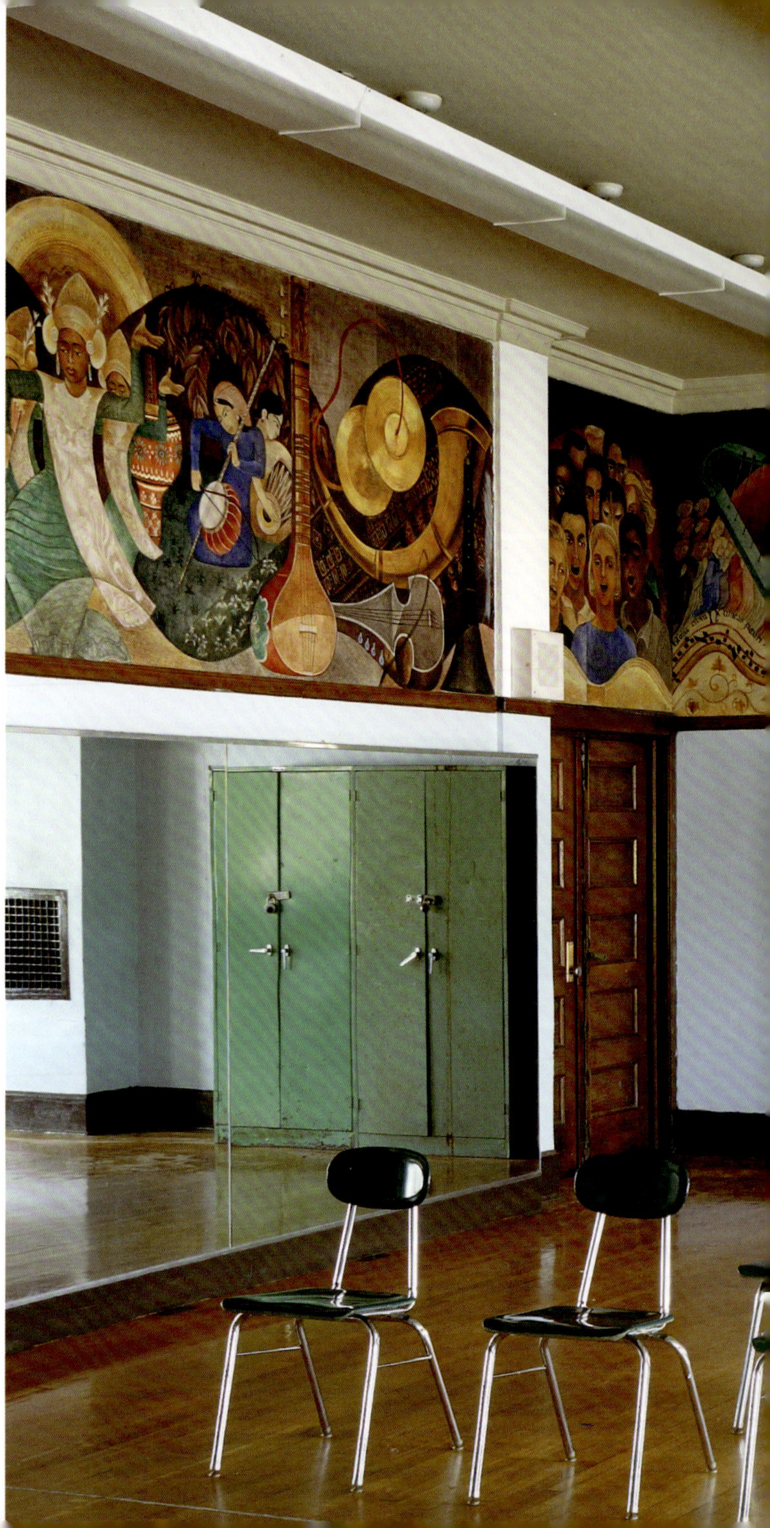

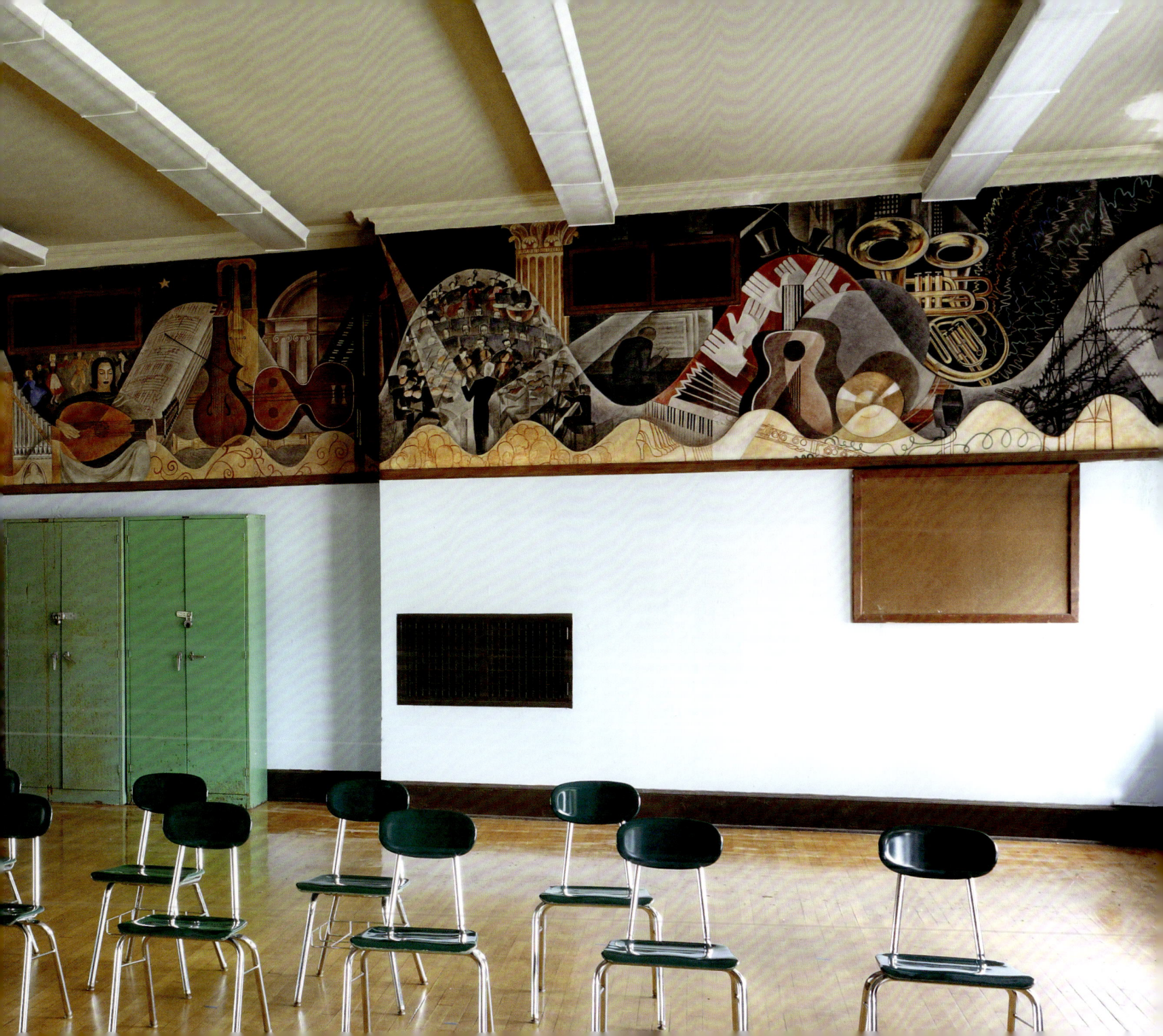

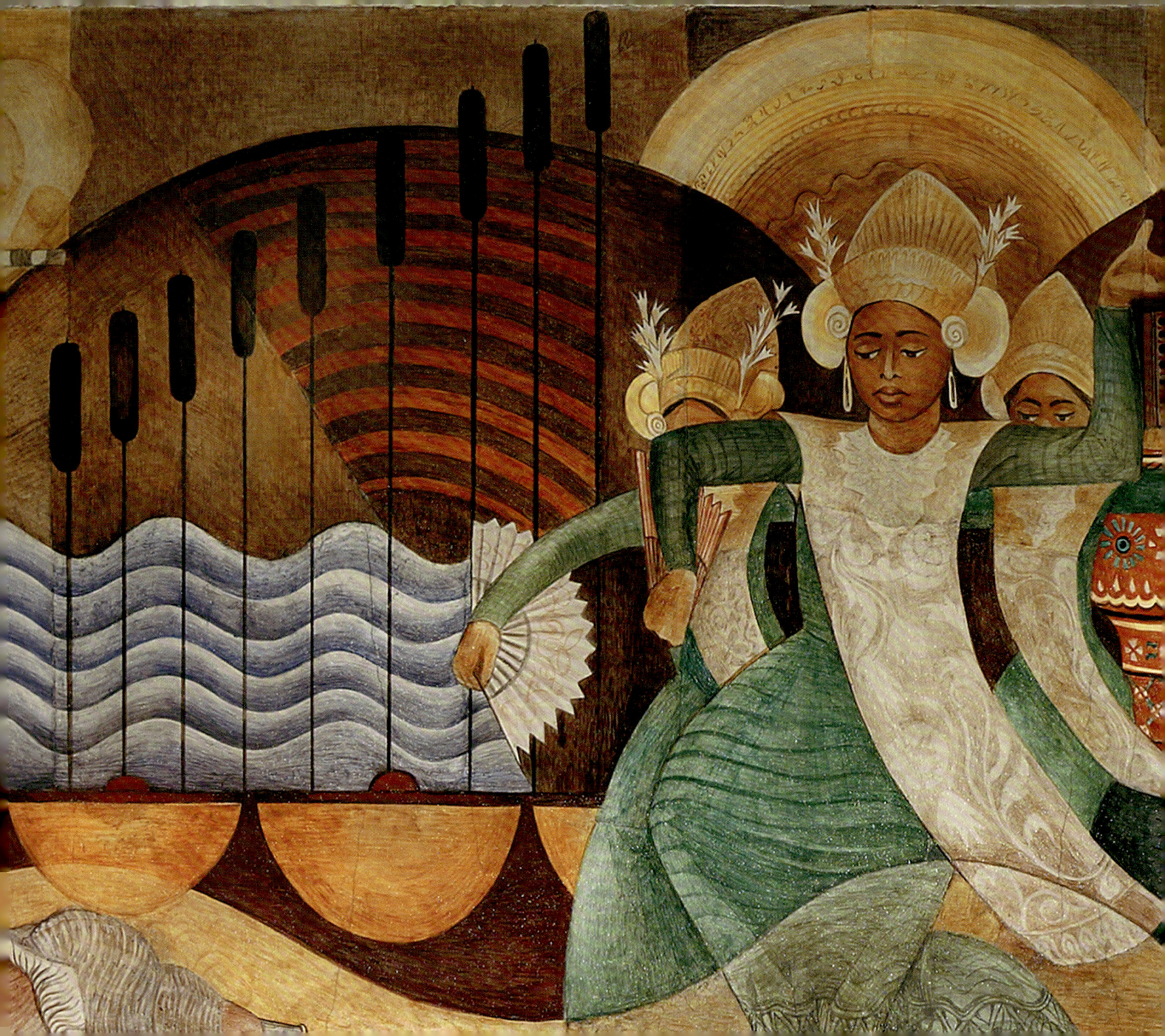

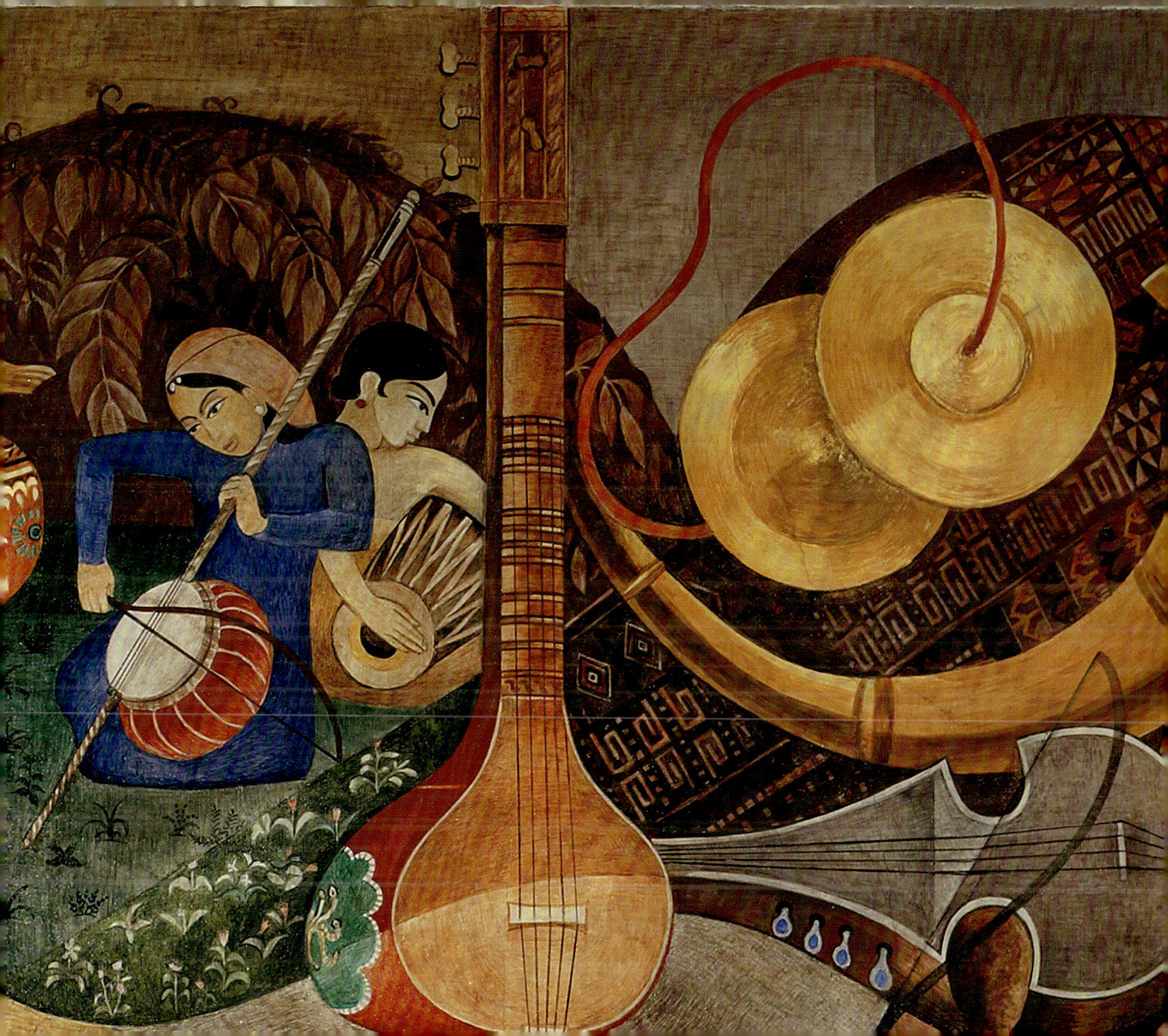

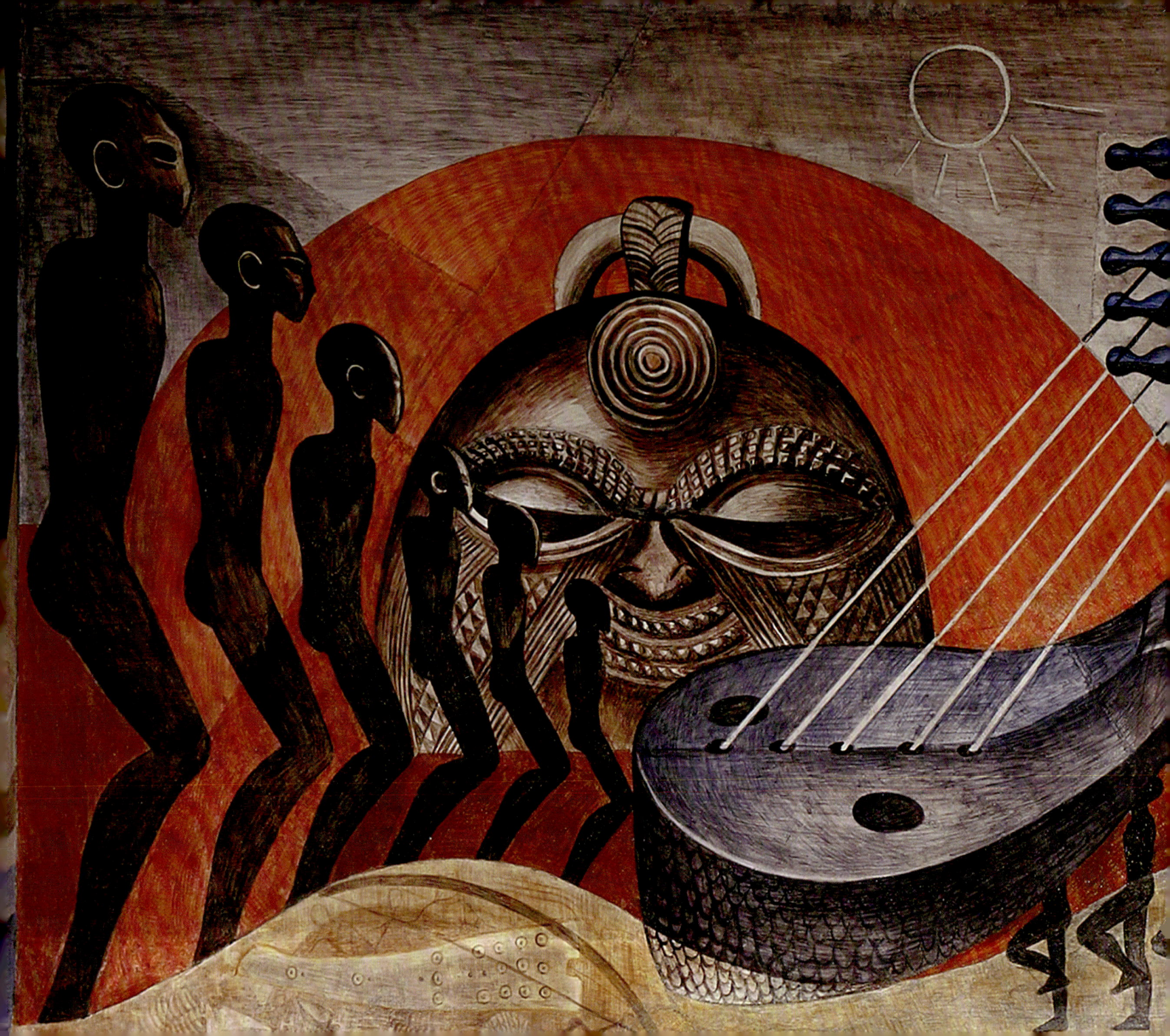

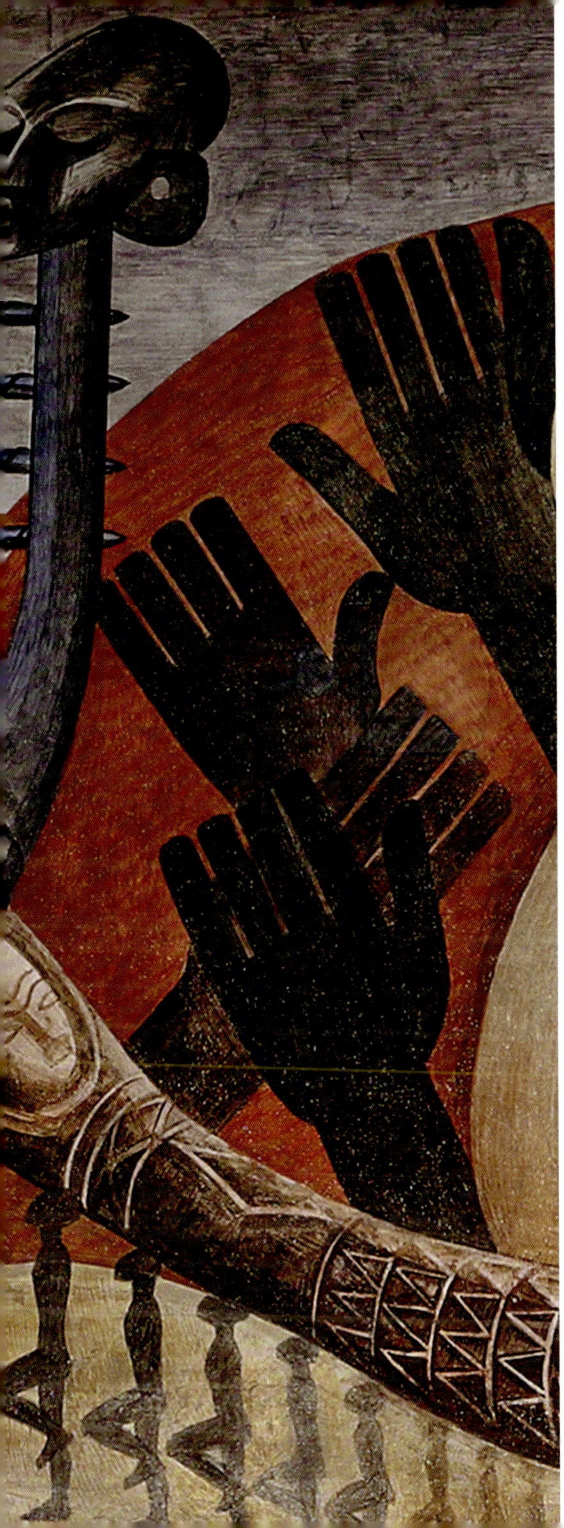

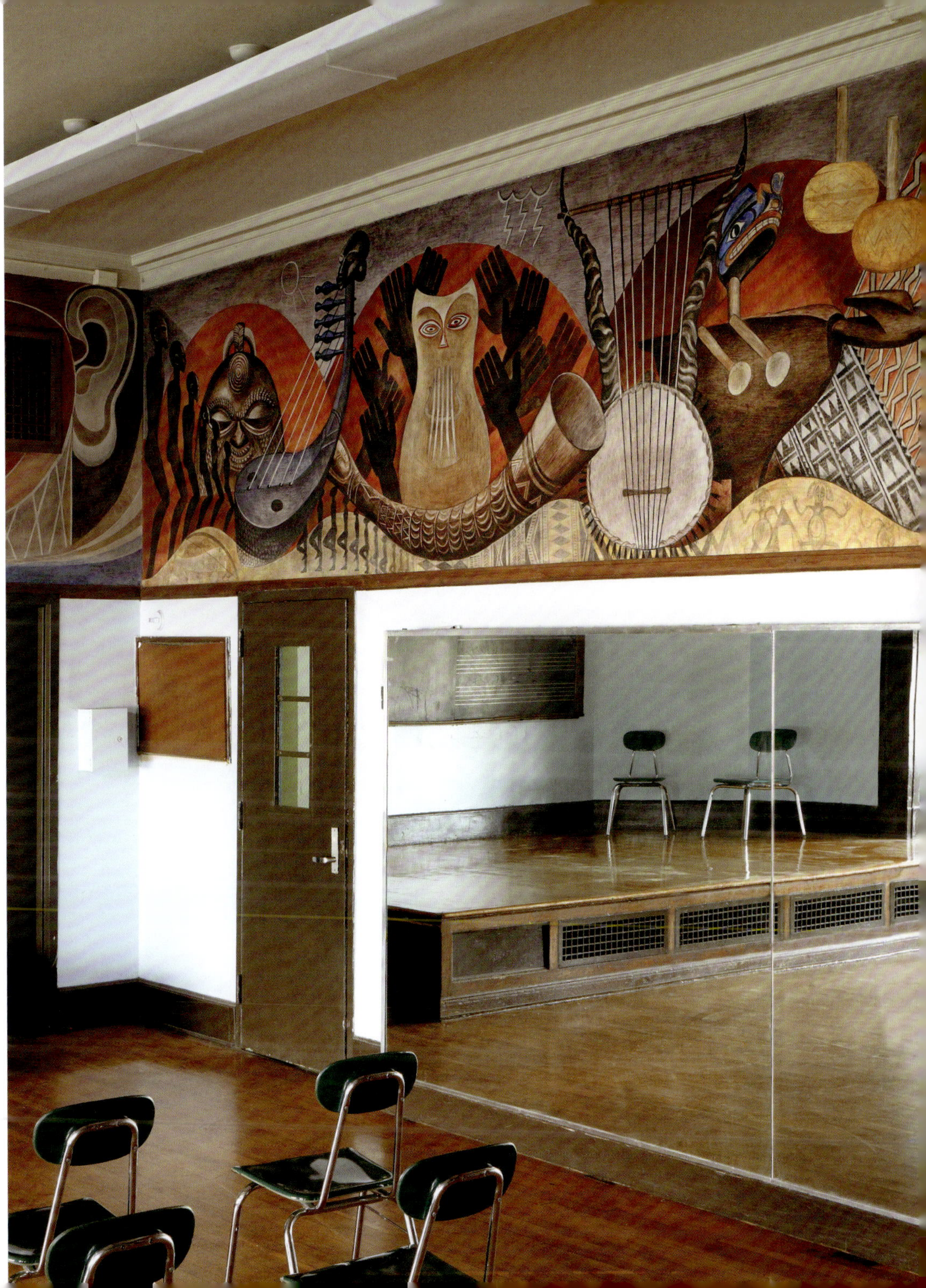

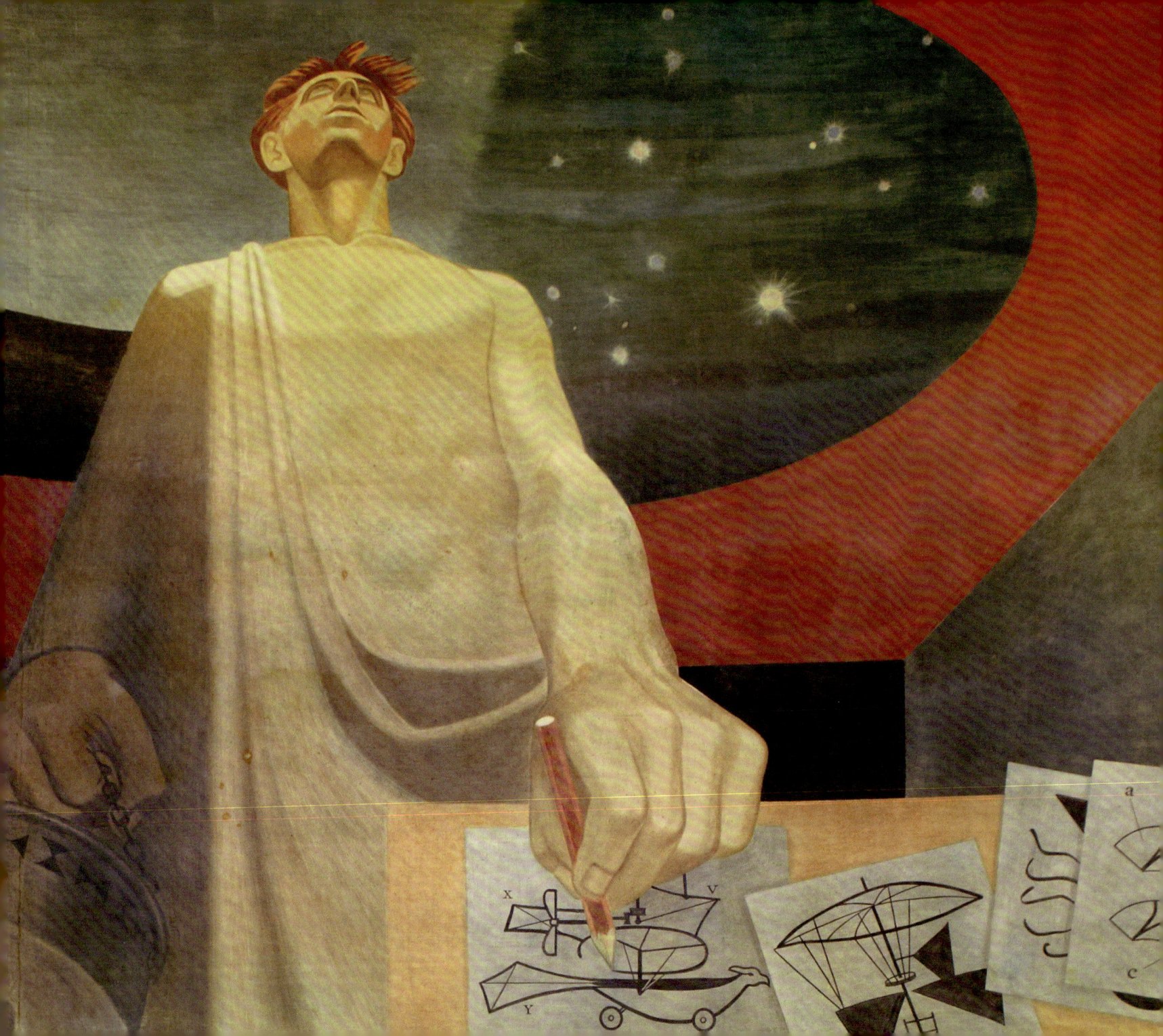

MARINE AIR TERMINAL

LaGuardia Airport, Queens • JAMES BROOKS

The Marine Air Terminal at LaGuardia Airport, designed by society architect William Adams Delano, echoed the Art Deco elegance of Rockefeller Center. This showplace, like the lobby of 30 Rockefeller Plaza, needed a magnificent mural to balance the marbled severity of its rotunda.

The WPA chose James Brooks for the commission. This was Brooks's third project for the WPA, and it was clearly in tune with his Social Realist style. Painted between 1940 and 1942, *Flight* was the last and largest mural produced under the auspices of the WPA. The painting, measuring 237 feet long by 12 feet high, depicts the evolution of man's quest to conquer the skies, from legends to prehistory to transoceanic air travel. The narrative flows from the mythology of Icarus and Daedalus to the genius of da Vinci and the Wright brothers. Pre-World War II aerial navigators are shown plotting their routes with paper maps and rulers. The culmination of man's dream arrives at the golden age of the "flying boat," when glamorous Pan Am Clipper seaplanes would land on water after a flight from Lisbon, Rio, or any city with a sheltered harbor, and taxi up to the Marine Air Terminal dock.

Flight reigned over the terminal rotunda for only a decade. In 1952, at the height of McCarthy anti-Communist fervor, when creative people in all disciplines were being persecuted for their real—or imagined—political beliefs, the Port Authority bureaucracy found the mural's strong and muscular depiction of workers too socialist. In particular, these self-appointed art critics took exception to the mural's suggestion that air travel would be available one day for ordinary people and not just the military and the rich. The Port Authority officials ordered the mural to be painted over. Fortunately, Brooks had sealed the mural with varnish, so the coat of appropriately bureaucratic-gray house paint couldn't penetrate the surface; nevertheless, the painting was lost to a generation of New Yorkers and travelers passing through the terminal.

As the years ticked by, the vandalized mural was forgotten until amateur aviation historian Geoffrey Arend, who was also the publisher of *Air Cargo News* and whose offices were in the building, ran across photographs taken at the terminal's inauguration. In the late 1970s, on his own initiative, he launched a campaign to restore the mural. He displayed those photographs in the terminal lobby so that wealthy New Yorkers on their way to their private planes would see the censored treasure hidden around them and that awareness might spark an interest in uncovering it.

The gambit worked. In 1980, Laurence Rockefeller and *Reader's Digest* founder DeWitt Wallace put up $75,000 to have the long-lost mural restored. Brooks, then in his eighties, was overjoyed with the resurrection of his masterpiece. It was rededicated on September 18, 1980, and has since been designated a New York City landmark and is listed in the National Register of Historic Places.

Today, in contrast to our perspective of democratized opportunity, *Flight* offers a glimpse into a time when air travel was considered a luxury reserved for the rich—and when the thought of ordinary people enjoying that freedom was dangerously subversive.

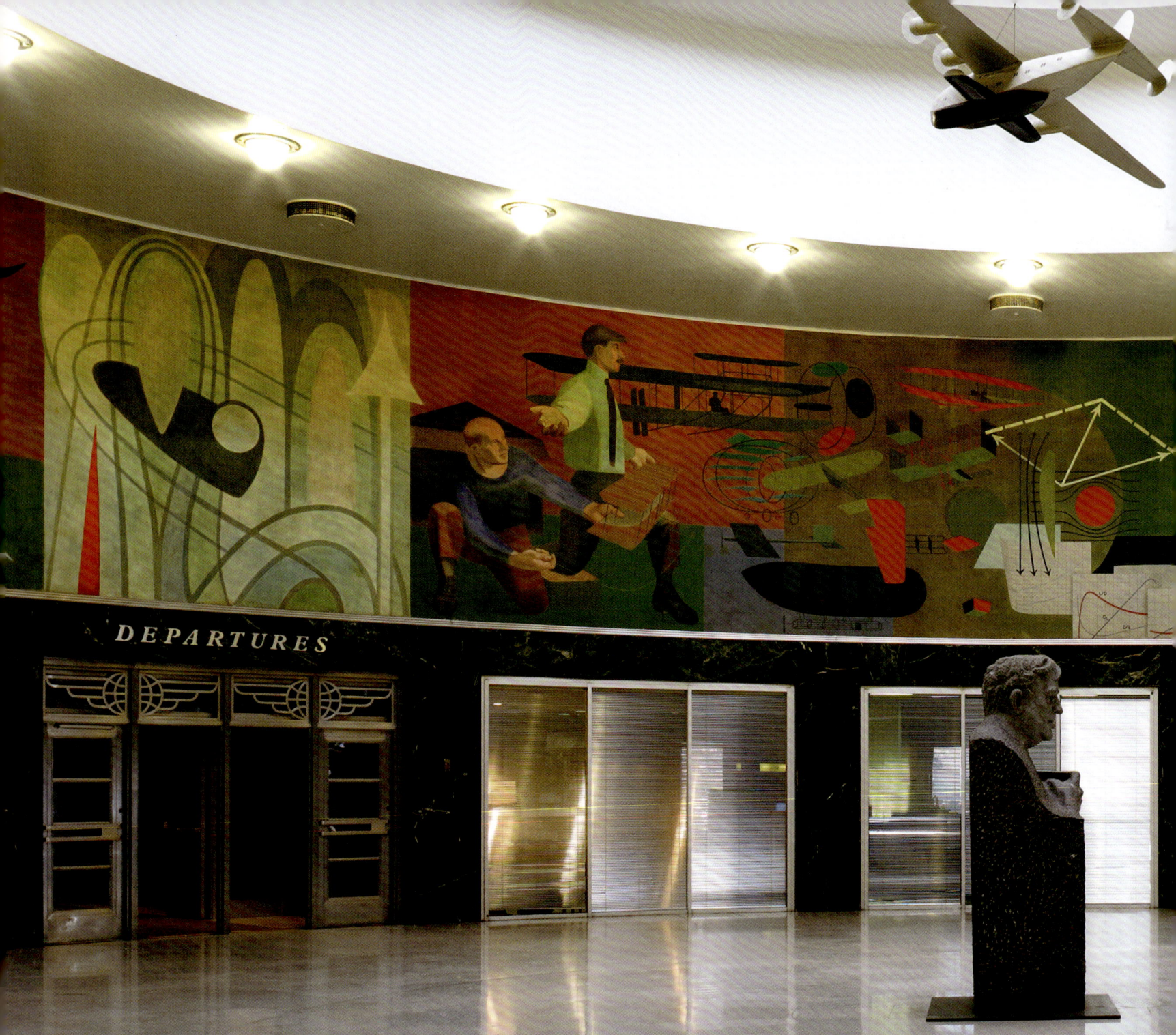

DEPARTURES

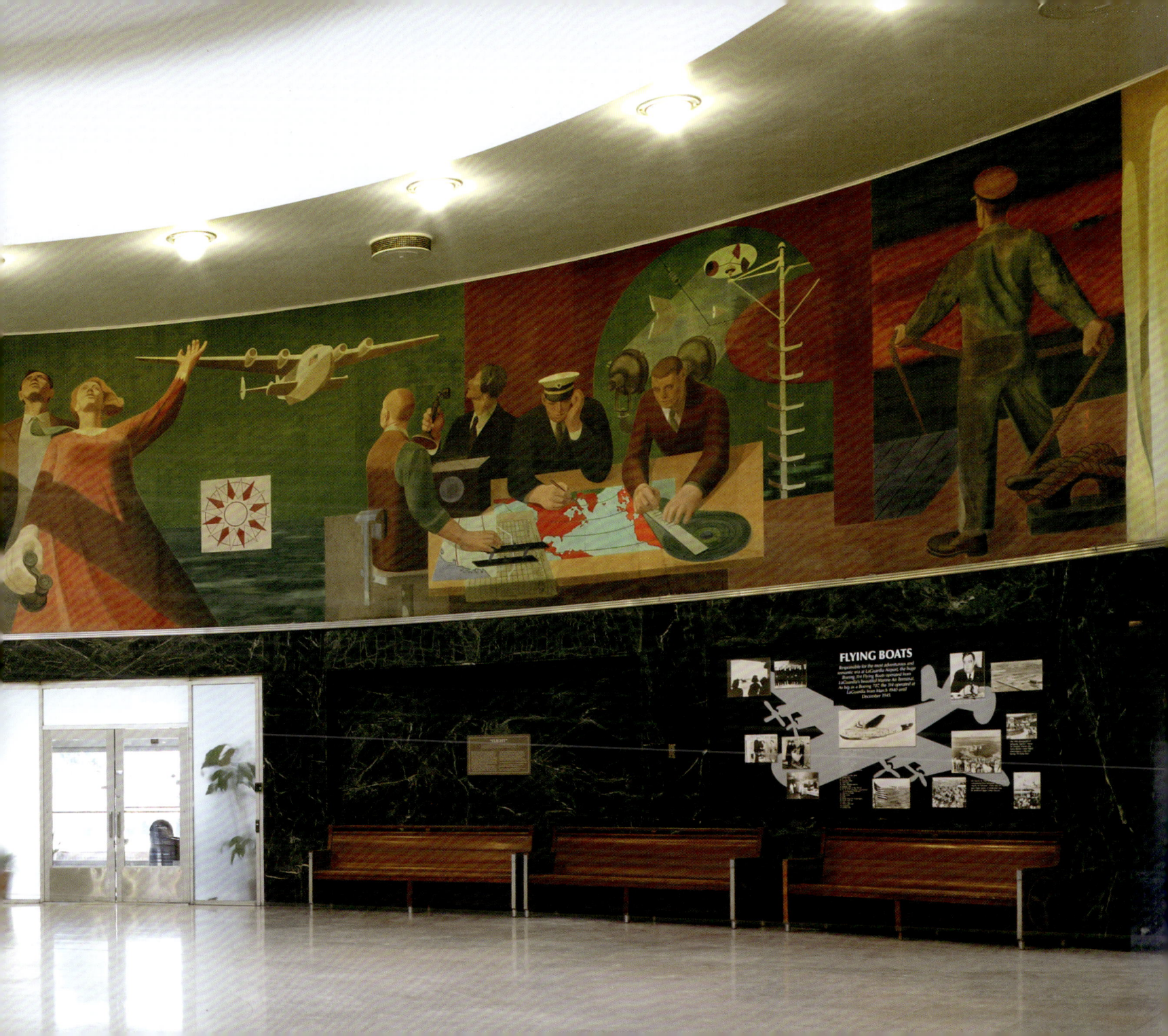

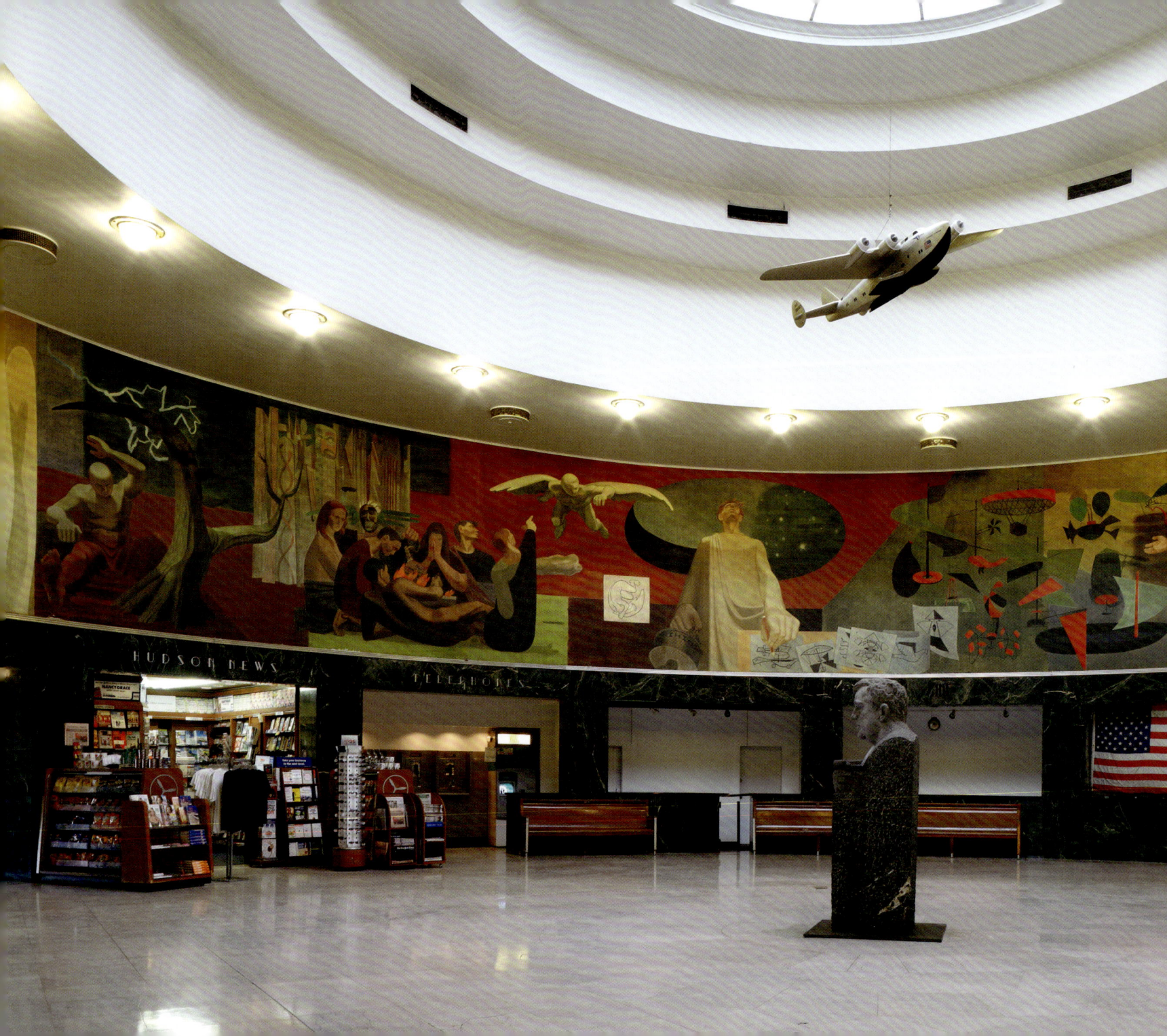

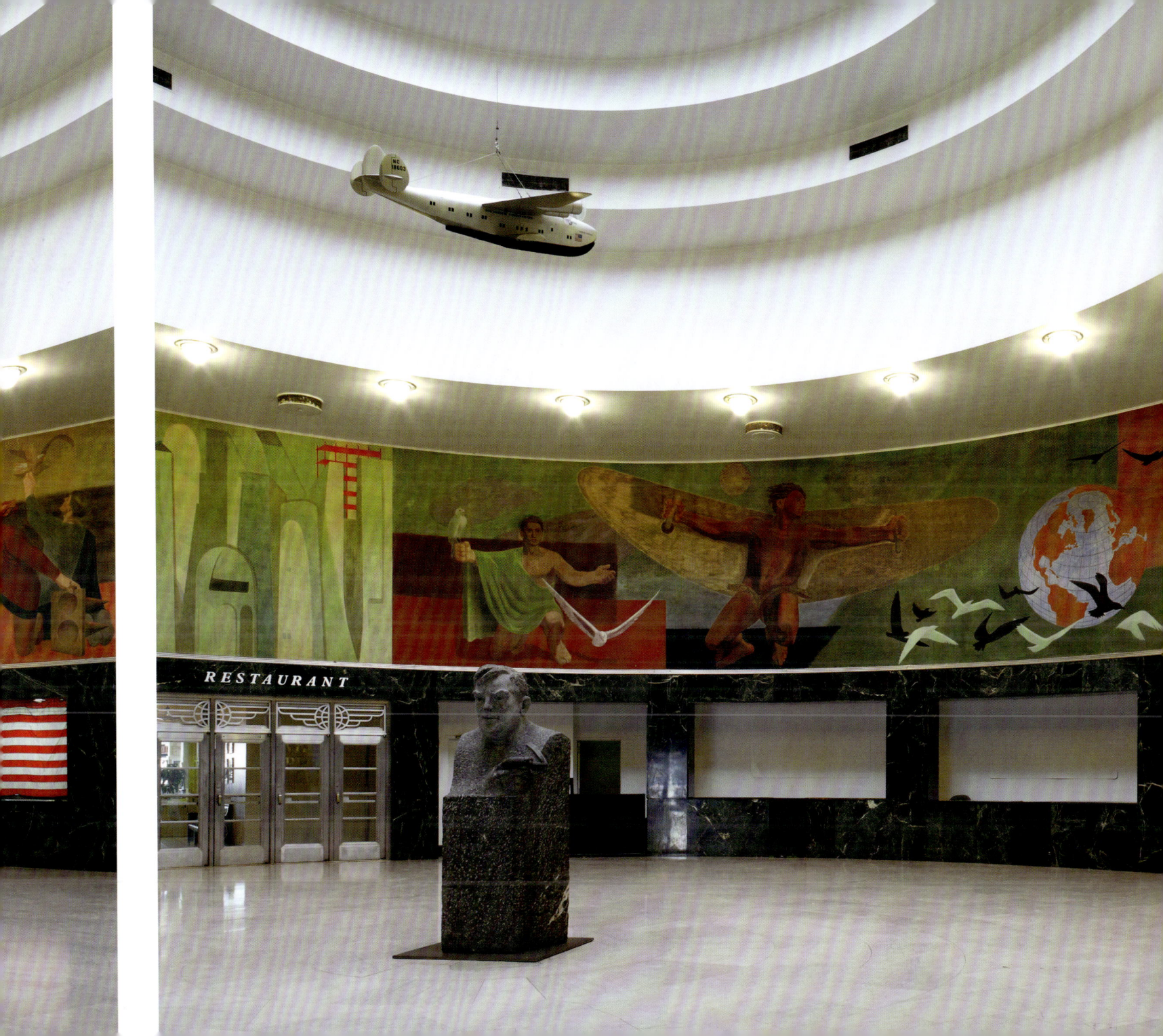

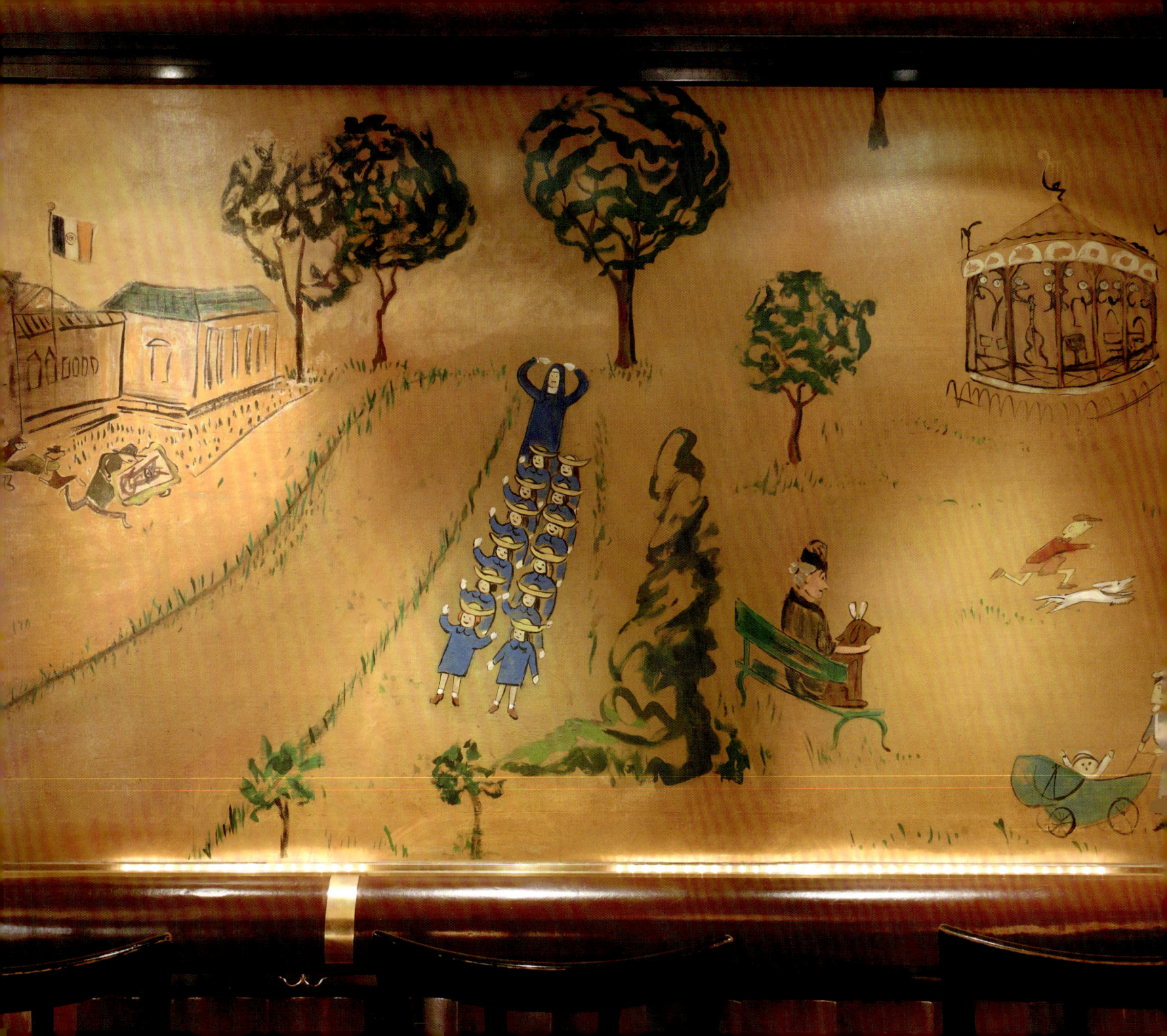

BEMELMANS BAR

35 East 76th Street, Manhattan · LUDWIG BEMELMANS

Fabulist. Fab-u-list, noun. 1: a creator or writer of fables 2: liar

Ludwig Bemelmans was a fabulist. Much of what he wanted us to know about his eventful life came from his vibrant imagination. What we do know as fact is that he left his troubled childhood in Europe to become the consummate New Yorker: an energetic, charming, nonconforming, spirited, free-spending, restless bon vivant who was always on the go and getting himself in and out of all sorts of fascinating situations.

According to history, or in his case, his story, he escaped a terrible childhood in Germany and began his life in America working at New York's famed Astor Hotel as a busboy, eventually moving up the ranks and to the Ritz, where he worked for fifteen years. He lived in William Randolph Hearst's private suite while Hearst was in California, bought a Hispano-Suiza touring car, and employed a Senegalese chauffeur and a personal valet—all while he also freelancing as an illustrator and cartoonist.

After Bemelmans quit the hotel business to become a full-time artist, book editor May Massee came to dinner at Bemelmans's flat on Gramercy Park. Captivated by the whimsical vision and humor she saw in his painted furniture and walls, especially the straw-hatted donkeys parading along the dining room wall, she insisted he write children's books.

By 1938 he was remarried and flush enough to take his second wife, Madeleine, and little daughter to France on holiday. While convalescing in the hospital on the island of Île d'Yeu after colliding on his bicycle with a car, he met his muse, a precocious little girl who had had her appendix removed. He returned to New York with an idea for a children's book and wrote the now-famous introductory rhyme to *Madeline* on the back of a menu in Pete's Tavern on 18th Street and Irving Place. "It's always wonderful," he is quoted as saying, "when something altogether wrong ends right, without the help of religion or the police."

In 1947, he was approached by Robert Dowling, who owned the Hotel Carlyle at the time and wanted him to paint his whimsical designs on the walls of the hotel bar. Bemelmans traded his work for free rent in one of the luxury apartments in the hotel for a year and a half.

The mural is a four-season Central Park fantasy. Like an adult version of a children's picture book, there are rabbits tobogganing and smoking cigars, a monkey in a top hat staring at a caged banker, two cats looking at a naked woman, and elephants ice-skating in front of high-rises as the snow drifts down on them. On the base of an equestrian statue is his signature: "Bemelmans 47." And, of course, Madeline and her convent-school classmates have a cameo.

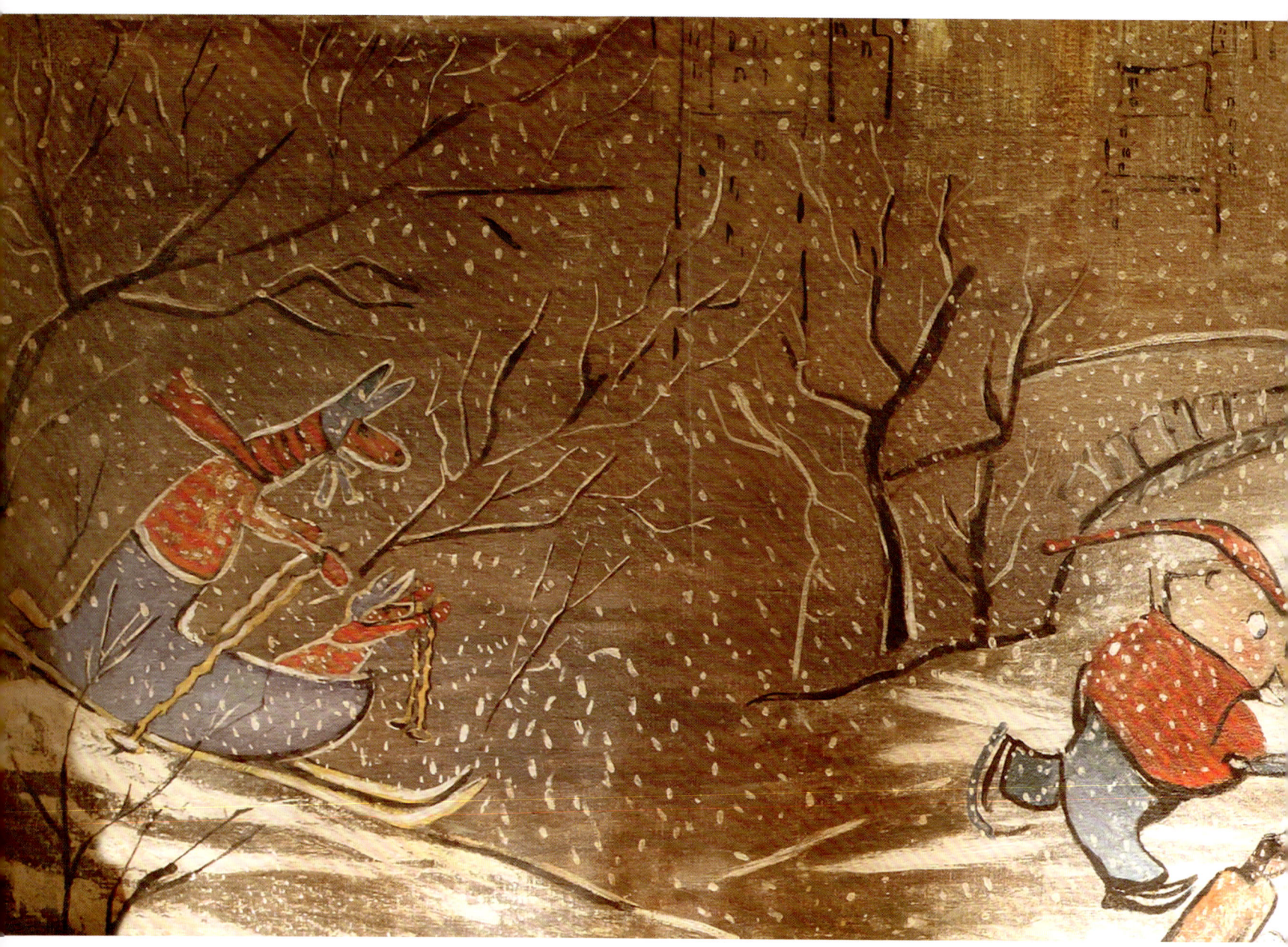

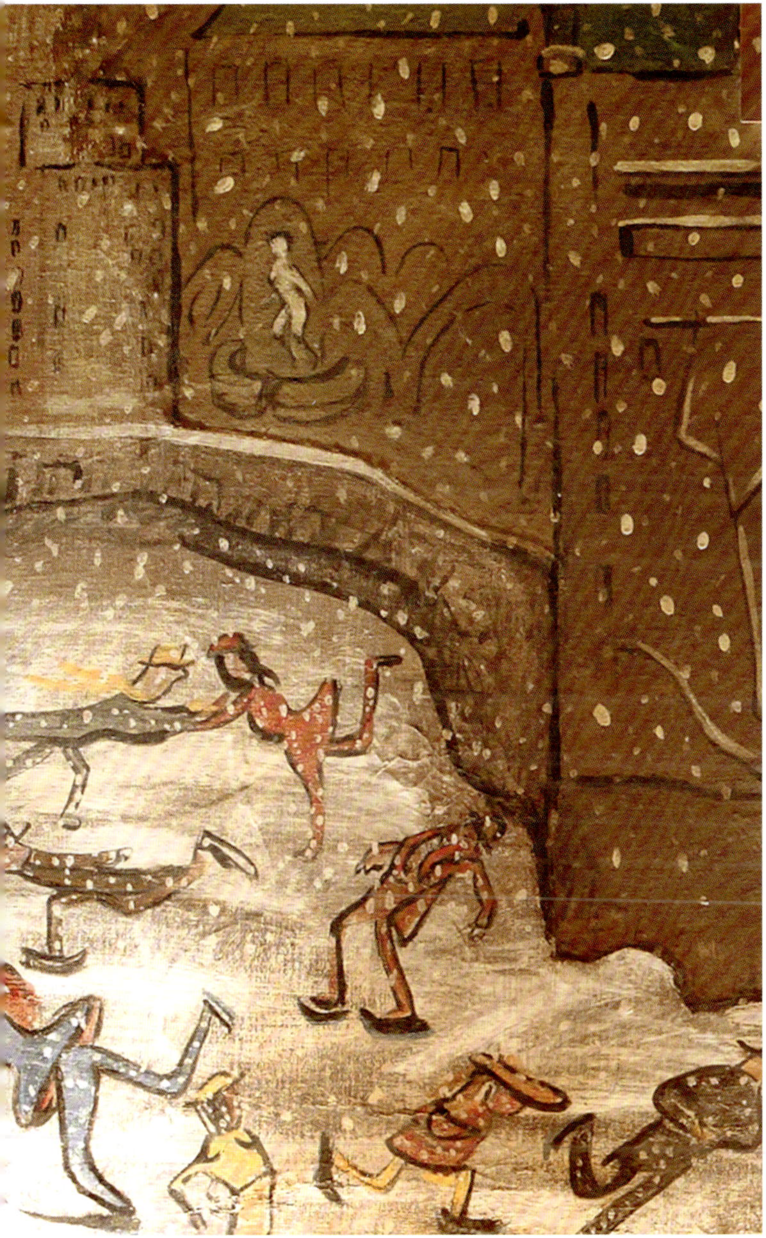

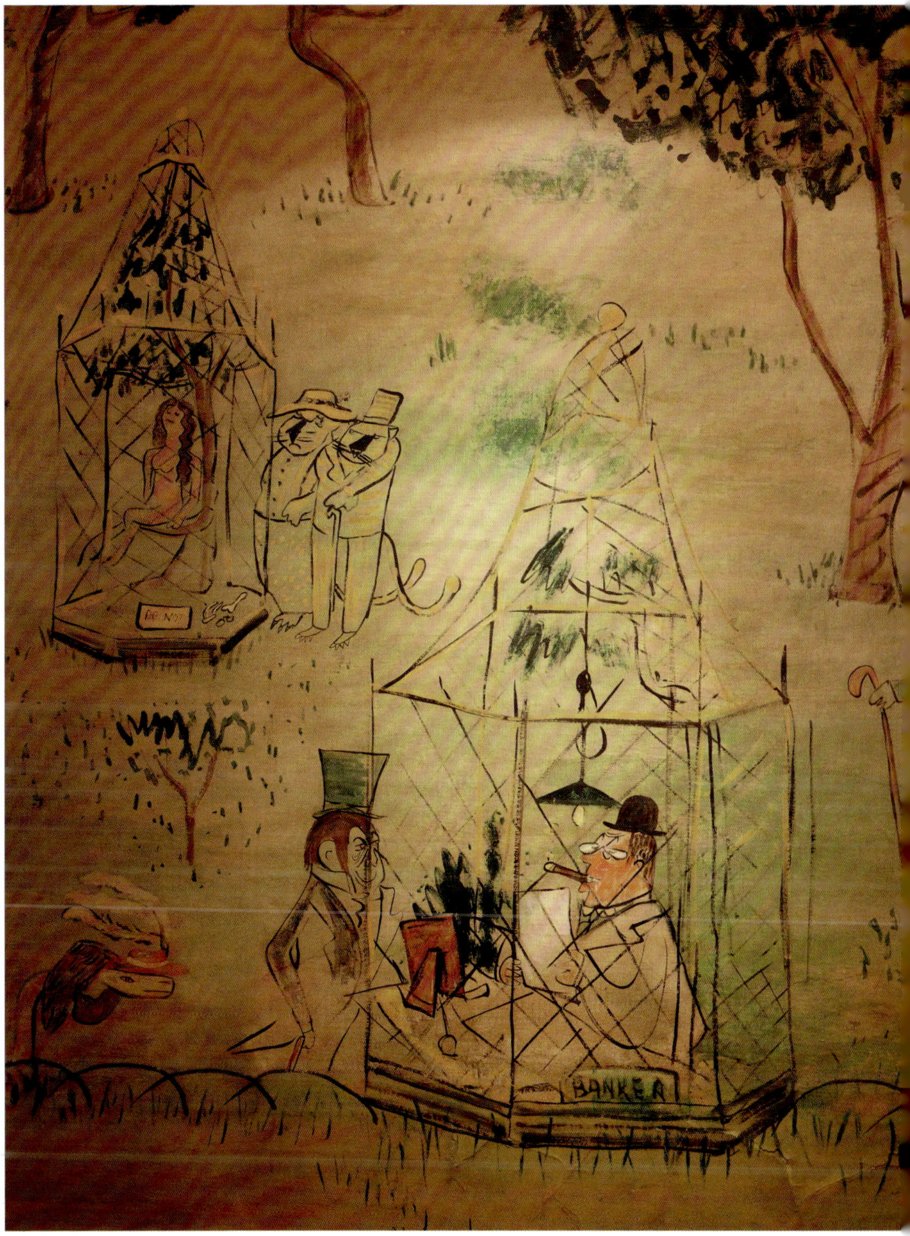
BANKER

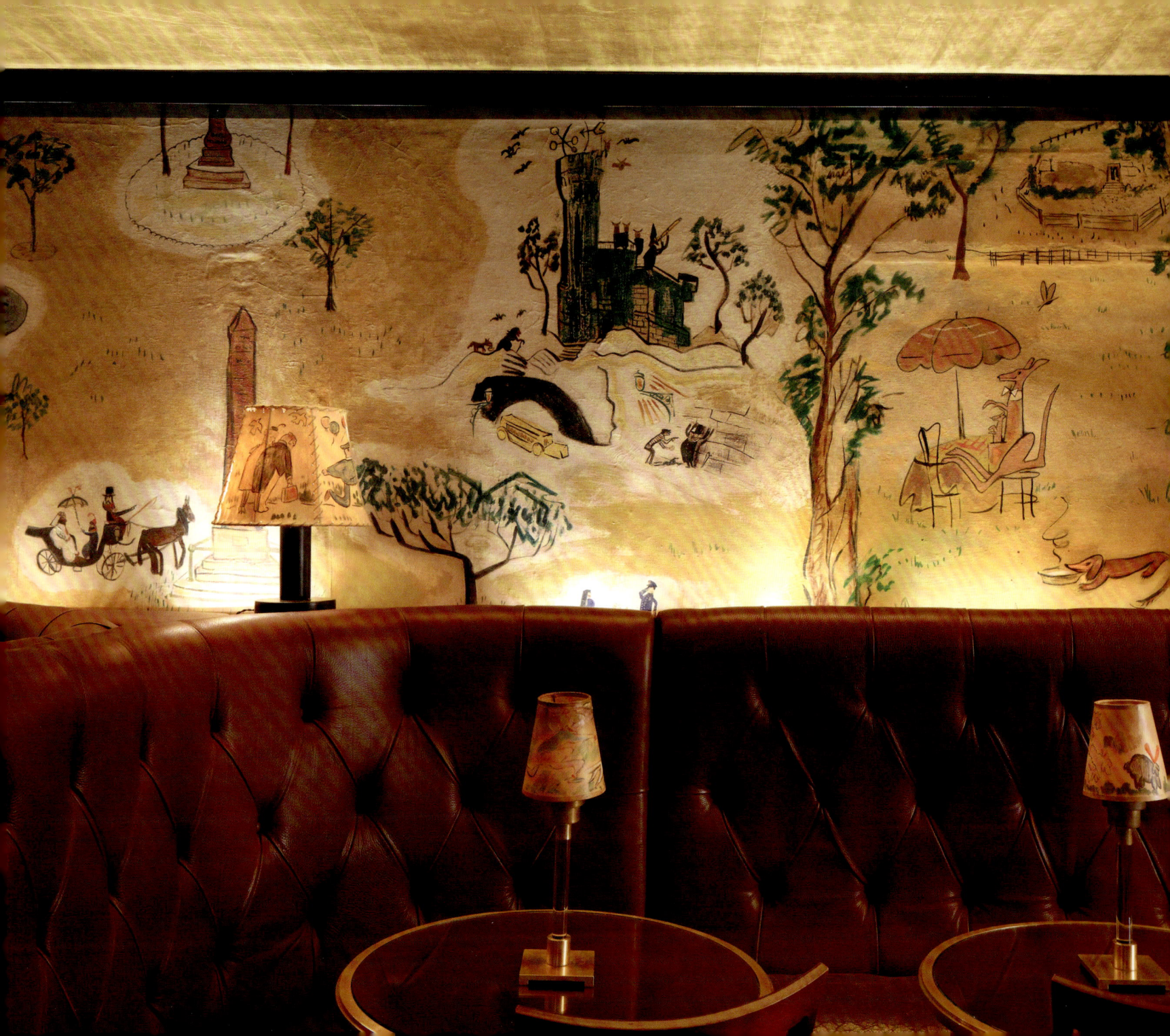

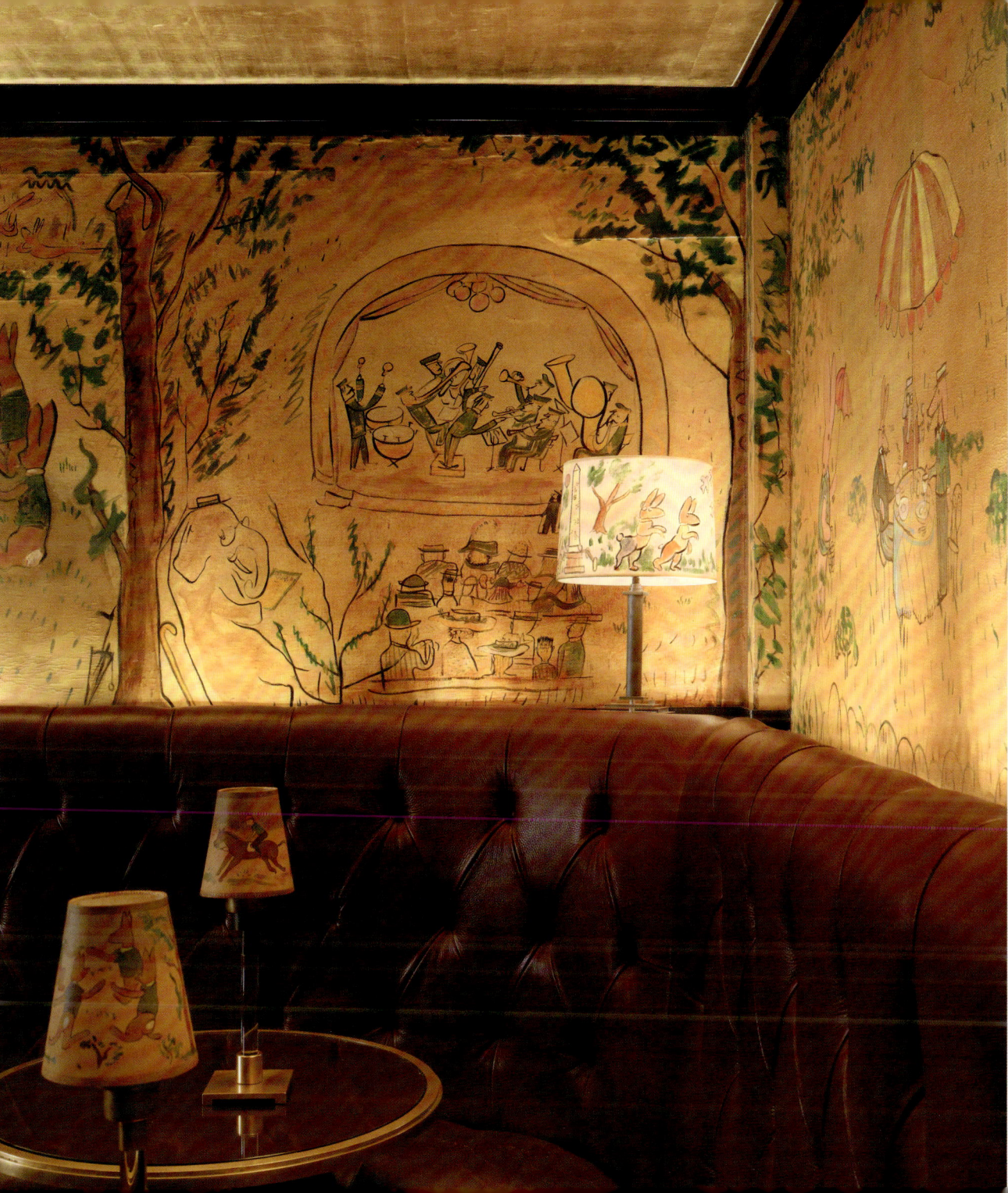

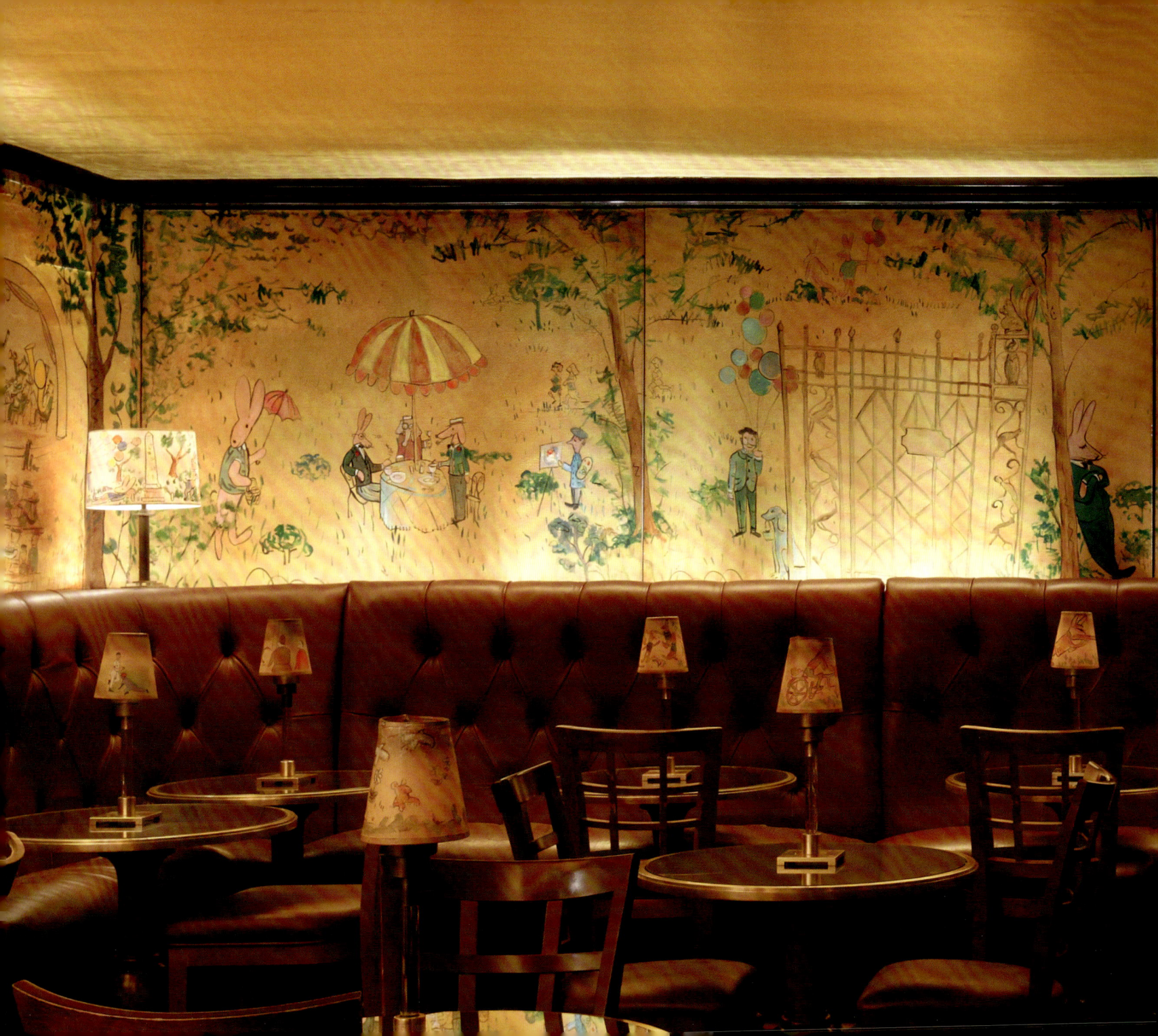

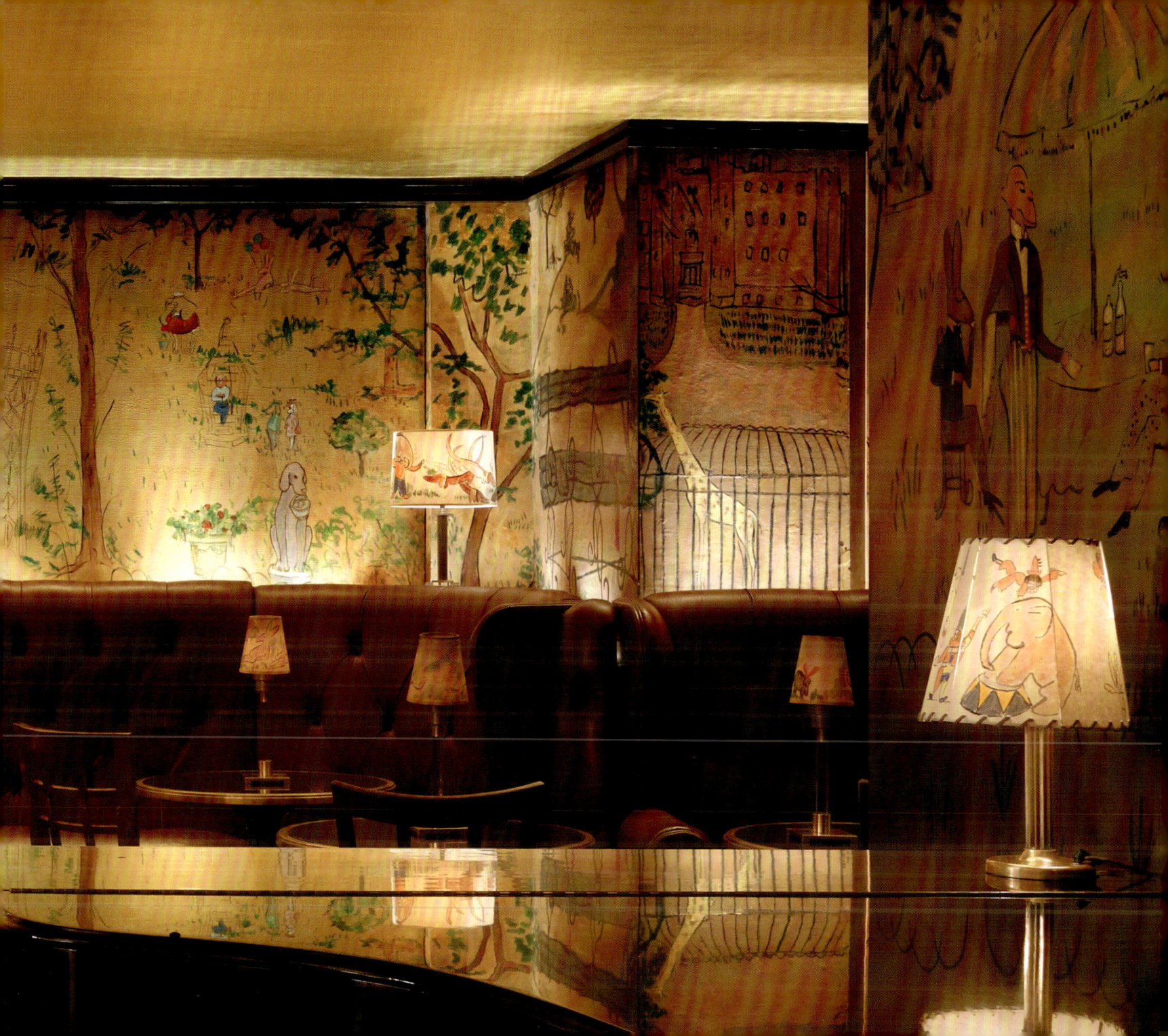

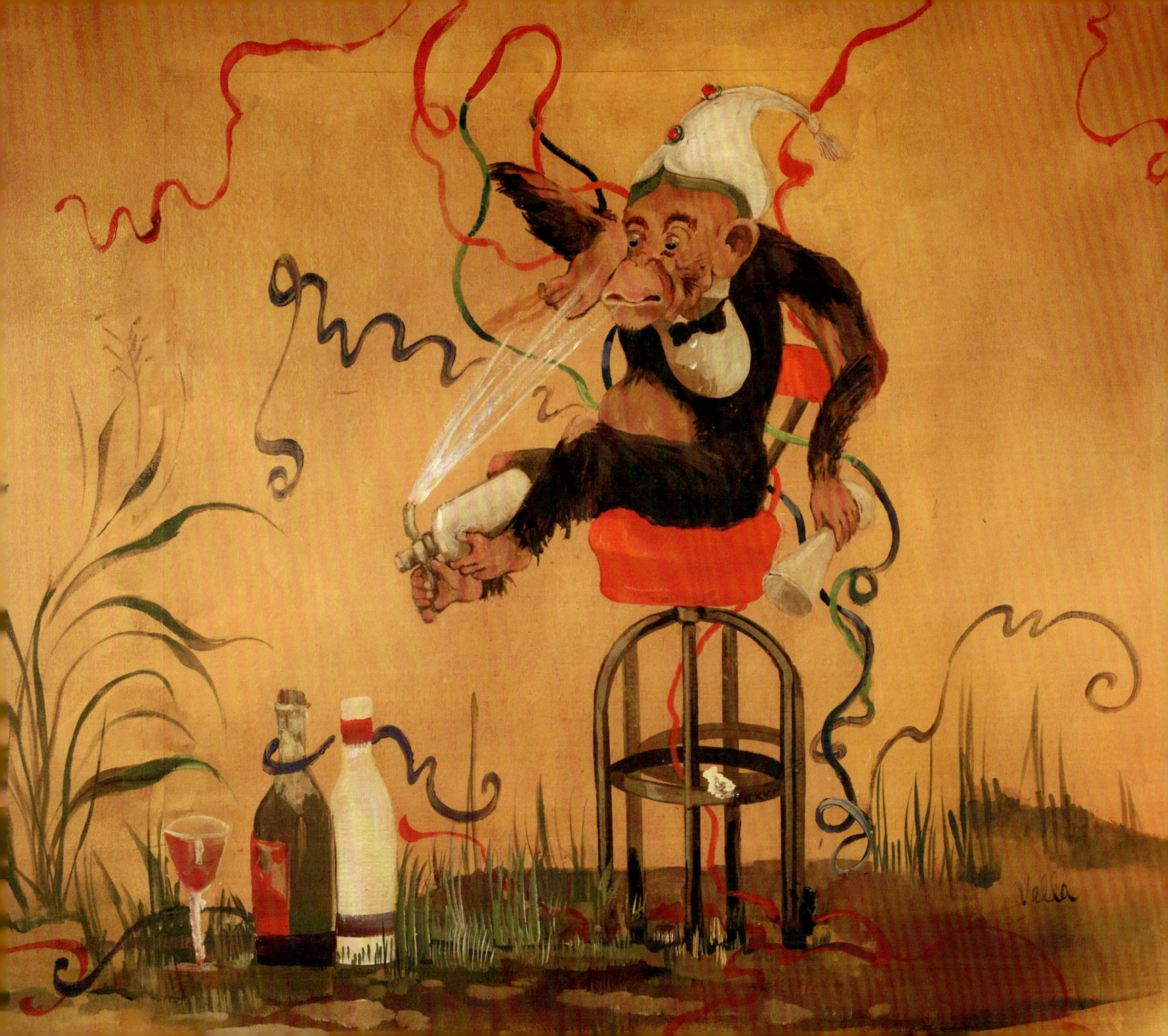

MONKEY BAR

EDWARD SOREL • CHARLES VELLA • DIANE VOYENTZIE

If Woody Allen had made *Midnight in New York* instead of *Midnight in Paris*, he would have filmed in the Monkey Bar at the Hotel Elysée, once a haunt for New York's glitterati, including Tallulah Bankhead and Tennessee Williams. The Monkey Bar was originally a piano bar, but after someone affixed monkey decals to the mirrors behind the bar, presumably to remind people that they might be acting like monkeys, it became much more than that.

In the late 1940s, the owner, Leon Quain, asked a Russian painter, Eugene Zaikine, to paint a couple of monkeys for the bar. It must have resonated with the clientele because Quain then asked his friend Charles Vella, a caricaturist, to paint a few more. In 1984, muralist Diane Voyentzie was commissioned to add to the simian theme. She painted monkeys directly onto canvas that had been affixed to the walls, capturing both Vella's style and the spirit of the venue. Then, ten years later, architect David Rockwell redesigned the space and Voyentzie was asked to unify the room with more simian art, palm trees, and foliage.

Though the monkeys have the style and charm of a sweet children's book illustrations from the 1920s and '30s, they're engaging in behavior ill suited for any nursery. Monkeys are pulling an elephant's trunk, having a birthday party, and tormenting a zebra. They are also making daiquiris and nursing hangovers with an ice bag.

Just across the lobby from the Monkey Bar is the main dining room, where Edward Sorel's ingenious caricatures of the larger-than-life celebrities of the 1920s and '30s reside. Starting in the lower-left corner, Tennessee Williams's cigarette smoke drifts toward his Stanley Kowalski and Blanche DuBois. Above Williams is Isadora Duncan, accessorized in her signature flowing red scarves; she's in a boxing ring with Joe Lewis, the greatest heavyweight boxer of all time. Overlooking them is moon-faced humorist Alexander Woollcott. The greatest jockey in history, Eddie "Banana Nose" Arcaro, is pictured on horseback near Richard Rodgers, who sits impatiently at his piano, looking at his watch and waiting for his cigar-chewing collaborator, Lorenz Hart, to write more lyrics.

In the next panel Langston Hughes leans on a balustrade while Kate Smith belts out "God Bless America." In the lower left, Peter Arno is drawing a cartoon for *The New Yorker*. The dominant figure, Fats Waller, performs for Frank Sinatra and Ella Fitzgerald. Florenz Ziegfeld holds back the curtain of the *Ziegfeld Follies* for beautiful Lillian Lorraine, while Clifford Odets types another master-piece. Henry Luce, the father of magazine publishing, scowls at *The New Yorker* founder Harold Ross, while Luce's wife, Clare Boothe Luce (whose face is now covered by a fire alarm), looks on. Publisher Adolph Ochs reads his paper, the *New York Times*, near Edna Woolman Chase, *Vogue*'s editor in chief. Publishing giant Condé Nast stolidly looks on as showman Billy Rose delights in Zelda Fitzgerald's tabletop dance. Her husband, F. Scott Fitzgerald, sits beside Robert Benchley, the deadpan *The New Yorker* humorist, and across from the Algonquin Round Table's own Dorothy Parker. Gossip columnist Elsa Maxwell listens to Cole Porter tickle the ivories of his Steinway near marquees of Broadway theaters. Katharine Cornell, known as the "the first lady of the theater," comforts brooding Eugene O'Neill near George S. Kaufman and Moss Hart.

A young John Barrymore holds the Yorick-like head of an old John Barrymore. Louis Armstrong, Billy Holiday, and Rudy Vallee gather near George Gershwin as Irving Berlin watches in admiration. Duke Ellington plays the piano near classical pianist Vladimir Horowitz, who is being conducted by his father-in-law Arturo Toscanini. Nestled between the two pianos is a vase of flowers with "The Little Flower," the diminutively nicknamed mayor of New York City, Fiorello La Guardia, placed in the center. Observing these piano virtuosi are the great jazz musician "Bix" Beiderbecke and a round-faced Oliver Hardy. Monkey paparazzi are snapping away at Babe Ruth in a raccoon coat. David Sarnoff, the president of RCA and NBC, can be seen in a poster, while William Paley, who built

CBS, rides in a convertible. Dancing siblings Adele and Fred Astaire sidestep King Kong as Alfred and Blanche Knopf walk their dog near a poster of Paul Robeson as the Emperor Jones. Meanwhile, at the Stork Club Bar, Ernest Hemingway engages Walter Winchell, the most feared gossip columnist of his day. Cary Grant and Tallulah Bankhead draw attention to perhaps the least famous man at the table, Stork Club owner Sherman Billingsley. And finally, Mae West, who is waiting for a cab, reminds us that it's important to know when to leave a party.

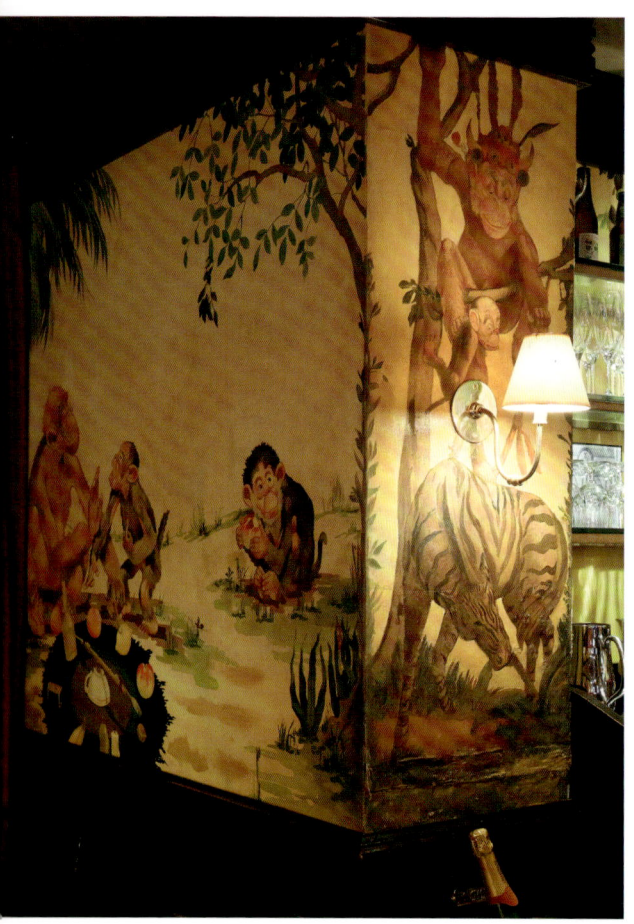

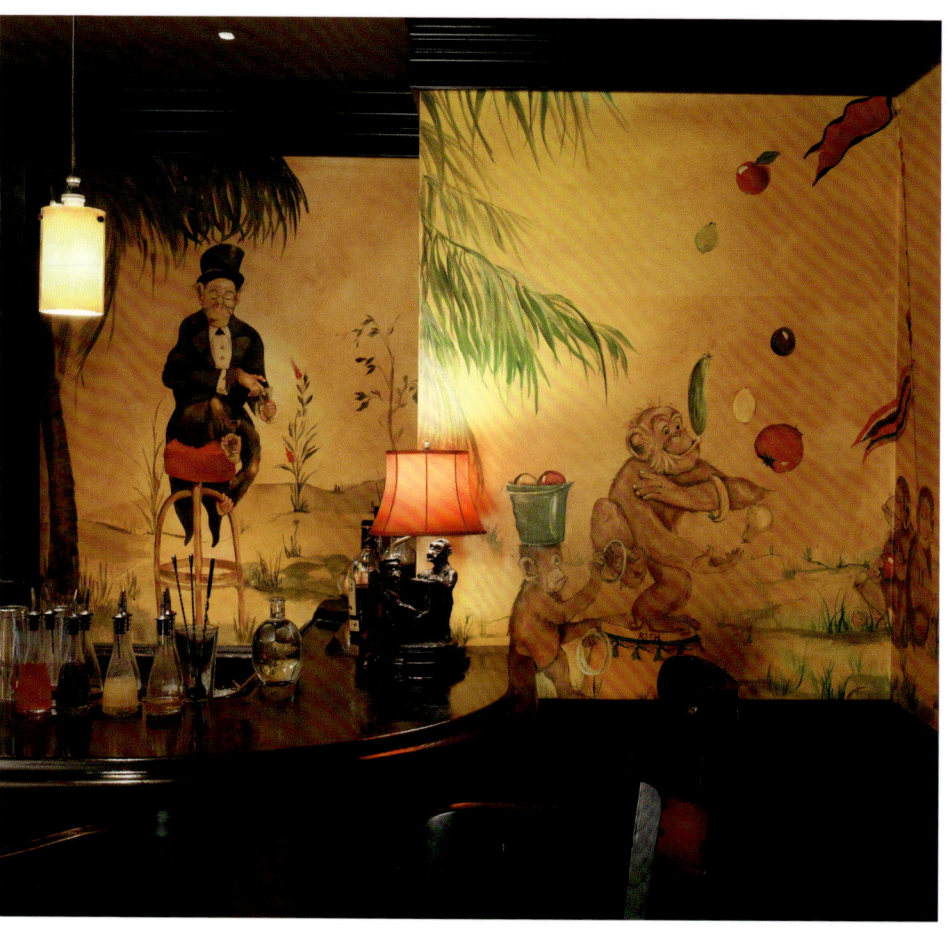

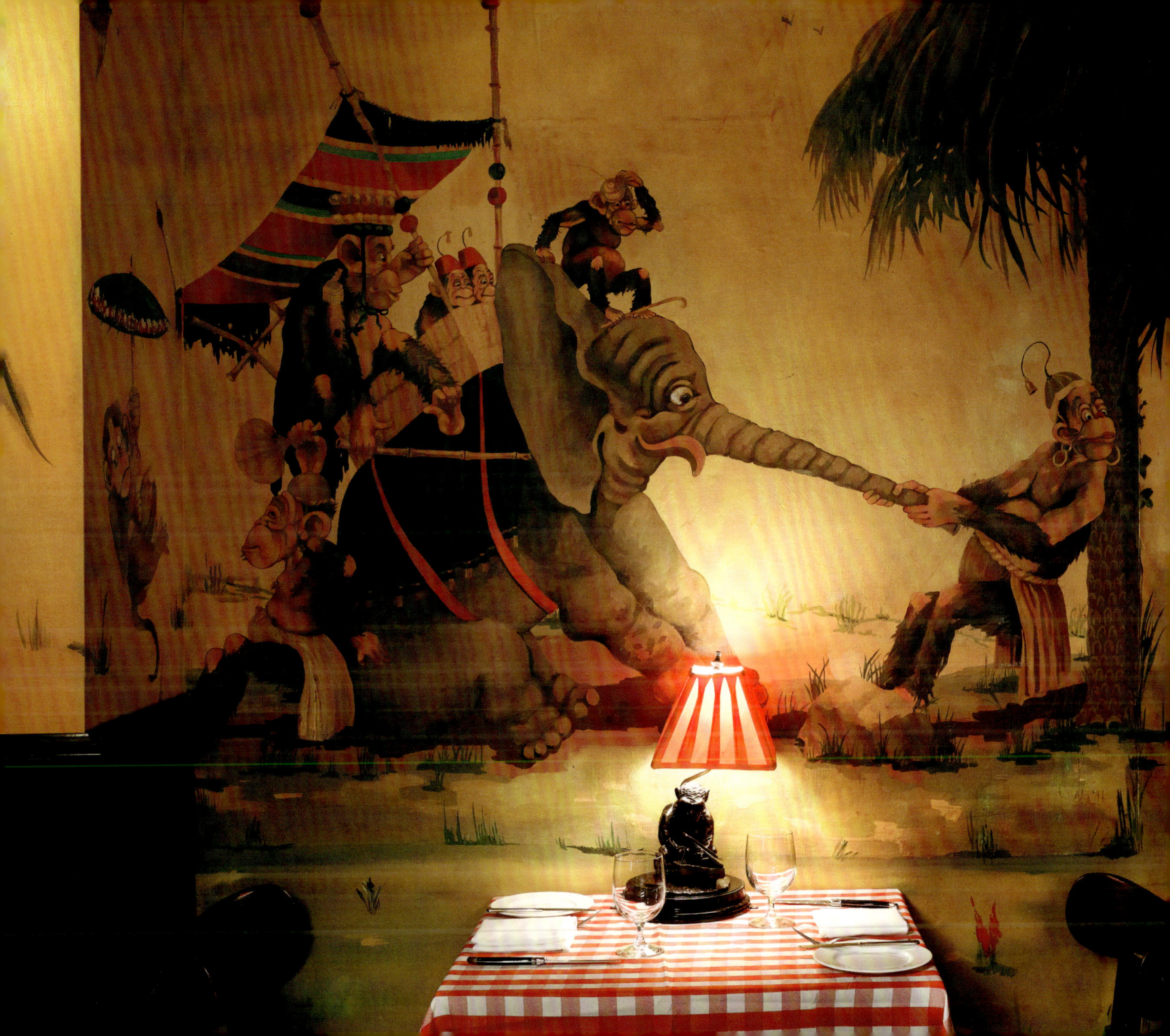

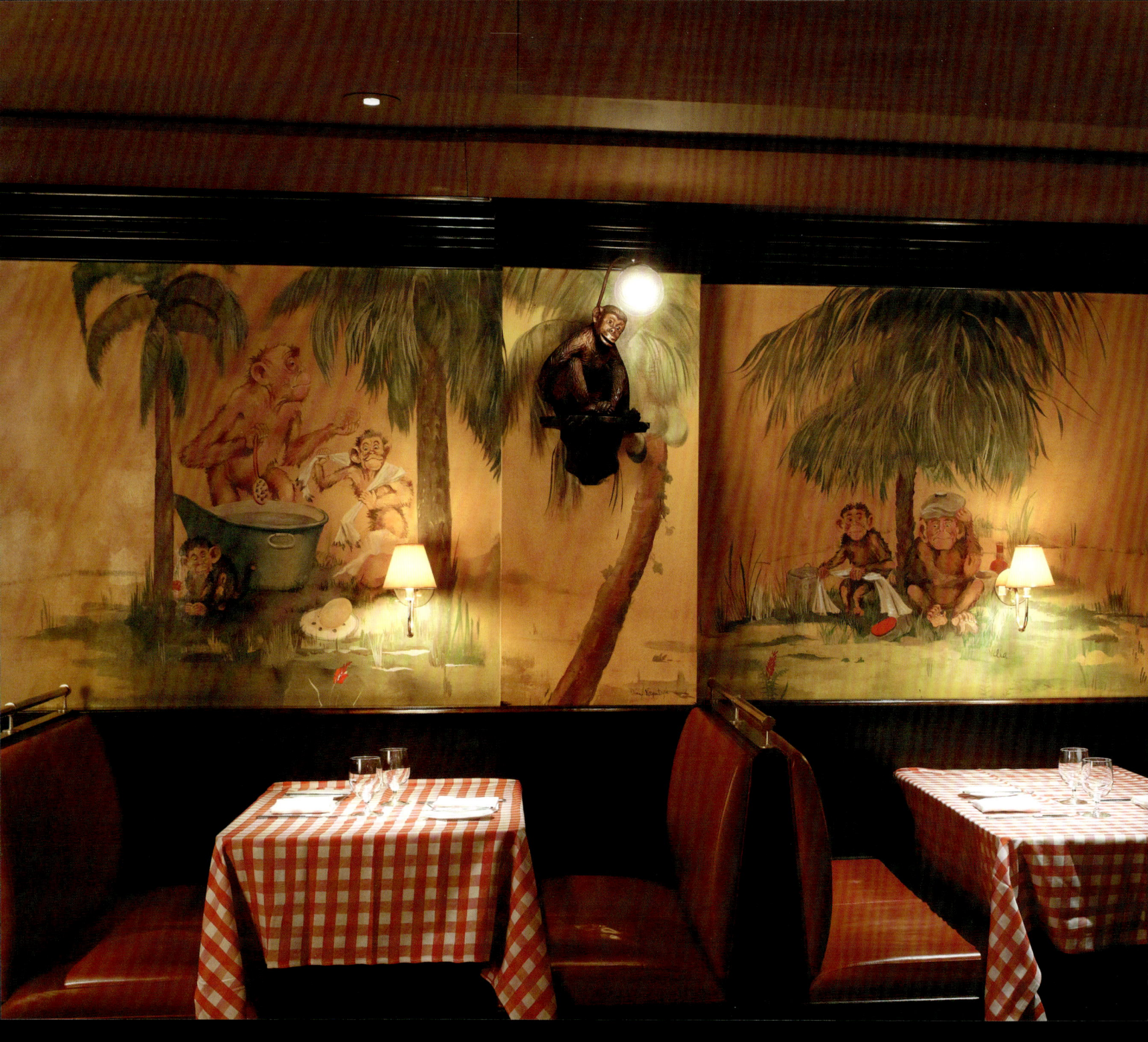

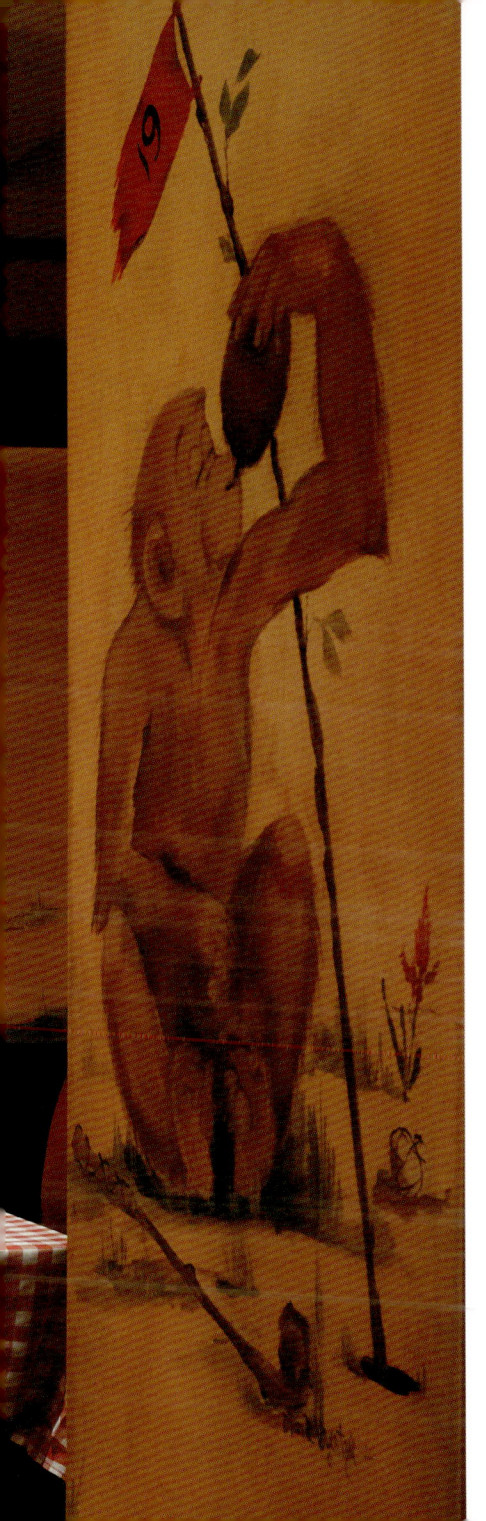

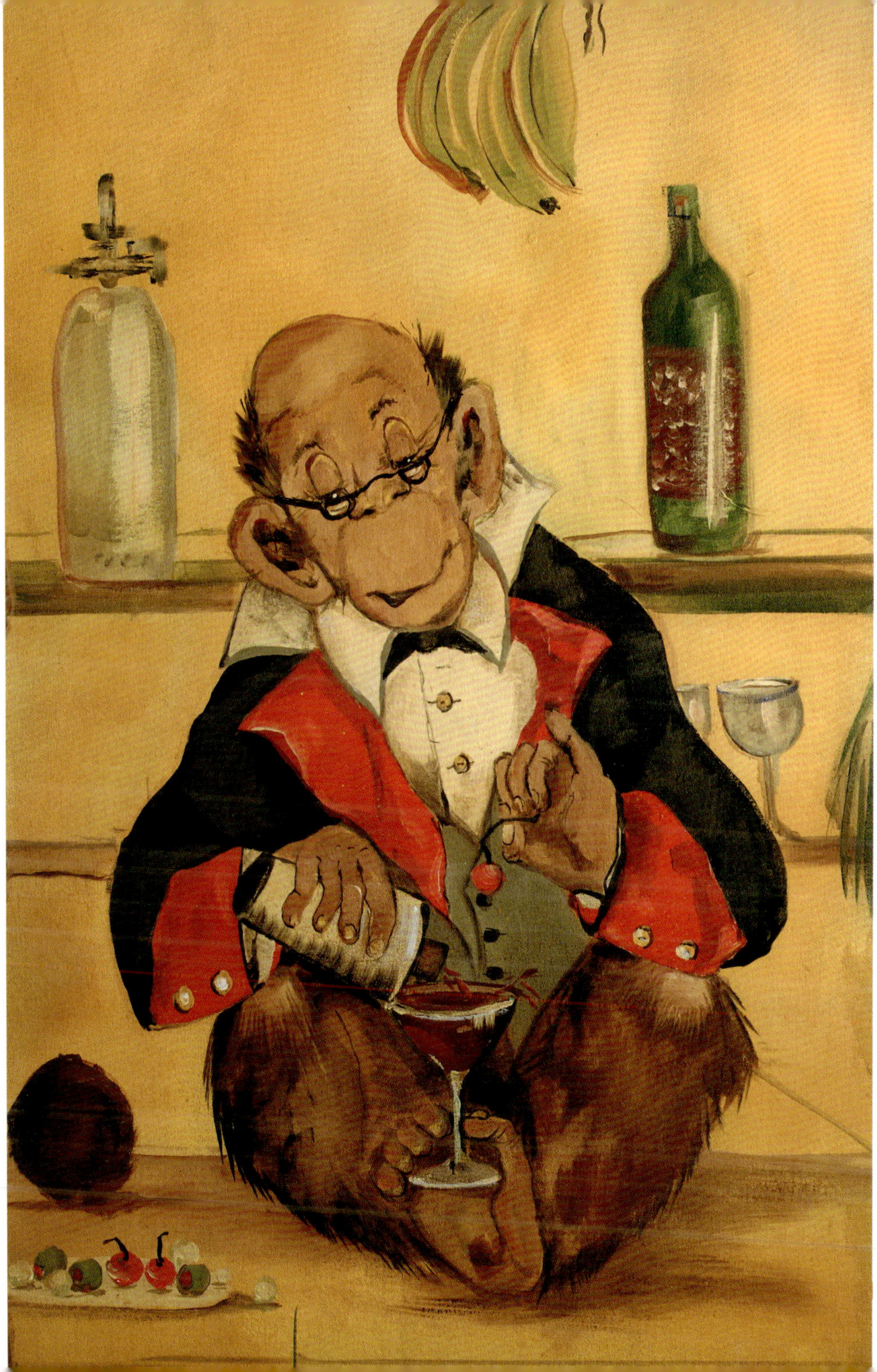

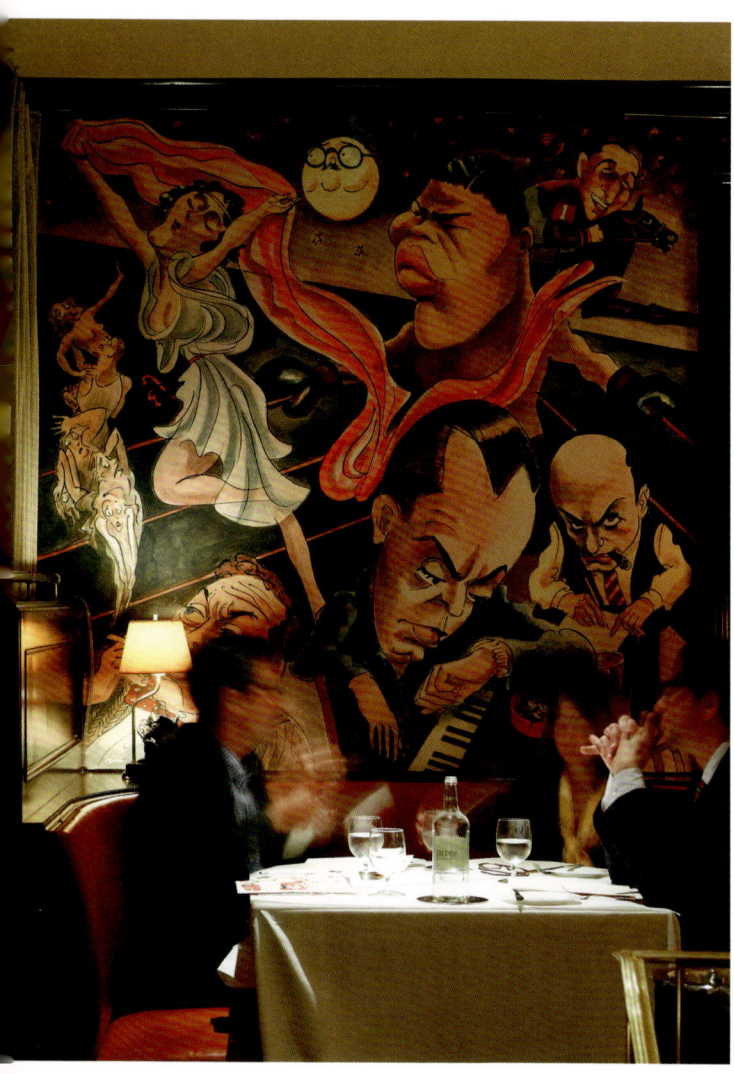
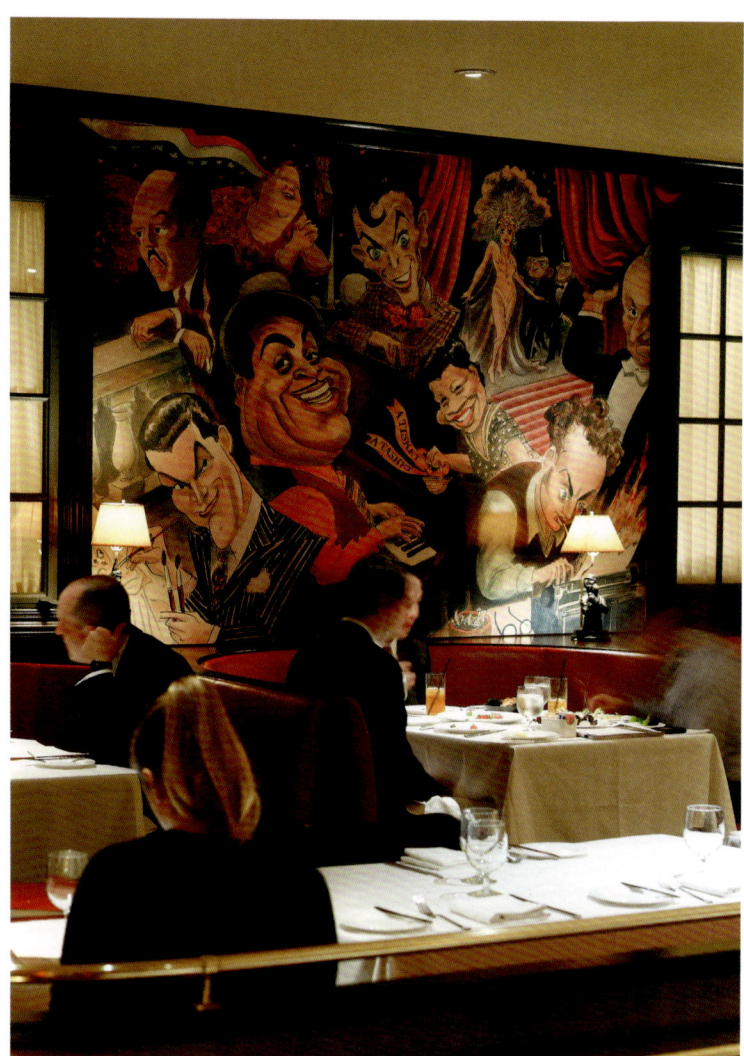

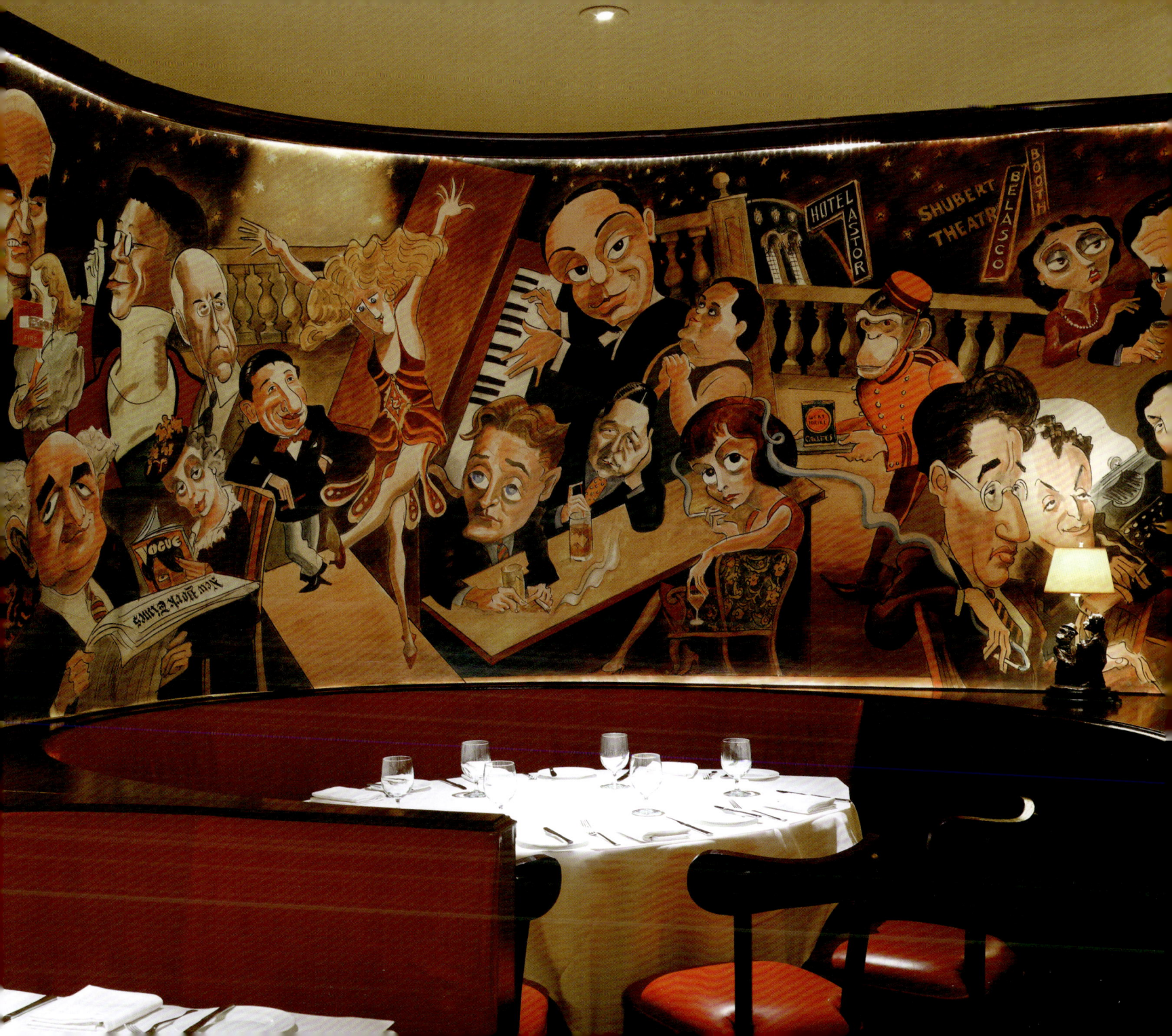

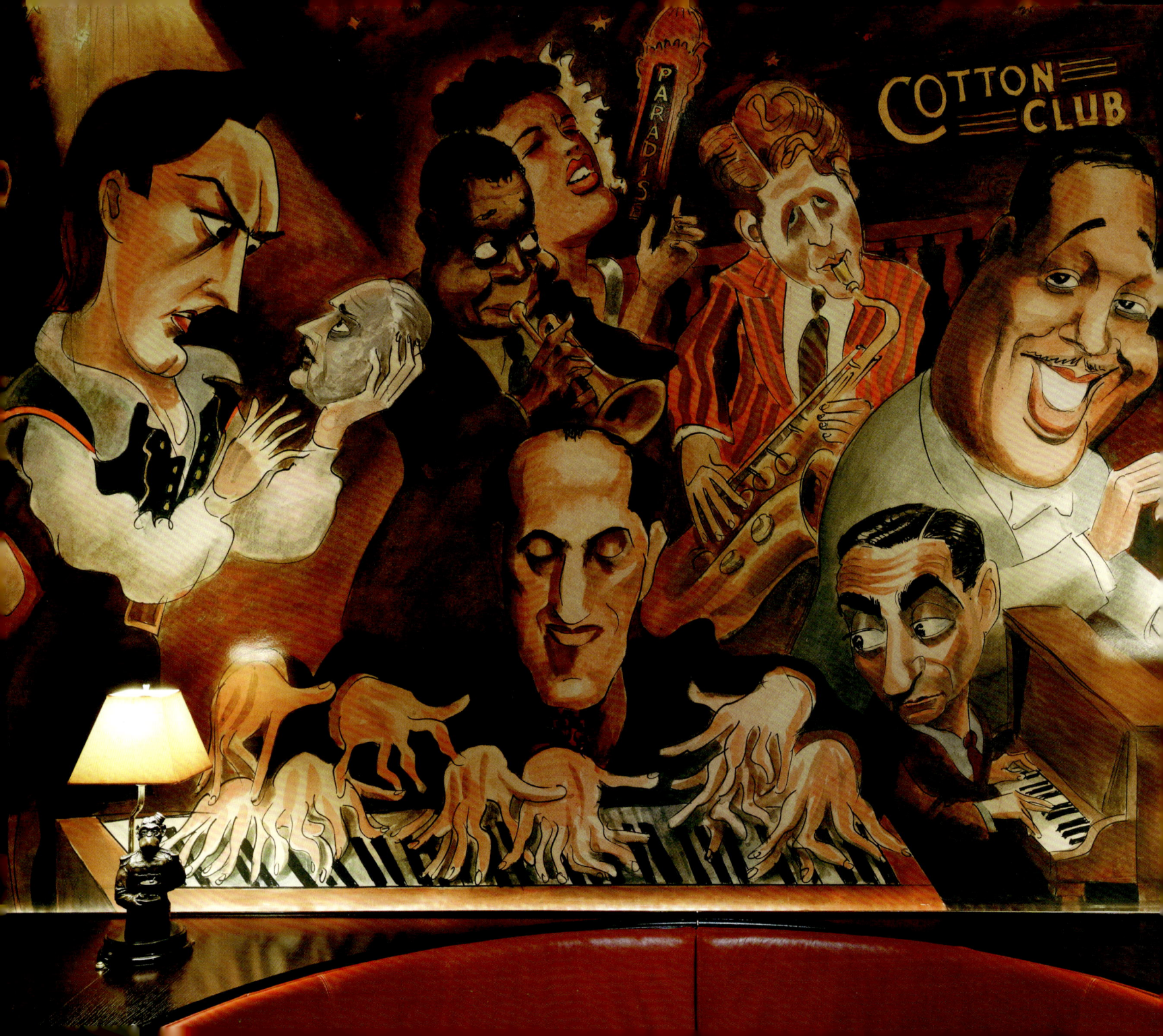

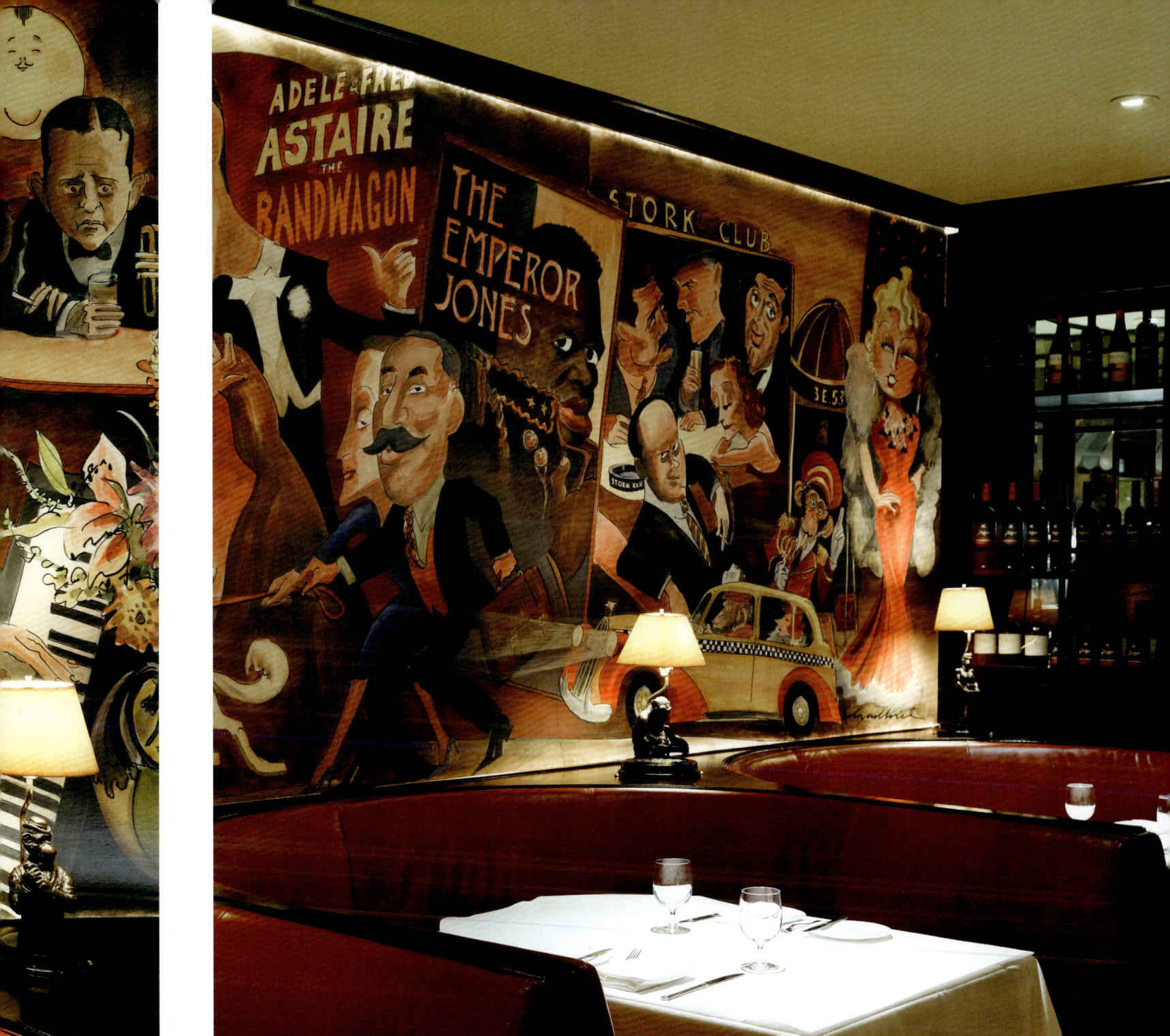

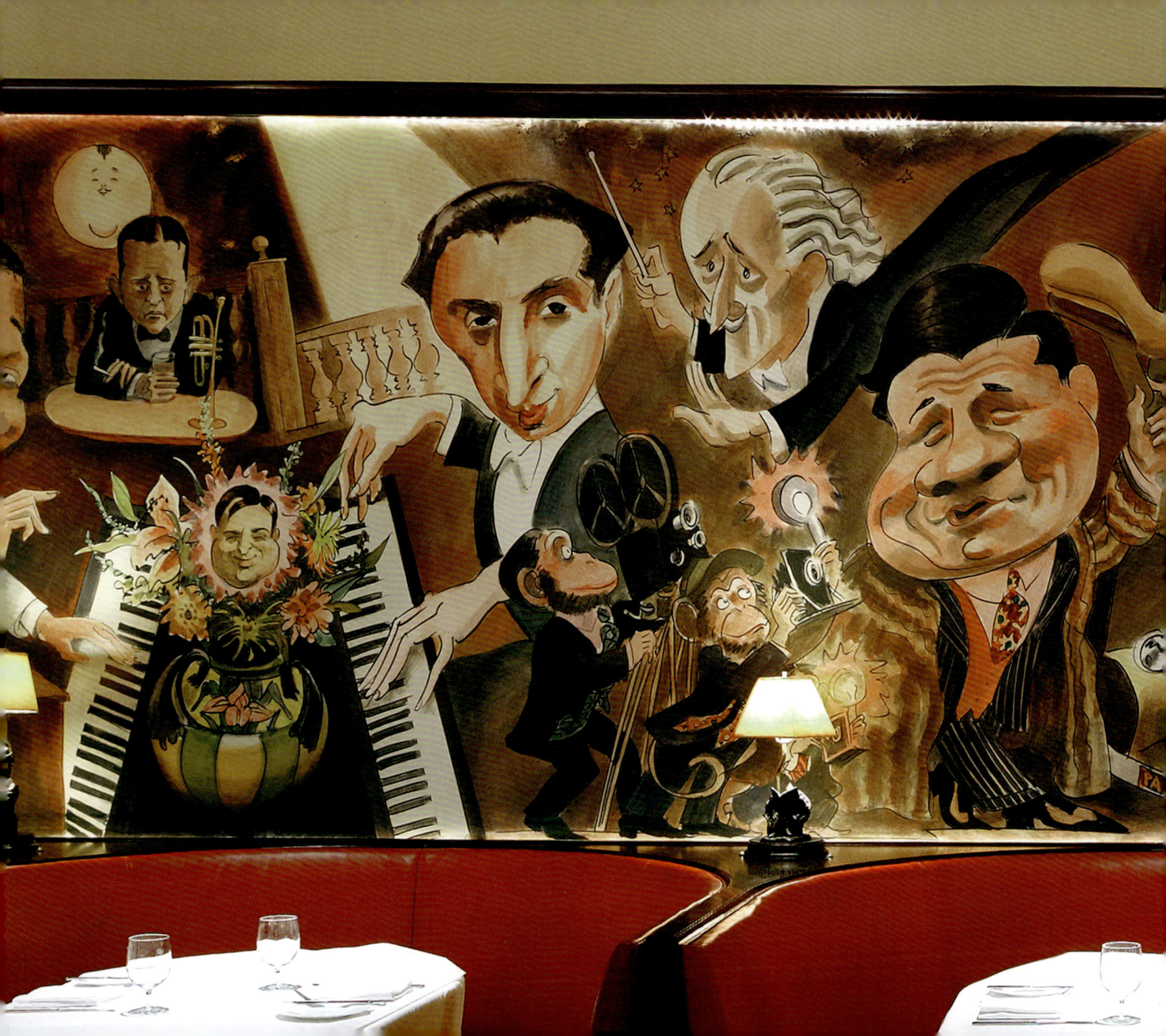

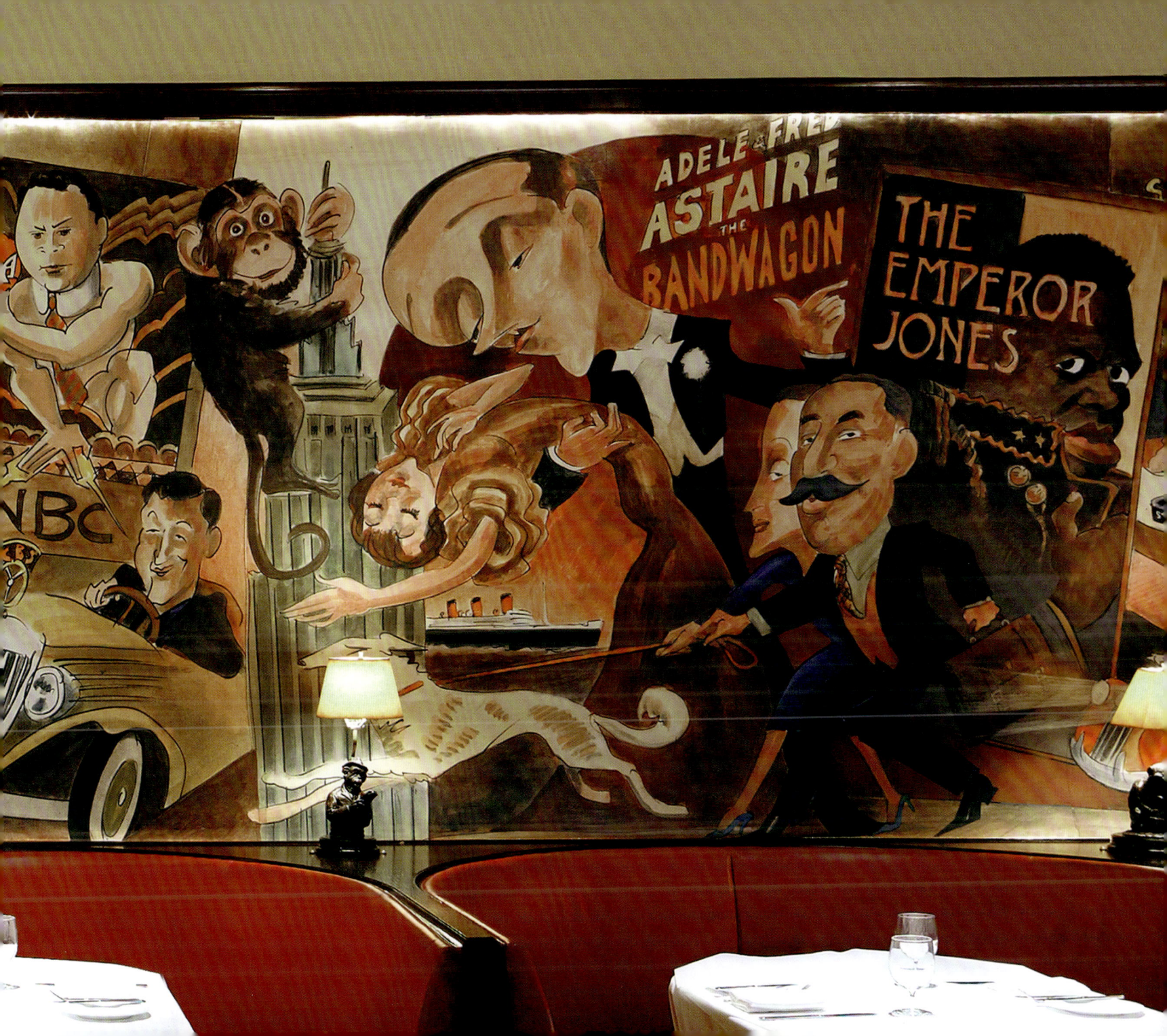

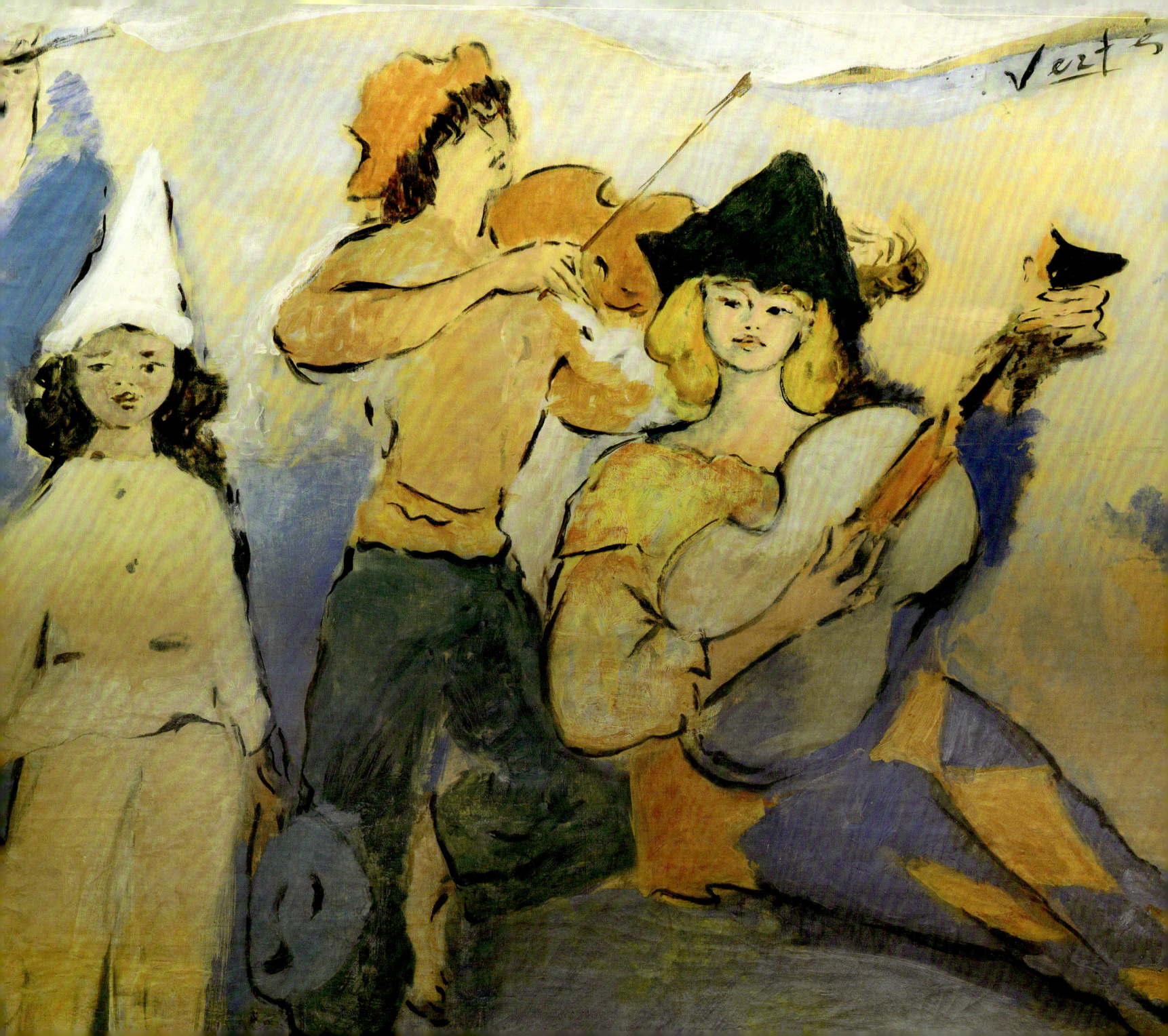

CAFÉ CARLYLE

In the autumn of 1955, Robert Huyot, the general manager and president of the Hotel Carlyle, commissioned a Hungarian expatriate, Marcel Vertès, to paint murals for his new Café Carlyle. Huyot, a Frenchman, connected with the Hungarian Vertès because of their shared Parisian background and love of cabaret. Vertès had immigrated to Paris after World War I to pursue the life of an artist in the Latin Quarter, where he embraced—and was embraced by—the art and social worlds of the 1920s. He was dashing, stylish, and charming, and he became the darling of the fashion world, his paintings both in vogue and on the covers of *Vogue*.

In the 1930s he started a foray into French films as an art director and designer, a successful venture that followed him on his immigration to America right before World War II. His aesthetic was a perfect fit for the heyday of dazzling MGM musicals, and he went on to win Oscars for Art Direction and Costume Design in 1952 for his work on John Huston's *Moulin Rouge*.

The Café Carlyle was, and still is, the apotheosis of New York cabaret nightlife. It is as sophisticated and polished as it gets. Bobby Short played and sang there for thirty-six years. Judy Collins, Elaine Stritch, and a marvelous list of artists perform there regularly, as did Eartha Kitt. Woody Allen plays clarinet every Monday night and, every once in a while, when the memory of the price of the last visit fades, I join seventy other lucky people to savor the luxury of an evening of music accompanied, as always, by the mural of Marcel Vertès.

Vertès's beautifully lit mural encircles the room in a glowing Chantilly froth (the dessert, not the lace). A brilliant band of cerulean blues, ochres, and warm oranges, it is the perfect accessory to what would have been the perfect venue for the cast party of *An American in Paris*. His staccato brush outlines ballerinas, troubadours, children, gypsies, and dancing dogs, all floating in a theatrical limbo with the suggestion of a just-raised curtain. It is a celebration of performance. It is Cole Porter made visible. It is high *Gigi*.

In the summer of 2007, I was chosen to restore the Vertès murals as a part of the total makeover of the Café. James McBride, the general manager of the hotel, fought not only to keep the café from destruction but also to restore the murals and renovate the space. When I first walked into the gutted space to begin work, the murals were all that remained of the original room. Huge speaker enclosures had been ripped out of the wall in the two corners flanking the stage, leaving gaping holes in the mural's canvas. The mural itself was coated in a dingy patina from years of cigar and cigarette smoke. I removed the sticky mess and patched and repainted the damage caused by decades of abuse. Once cleaned, the original colors glowed beautifully.

The huge gaps in the wall were replastered and covered with canvas and, to create an unbroken continuity throughout the room, I added new images in Vertès's style. After researching paintings, lithographs, and the artist's life, I learned that in *Moulin Rouge*, the close-up of Toulouse-Lautrec's hand was not that of the actor José Ferrer's, but actually Vertes's own. So when it came time for me to actually re-create Vertes's work, I mimicked his hand using his own wonderful, sketchy brushwork to outline the figures. I like to think he would have been pleased.

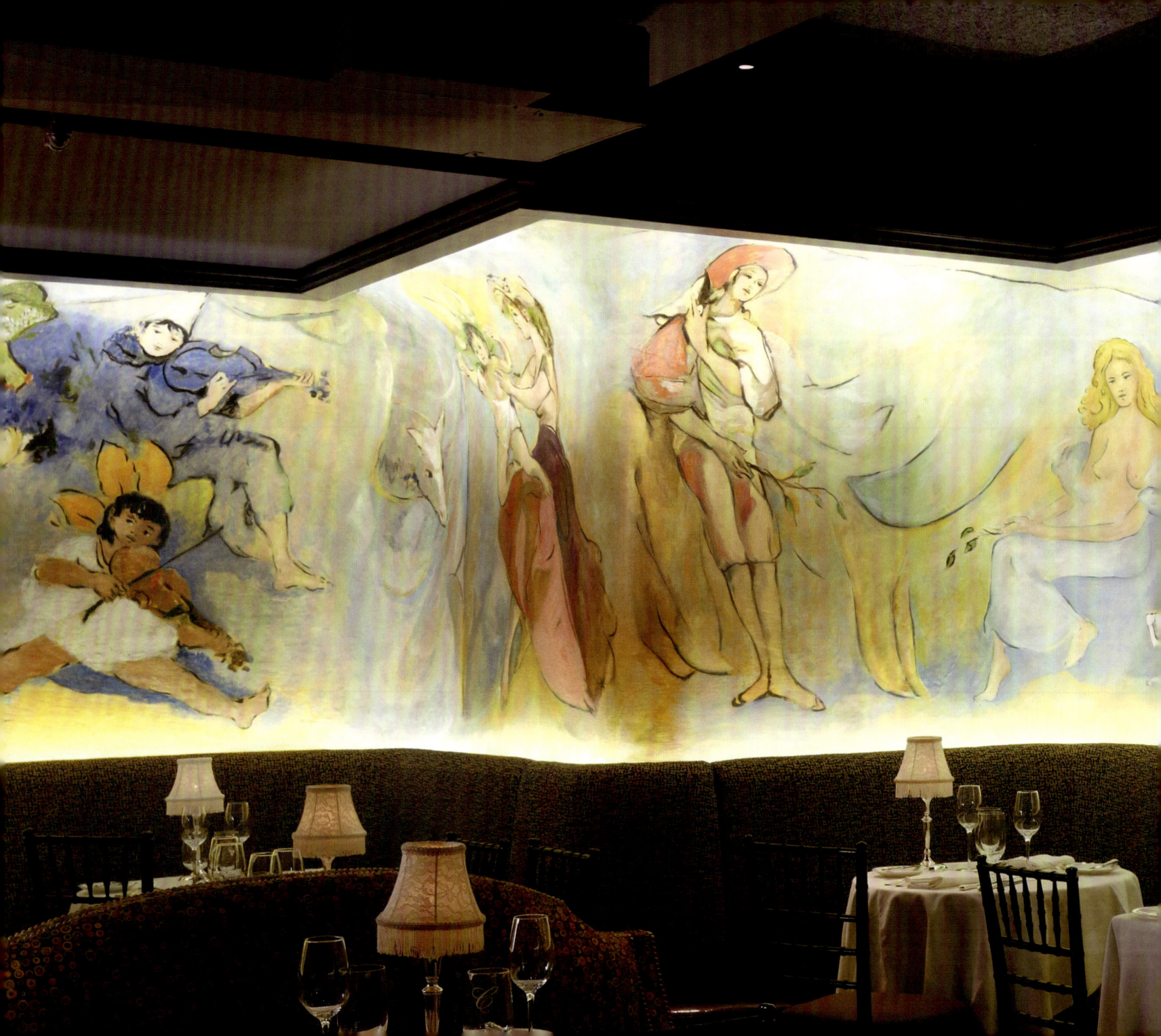

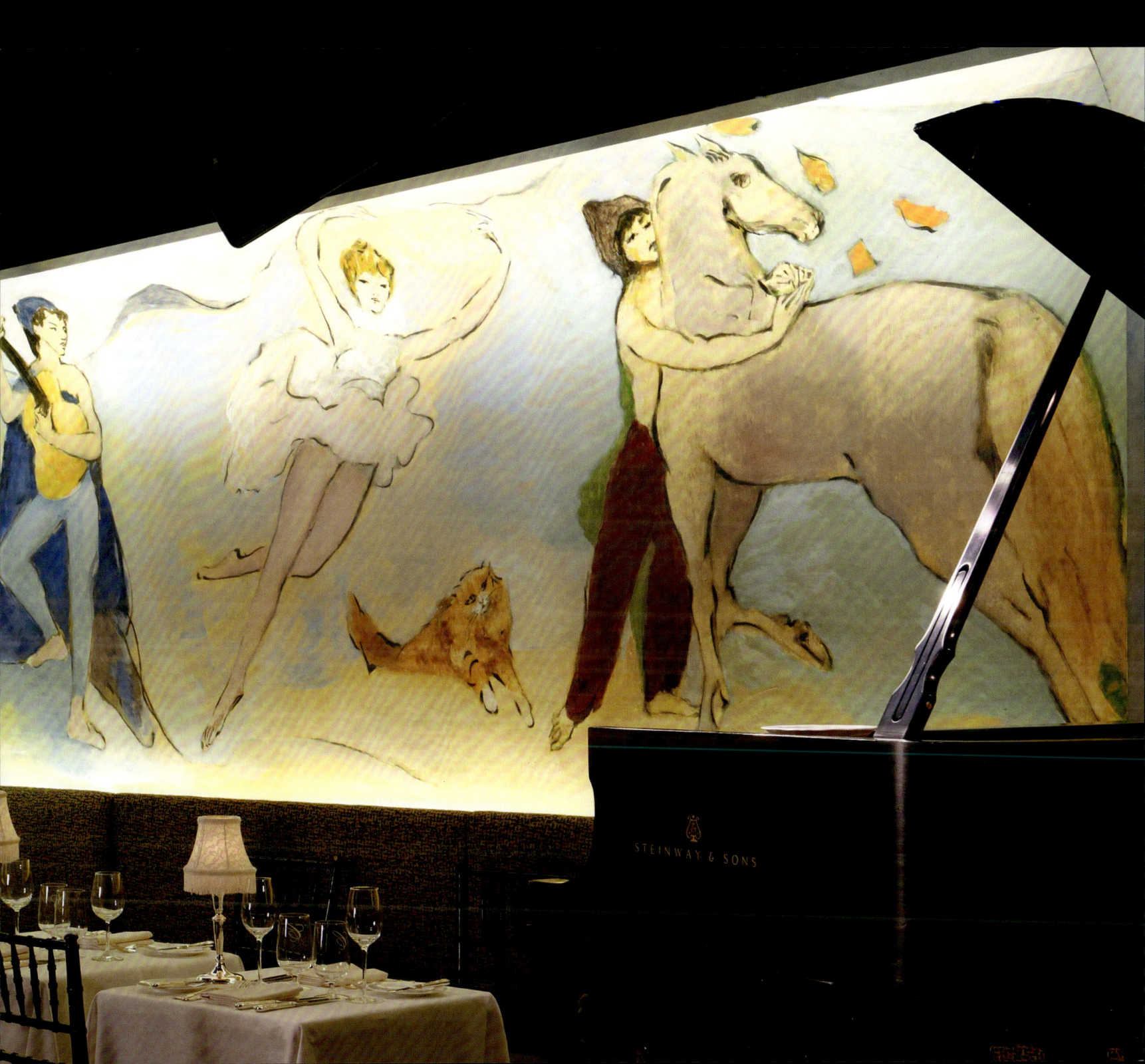

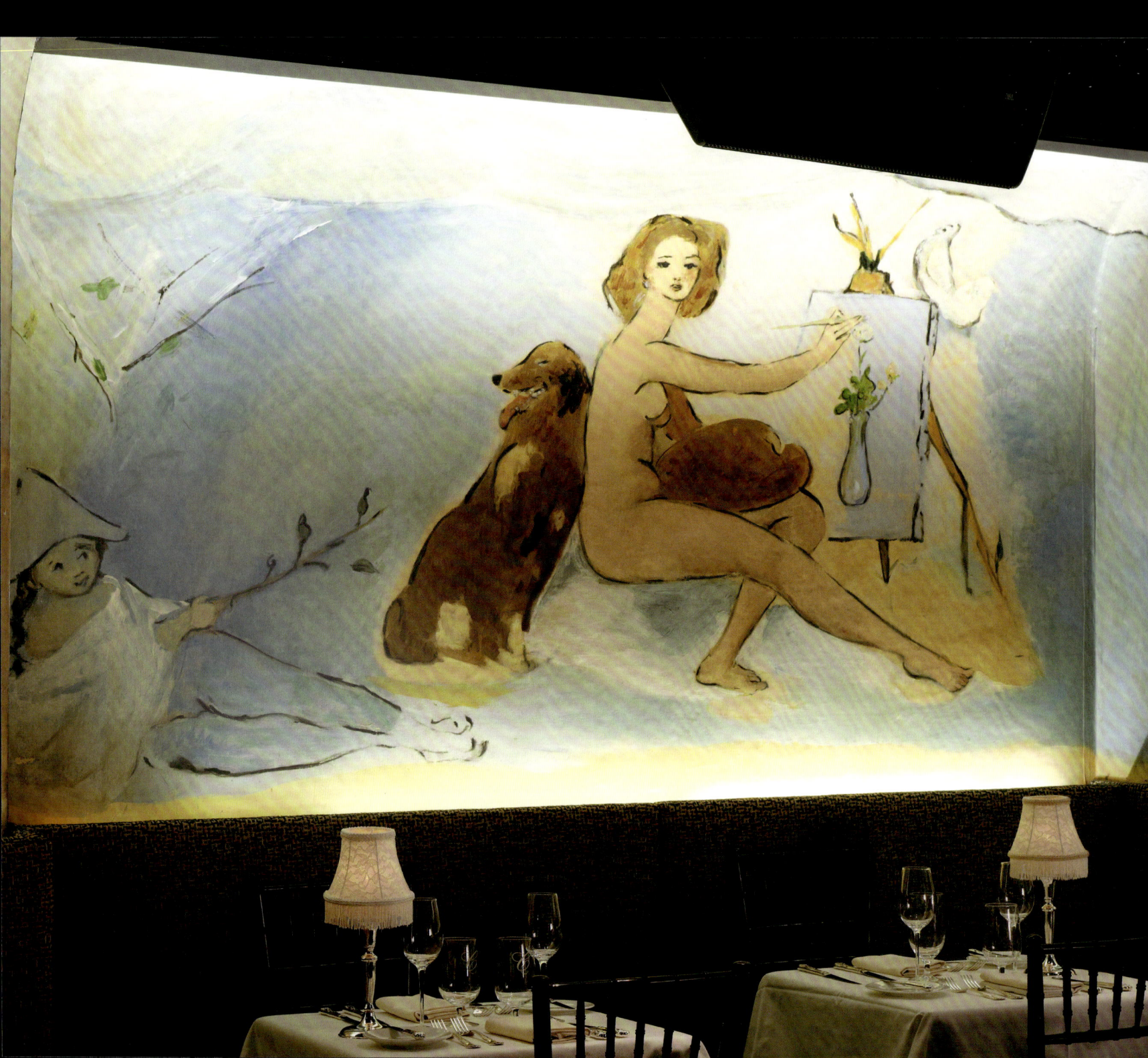

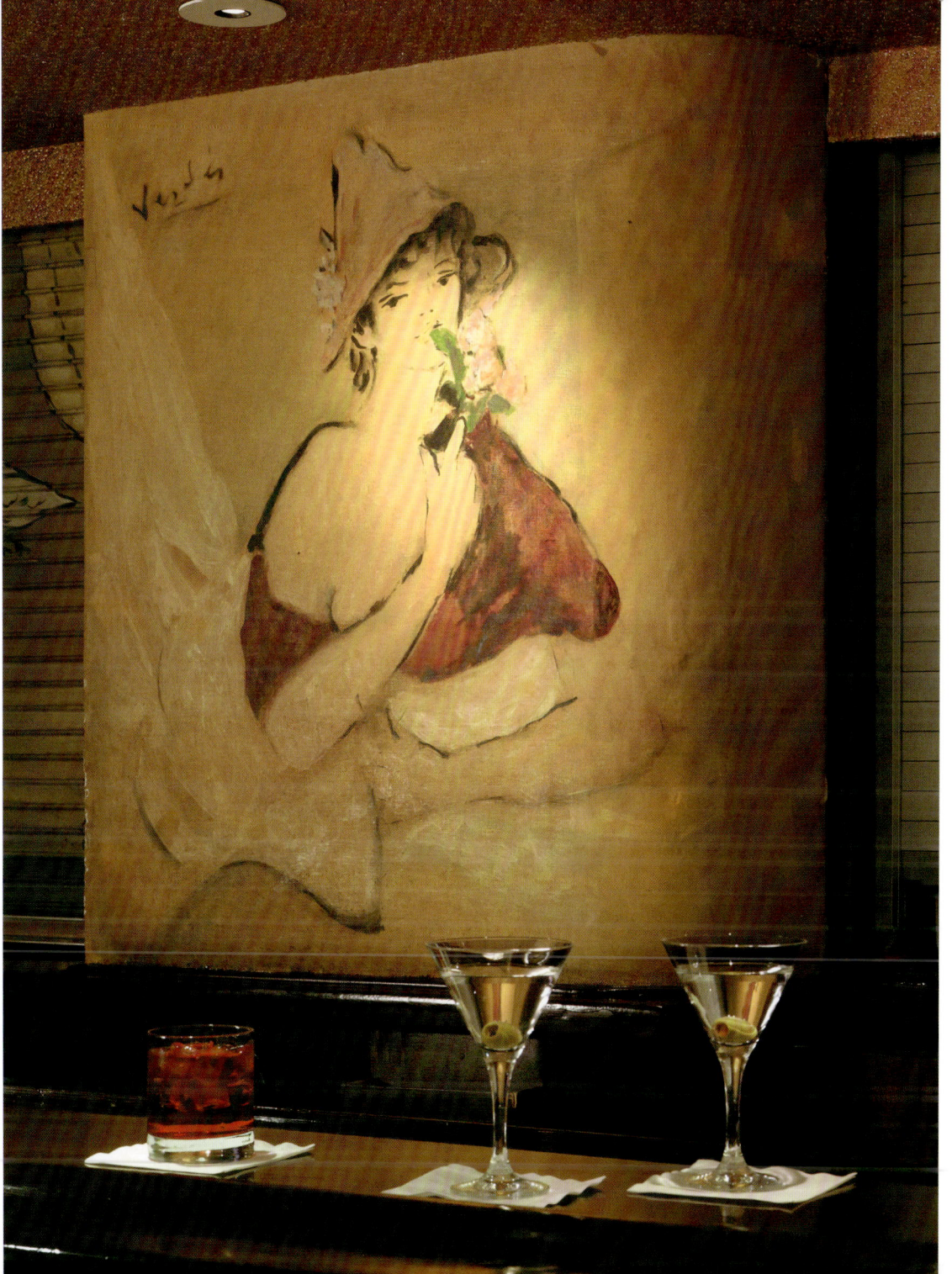

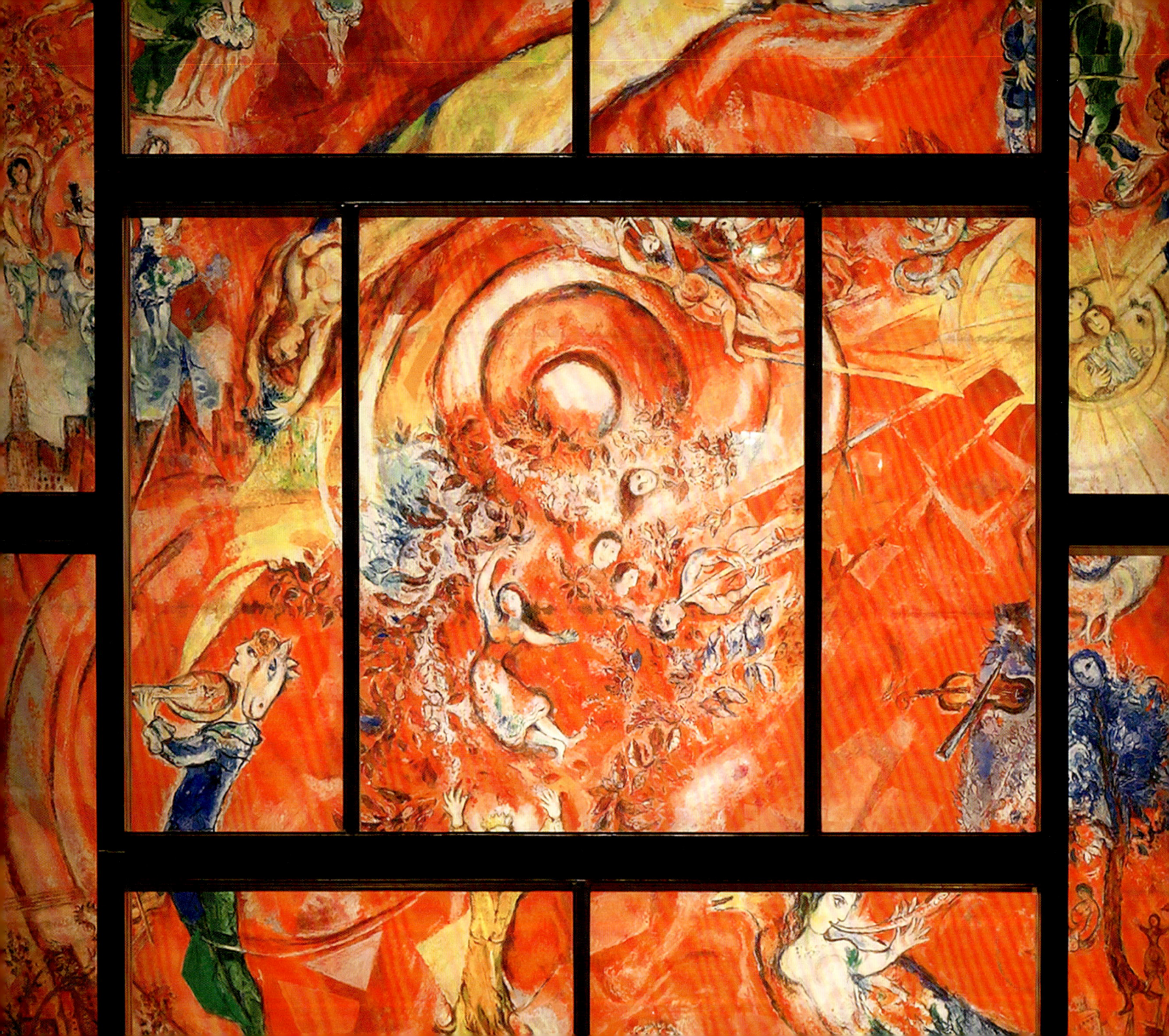

THE METROPOLITAN OPERA

Lincoln Center Plaza, Manhattan • MARC CHAGALL

Born to a devout Hasidic family in the picturesque city of Vitebsk (now in Belarus) in 1887, Marc Chagall grew to be, as Robert Hughes has called him, "the quintessential Jewish artist of the twentieth century." Chagall worked and lived in Montparnasse during the golden age of Modernism in a decrepit studio complex. Everything in the city of light intoxicated his senses, and he synthesized all the Modernist influences—Cubism, Symbolism, Surrealism, and Fauvism—into his own evocative dreamlike fantasy images. As he put it, "Poetic without poetry. Mystic without mysticism."

Shortly after the Nazis invaded France, Chagall and his family were smuggled out of France with forged papers. They arrived in New York on June 23, 1941, the day after Germany invaded Russia. Twenty-five years later, in 1966, Chagall gifted New York, the city that sheltered him from the war, two murals for the Metropolitan Opera. *The Sources of Music*, located on the north wall, and *The Triumph of Music*, on the south, each measure a monumental 30 by 36 feet; they dominate the enormous windows of the Opera House and can be seen from any location in Lincoln Center's main plaza.

Both paintings are filled with mythological figures, exotic wildlife, and symbols of music and life floating on luxuriant seas of reds and yellows. In the upper-left corner of *The Triumph of Music* is the ballet corps. To the right, is the firebird from the ballet of the same name by Igor Stravinsky. Directly below the firebird is a large angel with a horn, while just below it are smaller musicians celebrating the "Song of the Peoples." To their right is Chagall's homage "a la musique Americaine," and to the left are multiple figures and his homage "a la musique Francaise." Chagall includes a respectful nod to Rudolph Bing, the general manager of the opera at the time. In the bottom-left corner of the painting is a blue-green, two-headed musician floating to the right of Chagall's beloved New York City. In the lower-right portion, a woman-bird, representing Russian music, floats beneath an image of the Tree of Life, Chagall, and his wife, Bella.

On the north wall of the Grand Tier is *The Sources of Music*. The upper-left section is a tribute to Beethoven and his opera *Fidelio*. The large central figures are a two-headed Orpheus and a lyre-playing King David. Immediately to their right, below an image of a New York bridge, are Romeo and Juliet, surrounded by representations of various forms of music; figures portraying Bach's sacred music and Wagner's *Tristan and Isolde* can be seen to the left. Mozart, the large angelic female figure across the lower central part of the painting, is surrounded by musicians playing music from *The Magic Flute*. At the bottom, a fallen Tree of Life is near another image of New York and an homage to Verdi.

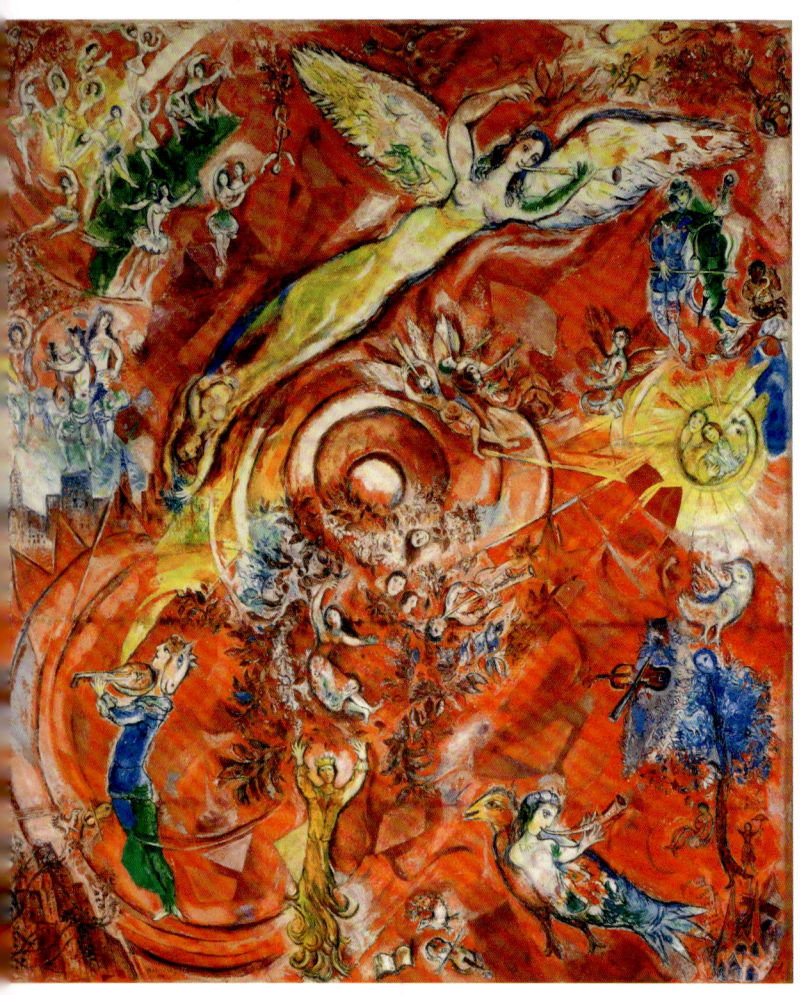

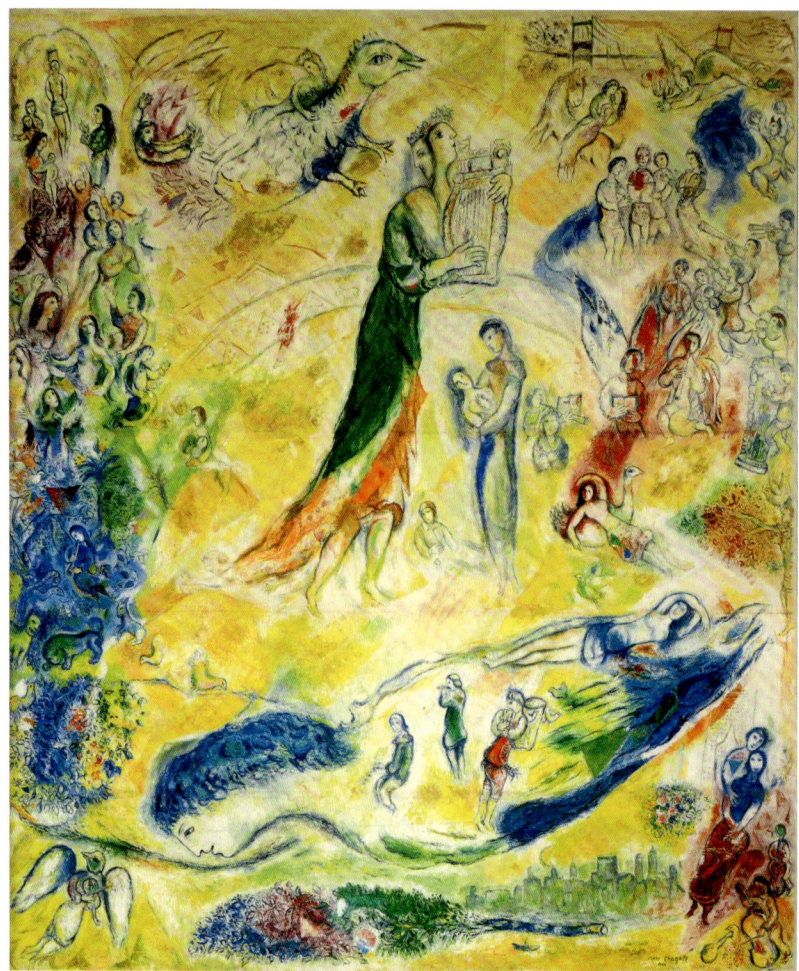

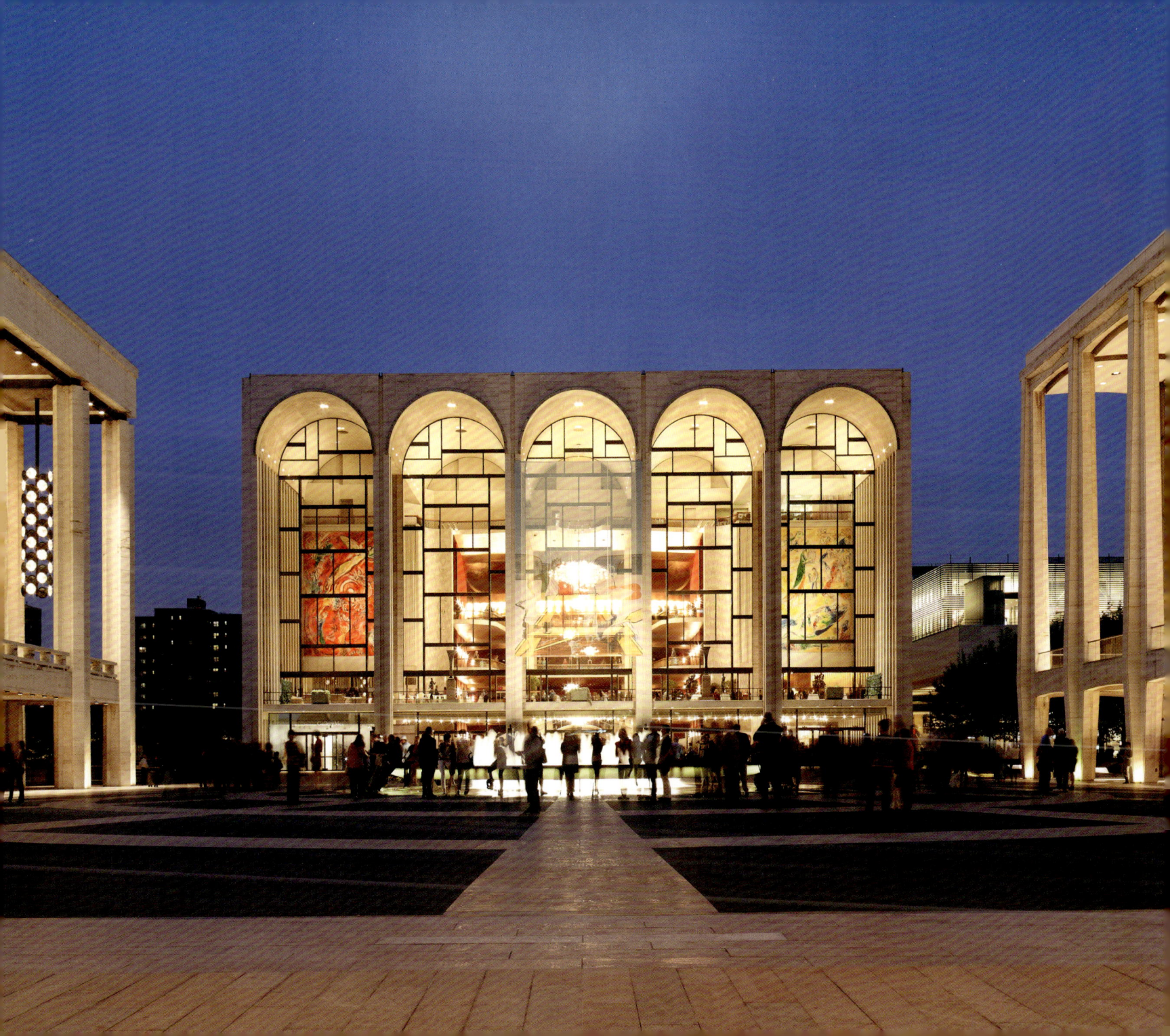

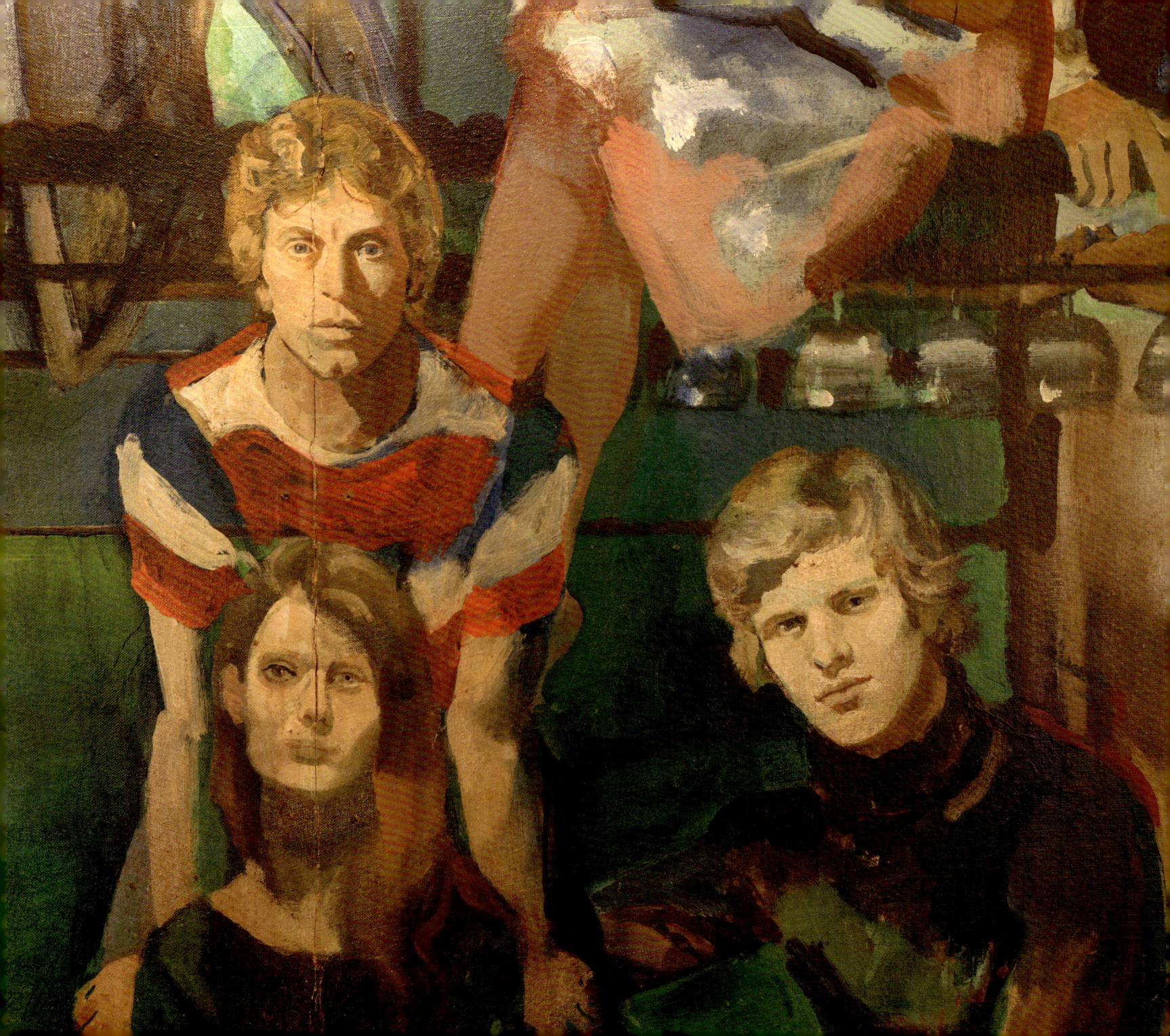

NEW YORK CITY BALLET

Lincoln Center Plaza, Manhattan • ROBERT CROWL

In 1967, the actor Patrick O'Neal and his brother, Michael, opened a saloon on West 63rd Street, a quick hop across Columbus Avenue from Lincoln Center. They wanted to call it "O'Neal's Saloon," but a Prohibition-era blue law still on the books prohibited naming a saloon a saloon. So they named it "O'Neal's Baloon," instead. It quickly became the hangout not only for dancers performing at Lincoln Center but also for everyone in the world of dance.

Patrick's wife, Cynthia, a decorator and a big ballet fan, came up with the idea to paint a mural of the dancers who frequented the bar. She asked her artist friend Robert Crowl to do the painting. Of all the painters written about in this book, Crowl is perhaps the most mysterious. Little is known about this talented artist who never managed to craft a full-fledged career as one. *Dancers at the Bar*, his 8-foot-by-16-foot painting at O'Neal's, is his lasting—and only—contribution to the murals of New York.

Between 1969 and 1970, Crowl painted twenty-six of the era's most brilliant dancers, ballet conductor Robert Irving, the O'Neal brothers and their wives, and the restaurant's manager and the maître d'. Because of the dancers' rigorous rehearsal and performance schedules, Crowl had to paint each subject whenever each could find an hour to pose. Sittings usually took place in the relative quiet of the mornings before the restaurant opened. It was both the summer of Woodstock and the Age of Aquarius, so Crowl's subjects arrived wearing love beads, bell-bottoms, hot pants, and platform shoes. It was also the golden age of ballet, and the stars of the Royal Danish, and the Royal and Stuttgart companies, as well as the New York City Ballet and American Ballet Theatre, are all represented in the painting. Peter Martins sat, as did Cynthia Gregory, Carol Sumner, Edward Villella, and twenty-two other dancers. Rudolf Nureyev considered sitting for the painting but decided against it.

The mural gradually grew to include all of the subjects until, one day, it was completed. Although they weren't included, many of the great dancers of the Bolshoi hung out at O'Neal's after performances, in those pre-glasnost days, under the watchful eyes of the KGB. Imagine Leonard Bernstein and his entourage or George Balanchine and Jerome Robbins discussing the next New York City Ballet production in front of the painting. O'Neal's was a happy madhouse and the best choreographed bar in New York.

Ironically, in a world that thrives on theatricality, hoopla, and grand gesture, the painting commissioned to capture it was unveiled without any ceremony or commotion. It became a treasured part of the world it quietly represented. So quietly, in fact, that Crowl never even signed it.

After the "Baloon" closed, the painting was moved to the second O'Neal's Restaurant on West 64th Street. In 2010, when that restaurant was sold, stagehands walked it across Columbus Avenue. Peter Martins, now ballet master in chief of the New York City Ballet, accepted *Dancers at the Bar* as a permanent loan from the O'Neal family to the company, where the painting now hangs in its main rehearsal hall.

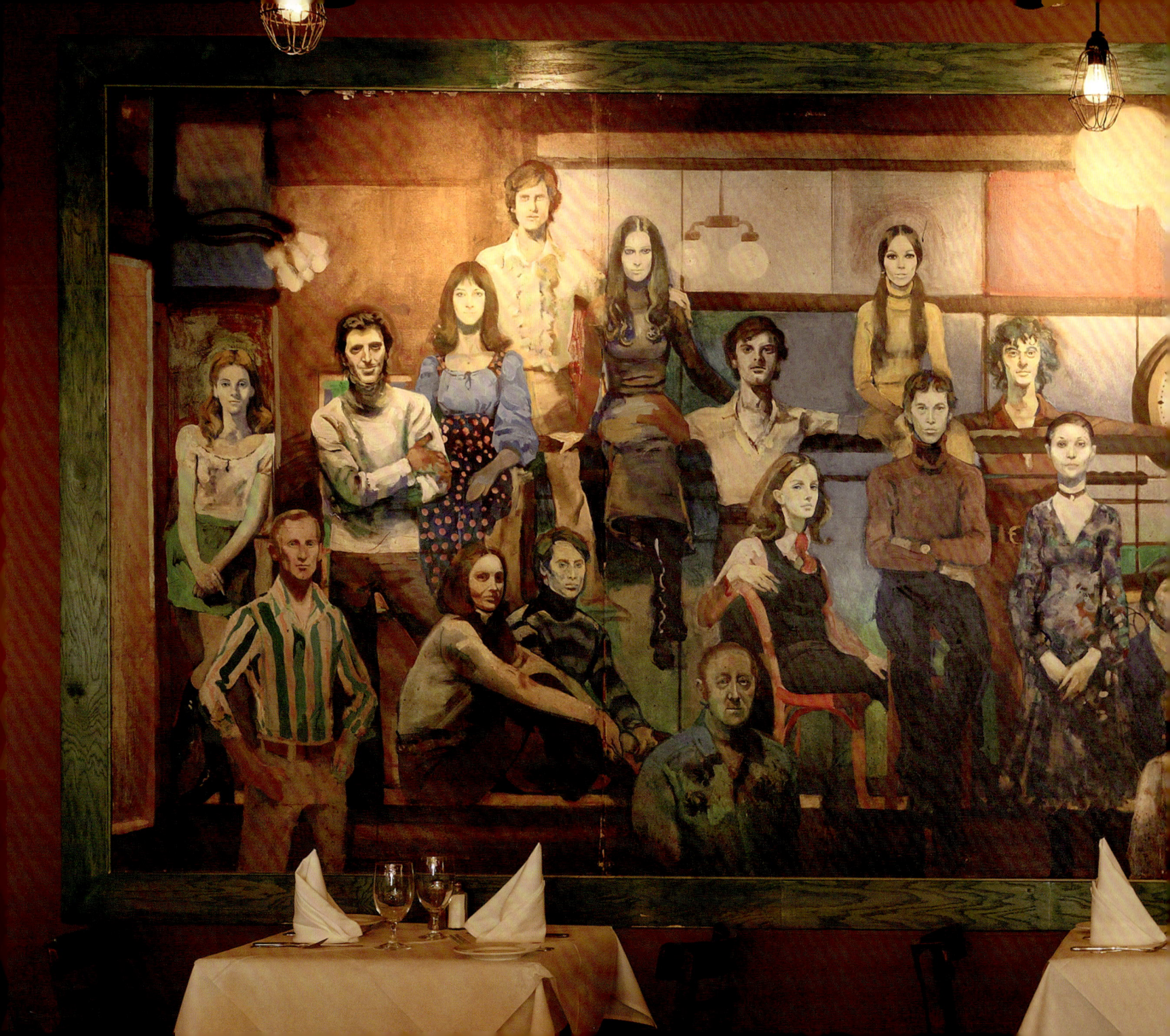

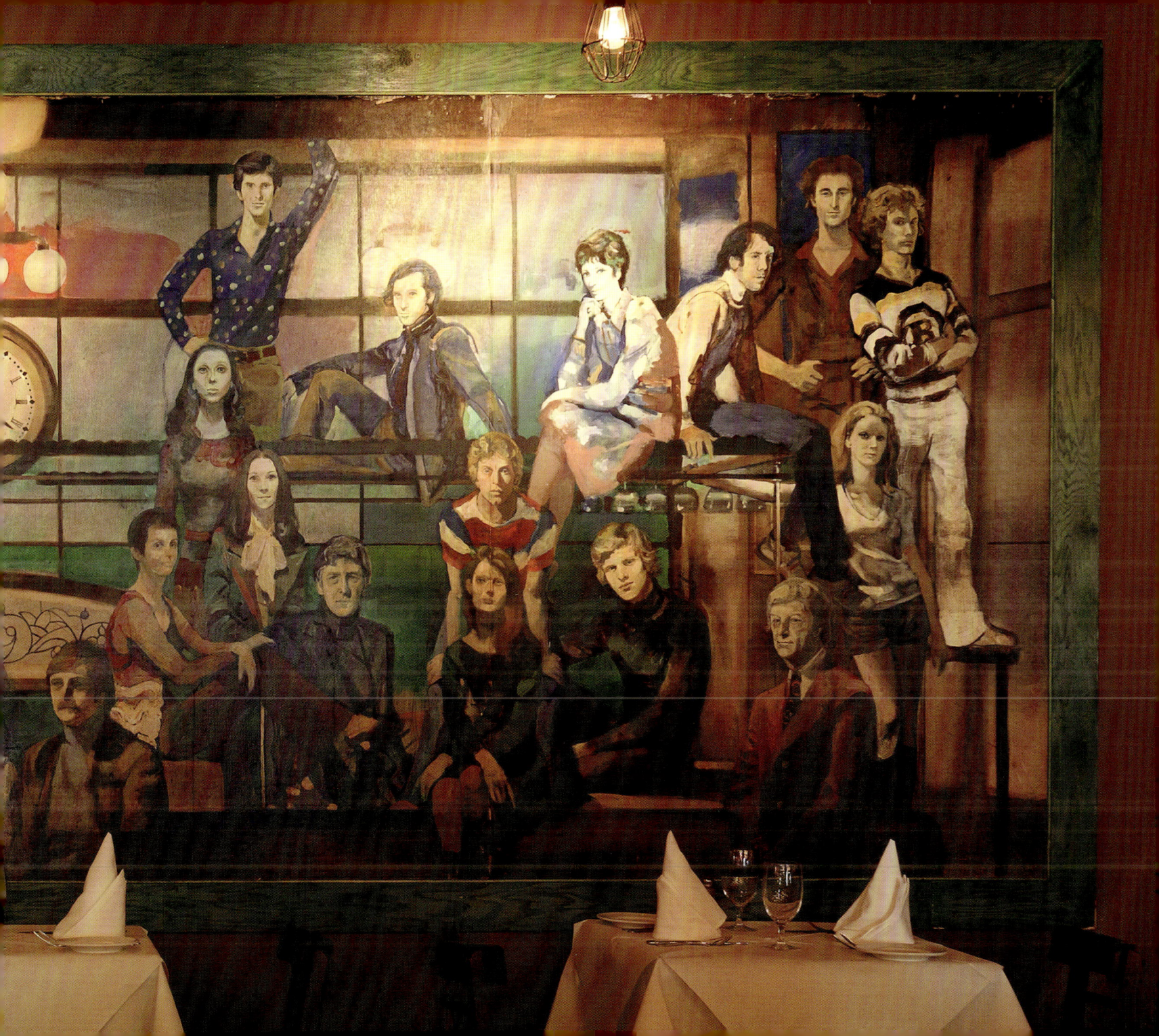

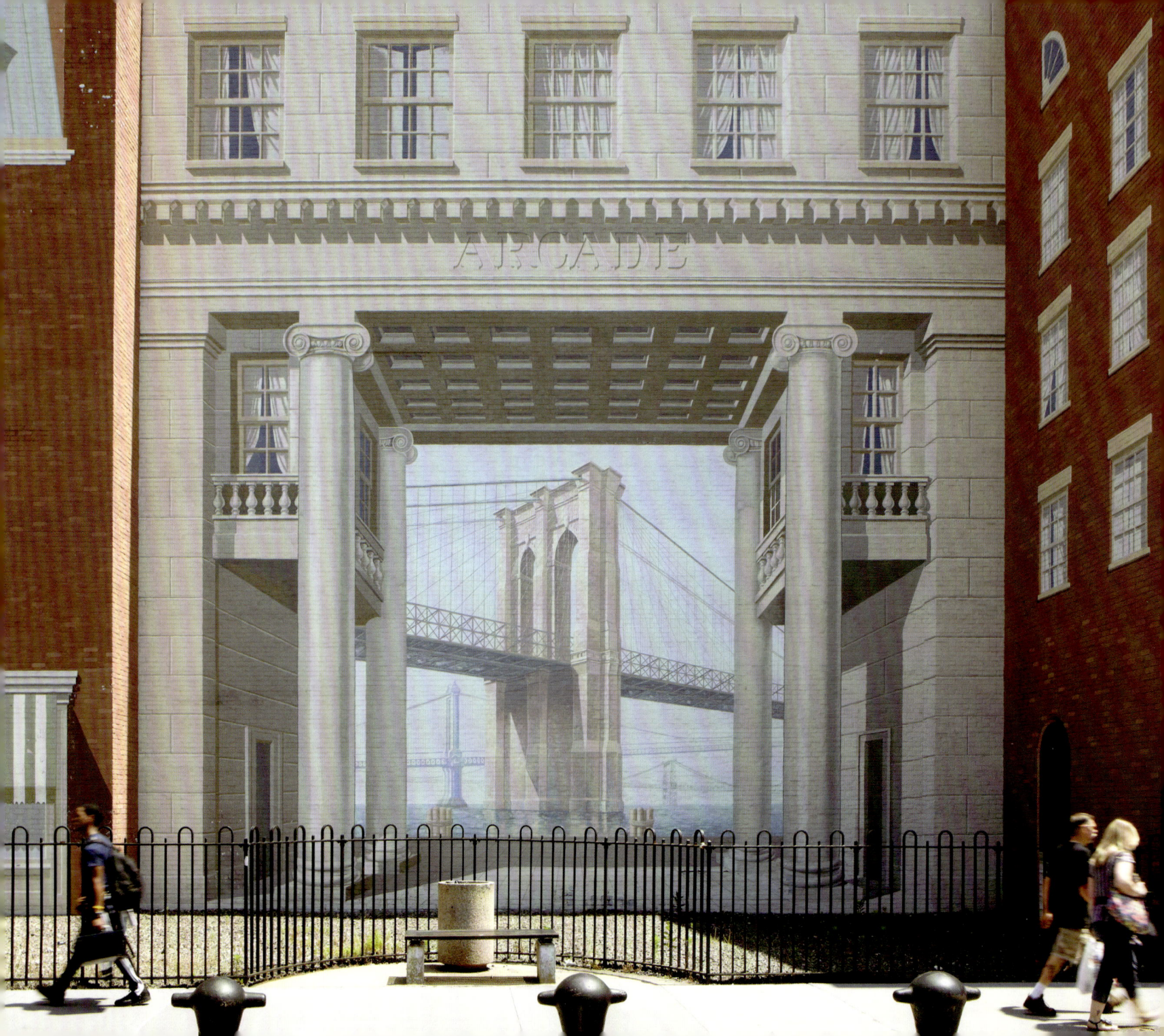

THE PECK SLIP ARCADE & GLOCKENSPIEL

RICHARD HAAS

43 Peck Slip, Manhattan • 83rd Street and York Avenue, Manhattan

The Romans claimed to have originated *quadratura* (a technique of painting that creates the illusion of architectural details on blank walls), but the Greeks might disagree. Either way, the practice of painting architectural illusion dates back millennia. When the Roman civilization declined and fell, so did *quadratura*, which then popped up again during the Renaissance, faded away for a bit, and surged back to reach its zenith during the Baroque period, when it was known as trompe l'oeil ("tricking the eye"). It last re-emerged in New York with the work of the visual magician Richard Haas.

After the bland fare of the plains, most midwestern artists find the complexity and variety of New York's architecture a visual feast. For Wisconsin-born Haas, architecture became an unwavering, lifelong passion. The city became his muse.

His first works were explorations into architectural illusion and art. He created shadow boxes, basically miniature three-dimensional dioramas of other artists' studios—Jackson Pollock, Henri Matisse, Johannes Vermeer—as well as Gertrude Stein in her Parisian dining room.

Influenced by Giovanni Battista Piranesi, Haas's work evolved into pencil drawings, paintings, and etchings of the art we live in. A closet Realist in a time of Abstract Expressionism, he created some of the best urban landscapes ever painted. A master printer, he faithfully captured anything that caught his voracious eye. Then, in 1975, he shifted gears again, and the city itself became his canvas.

Doris Freedman had founded the nonprofit City Walls, a latter-day Works Progress Administration, devoted to using public art to revitalize the downtrodden streets of New York of the late 1960s. Haas proposed a mural extending the façade of 112 Prince Street around to the side of the building to cover a wall left scarred and exposed when the building next door had been razed. With a grant from the National Endowment for the Arts, the mural, an illusion of reality, became a reality.

Working from a maquette, sign painters dangled from scaffolds off the side of the building, transforming the crude brick into a beautiful continuation of the adjacent 1889 cast-iron architecture. Haas struggled with detachment, watching others painting his vision. He hovered nearby in Fanelli's to eat pub grub and periodically stepped out onto the street to join the crowd watching the progress as the "new" building emerged.

The final effect was magical or, as the self-effacing Haas describes it, "plausible." He included faux air-conditioning units and, in one window, two cool cats pose on a sill observing the street below. There are two actual windows on the wall, which were incorporated into the composition, adding to the illusion. After nearly four decades, the elements and the disfigurations of graffiti have tarnished the beauty of Haas's work but, luckily for New York, there are currently restoration efforts in motion.

In 1978, Consolidated Edison commissioned Haas to paint its clunky electrical substation at the Peck Slip to blend with the landmarked buildings of the South Street Seaport. Haas made it vanish by not only re-creating a street of two-hundred-year-old buildings, but by adding a trompe l'oeil vision of the Brooklyn Bridge appearing in the distance beyond the painted arcade. By marrying the painted architecture to its surroundings, he neutralized the substation's twentieth-century utilitarian intrusion into one of New York's treasures. Haas's painted fantasy achieved a reality with a life of its own.

In 2005, the Cielo, a luxury high-rise, arose on an Upper East Side corner. The refined atmosphere of the building was marred by its neighbor: a graffiti-covered

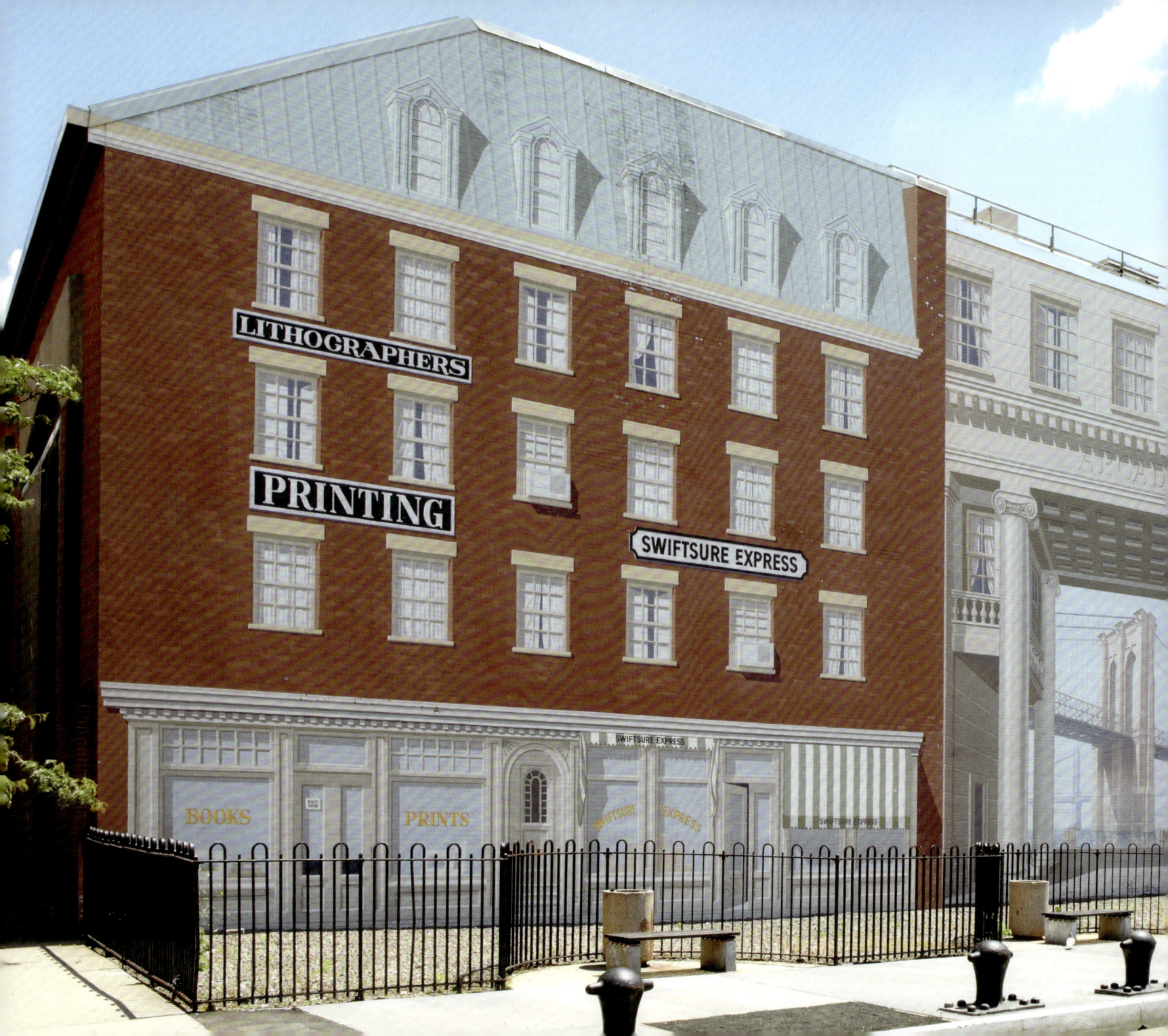

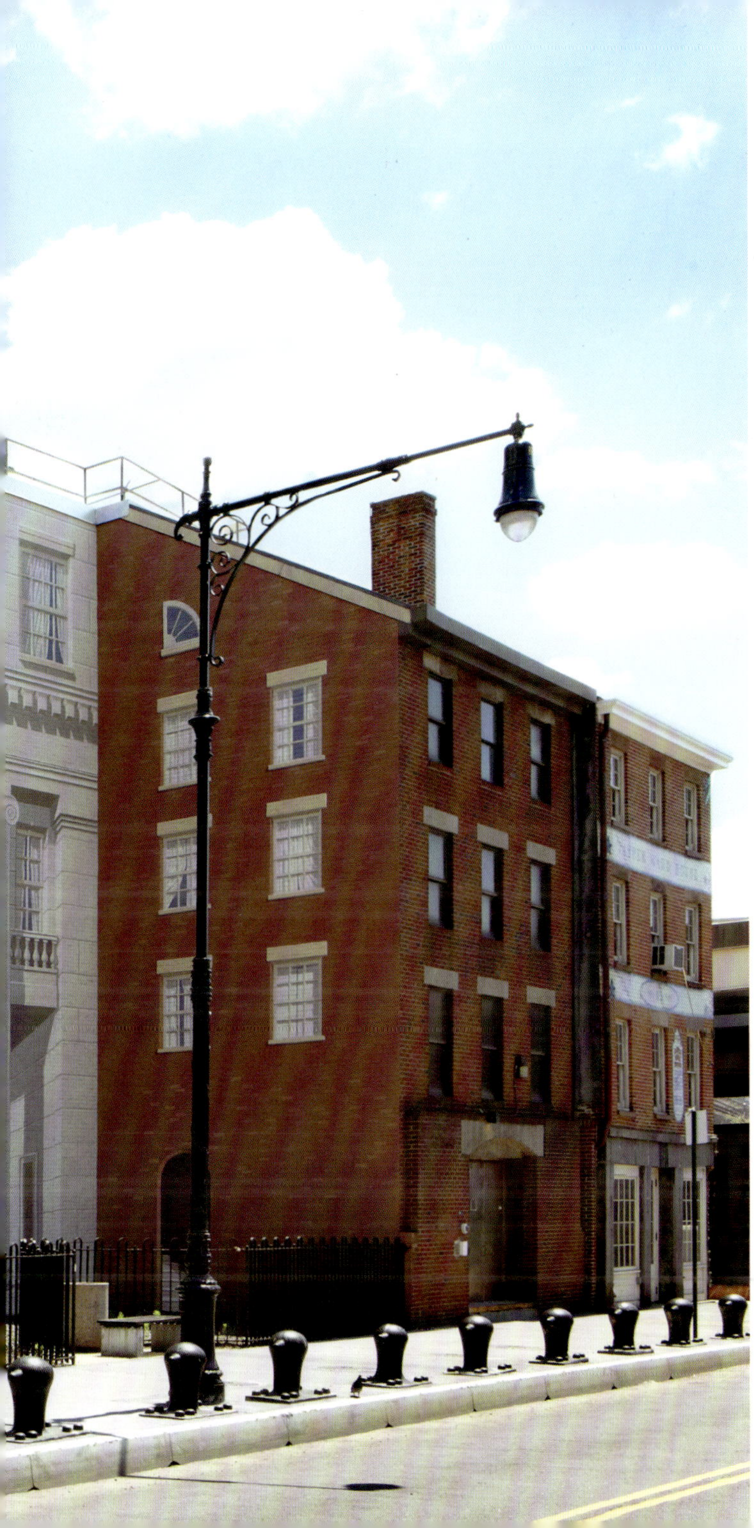

tenement. The developer, Jules Demchick, approached George Papoutsis, the owner of the offending edifice, and asked permission to paint a mural on the side of his building to give the illusion that the neighborhood was upscale enough to justify the price of the apartments.

Papoutsis agreed, and Richard Haas was commissioned. Haas painted *Glockenspiel* as a tribute to the Germanic history of the Yorkville neighborhood. He painted a side of a building rich in architectural detail, such as a three-story bay window and a clock with painted "movable" mechanical figures, which, reflecting the city theme, are two New York City mounted policemen.

A mural is dependent on the walls of its host building. No building, no mural. Sadly, because our restless urban landscape is in constant flux and buildings are forever being torn down and replaced, most of Richard Haas's 120 major murals no longer exist. How lucky are we, then, to still have these three.

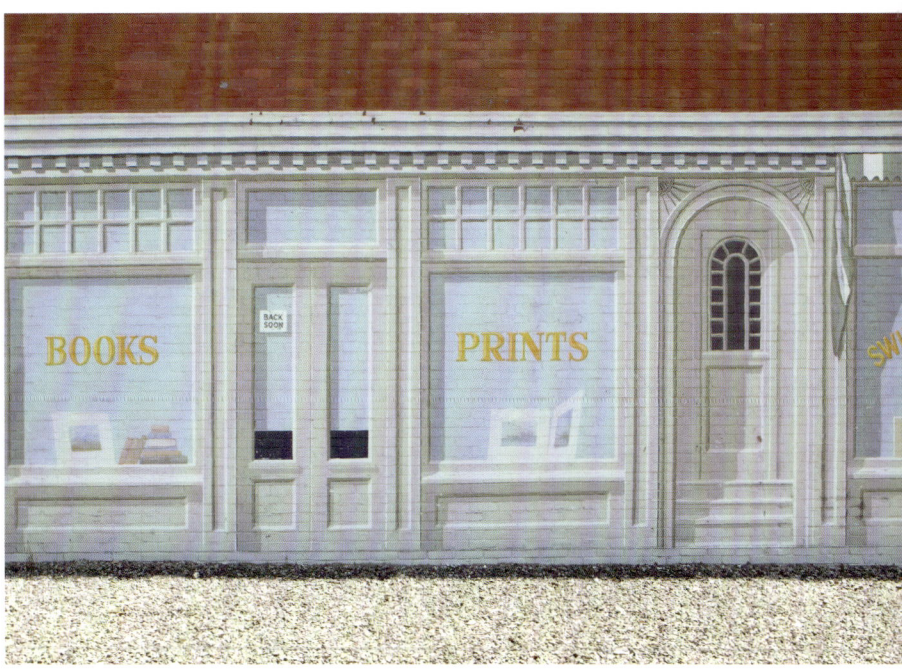

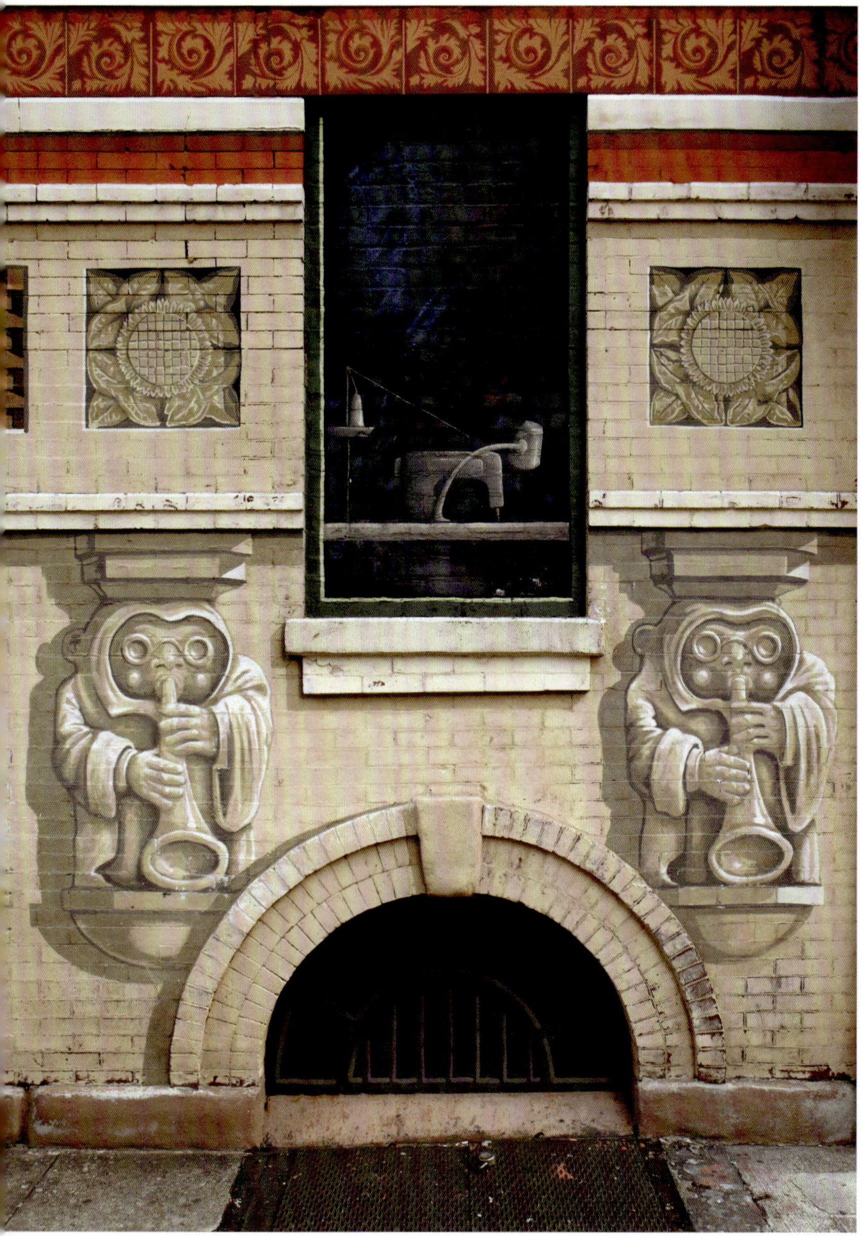

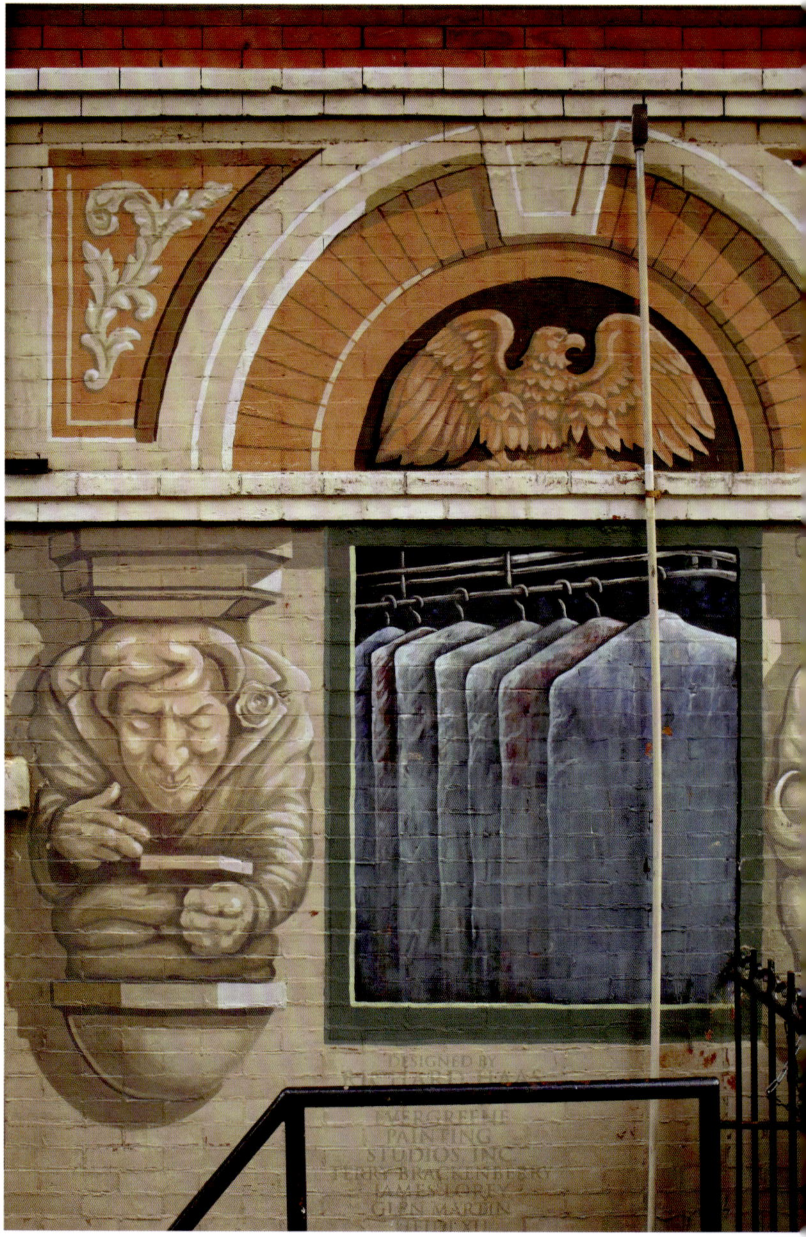
DESIGNED BY
EVERGREENE
PAINTING
STUDIOS, INC
GLEN MARBIN

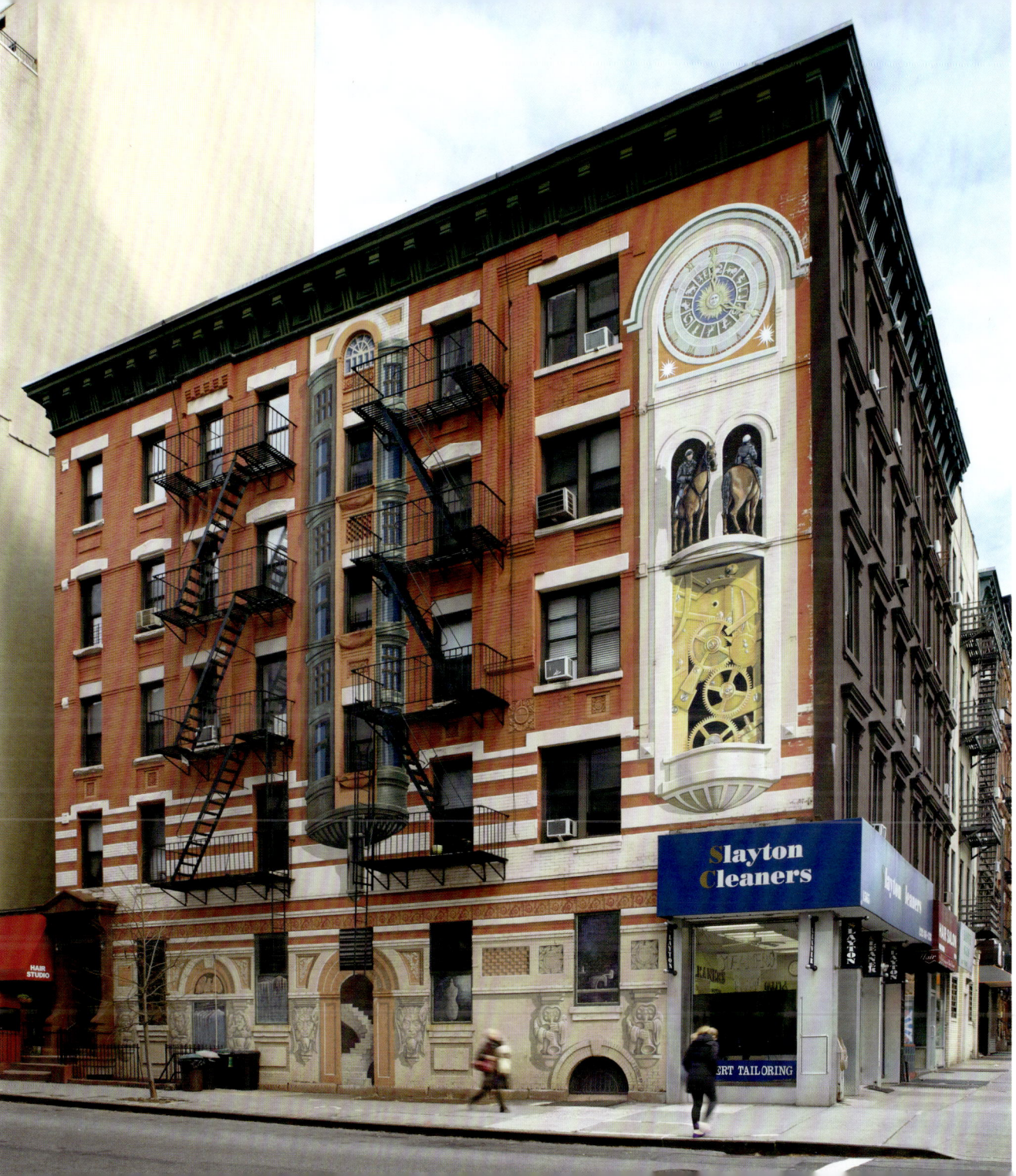

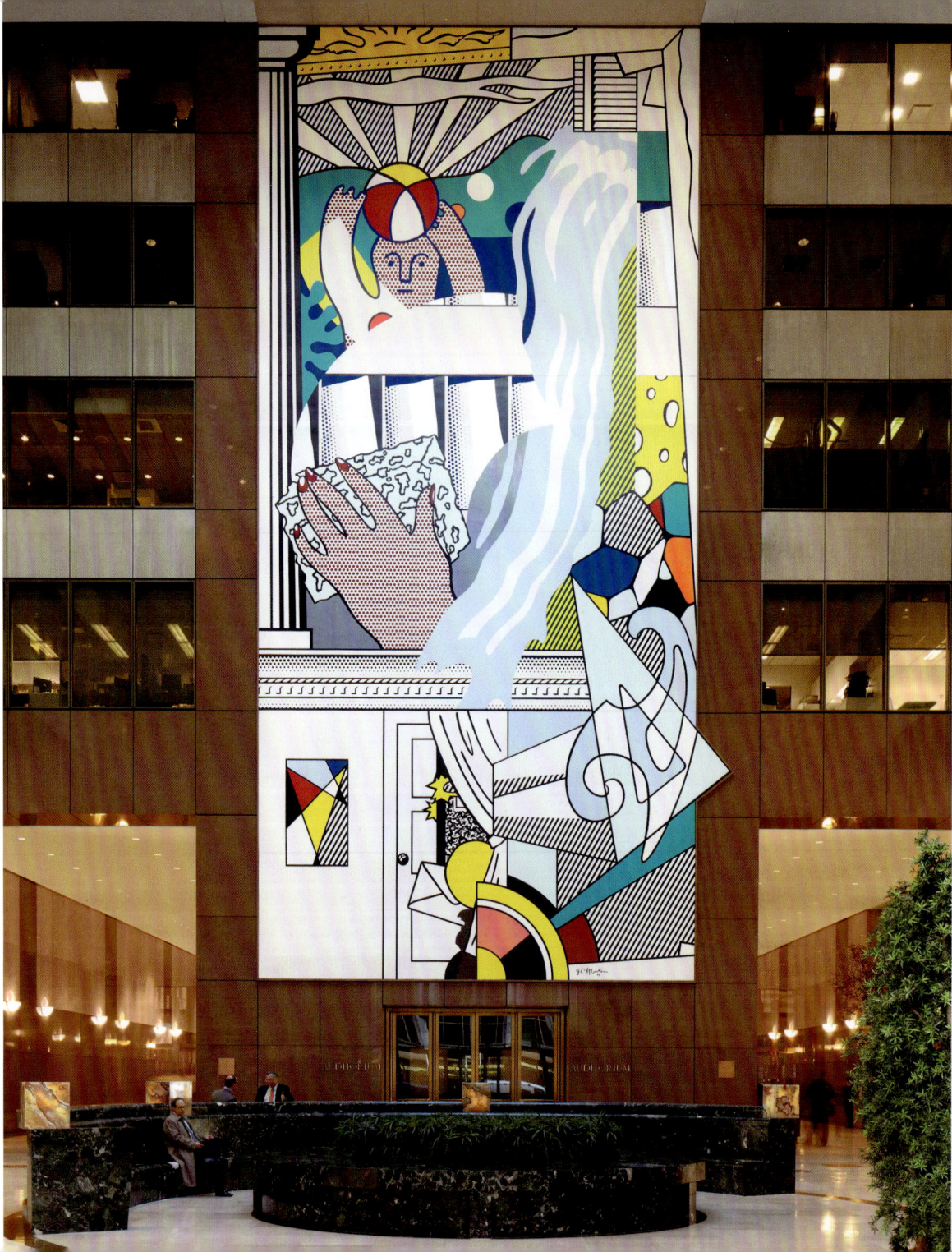

AXA EQUITABLE CENTER

The cliché that all artists hail from rigid lower-middle-class families that reside in places like Cody, Wyoming (Jackson Pollock), Pittsburgh, Pennsylvania (Andy Warhol), or Monroe, Washington (Chuck Close), and escape to New York to make art and "make it" was not the path of Roy Lichtenstein.

Born in Manhattan to a loving, upper-middle-class Jewish family, who encouraged his artistry, Lichtenstein was a mediocre student whose daydreaming and doodling were infinitely more compelling to him than chemistry tables. When he was sixteen, he took a class from Reginald Marsh at the Art Students League and, from then on, he knew that he wanted nothing other than to be an artist.

Though World War II interrupted his formal education, he spent the war drawing maps showing troop movements. He visited Paris after the war and, once, went by Picasso's apartment on rue des Grand-Augustins. He couldn't work up the nerve to ring the bell: "I walked away after a while thinking, 'Why would Picasso want to see me?'"

Back in the United States, he taught at Rutgers and painted mock historical paintings and tried Abstract Expressionism. He became friends with sculptor George Segal, and artists like Claes Oldenburg, Red Grooms, and Jim Dine, choreographers Merce Cunningham and Paul Taylor, and composer John Cage. And, as if by osmosis, he became liberated from the traditional view of what was art.

There are different stories of how Lichtenstein began his Pop Art painting, but no matter how it originated, Lichtenstein abandoned Abstract Expressionism and began to appropriate and re-present popular images from cartoons and other commercial imagery. His breakthrough painting, *Look Mickey*, now hangs in the National Gallery of Art in Washington, D.C. In a 1963 *Artnews* interview, he said his own art is "anti-contemplative, anti-nuance, anti-getting-away-from-the-tyranny-of-the-rectangle, anti-movement and anti-light, anti-mystery, anti paint-quality,

anti-Zen, and anti-all of those brilliant ideas of preceding movements which everyone understands so thoroughly."

In 1984, the Equitable Life Assurance Society of the United States commissioned Lichtenstein to paint a mural for the atrium of their building. Measuring 62 feet high by 35½ feet wide, it is one of the largest public paintings in New York. *Mural with a Blue Brushstroke* is a witty tour de force. Lichtenstein pays homage to famous artists of the twentieth century, including Fernand Léger, Ellsworth Kelly, Henri Matisse, Jean Arp, Jasper Johns, Georges Braque, and Frank Stella by assembling elements of their art into a one-man group show.

The dominant element of the mural, for which it is named, is a long, diagonal blue brushstroke. Before undertaking the mural, he had completed a series of large paintings of different artists' brushstrokes. Of course, the brushstrokes he created had little to do with the actual brushwork of the artists he saluted, but therein was his subtle, sophisticated humor. He parodied his own work by painting two cartoon starbursts in front of a door at the bottom of composition with the words "Knock! Knock!" For some reason, the powers that be took exception to these words. Ever affable and unflappable, Lichtenstein painted out the offending words and the bursts are now a flat, and for some corporate art critics, comforting yellow.

It is unknown how much Lichtenstein was paid for the Equitable Life mural but in 1994, three years before his death, he created a mural for the Times Square subway station, entitled *Times Square Mural*, made of porcelain enamel on steel and measuring 6 feet high by 53 feet long, for which he was offered $250,000. He declined the fee, making a gift of the piece to the people of New York.

By all accounts he was soft-spoken, self-deprecatingly humorous, charming, warm-hearted, and unfailingly polite. "I don't have any big anxieties," he once said. "I wish I did. I'd be much more interesting."

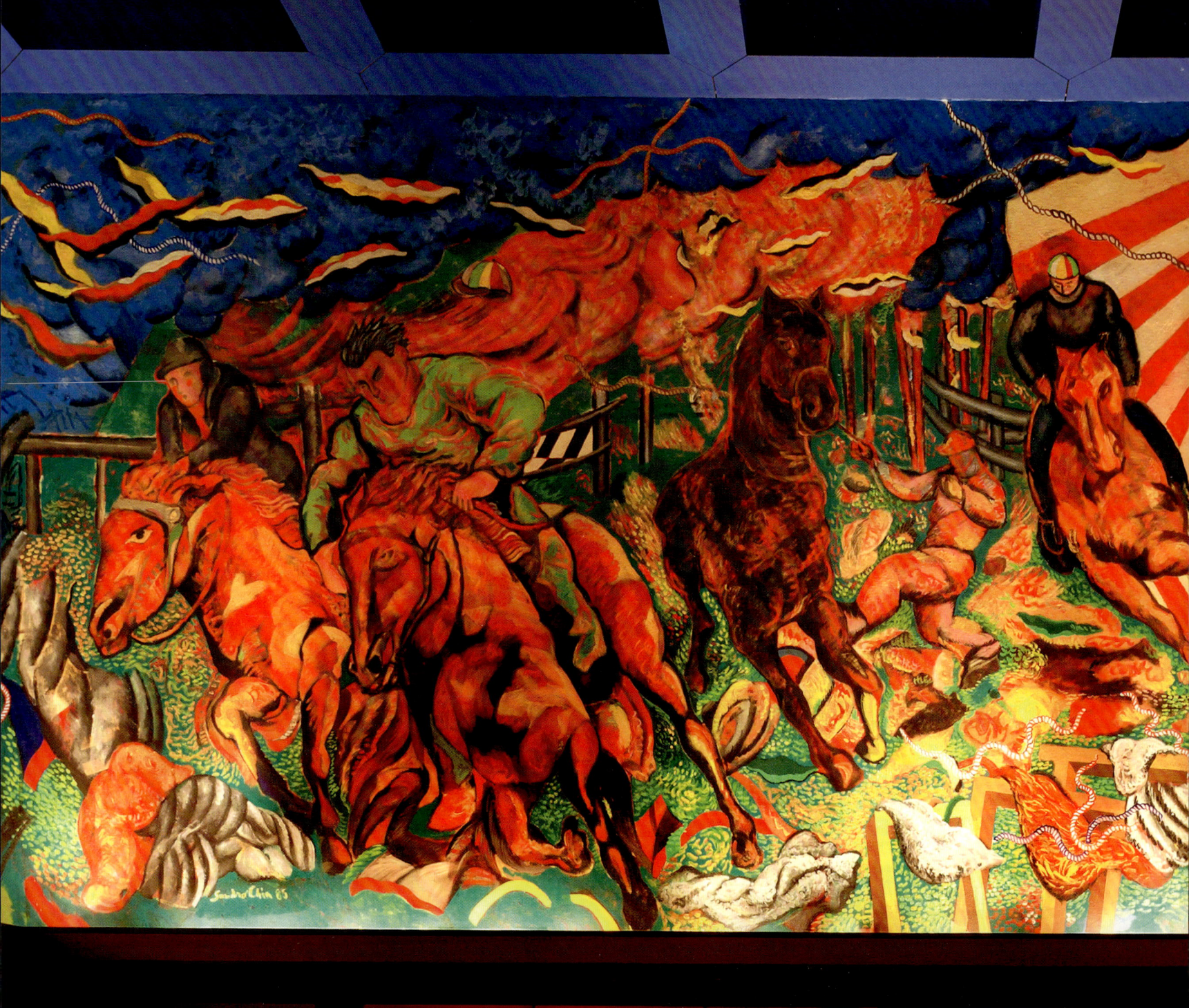

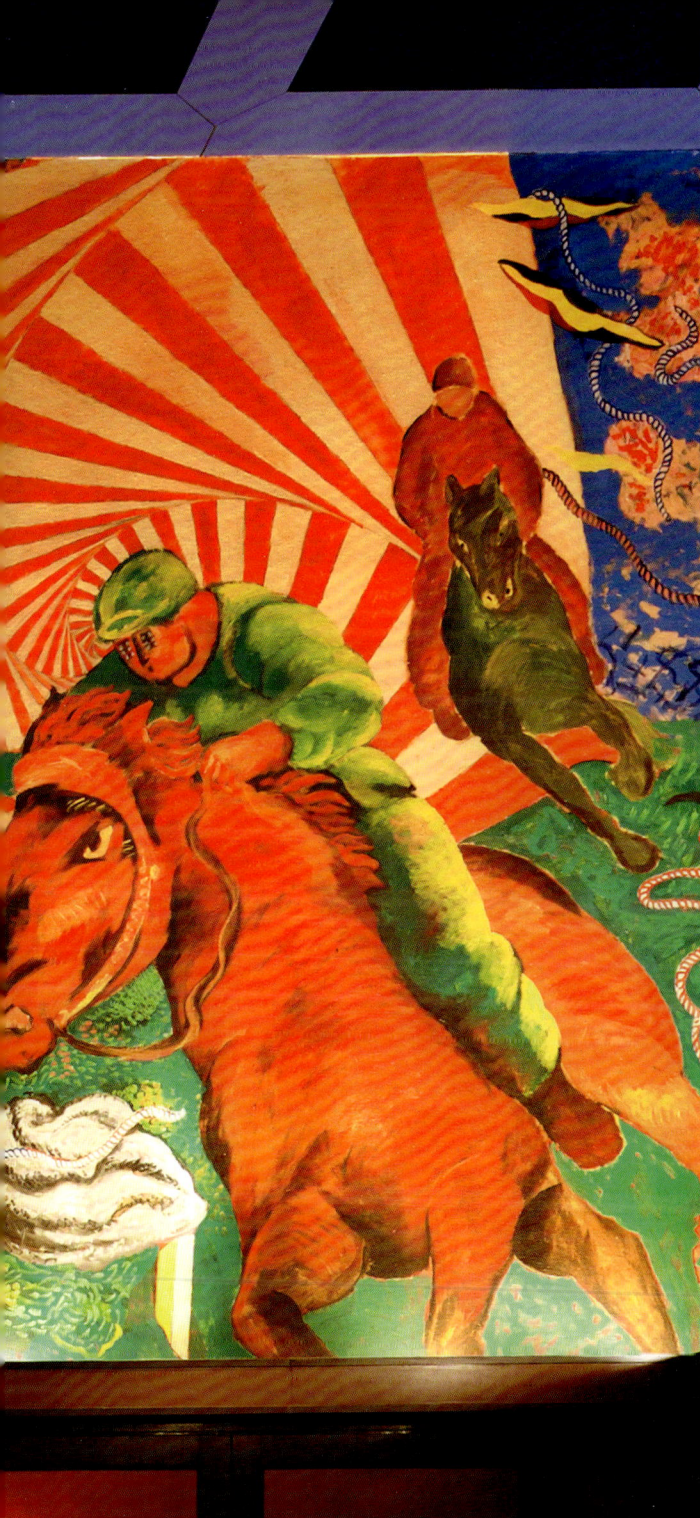

PALIO BAR

151 West 51st Street, Manhattan · SANDRO CHIA

In 1985, the chairman of the Equitable Life Assurance Society of the United States, Benjamin D. Holloway, commissioned art to decorate his office building. Taking a cue from Rockefeller Center, he asked Roy Lichtenstein to create a painting for the building's atrium, and Sandro Chia, arguably the most famous Neo-Expressionist painter in the world, to paint a 128-foot-long mural for a restaurant space.

He asked Chia to paint the skyline of Siena's Piazza del Campo around the top third of the double-height room. Holloway explained his vision for a polite, decorative depiction of the beautiful piazza so diners might briefly, be lulled into believing they were in a medieval walled city instead of a restaurant in Manhattan.

When the canvas was delivered, Holloway found not a quaint Italian cityscape but a soaring, riotous painting of the Palio horse race, an event run in Siena every year since 1590. Instead of languidly relaxing in the peaceful Piazza del Campo, patrons would be sitting in the middle of a Neo-Expressionist masterpiece of galloping horses and the explosive frenzy of a race, a thunderous, celebratory Italian metaphor for living life to the fullest. Rather than a calming and tranquil oasis, in a palette of intense late-afternoon scarlet oranges, fiery yellows, and crimsons, Chia depicted a rowdy competition between seventeen neighborhoods, or contrade, filled with a spectacle of Renaissance splendor whose participants are dressed vibrantly in colored silks and waving their contrada's banner.

Neapolitan restaurateur Tony May loved the energy of the painting and the magic of the room and opened the Palio Bar in 1986. Sadly, after twenty-five years, May discontinued operations, and the space awaits the next entrepreneur to treat another generation to this unique treasure. Like Reginald Marsh's U.S. Customs House murals, which were shuttered for twenty-five years, Sandro Chia's riotous masterpiece is resting quietly in the dark, waiting to dazzle us all anew.

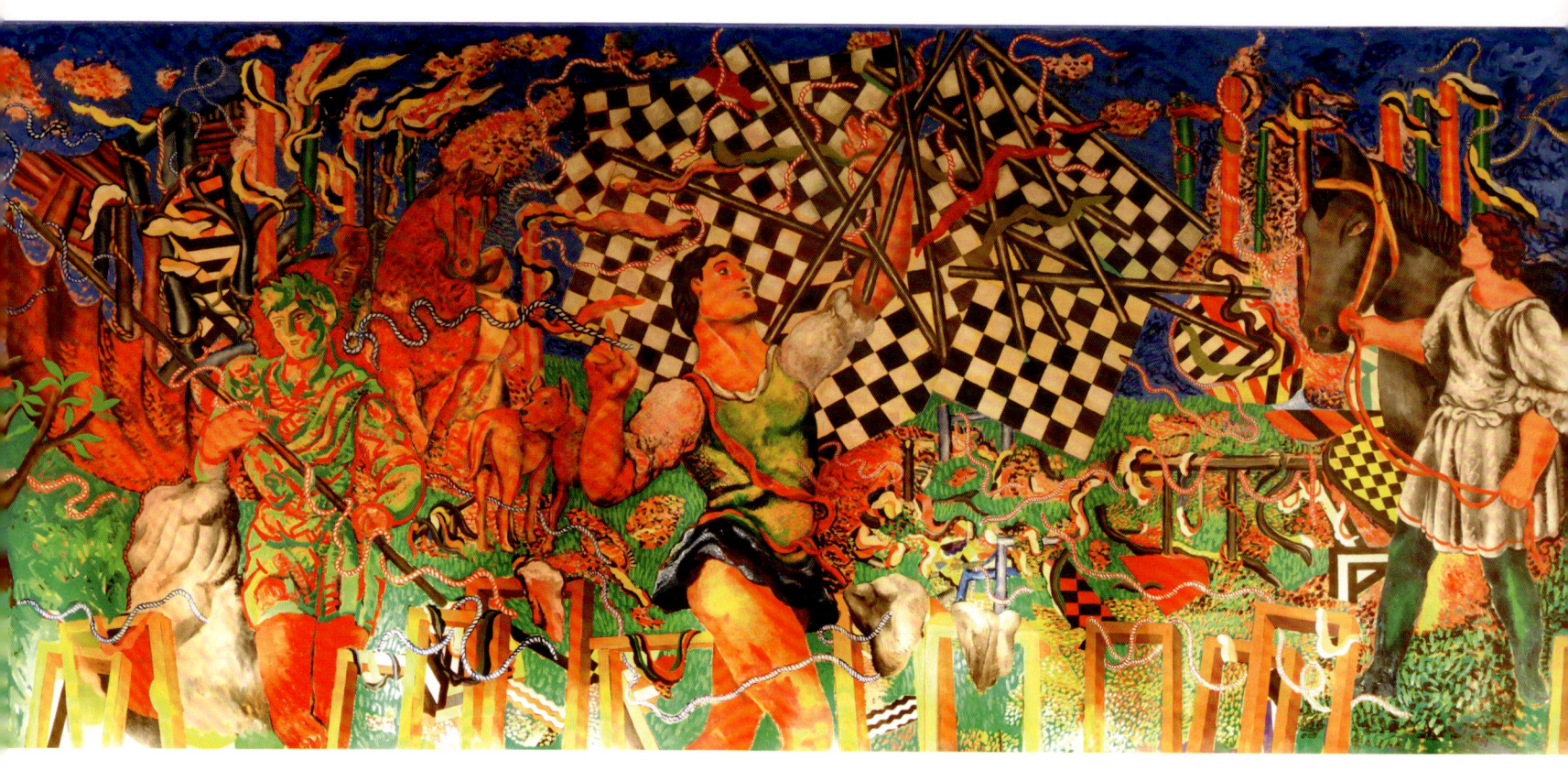

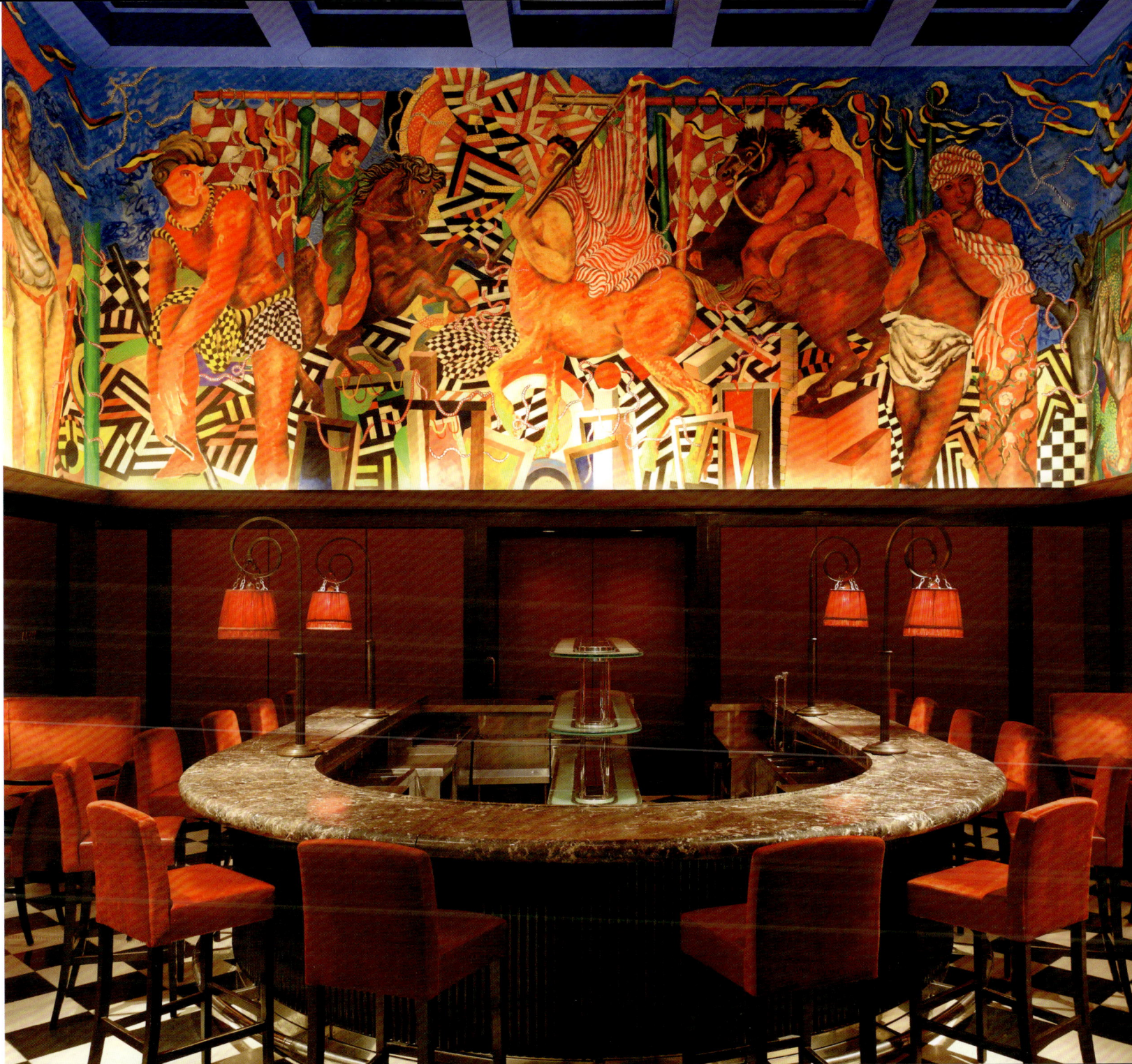

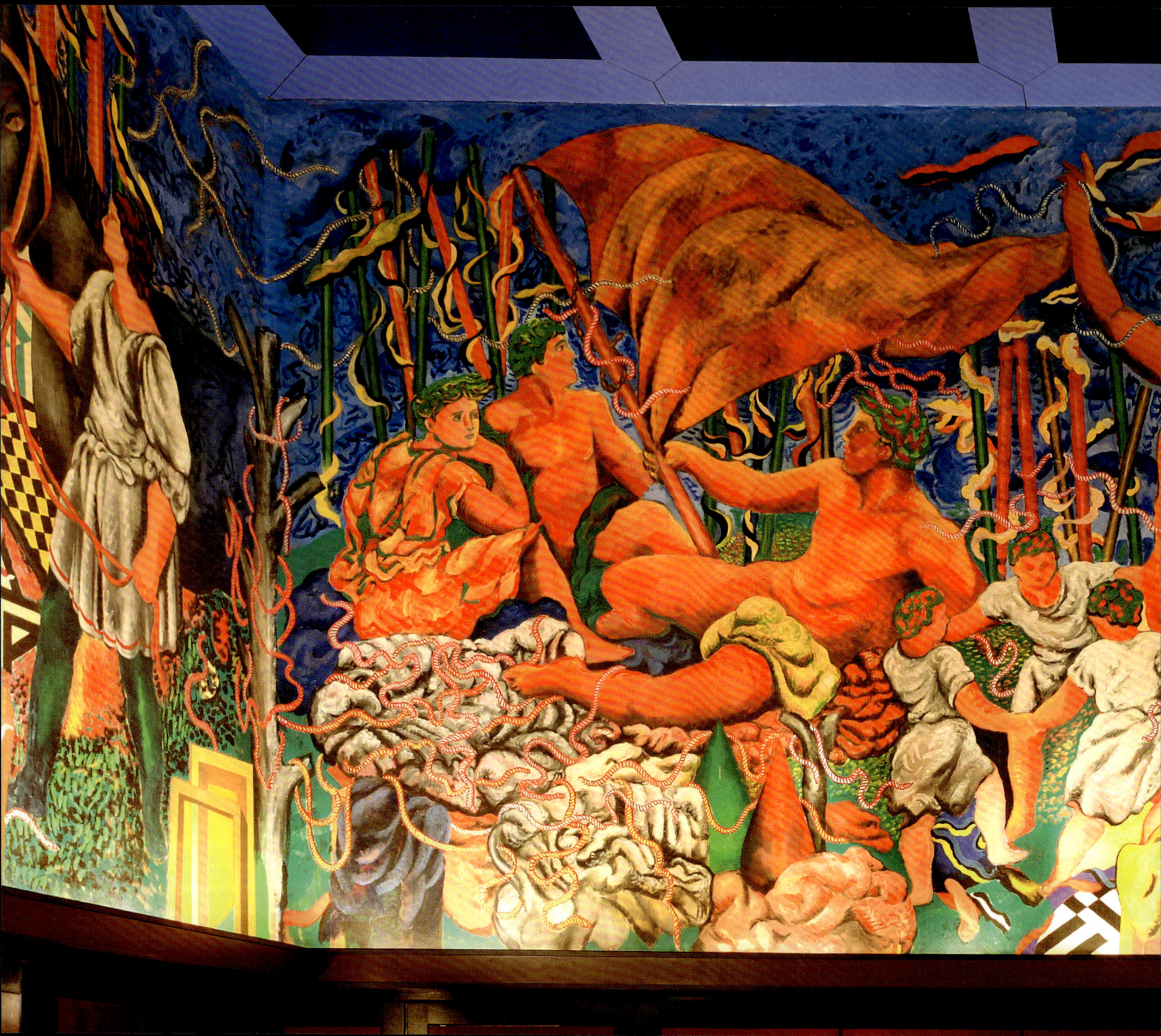

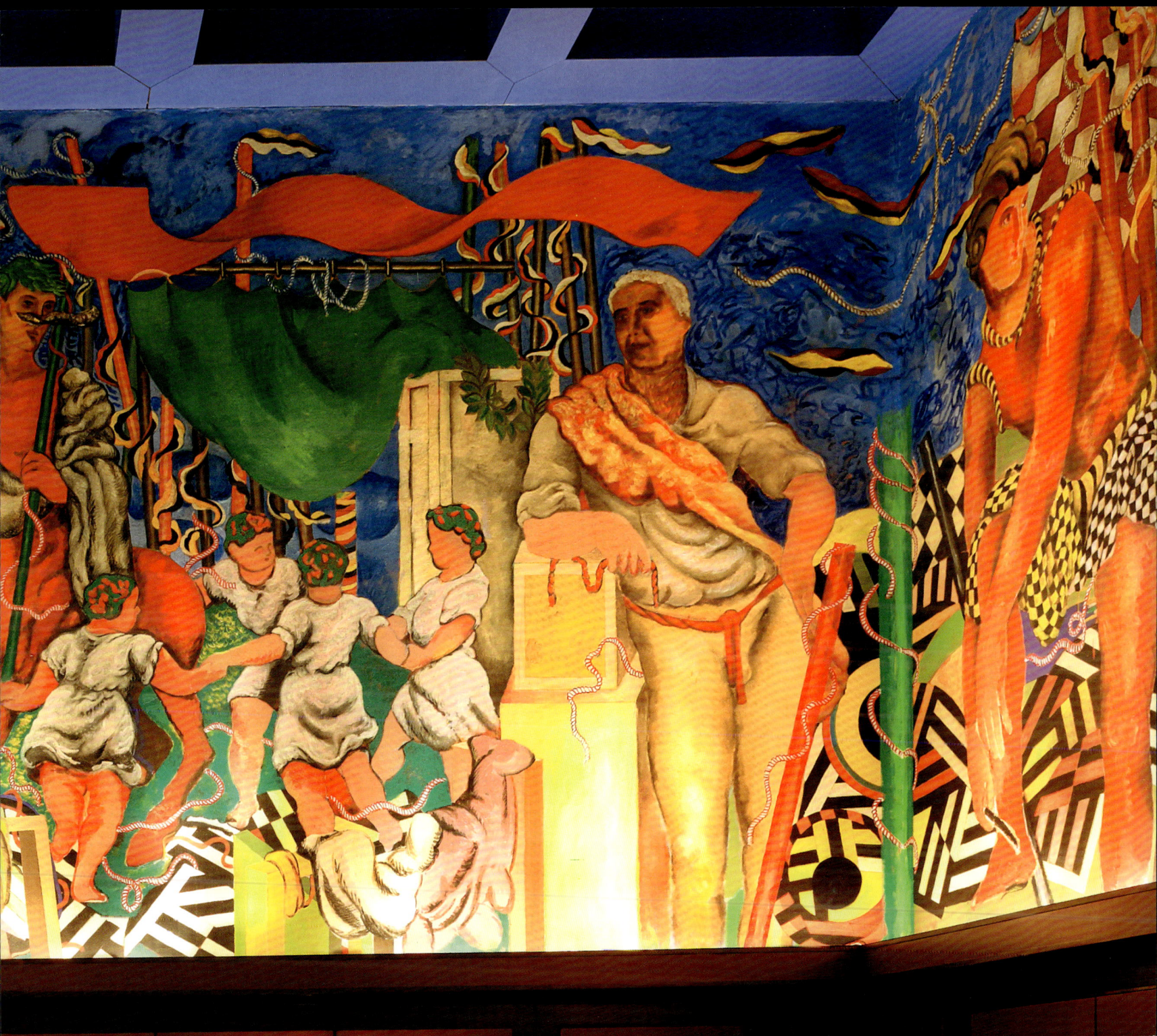

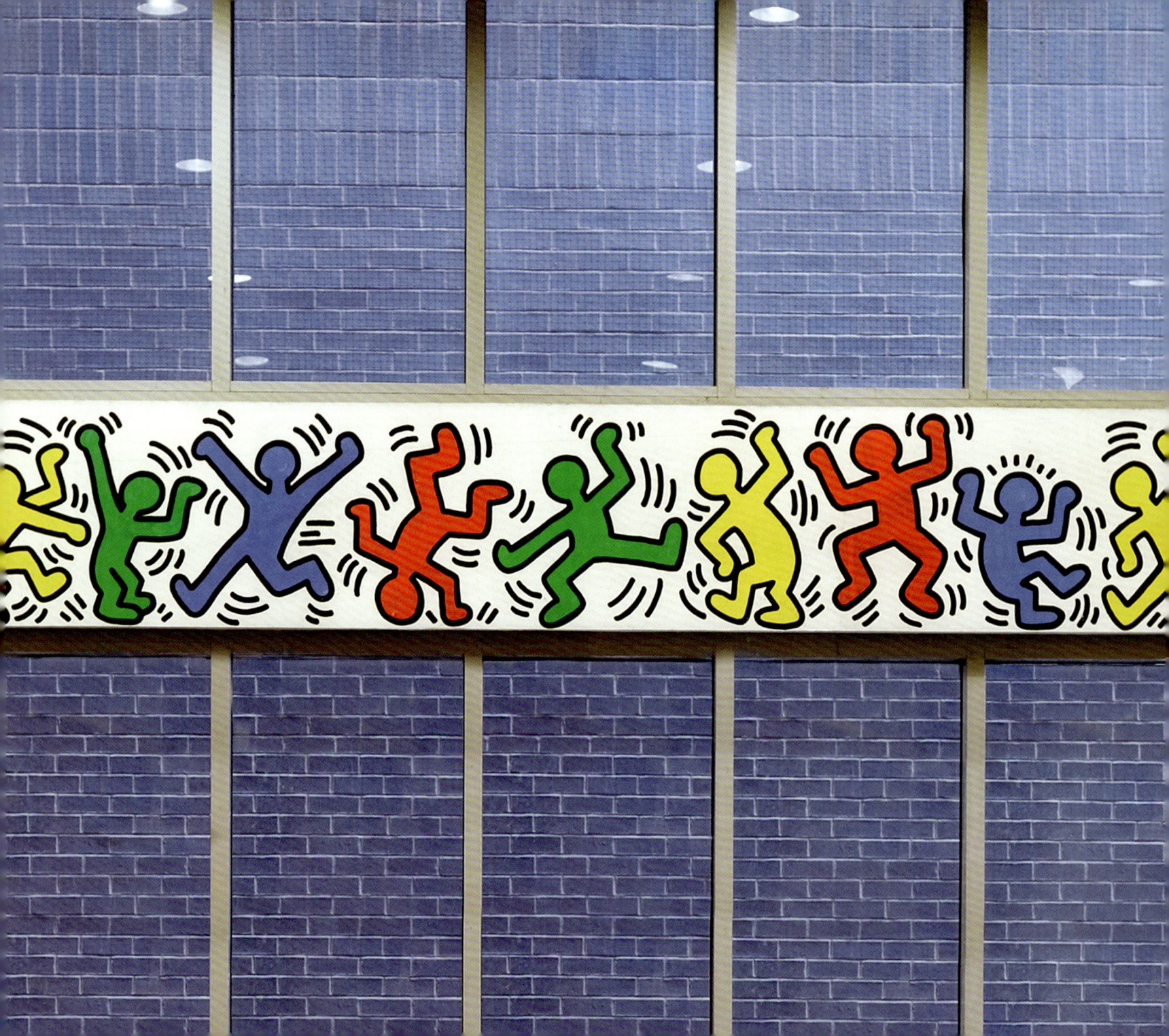

A MUSEUM, A PARK & A HOSPITAL

KEITH HARING

New York Historical Society, 170 Central Park West, Manhattan   •   128th Street and FDR Drive, Manhattan

Woodhull Medical & Mental Health Center, 760 Broadway, Brooklyn

In 1986, Keith Haring was arrested for disorderly conduct and fined twenty-five dollars for painting an unauthorized mural on the wall of a handball court on 128th Street at the edge of the FDR Drive. The bright orange background of Haring's iconic black outlined cartoon figures came with the warning "Crack Is Wack," a reaction to the drug epidemic that was then sweeping the city. When another street artist changed the wording to "Crack Is It," maintenance crews promptly painted over the entire mural with gray paint. After New York City Parks Commissioner Henry Stern learned that a work by one of the most famous and prolific artists in the world had been obliterated, he called Haring, with apologies, and offered him a choice of eight different sites, paint, and the use of a van to paint anything he wanted. Haring insisted on repainting that mural on that wall. Now a New York City landmark, the adjacent park is officially named "Crack Is Wack Playground."

At the time, Haring's work frequently made statements about drug abuse, apartheid, and AIDS decimating a generation of young men. Ironically, four years later, the AIDS virus ended Keith Haring's life. But, fueled by an incandescent energy, he accomplished more in his brief time on earth than most could hope for.

When Haring was growing up in Kutztown, Pennsylvania, his father, an amateur cartoonist, taught him to draw with his eyes closed so that he could trust his hand in the same way a musician plays without looking at the instrument. When he arrived in New York to study at the School of Visual Arts, he was dazzled by the vitality of the ubiquitous graffiti that covered the city's walls and subways. So Haring joined in, becoming a contemporary paleolith decorating the walls of his adopted tribe's caves. He roamed subway platforms in search of empty black panels awaiting advertisements and, with a large piece of chalk, would draw one of his cartoonlike creations. The city became his canvas, his gallery, and his museum and the straphangers his audience. New Yorkers, most of whom would rarely, if ever, attend an art opening or visit a museum, came to know his bold line drawings and his "Radiant Baby," a symbol of life, happiness, and new energy.

His talent was so extraordinary, his confidence so absolute, his instincts so tuned that he never did any preparatory drawings for his paintings. He painted and drew as his father had taught him, trusting his hand, intuition, and rhythm. There was never a false move, never a correction. He approached a surface the same way he approached people, with the total openness and playfulness of a child.

Haring's self-generated fame allowed him to bypass the traditional gallery system, and by his mid-twenties he was a star. The same cartoon calligraphy that had lead to multiple arrests for vandalism elevated him to international celebrity. Over time he became the most prolific and widespread muralist of all time. Whenever he had an exhibit, he would pressure his art dealer in that city to arrange for him to do a mural as well. Between 1982 and 1989, he created public works in over fifty cities including Paris, Sydney, Tokyo, Rio de Janeiro, and Berlin.

His line silhouettes of figures and, in particular, "Radiant Baby" underscored his belief that art could heal. In 1986, he donated a mural, a joyous painting with colorful splashes behind dancing figures and images of families and pregnant women and his famous barking dog, to the Woodhull Medical Center in Brooklyn to acknowledge their dedication to pediatric AIDS research and treatment.

Andy Warhol encouraged Haring to take the "Factory" concept one step further and open a factory/store. The Pop Shop opened in 1986 and sold his iconic

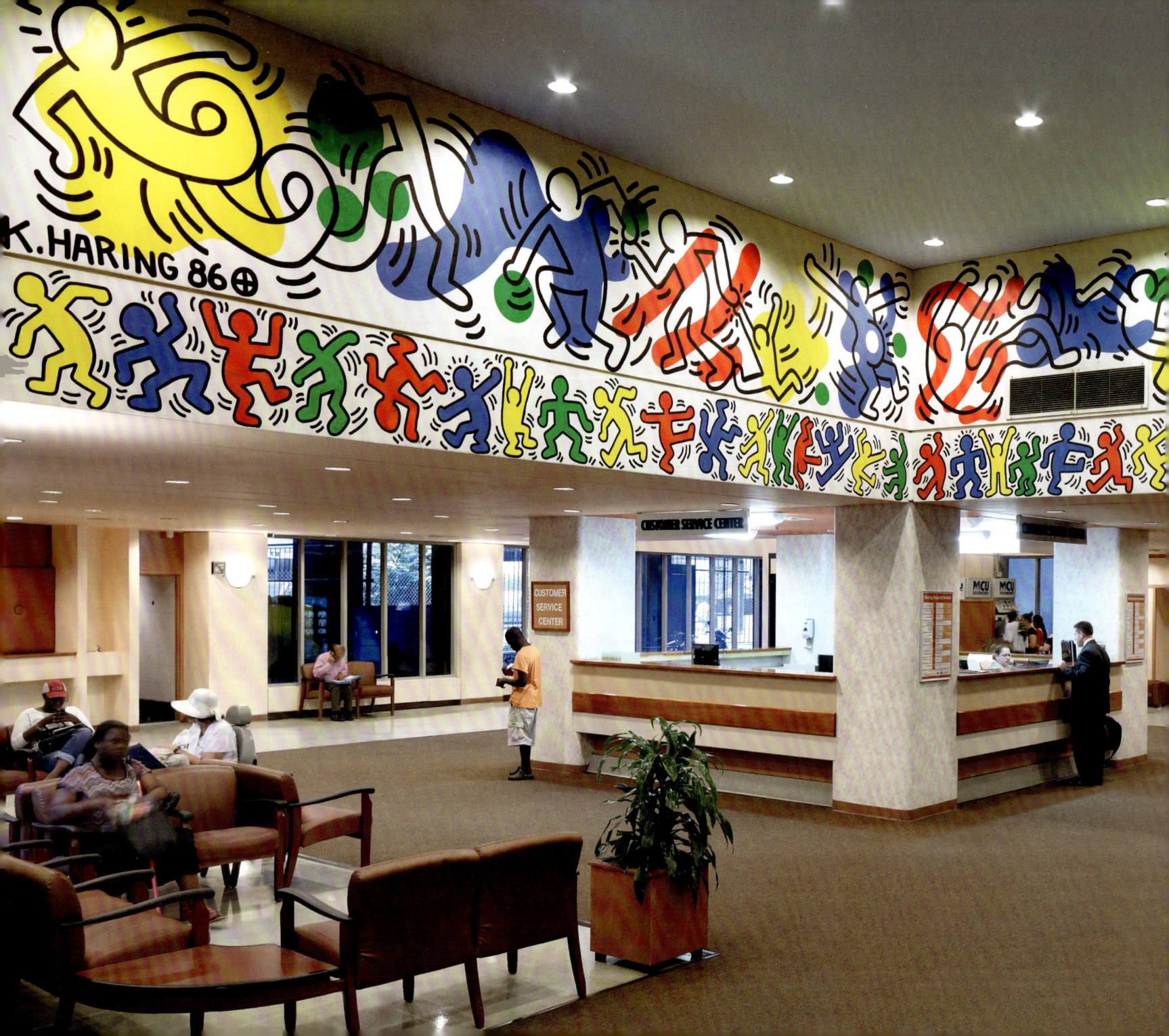

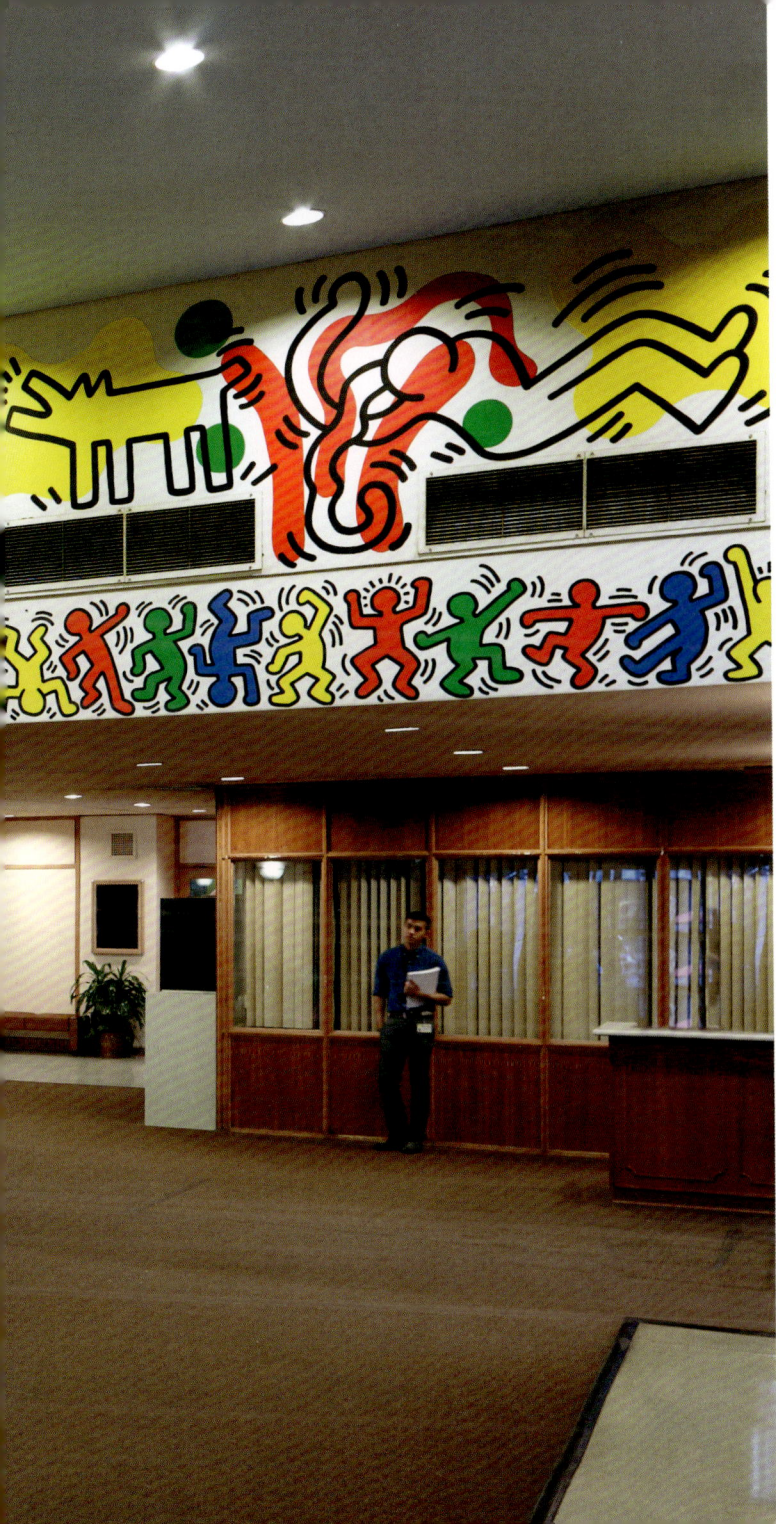

images on T-shirts, toys, and posters, blurring the distinction between high and low art. When it closed in 2005, a section of the store's painted ceiling was preserved and stored until 2011, when the Keith Haring Foundation donated a section of it, unofficially called "Doodle Ceiling," to the New-York Historical Society, where it can be seen today.

In 1989, Haring painted an erotically charged mural to commemorate the 20th anniversary of the Stonewall Riots for the Gay, Lesbian, Bi-Sexual and Transgender Community Center in Greenwich Village.

In the twentieth century, four artists made thier international reputations as catalysts for new trends in art: Warhol, Pollock, Basquiat and Haring. Each artist had their own highly distinctive style and media savvy personality. Of the four, perhaps it is the influence of Basquiat and Haring that has continued on into the twenty-first century. Their work served to energize graffiti street art, a relatively new worldwide phenomenon that both literally and figuratively brings outsiders and outside art into galleries, museums, and private collections. One of the direct descendants of their groundbreaking work is the last painter in this book, Barry McGee.

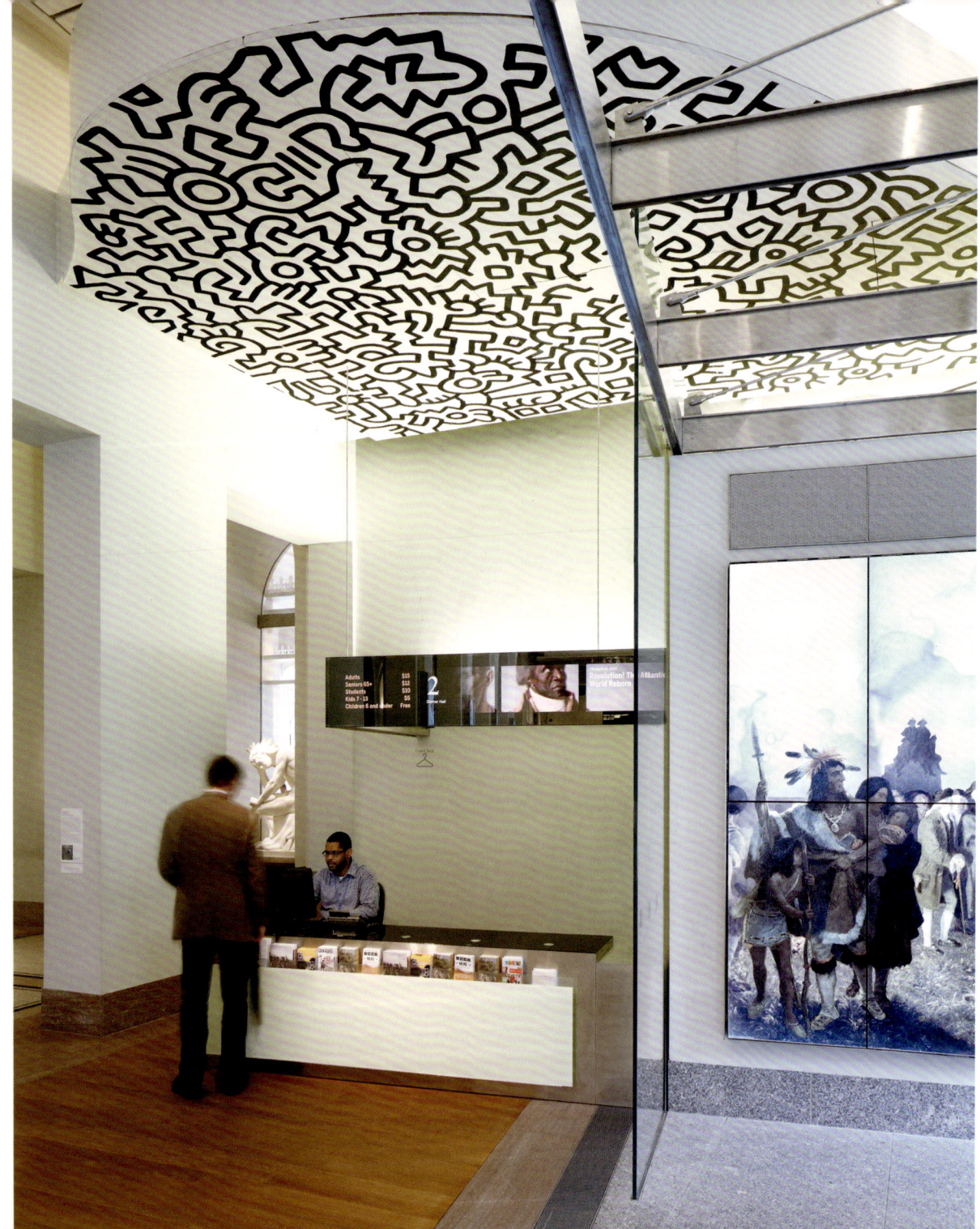

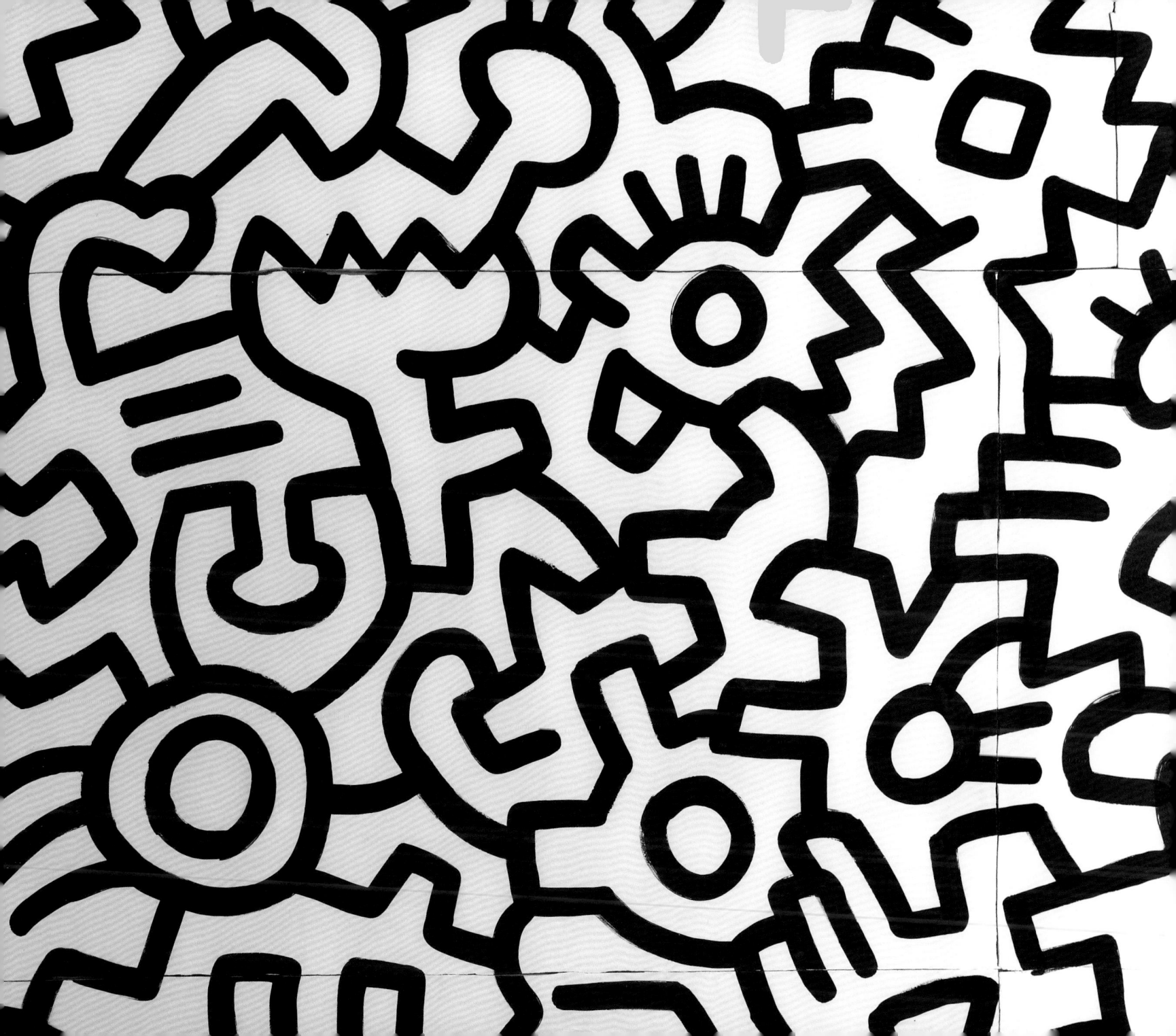

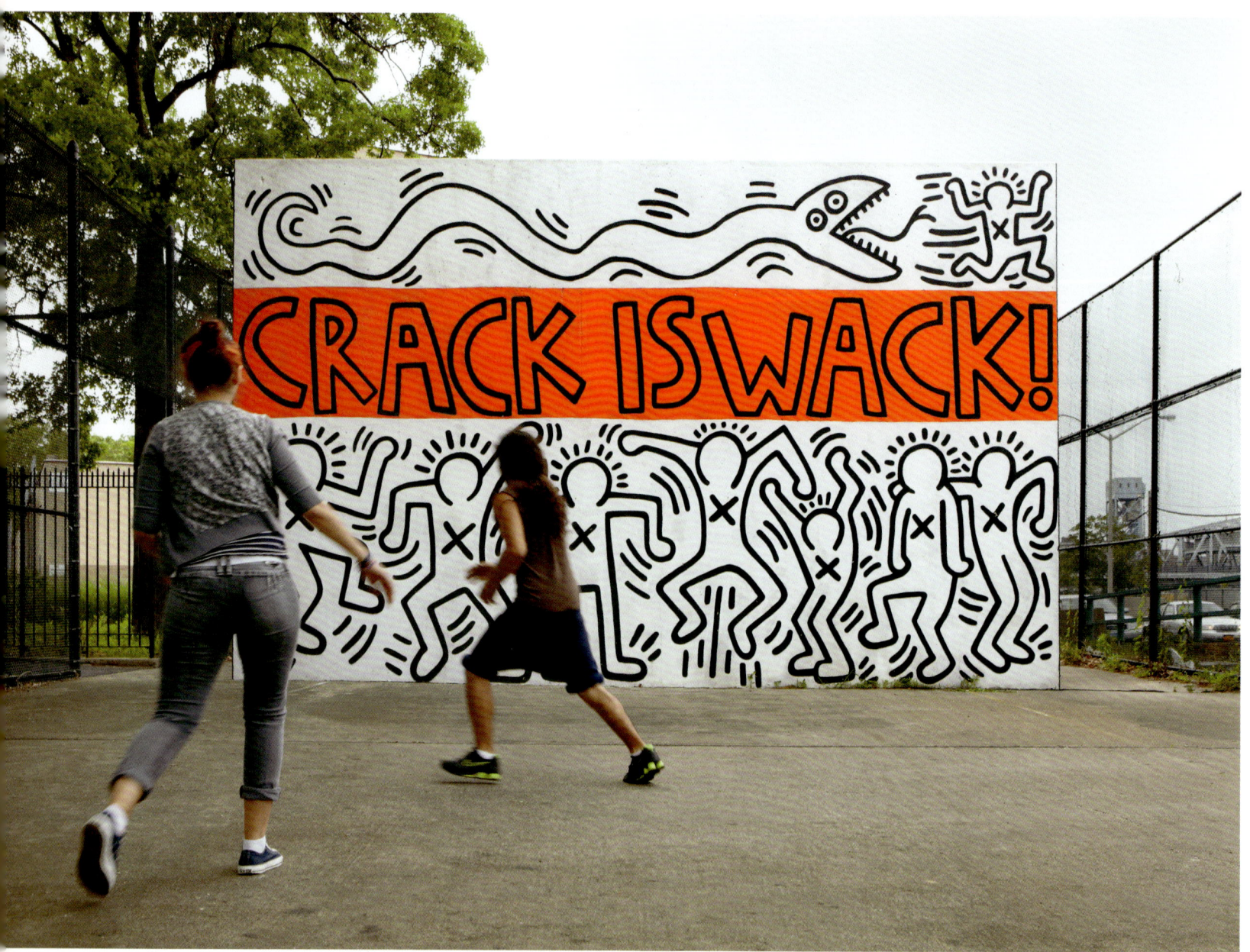

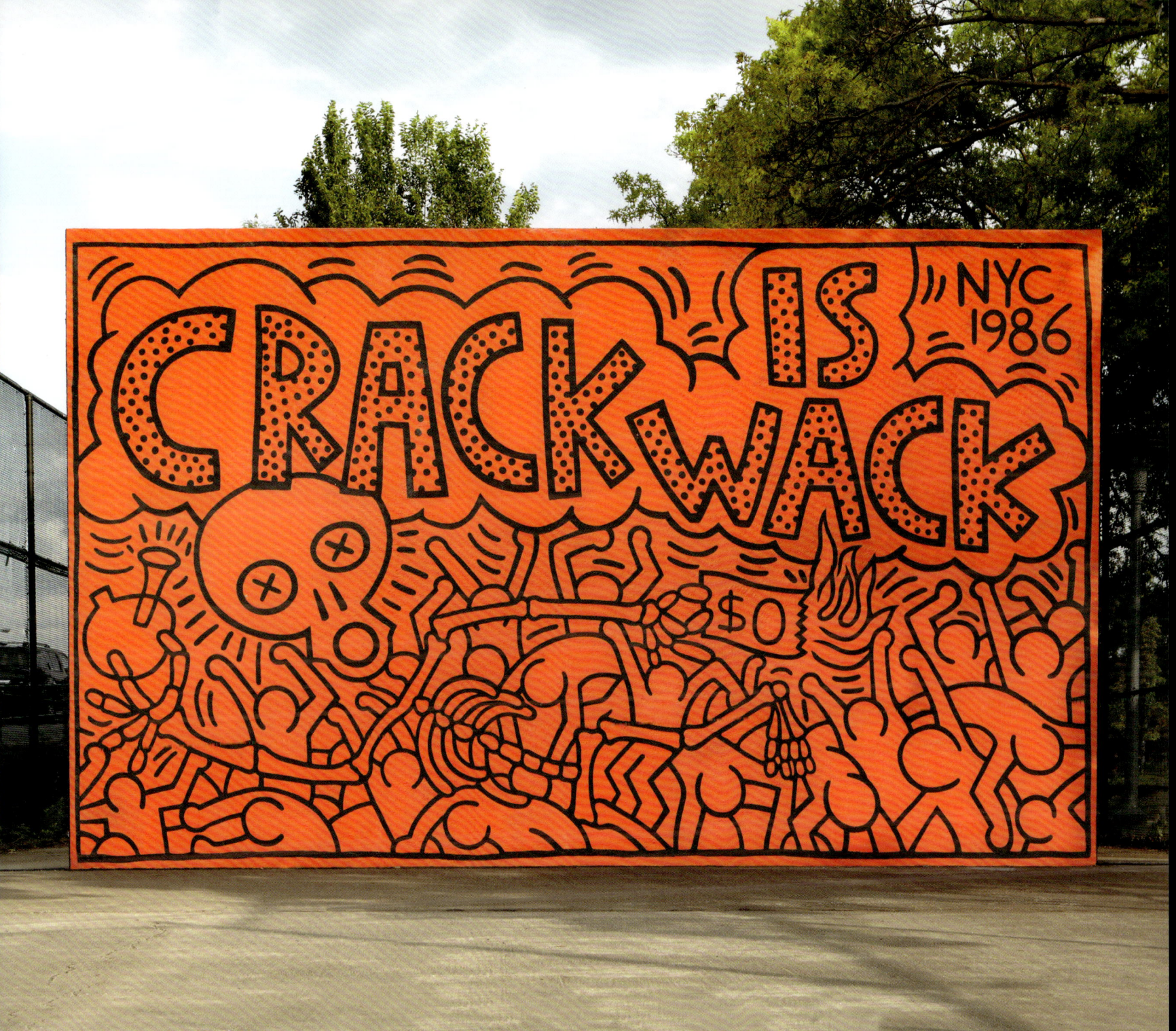

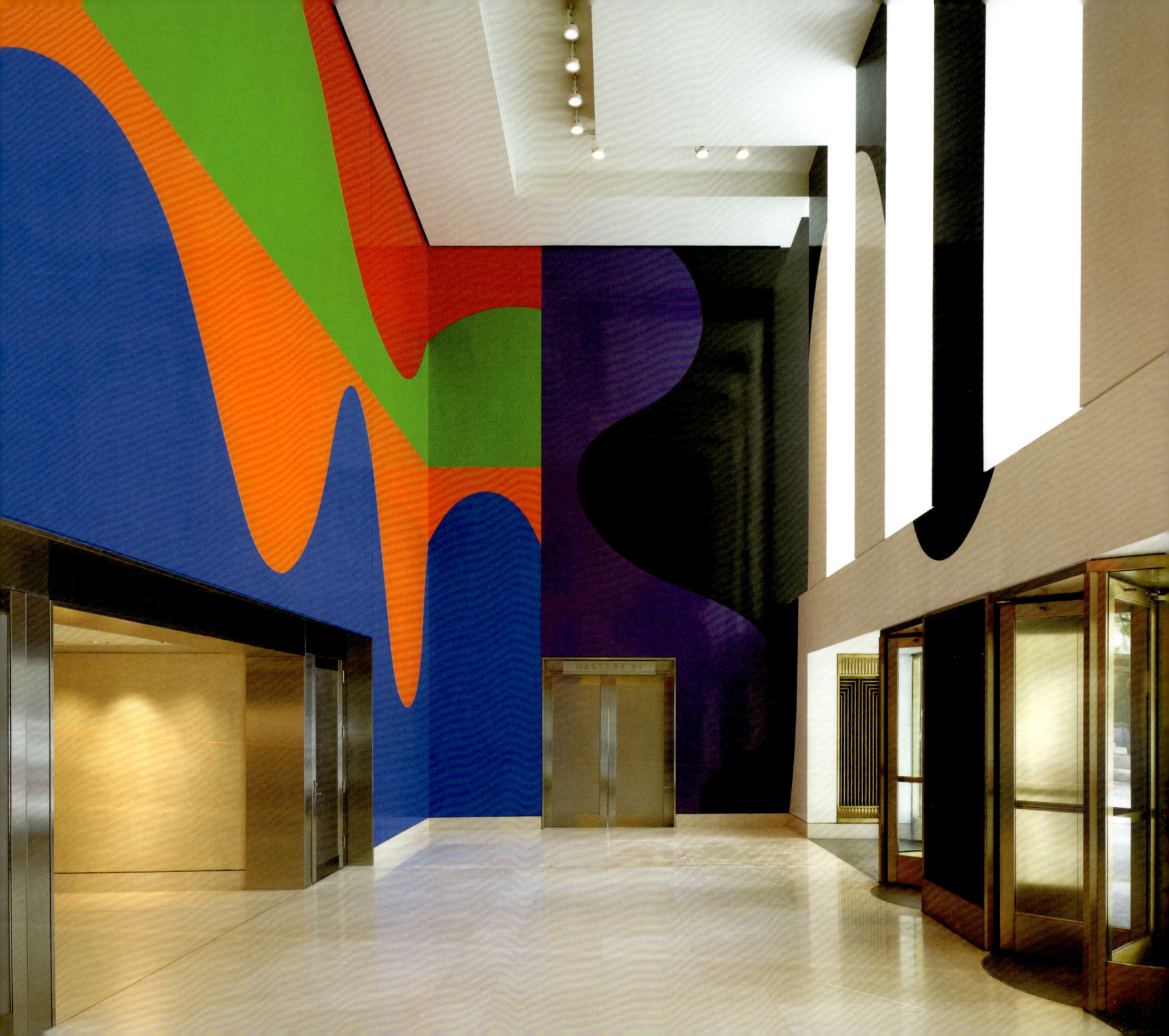

CHRISTIE'S
NEW YORK

20 Rockefeller Plaza, Manhattan • SOL LEWITT

The first new murals since 1946 at Rockefeller Center were installed in the soaring three-story lobby of Christie's auction house in March 1999. Sol LeWitt's *Wall Drawing #896, Colors/Curves* was painted with acrylic paints directly on the walls.

Solomon "Sol" LeWitt enjoyed an ordinary, happy childhood in Hartford, Connecticut, and decided to major in art at Syracuse because he "didn't know what else to do." After serving in the Korean War, he worked as a night receptionist at the Museum of Modern Art. Both a Conceptualist and Minimalist, LeWitt's style grew out of his loose collaboration with fellow artists (and fellow MoMA employees) Robert Ryman, Dan Flavin, and Robert Mangold, and were reactions to, and rejections of, personality-drenched Abstract Expressionism. The goals of Conceptualism and Minimalism were to reduce art to the most essential colors and shapes, and to remove the brush or the presence of any physical device that might detract from the clarity of concept and its final, visual form.

Throughout his career, LeWitt employed teams of assistants so that the resulting artwork would be further insulated from the unnecessary visual noise of his own hand. He encouraged creative input from his team so their efforts would be a part of his creative process. He was the composer, but his crew and collaborators were the visual musicians who brought the work to life. Musicians say that Bach is Bach regardless of the musician performing or the instrument played—Bach whistled in the shower is still Bach. So Sol LeWitt's concepts, or "wall drawings" as he called them, are uniquely LeWitt's regardless of how the paint reached the wall.

Christie's felt that a mural would keep with the history of public art in Rockefeller Center. Through his gallery, PaceWildenstein, LeWitt submitted four different designs. The one they chose was his personal favorite, with a highly saturated palette of orange, black, red, yellow, blue, lavender, and green. His crew of artisans painstakingly prepared the walls for the painting by sanding and resanding them six days a week for three straight weeks until the surfaces rivaled the finish of a new Ferrari. Any blemish would be a glaring distraction to the pristine simplicity of the painting, and the resultant, luxurious colors are so glossy it's tempting to touch the surface to see if the paint is still wet.

The enormous sweep of vibrant colors envelops the lobby and seems to expand the room beyond its 30-by-49-foot dimensions. Initially, the colors and design appear random, but there are actually exacting guidelines dictating the proportions of the horizontal and vertical bands. No color touches the same color at any point in the composition.

LeWitt is widely considered to have been the opposite of a spotlight-glomming art star. He avoided any media attention, denied reports of his precocity, shuddered at the word "masterpiece," and refused to be photographed. Then *New York Times* art critic Peter Schjeldahl wrote in his book *Columns & Catalogues* (The Figures, 1994), "Sol LeWitt is a very nice man. . . . I wonder if we can't just reconfigure our sense of the movement with him as king and the other fellows as squires. (LeWitt would be the Scandinavian type of royal who drives his own car.)"

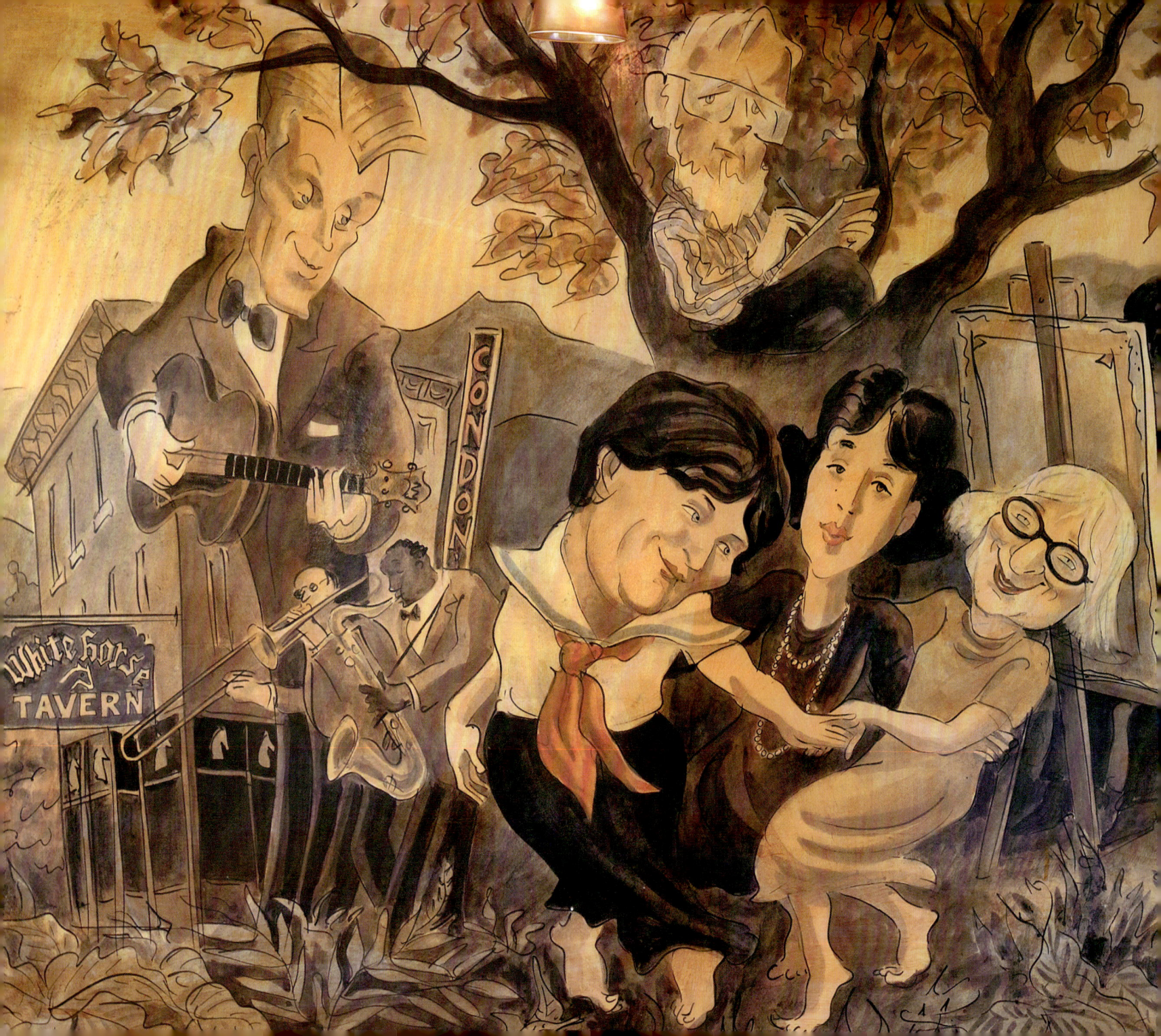

THE WAVERLY INN AND GARDEN

16 Bank Street, Manhattan • EDWARD SOREL

Ye Waverly Inn opened in a pre–Civil War redbrick townhouse on Bank Street a year after Prohibition became law. As decades passed, the Inn became a musty artifact of its former self, until 2006, when Graydon Carter resuscitated it with taste, charm, and wit, not the least of which was commissioning the brilliant Edward Sorel to execute a mural for the main dining room.

Sorel's wickedly clever caricatures spontaneously flow from his pen in a style he calls "direct drawing." The mural, originally a watercolor drawing, was digitally enlarged and installed, like wallpaper, directly on the walls. This became particularly practical when, in 2012, a portion of the mural that had been destroyed in a fire was simply replaced with its exact duplicate.

Sorel depicted forty-three of Greenwich Village's most colorful, fascinating, and influential people from the last 150 years: Allen Ginsberg shares the boughs of a tree with E. E. Cummings, who stares down at a naked Anaïs Nin. Margaret Sanger rejects a pamphlet proffered by Djuna Barnes. Edward Albee, perched in the window, observes a *Variety*-reading Marlon Brando as Fran Lebowitz enters the restaurant. Dawn Powell flutters above, while Jackson Pollock jets off to splatter. Political cartoonist Art Young, as a portly knight in armor, shares his steed with William Burroughs.

Eugene O'Neill writes while a winged Edmund Wilson embraces a naked Edna St. Vincent Millay. Marcel Duchamp plays chess while a Pan-like Dylan Thomas stares into oblivion. A raven-like Edgar Allan Poe is seen near Dashiell Hammett, who is carrying a black Maltese falcon. Eleanor Roosevelt listens to Thelonious Monk's music as Emma Goldman becomes enraged, probably, at a toga-wearing Bob Dylan. At his feet, Norman Mailer, as Narcissus, gazes at his own reflection in a pond, while, to their right, Jack Kerouac types on a continuous roll of paper that swirls around S. J. Perelman and Theodore Dreiser. Behind Dreiser is Cole Porter and Joan Baez. As Walt Whitman gazes up at a Truman Capote butterfly, Martha Graham dances near James Baldwin, who seems to be disturbed by naked heiress Mabel Dodge and the equally naked (but more political) John Reed, the only American buried in the Kremlin. Joseph Papp is seen near jazz guitarist Eddie Condon and writers Donald Barthelme and Willa Cather. Gertrude Vanderbilt Whitney, who founded the Whitney Studio Club, which eventually became the Whitney Museum of American Art, is pictured near Jane Jacobs, a devoted New Yorker who brought the most powerful man in New York, Robert Moses, to his knees. Though the mural ends with John Sloan looking away from his own painting to Andy Warhol wheeling a Brillo Box, we can never look away from this mural, Sorel's ode to New Yorkers.

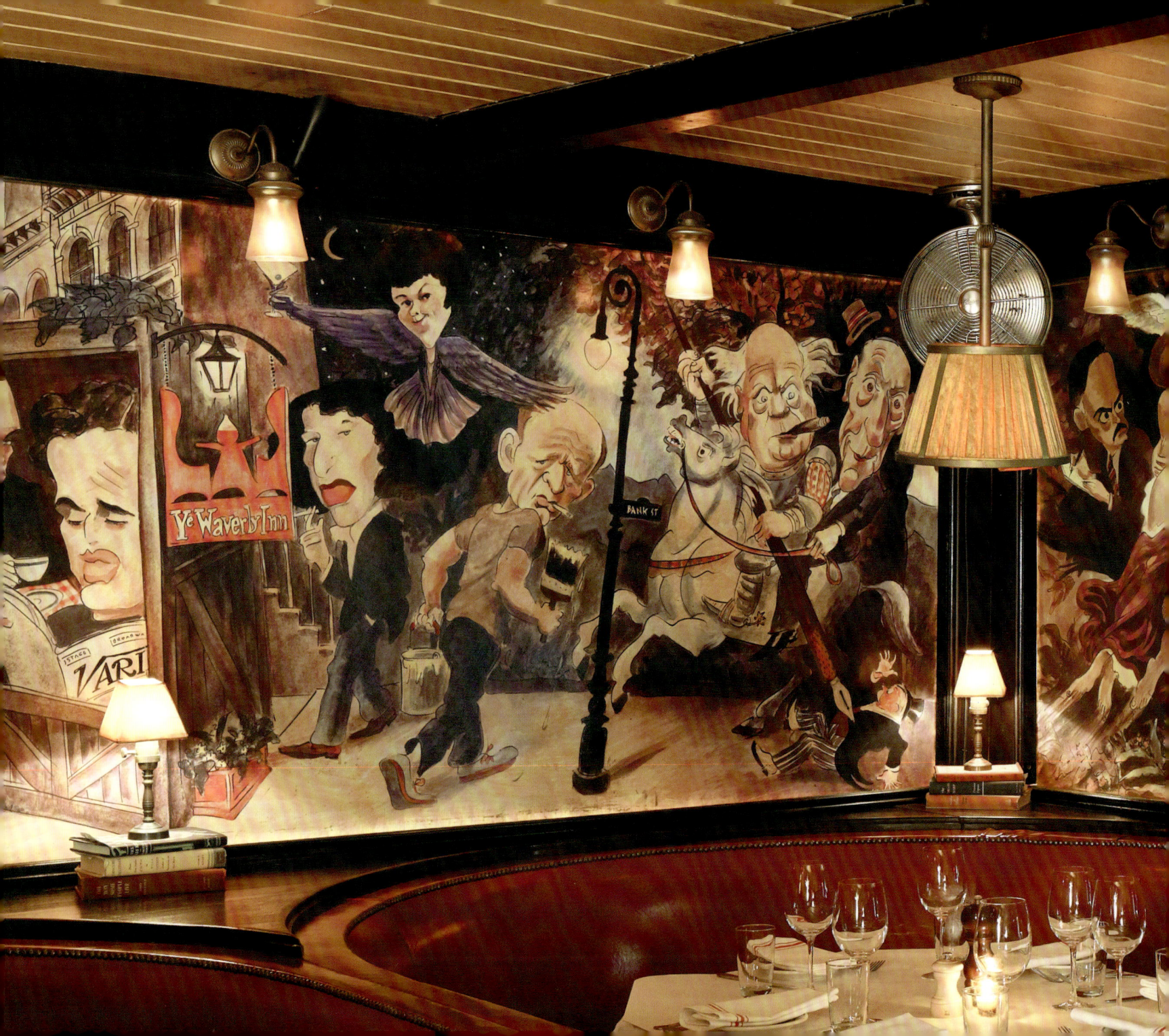

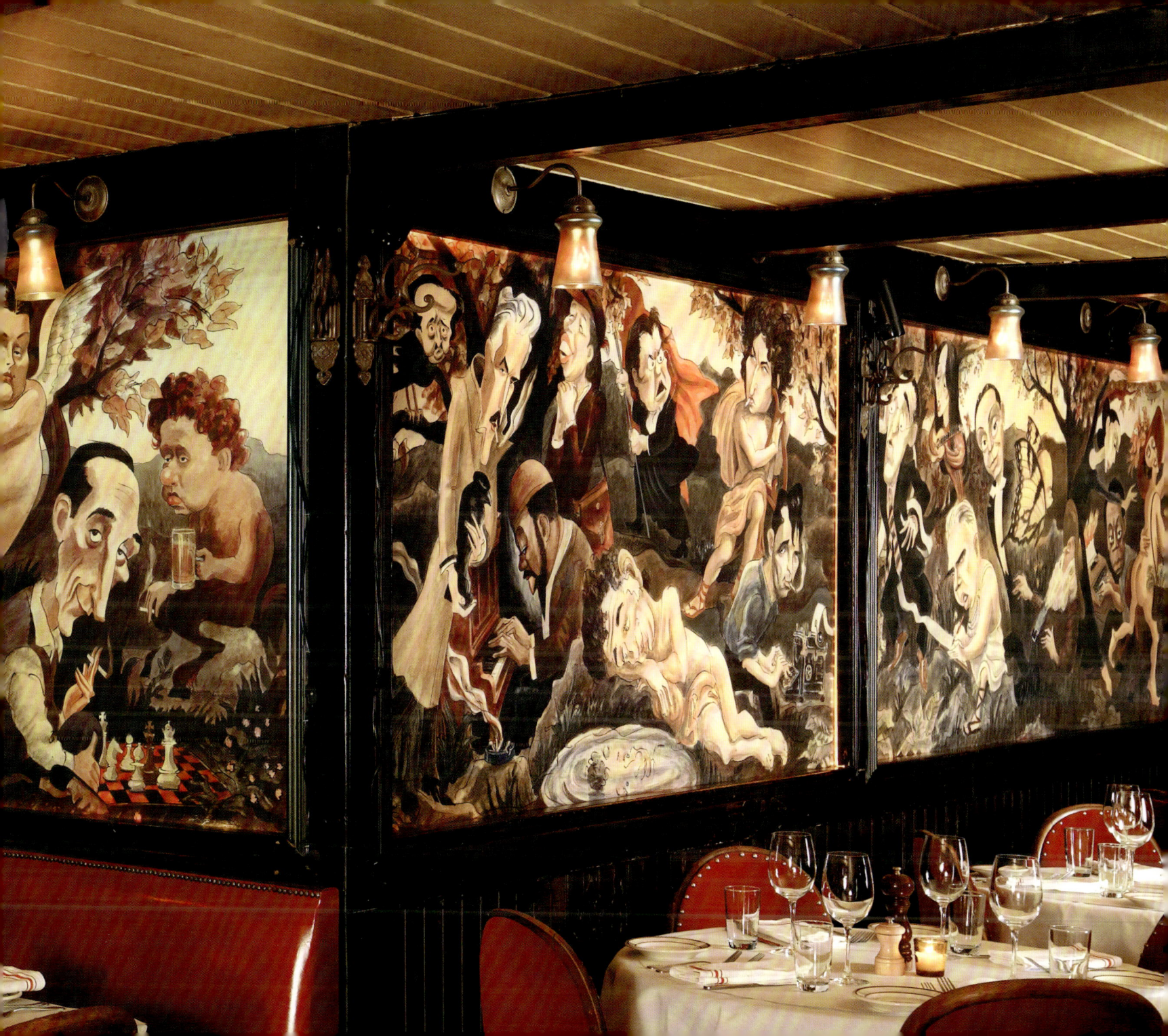

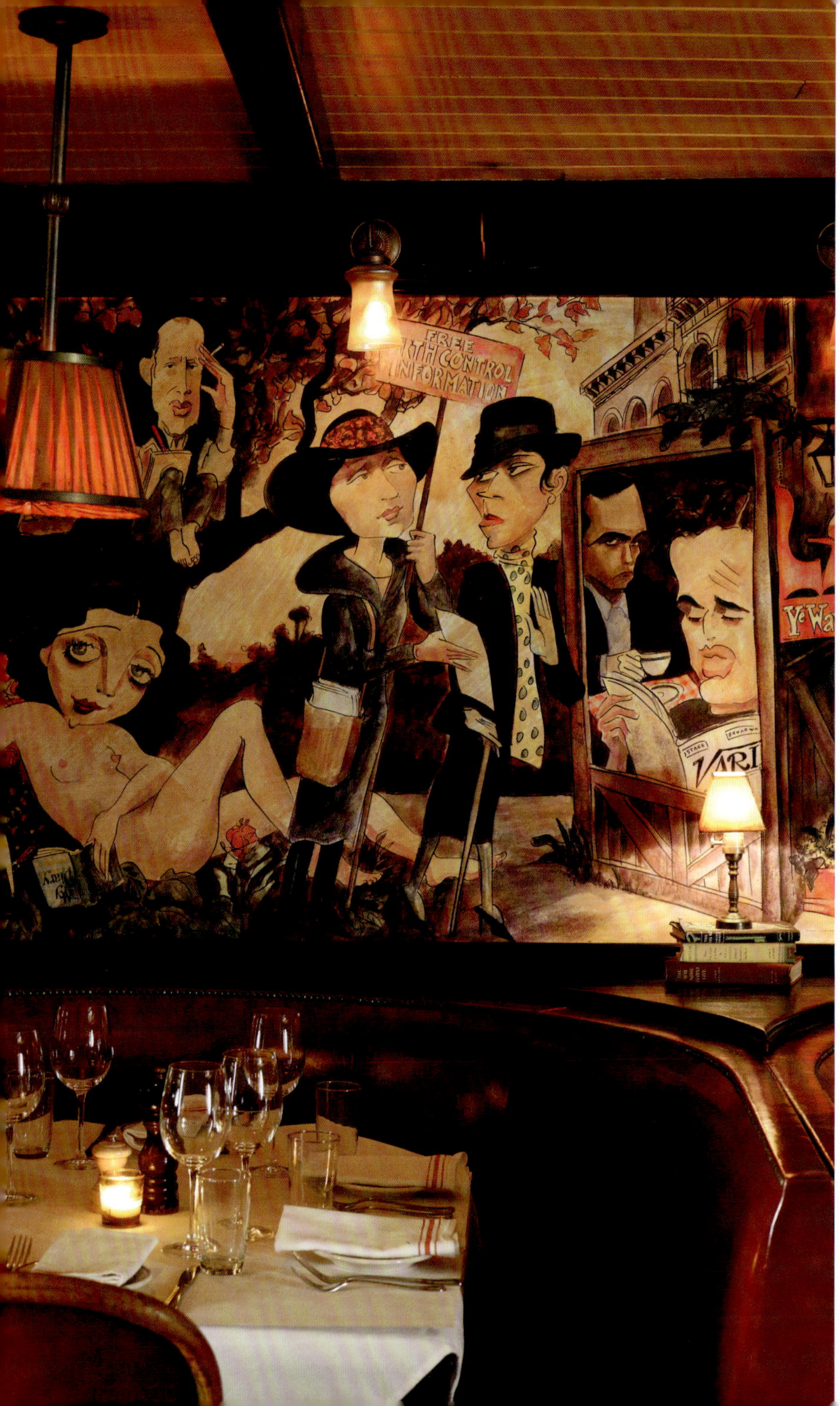
FREE
INFORMATION

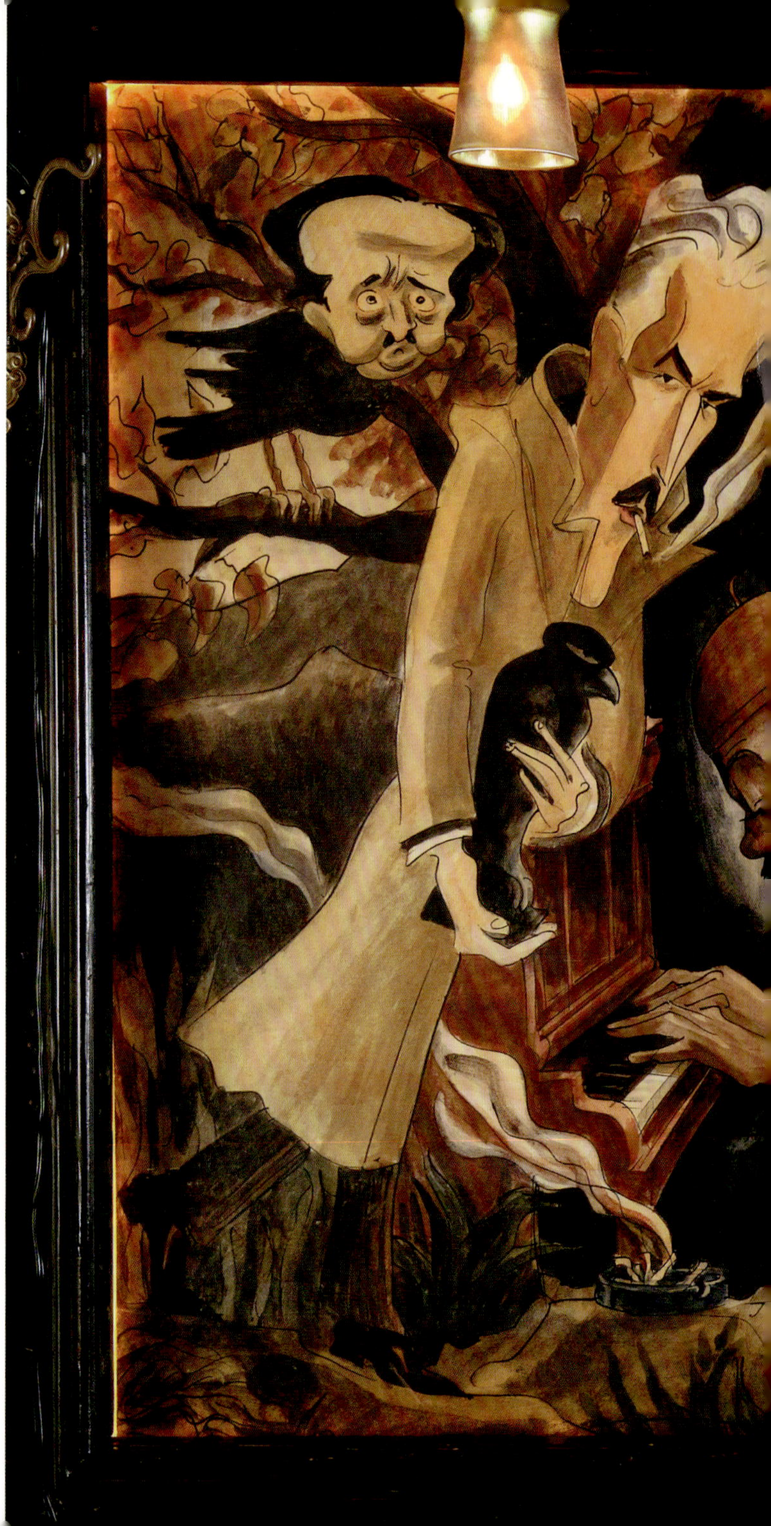

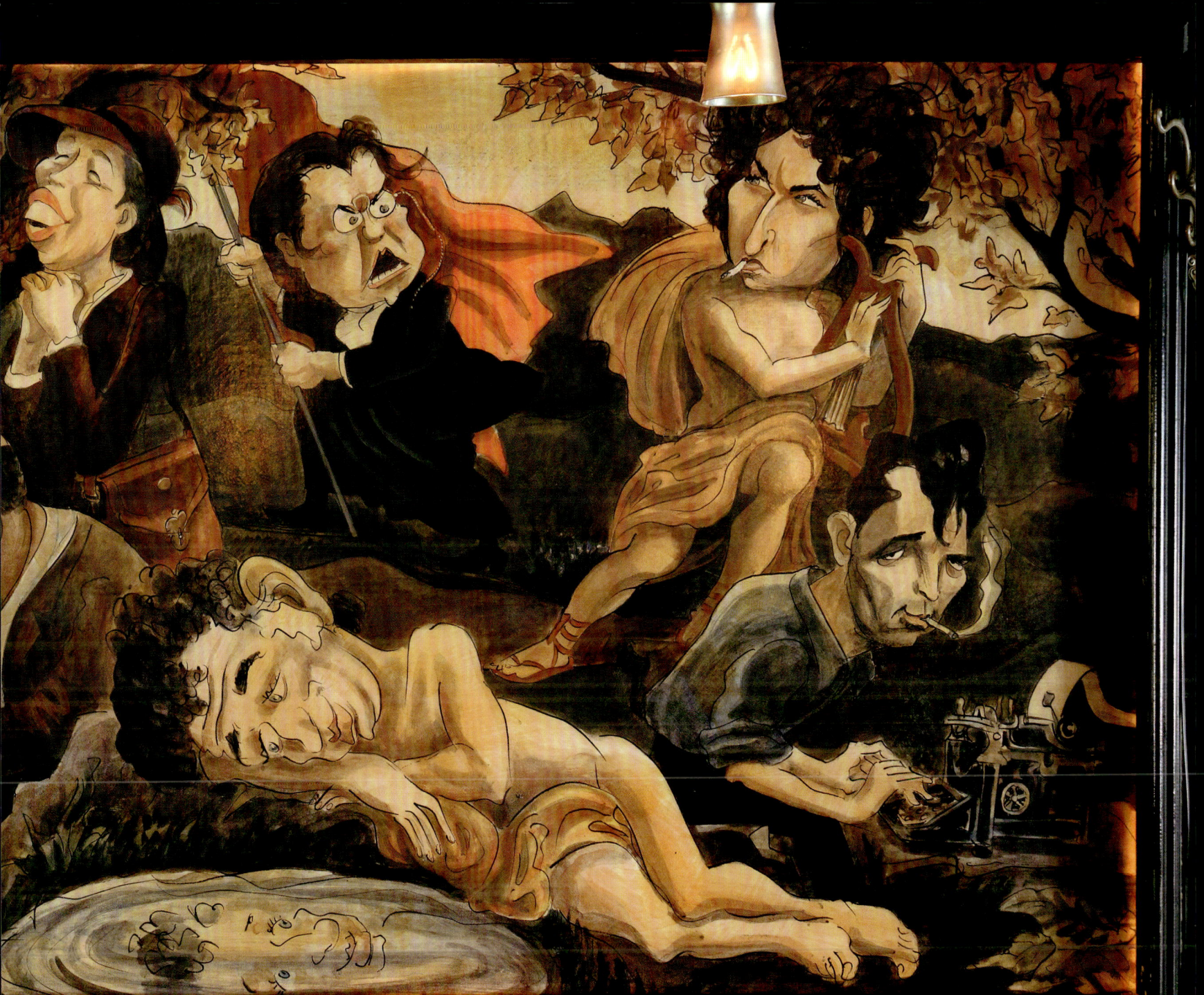

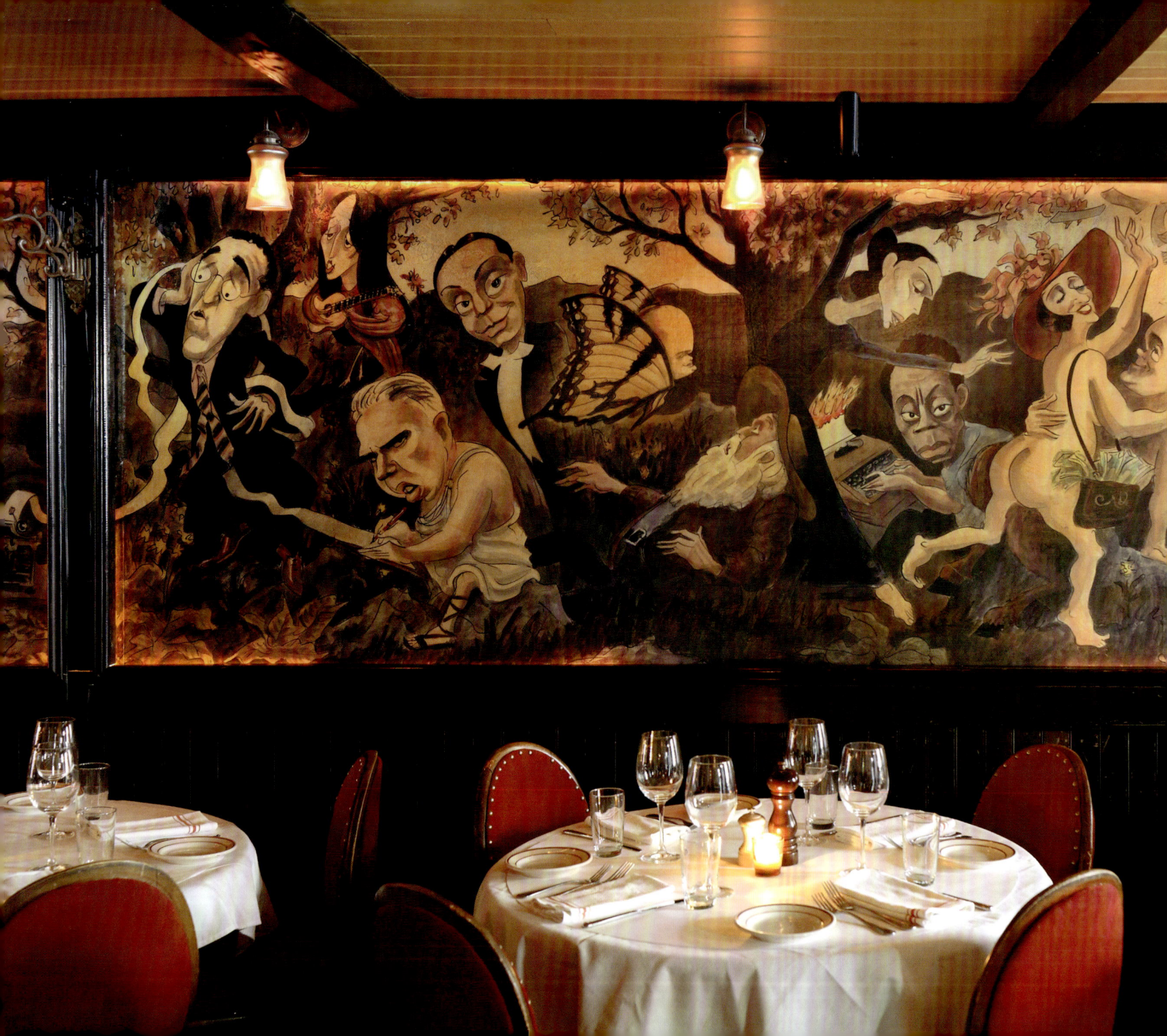

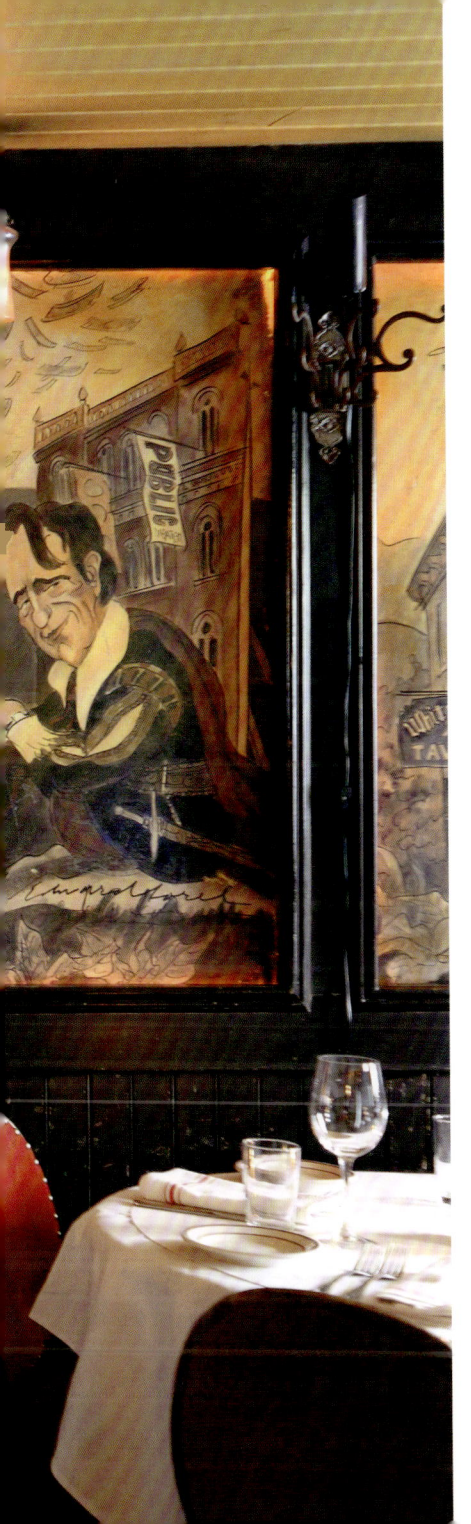

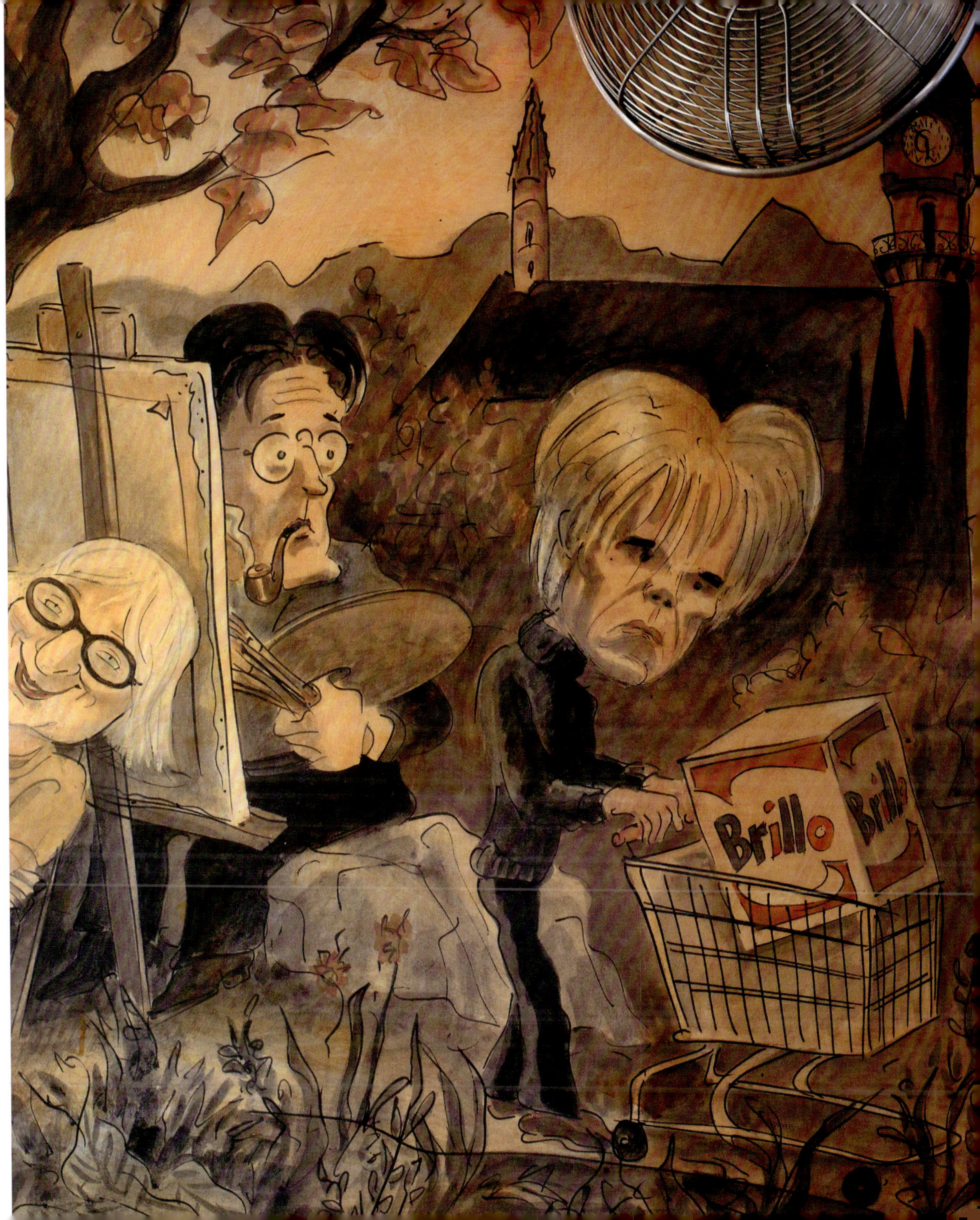

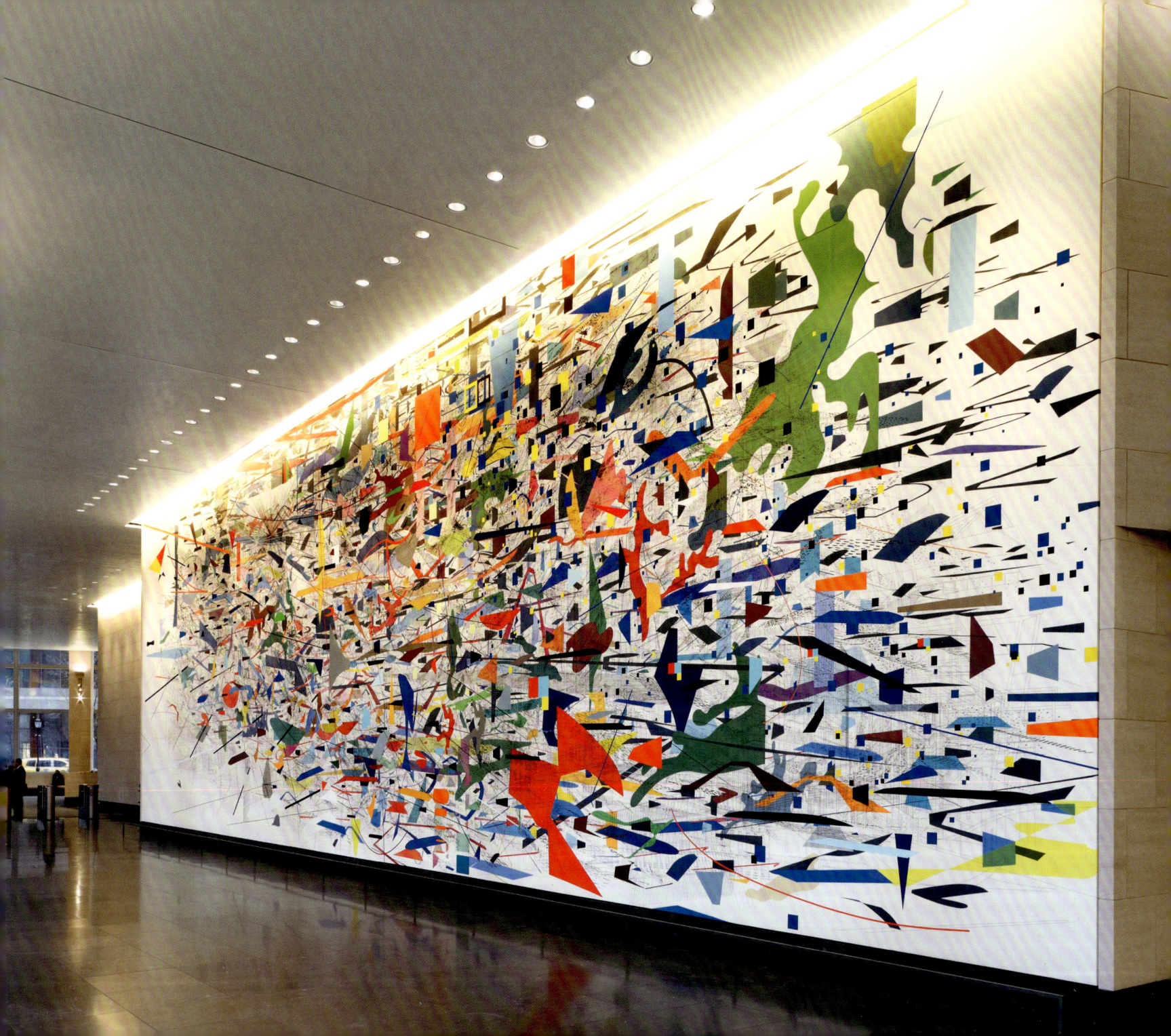

GOLDMAN SACHS

Julie Mehretu's *Mural*, 80 feet long by 23 feet high, dominates the glass and steel lobby of Goldman Sachs. It is, if not the most ambitious and dynamic public art to grace New York City in many decades, then certainly the most important public painting of the twenty-first century. Architect Henry N. Cobb, a strong proponent of public art in architecture, designed a row of 20-foot-square windows on the east wall of the lobby so the grand mural would be visible from the outside, making it both private and public art.

To create a giant canvas required a giant studio. Mehretu leased a mammoth former Lugar pistol factory in Berlin to produce the painting. Because of its enormous size, it was painted on five separate panels that were eventually rolled, shipped, and installed on site. Nearly 80 percent of the $5 million fee went to the cost of the production, which included up to thirty assistants working full time for fourteen months.

Mehretu's mesmerizing, incredibly complex composition features four beautiful layers of abstract signs and symbols that advance and recede, referencing the history of finance, trade, institutions, and social networks. In a process similar to traditional glazing techniques, each of the four layers was sprayed with a clear coat of silica and acrylic paint and sanded smooth, allowing the colors to overlap and glow through to the new layers, resulting in a deliciously luminous and rich surface. Multitudes of lines, reminiscent of airline routes mapping global connections, shoot between critical hubs of commerce. Underlying layers of ink drawings of architectural details of institutions like the New York Stock Exchange, the Greek city of Miletus, the New Orleans Cotton Exchange, and the London Stock Exchange compete for attention with horizontal and vertical lines. The calligraphic marks, which Mehretu calls "characters," reference the layers of Lower Manhattan's history and growth fueled by commerce. The hyperactive surface shimmers with hundreds and hundreds of free-form configurations in 215 different colors. Some of the colors are opaque, others transparent. After the painting was finished and installed in the Goldman Sachs lobby in 2009, she spent the month of September on a ladder altering and adding to the composition by masking off shapes and airbrushing colors to bring them back to the surface from their muted presence under earlier layers.

Mehretu was born in Addis Ababa, Ethiopia, in 1970 to an Ethiopian economic geography professor and an American teacher, and her family fled the 1977 revolution to Michigan. Her fascination with travel, architecture, and history, perhaps fueled by her early migration and later travels to Senegal, San Francisco, Rhode Island, Berlin, and New York, imbues her paintings with abstract metaphors of the incredibly complex interconnection of world economies and societies in the twenty-first century.

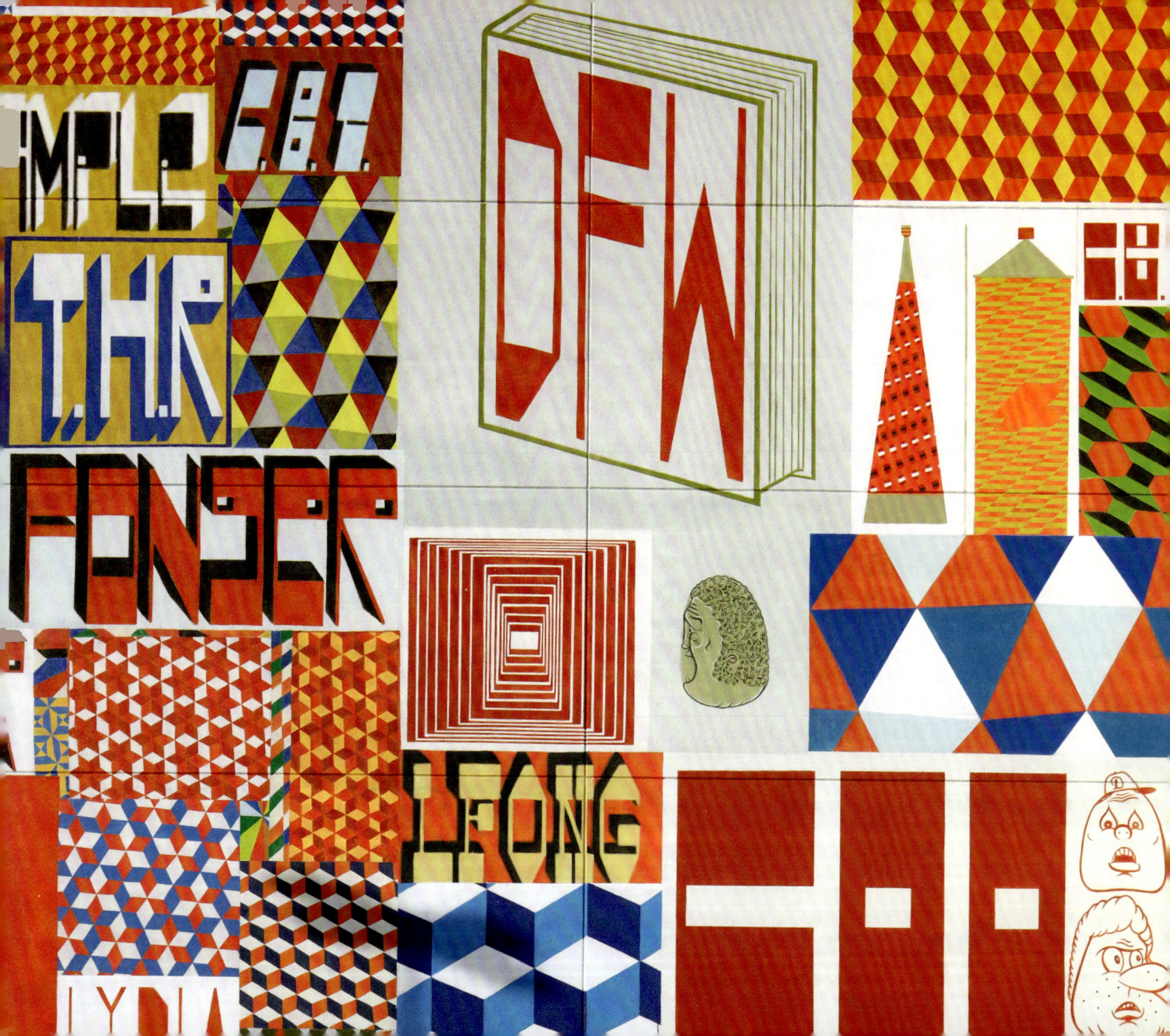

MARK MORRIS
DANCE CENTER

3 Lafayette Avenue, Brooklyn • BARRY MᶜGEE

Barry McGee, aka Ray Fong, Lydia Fong, Bernon Vernon, Robbie Pimple, P. Kin, Ray Virgil, Twister, Twisty, Twisto, and Twist, emerged from the Mission School movement and the graffiti boom of the 1990s in the San Francisco Bay Area.

As a spray-painting graffiti vandal, he left his mark by painting his tag on anything that didn't (or did) move. Freight trains, bathroom mirrors, highway overpasses, buses, abandoned cars, and the walls of the city bore his brand.

Like his fellow street artists, he had a role in advancing the movement begun in the 1970s in New York. By the time McGee received his bachelor's degree from the San Francisco Art Institute in 1991, street graffiti had begun to sputter into derivative, repetitive graphics. But McGee expanded on what had preceded him and, like Jean-Michel Basquiat and Keith Haring, elevated his vivacious street art into something aesthetically and intellectually compelling. Inspired by the socially conscious Beat poets of the 1940s and '50s and the Mexican muralists of the 1930s, McGee's style began to draw from comics, hobo art, and sign paintings.

He and his partner and wife, Margaret Kilgallen, defended their additions to the urban landscape. Not only did their art have greater artistic value than the clutter of corporate advertising, but it was also available, for free, to a large, diverse audience in public spaces rather than cloistered in museums and art galleries.

In 2003, two years after Kilgallen's death, McGee shifted gears yet again and adopted Op Art pattern painting as the fundamental element of his work. Museums and galleries offering him exhibitions had to agree to installations that included overturned cars, trucks, and Dumpsters as he brought the gritty urban reality inside.

In 2012, *Vanity Fair* and Cadillac, under the auspices of the street-art project *Art in the Streets*, awarded McGee the commission to paint an exterior wall of the Mark Morris Dance Center across the street from the Brooklyn Academy of Music.

The wall, which was obscured by development on the neighboring property in 2017, was 70 feet high by 100 feet long and a colorful cacophony of geometric shapes, patterns, cartoon characters, and calligraphy. His street names, Pimple and Fong, were repeated along with "D.F.W." (Down for Whatever) and "T.H.R." (The Harsh Reality). It was a vivid symbol of both the area's artistic life and the creativity taking place on the other side of the wall in the dance center.

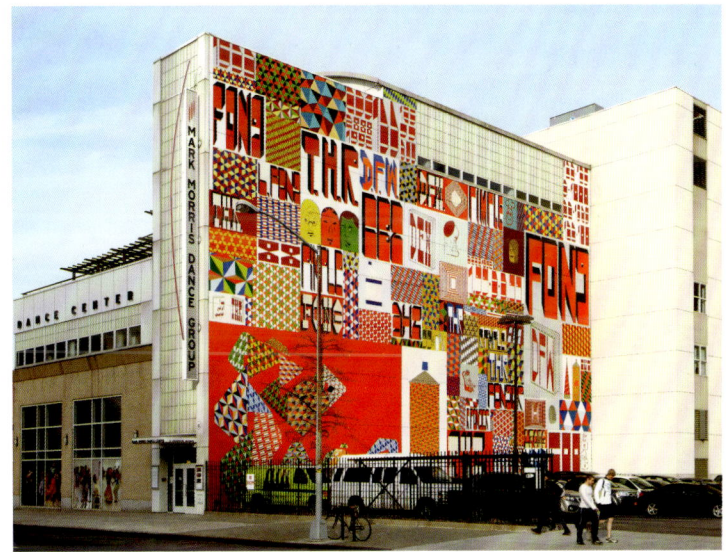

ACKNOWLEDGEMENTS

Thanks to my partner, Joshua McHugh. His splendid photography, cheery nature, and nuclear energy made this a happy adventure. Thanks, Rob Passal, for introducing us. We owe our gratitude to our dedicated editor and champion, Robb Pearlman, who, with oft-tested patience and impeccable taste, guided us through this journey. Thank you to Charles Miers of Rizzoli for green-lighting the project. We deeply appreciate Graydon Carter writing the foreword. Kudos to Susi Oberhelman for our book's beautiful design. None of the above would have happened without our angel agent, Jane Lahr, and her partner Lyn DelliQuadri. Thanks to Anne VanRensselaer for introducing me to Jane, and Stephanie Gunning for molding the idea into an irresistible proposal.

Our thanks to the following people who helped along the way: Martin Henry of the Appellate Court and Librarian Gene Prudhomme. Meg Connolly and Austin Jacobson of the St. Regis Hotel. The Morgan Library's Jennifer Tonkovich, Patrick Milliman, Marilyn Palmieri, Simone Grant, and Alanna Schindewolf. At Grand Central Terminal, Lester Freundlich, Mark Heavy, Meredith Conti, Dan Bruckner and Charles Gulbrandsen. The Hispanic Society Executive Director Dr. Mitchell Codding and curator Daniel Silva. Julie Zeftel and Dina Selfridge of the Metropolitan Museum of Art. Pari Stave of AXA Equitable Life. Anna Dinces of Rubenstein Public Relations. Silvia Rocciolo and Katherine Bailey of the New School. Rick Tejada-Flores of Paradigm Productions. At Rockefeller Center, Brooke Smy of Tishman Speyer, Mimi Gonzales, and author Christine Roussel. Aubrey Miller and Michael Walker of The American Museum of Natural History. Jessica Helfand's input on Ezra Winter. Jeff Greene of EverGreene Architectural Arts. Chloe Stewart, Jennifer Bretschneider at Radio City. Gerard Picaso of the Hotel des Artistes. James Head, biographer of Howard Chandler Christy. At 60 Centre Street, Major Gerard Fennell. The Department of Citywide Administrative Services' Rebecca Seale. Tiffany Forrest and Gigi Davis of the Harlem YMCA. Deborah Thornhill and Sylvia White of Harlem Hospital. Cynthia Gilbert and Charlotte Cohen of General Services Administration. Dianne Jones of the Bronx General Post Office. At the Staten Island Borough Hall, Nick Dmytryszyn. Nick Politis, principal of George Washington High. Lucienne Allen, grandaughter of Lucienne Bloch. April Gaspari of the Port Authority. Larry Elkin, for his article on James Brooks. Maureen Stella and Jamie Beck of the Rosewood Hotels. The Monkey Bar's Ken Friedman and Diane Voyentzie, painter of the monkeys. Peter Clark of the Metropolitan Opera.

Cynthia O'Neal and Michael O'Neal, for providing background for the essay on *Dancers at the Bar*. Richard Haas for his interview. Shelley Lee of The Estate of Roy Lichtenstein. Beck Papraniku, building manager of AXA Equitable. Annelise Ream at the Keith Haring Foundation. Lynn Schulman of the Woodhull Medical Center. Laura Washington and Timothy Wroten of The New-York Historical Society. Gabriel Ford of Christie's and the Paula Cooper Gallery. Randy Neff and Emil Varda at the Waverly Inn. Lissa McClure of the Marian Goodman Gallery. Timur Galen, Karen Holm, and Emily Silver of Goldman Sachs. Howard Read, Adam Sheffer at the Cheim & Read Gallery.

Gratitude overflowing for Silvia, the light of my life, who was with me every step of the way. Austin and Nolan, formerly the greatest kids in the world, now men I am proud to call my friends. My beautiful daughters (step- and in-law aside) Francesca and Dimity. And Eddie, paperweight and muse.

—GLENN PALMER-SMITH

This book would not have been possible without the enthusiastic participation of the murals' stewards; their commitment to these rich cultural icons of our city remains invaluable. Their embrace of this volume has been critical to its creation.

It has been a true pleasure collaborating with Glenn Palmer-Smith in fostering this book. His exuberance and passion for the murals are boundless and have made our journey to document them both joyful and enlightening.

Scott Irvine and Stewart Isbell each played an essential part in helping to capture the images for this book; my heartfelt thanks for their assistance.

My gratitude extends to all of those who played a key role in the book's development: Charles Miers for publishing this celebration of New York's murals, Robb Pearlman for deftly shepherding it along the editorial path with wisdom and insight, Susi Oberhelman for articulating our vision with her elegant design, Graydon Carter for penning the introduction, Jane Lahr for her tenacity in bringing this project to fruition, Robert Passal for introducing Glenn to me, and Marc Joseph Berg and Donna Wingate for their guidance as I navigated this process.

Above all, my deepest thanks goes out to Hilary Easton and Calder McHugh, whose unwavering support, encouragement, and love I am blessed with daily.

—JOSHUA McHUGH

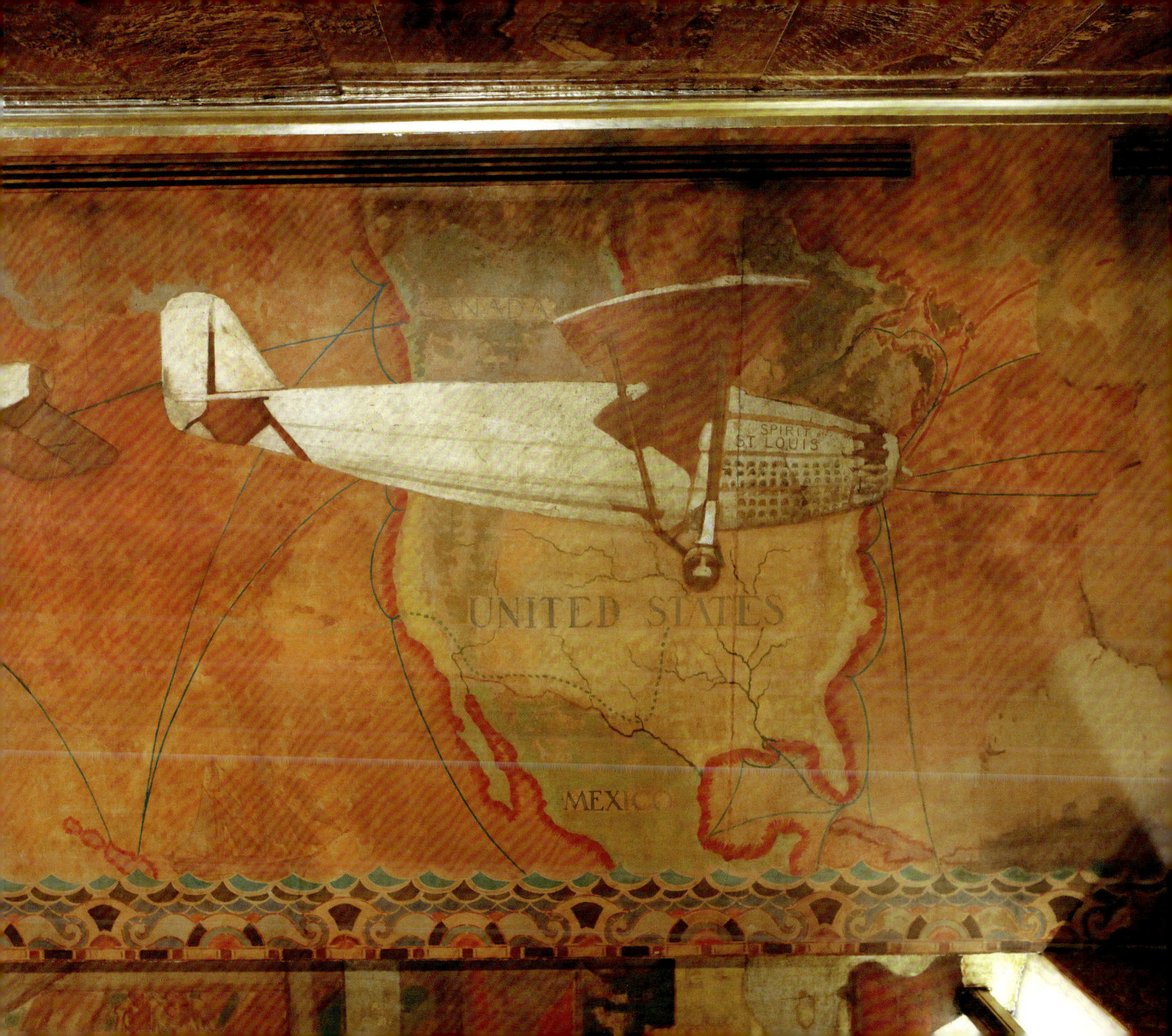

CREDITS

KING COLE BAR

Front Cover: Maxfield Parrish, *Old King Cole*, 1906. All art by Maxfield Parrish is © Maxfield Parrish Family, LLC/Licensed by VAGA, New York, NY. The St. Regis New York.

CAFÉ CARLYLE

Front Flap: Marcel Vertès, untitled (detail), 1955. The Carlyle, A Rosewood Hotel.

GEORGE WASHINGTON HIGH SCHOOL

Page 1: Lucienne Bloch, *The Evolution of Music* (detail), 1938. George Washington High School.

CHRISTIE'S NEW YORK

Page 2: Sol LeWitt, *Wall Drawing #896 Colors/Curves*, 1999. © 2013 The LeWitt Estate/Artists Rights Society (ARS), New York. Christie's New York.

GOLDMAN SACHS

Page 5: Julie Mehretu, *Mural* (detail), 2009. Goldman Sachs.

NEW YORK STATE SUPREME COURT, APPELLATE DIVISION

Page 6: Henry Siddons Mowbray, *Transmission of the Law* (detail), 1900.
Page 8: Robert Lewis Reid, *Justice*, 1900.
Page 9: Henry Siddons Mowbray, *Transmission of the Law*, 1900.
Pages 10-11: Henry Siddons Mowbray, *Transmission of the Law* (details), 1900.
Pages 12-13: Edward Emerson Simmons, *The Justice of the Law*, 1900; Henry O. Walker, *The Wisdom of the Law*, 1900; Edwin Blashfield, *The Power of The Law*, 1900.

KING COLE BAR

Pages 14-17: Maxfield Parrish, *Old King Cole*, 1906. All art by Maxfield Parrish is © Maxfield Parrish Family, LLC/Licensed by VAGA, New York, NY. The St. Regis New York.

THE MORGAN LIBRARY & MUSEUM

Pages 18-25: Henry Siddons Mowbray, untitled, 1906.

GRAND CENTRAL TERMINAL

Pages 26-31 and Back Flap: Paul César Helleu, *Sky Ceiling*, 1912. Imagery of Grand Central Terminal includes trademarks of the Metropolitan Transportation Authority. Used with Permission.

THE HISPANIC SOCIETY OF AMERICA

Pages 32-41: Joaquín Sorolla y Bastida, *Vision of Spain*, 1919.

CHRYSLER BUILDING

Pages 42-51: Edward Trumbull, *Transport and Human Endeavor*, 1930. Courtesy of Tishman Speyer.

THE METROPOLITAN MUSEUM OF ART

Page 52: Thomas Hart Benton, *America Today: Deep South* (panel d), 1930-31. The Metropolitan Museum of Art, Gift of AXA Equitable, 2012 (2012.478a-j) Image © The Metropolitan Museum of Art.
Page 54, top left: Thomas Hart Benton, *America Today: Steel* (panel h), 1930-31. The Metropolitan Museum of Art, Gift of AXA Equitable, 2012 (2012.478a-j) Image © The Metropolitan Museum of Art.
Page 54, bottom left: Thomas Hart Benton, *America Today: Instruments of Power* (panel a), 1930-31. The Metropolitan Museum of Art, Gift of AXA Equitable, 2012 (2012.478a-j) Image © The Metropolitan Museum of Art.
Page 55: Thomas Hart Benton, *America Today: City Activities with Subway* (panel c), 1930-31. The Metropolitan Museum of Art, Gift of AXA Equitable, 2012 (2012.478a-j) Image © The Metropolitan Museum of Art.

THE NEW SCHOOL

Page 56: José Clemente Orozco, *Science, Labor, and Art* (detail), 1931. The New School Art Collection, New York City. © 2013 Artists Rights Society (ARS), New York/ SOMAAP, Mexico City.

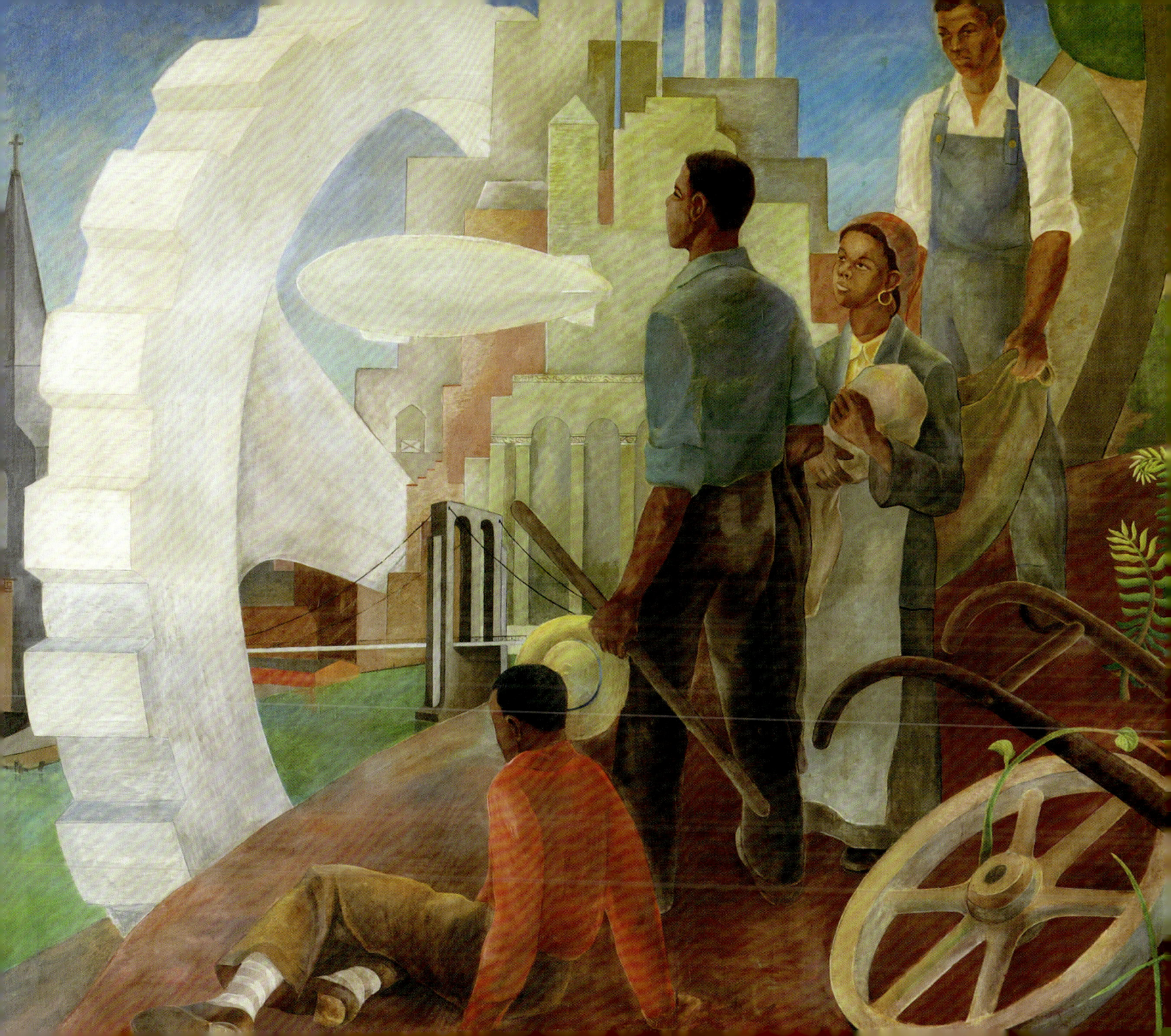

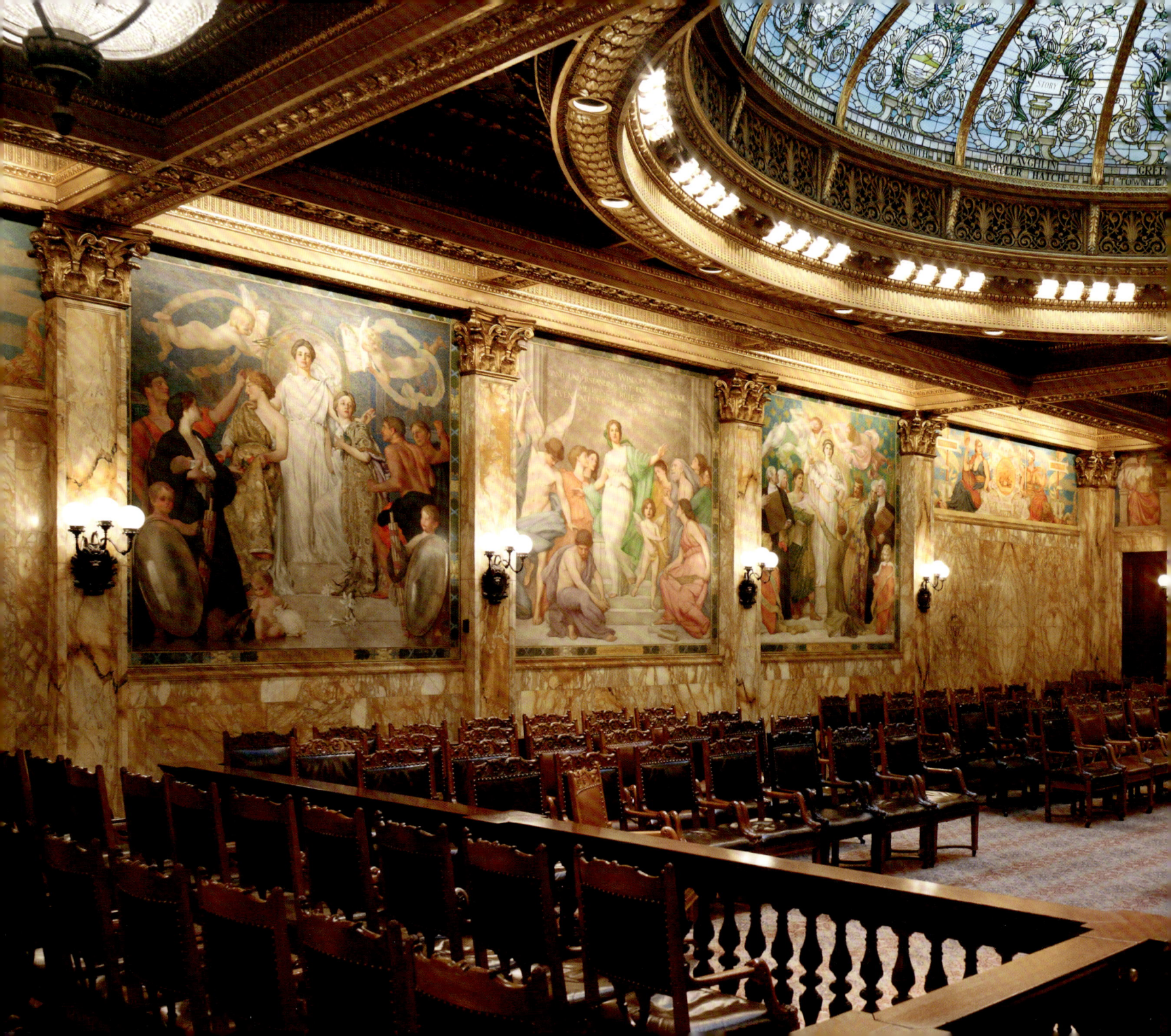

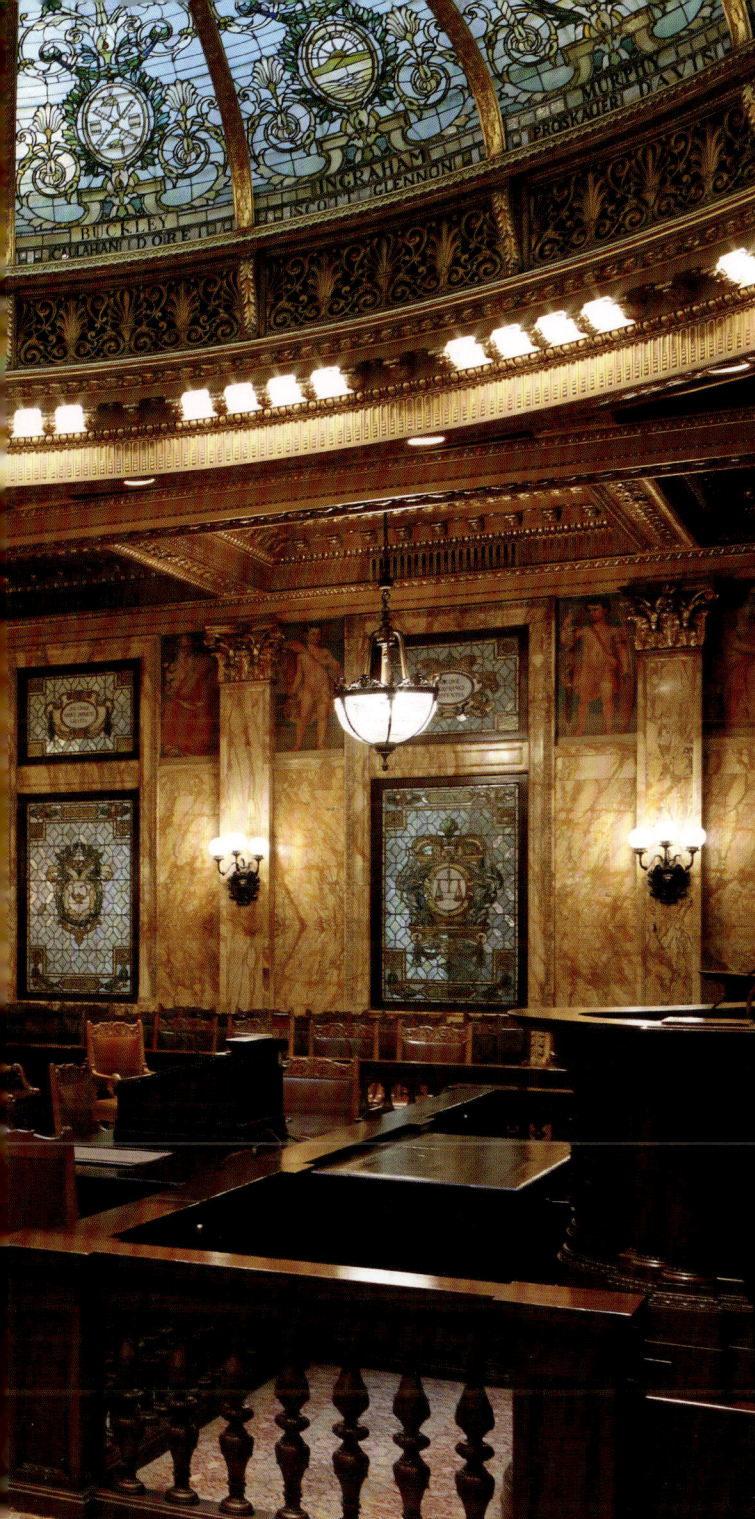

Pages 58–59: José Clemente Orozco, *Struggle in the Occident*, 1931. The New School Art Collection, New York City. © 2013 Artists Rights Society (ARS), New York/ SOMAAP, Mexico City.

Page 60: José Clemente Orozco, *Struggle in the Orient*, 1931. The New School Art Collection, New York City. © 2013 Artists Rights Society (ARS), New York/SOMAAP, Mexico City.

Page 61, top right: José Clemente Orozco, *Homecoming of the Worker of the New Day*, 1931. The New School Art Collection, New York City. © 2013 Artists Rights Society (ARS), New York/SOMAAP, Mexico City.

Page 61, bottom right: José Clemente Orozco, *Science, Labor, and Art*, 1931. The New School Art Collection, New York City. © 2013 Artists Rights Society (ARS), New York/SOMAAP, Mexico City.

Pages 62–63: José Clemente Orozco, *Table of Universal Brotherhood*, 1931. The New School Art Collection, New York City. © 2013 Artists Rights Society (ARS), New York/ SOMAAP, Mexico City.

RADIO CITY MUSIC HALL
Pages 64–67: Ezra Winter, *Quest for the Fountain of Eternal Youth*, 1932.
Page 68: Yasuo Kuniyoshi, *Exotic Flowers*, 1932. Art © Estate of Yasuo Kuniyoshi/ Licensed by VAGA, New York, NY.
Page 69: Stuart Davis, *Men without Women*, 1932. Art © Estate of Stuart Davis/ Licensed by VAGA, New York, NY.
Photographs taken on location at Radio City Music Hall. Special Thanks to Radio City Music Hall and Madison Square Garden Entertainment.

ROCKEFELLER CENTER
Pages 70: José María Sert, *Time*, 1937.
Pages 72–73: José María Sert, *American Progress*, 1937.
Page 74: José María Sert, *Man's Triumph in Communication*, 1933.
Page 75, left: José María Sert, *Fraternity of Men*, 1937.
Page 75, right: José María Sert, *Contest*, 1940.
Pages 76–77: Sir Frank Brangwyn, *Untitled South Corridor*, 1934.
Page 78: José María Sert, *Abolition of War*, 1933.
Page 79: José María Sert, *Abolition of Bondage*, 1933.
Courtesy of Tishman Speyer.

CAFÉ DES ARTISTES

Page 80: Howard Chandler Christy, *The Swing Girl*, 1934.

Page 82: Howard Chandler Christy, *Ponce de León* and *Parrot Girl*, 1934.

Page 83: Howard Chandler Christy, *The Fountain of Youth*, 1934.

Page 84: Howard Chandler Christy, *Spring*, 1934.

Page 85: Howard Chandler Christy, *Tarzan*, 1934.

AMERICAN MUSEUM OF NATURAL HISTORY

Pages 86-93: William Andrew Mackay, untitled, 1935.

HARLEM YMCA

Pages 94-95: Aaron Douglas, *Evolution of Negro Dance*, 1935. Art © Heirs of Aaron Douglas/Licensed by VAGA, New York, NY.

HARLEM HOSPITAL

Pages 96-102 and 223: Vertis Hayes, *Pursuit of Happiness*, 1937.

Page 103: Alfred D. Crimi, *Modern Surgery and Anesthesia*, 1936.

Pages 104, left and 105: Charles Alston, *Modern Medicine*, 1940.

Page 104, right: Charles Alston, *Magic in Medicine*, 1940.

Pages 106-107: Georgette Seabrooke, *Recreation in Harlem*, 1937.

NEW YORK STATE SUPREME COURT

Pages 108-111: Attilio Pusterla, *The History of Law*, 1936.

Pages 112-113: Attilio Pusterla, untitled, 1936.

Page 114, left: Andrew Thomas Schwartz, *Manhattan End of Brooklyn Bridge*, 1936.

Pages 114-115, center: Attilio Pusterla, untitled, 1936.

Page 115, right: Andrew Thomas Schwartz, *Trinity Church from Wall Street*, 1936.

Page 116, left: John Edwin Jackson, untitled, 1936.

Pages 116-117: Andrew Thomas Schwartz, *Trinity Church from Wall Street*, *Columbia University Low Memorial Library*, *The Woolworth Building from Municipal Building*, 1936.

ALEXANDER HAMILTON U.S. CUSTOM HOUSE

Pages 118-123: Reginald Marsh, *The Rotunda Murals*, 1937. © 2013 Estate of Reginald Marsh/Art Students League, New York/Artists Rights Society (ARS), New York. Courtesy of U.S. General Services Administration, Public Buildings Service, Fine Arts Collection.

BRONX GENERAL POST OFFICE

Pages 124-129: Ben Shahn, *Resources of America*, 1938. All art by Ben Shahn is © Estate of Ben Shahn/Licensed by VAGA, New York, NY. Post Office™ Murals reprinted with the permission of the United States Postal Service. All Rights Reserved. Written authorization from the Postal Service is required to use, reproduce, post, transmit, distribute, or publicly display these images.

STATEN ISLAND BOROUGH HALL

Page 130: Frederick Charles Stahr, *Bayonne Bridge under Construction*, 1938.

Page 132, left: Frederick Charles Stahr, *Giovanni da Verrazzano Discovers Staten Island, 1425* (detail), 1938.

Pages 134-135: Frederick Charles Stahr, *Henry Hudson Anchors Off "Staaten Eylandt," 1609*; *Fight at St. Andrew's Church, 1776*; *Castleton Hotel Fire at New Brighton, British Troops Evacuate Staten Island: Dec 5, 1783*, 1938.

GEORGE WASHINGTON HIGH SCHOOL

Pages 136-143: Lucienne Bloch, *The Evolution of Music*, 1938. George Washington High School.

MARINE AIR TERMINAL

Pages 144-149: James Brooks, *Flight*, 1942. All art by James Brooks is © Estate of James Brooks and Charlotte Parks/Licensed by VAGA, New York, NY. The Port Authority of New York & New Jersey.

BEMELMANS BAR

Pages 150-157: Ludwig Bemelmans, untitled, 1947. The Carlyle, A Rosewood Hotel.

MONKEY BAR
Pages 158–163: Charles Vella, untitled, 1949, and Diane Voyentzie, untitled, 1984, 1994.
Pages 164–169: Edward Sorel, untitled, 2009.

CAFÉ CARLYLE
Pages 170–175: Marcel Vertès, untitled, 1955. The Carlyle, A Rosewood Hotel.

THE METROPOLITAN OPERA
Pages 176 and 178, left: Marc Chagall, *The Triumph of Music*, 1966. © 2013 Artist Rights Society (ARS), New York/ADAGP, Paris.
Page 178, right: Marc Chagall, *The Sources of Music*, 1966. © 2013 Artist Rights Society (ARS), New York/ADAGP, Paris.

NEW YORK CITY BALLET
Pages 180–183: Robert Crowl, *Dancers at the Bar*, 1967.

THE PECK SLIP ARCADE & GLOCKENSPIEL
Pages 184–187: Richard Haas, *Peck Slip Arcade*, 1978. All art by Richard Haas is © Richard Haas/Licensed by VAGA, New York, NY.
Pages 188–189: Richard Haas, *Glockenspiel*, 2005. All art by Richard Haas is © Richard Haas/Licensed by VAGA, New York, NY.

AXA EQUITABLE CENTER
Page 190: Roy Lichtenstein, *Mural with a Blue Brushstroke*, 1984-86. © Estate of Roy Lichtenstein.

PALIO BAR
Pages 192–197: Sandro Chia, *Palio*, 1985-86. All art by Sandro Chia is © Sandro Chia/Licensed by VAGA, New York, NY. Acrylic on panel, 4 part mural, each part 13'x20'. Collection of AXA Equitable.

A MUSEUM, A PARK & A HOSPITAL
Pages 198, and 200-201: Keith Haring, *Woodhull Medical Center Mural*, 1986. © Keith Haring Foundation. Woodhull Medical & Mental Health Center. Used by permission.

Pages 202-203: Keith Haring, *Pop Shop Ceiling*, 1986. © Keith Haring Foundation. New-York Historical Society. Used by permission.
Pages 204-205: Keith Haring, *Crack Is Wack*, 1986. © Keith Haring Foundation. Used by permission.

CHRISTIE'S NEW YORK
Page 206: Sol LeWitt, *Wall Drawing #896 Colors/Curves*, 1999. © 2013 The LeWitt Estate/Artists Rights Society (ARS), New York. Christie's New York.

THE WAVERLY INN AND GARDEN
Pages 208-215: Edward Sorel, untitled, 2007.

GOLDMAN SACHS
Page 216: Julie Mehretu, *Mural*, 2009. Goldman Sachs.

MARK MORRIS DANCE CENTER
Pages 218-219: Barry McGee, untitled, 2012. Courtesy of the artist, Ratio 3, San Francisco, Cheim & Read, New York, and Modern Art, London. Presented by Cadillac.

CHRYSLER BUILDING
Page 221: Edward Trumbull, *Transport and Human Endeavor* (detail), 1930. Courtesy of Tishman Speyer.

HARLEM HOSPITAL
Pages 223: Vertis Hayes, *Pursuit of Happiness*, 1937.

NEW YORK STATE SUPREME COURT, APPELLATE DIVISION
Page 224-225: Edward Emerson Simmons, *The Justice of the Law*, 1900; Henry O. Walker, *The Wisdom of the Law*, 1900; Edwin Blashfield, *The Power of The Law*, 1900.

ROCKEFELLER CENTER
Page 228: José María Sert, *Time* (detail), 1937.
Back Cover: José María Sert, *American Progress*, 1937.

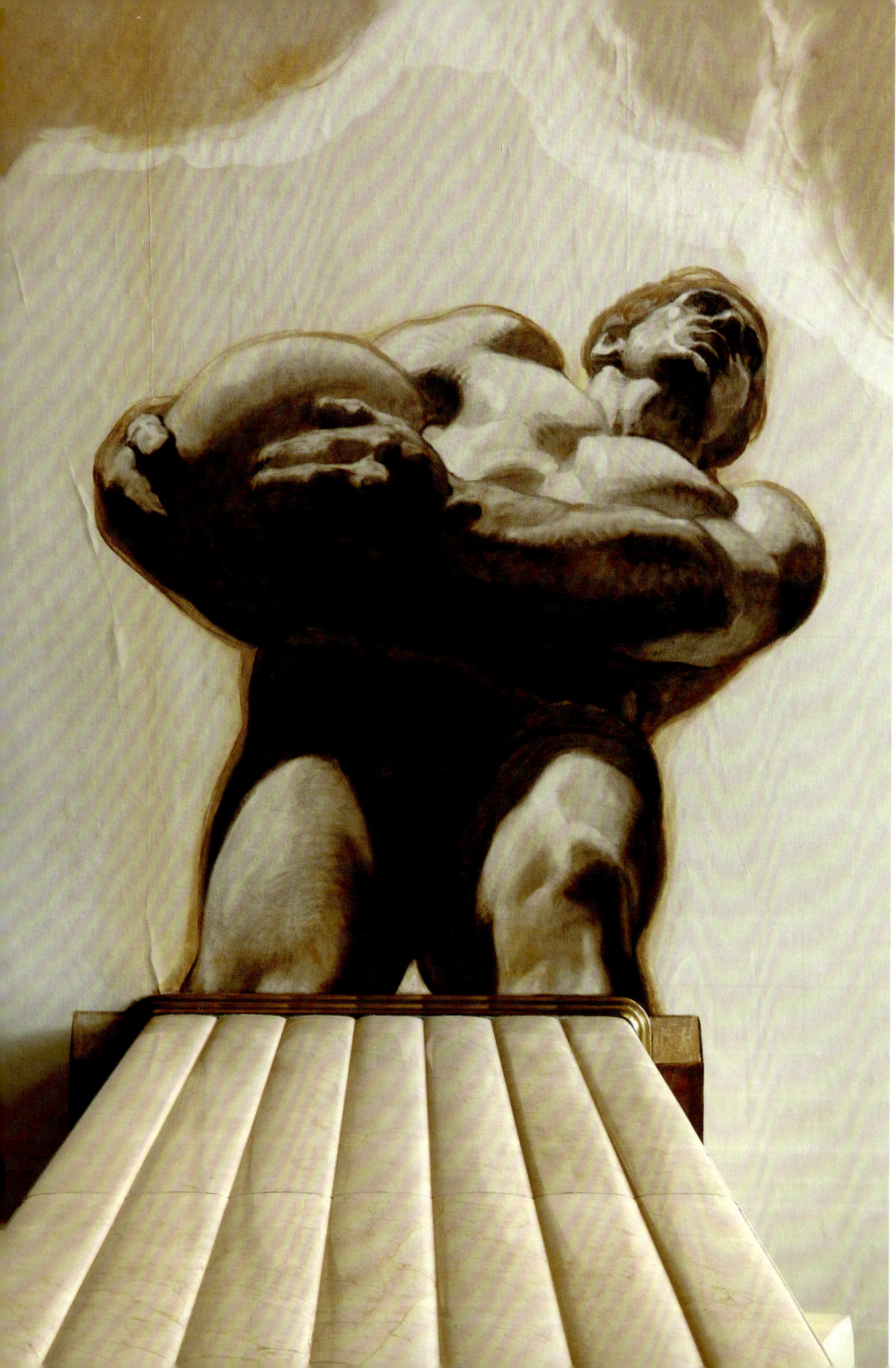

This edition published in
the United States of America in 2013 by
Rizzoli International Publications, Inc.
300 Park Avenue South
New York, NY 10010
ww.rizzoliusa.com

Project Editor: Robb Pearlman
Book Design: Susi Oberhelman

2019 2020 2021 / 10 9 8 7 6 5 4 3 2 1

Printed in China

ISBN: 978-0-8478-6806-3

Library of Congress Control Number: 2013934332